The

{WOMAN}

Advocate

The {WOMAN} Advocate

Editors
Jean Maclean Snyder
Andra Barmash Greene

Editorial Board
Miriam Kass
Janet S. Kole
Louise A. La Mothe
D. Jean Veta
Lynn S. Glasser

SECTION OF LITIGATION
AMERICAN BAR ASSOCIATION

Cover design by Richard Laurent.

Originally published in hardcover by Aspen Law & Business.

The materials contained herein represent the opinions of the authors and editors and should not be construed to be the action of either the American Bar Association or the Section of Litigation unless adopted pursuant to the bylaws of the Association.

Nothing contained in this book is to be considered as the rendering of legal advice for specific cases, and readers are responsible for obtaining such advice from their own legal counsel. This book and any forms and agreements herein are intended for educational and informational purposes only.

Library of Congress Catalog Card No. 95-83764
ISBN 1-57073-311-2

Discounts are available for books ordered in bulk. Special consideration is given to state bars, CLE programs, and other bar-related organizations. Inquire at Publications Planning & Marketing, American Bar Association, 750 North Lake Shore Drive, Chicago, Illinois 60611.

00 99 98   5 4 3

Table of Contents

Foreword

I look forward to the time when a book like this will be of solely historic interest to those chronicling the move of American society to true equality of the sexes. But although much great progress has been made, here is a book for lawyers that provides advice and encouragement for one of our profession's most vexatious problems: the failure of women lawyers to achieve complete equality.

The Woman Advocate tells the stories of women who have successfully overcome obstacles to become successful lawyers. One woman describes her journey from a large firm whose "ethos was predicated on distrust and fear" to a practice where she is able to be "a Gadfly lawyer, a Righter of Wrongs." Another lawyer describes how she uses "energy, efficiency, a thick skin, and a sense of humor" to balance her roles as litigator, wife, mother, and stepmother. A third lawyer describes how a woman's clothes, her voice, her manner, even the language she uses, can be used as tools to show her importance and trustworthiness in the courtroom.

Although targeted specifically at litigators (and containing excellent litigation tips), *The Woman Advocate* offers advice on subjects of interest to all lawyers: skills such as mentoring and developing business; professional issues such as making partner, going solo, or deciding what to do if your job won't take you where you want to go; advice from a judge who explains how to create confidence in a courtroom; and negotiating skills from experienced lawyers who know how to handle an overbearing adversary.

This is a great time for women lawyers in many ways, but there is no question that gender bias continues to be part of the reality we face. *The Woman Advocate* focuses on helping to advance professional skills—the important first step in combating bias.

Roberta Cooper Ramo
President
American Bar Association

Preface

The **Woman Advocate** should be read as you would read a good novel—from start to finish. Then it should be kept within arm's reach to be consulted again and again. This volume is truly a bible for women litigators. I venture to suggest that no woman litigator can afford not to devour it. The book contains page after page of on-point suggestions, lessons from the school of hard knocks, and success stories that will give confidence and inspiration to aspiring women advocates for decades to come.

The book examines strategies for successful advocacy both in and out of the courtroom. Separate chapters are devoted to every aspect of the litigation process, including depositions, settlements, courtroom techniques, and litigation styles. Each author—all are seasoned veterans—explains how women litigators can overcome stereotypes, deal with gender differences, establish their authority, and develop litigating approaches that are both effective and comfortable. Recognizing that it does little good to sharpen advocacy skills if they are never called to bear, the book also includes chapters on rainmaking and "what to do if your job won't take you where you want to go." There is something for everyone—those who want to go "solo," those in government, those in private practice, those in public interest work, and the part-time attorney mom, just to name a few.

This book details the often personal, humiliating, and agonizing experiences of discrimination and abuse. The obvious pain and suffering will capture readers' hearts. Yet, the ongoing struggle, which the authors share with many of you, and their accounts of the successes against discrimination achieved to date give hope to all that the corner had indeed been turned, and that the future will be much brighter. It is clear that the authors have chosen not to give in but to succeed.

Nor is **The Woman Advocate** a book for women alone. I wholeheartedly recommend it to all males who litigate with, supervise, or work with women litigators. I wish that I had had the occasion to read such a book many years ago. It would have been an immensely important resource for me and would have saved many less than cherished moments over the 25 years that I have managed and litigated with or against women lawyers.

While I first entered the profession there were few, if any, women litigators or judges in the legal community. It was an all-male and predominantly white club. When women began appearing—first as associates, then as first-chair trial lawyers, and then as judges—the adjustment was not easy. Clearly, these women were not given a level playing field. Among other things, they were excluded from "serious" case preparation sessions. There were few opportunities, if any, for women lawyers to stand up in court and take the lead. And the thought of including a woman in a client meeting where the possibility of new business was being considered did not even enter the equation.

The evolution from those days to today is well-described in the second chapter of **The Woman Advocate**, written by Tom Johnson, a prominent Los Angeles big firm trial lawyer and the only male among the contributing authors. My own experiences were similar to his. Fortunately, in the 70's, women began to enter legal practice in much greater numbers, and many turned their interest toward trial work. Their obvious abilities, their willingness to shoulder their fair share of the burdens and their successes quickly helped to turn the tide. Eventually, the more open members of the male litigation bar came to realize that not only could women do the work, they could do it "damn well."

Nevertheless, whether the playing field is still tilted toward male practitioners remains a fair question. The obvious improvement in the professional status of women lawyers as chronicled in **The Woman Advocate** is encouraging. Moreover, there is no major current case that does not actively involve many women advocates. Development and marketing activities always continue to include greater numbers of women. And women now hold leadership positions in law firms, the legal profession, and the community at large.

Finally, it should be added that this book is an outgrowth of the Woman Advocate Conferences co-sponsored by the American Bar Association Section of Litigation and Prentice Hall Law & Business during the past two years. Five such conferences have been held so far, drawing nearly 2,000 attorneys (mostly women). Two new conferences have been scheduled for early 1995 in New York and San Francisco. The success of these programs and the obvious need for the practicing bar to pay more attention to this vital area led to this masterful work.

Our Section is deeply grateful to the co-editors of **The Woman Advocate**, Jean Maclean Snyder and Andra Barmash Greene, who were also co-chairs of the first Woman Advocate Conferences, and to the editorial board of Lynn Glasser, Miriam Kass, Janet Kole, Louise LaMothe, and Jean Veta, who, with the exception of Ms. Glasser (a nonlawyer), are active Section of Litigation members and founders of the Section's efforts to assist the woman advocate. Without the dedication and foresight of Louise La-Mothe, Chair of the Section in 1992–1993, neither the Conferences nor this book would be a reality. As a result of those Conferences and with the publishing of this work, they have moved the cause of the woman advocate from the ante-room to the boardroom. No longer will bias and discrimination against women lawyers be so easily maintained and accepted. Our eyes and ears have been opened and they will never close.

David C. Weiner
Chair, Section of Litigation
American Bar Association

Introduction

Not long ago, a phone call came from one of our **The Woman Advocate** authors. "I'm having such fun writing my chapter," she said. "It isn't a legal discursive; it's like a play." Hmmmm, that sounded intriguing. The author continued, "Would you like to hear some of it? I'll pull it up on my computer screen until I find a portion I especially like."

The author read for several minutes, she read passionately for several minutes—modulating her voice to portray subdued tension, then outrage, and finally elation. "I feel rather sheepish making this story so personal," she finished. "I think there will be people who will never forgive me when they read it."

In one way or another, working on **The Woman Advocate** was an eye opener for all of us, editors and authors alike. Unexpectedly, it taught some of us things about ourselves that we had not known. And it gave a clarity to issues about our lives and the lives of other women lawyers that had been missing.

For one thing, writing this book showed the enormous effect that the fact of our sex, the fact of a vagina and not a penis, has had on our careers. If you did not believe that was so before reading this book, you likely will acknowledge it when you finish. Undeniably, for all of us, our femaleness affects our conduct as trial lawyers and as brief writers, and it affects how other lawyers respond to us.

For another thing, the intertwining of gender and career affects all parts of our lives, even our sense of personal identity. Again and again authors begin writing about their careers and end up writing about their families, their childhoods, their personal beliefs about what is important, their feelings of self worth.

It is fair to ask why this personal storytelling seems a particularly female thing to do. Imagine, if you can, a book called **The Male Advocate**. Is there a chance this book would contain tales of family demands that impinge on work obligations, of career changes made to contend with the sexist reactions of colleagues, of jobs that grind down a person's sense of self-esteem? Are any of your male colleagues' war stories about these kinds of battles?

For many of us, learning how strongly the fact of our sex affects our legal careers was a surprise. It was not what we expected when we started practicing law, ten to twenty-five years ago. At the beginning, many women thought that a law degree was a ticket to equal treatment. We believed that women lawyers could—and should—ignore their womanness during office hours. Femininity, and activism about women's issues, were strictly for extracurricular time. At work, we tried to blend in, hoping that no one, including ourselves, would notice that we were different. Even fashion reflected our attempt at camouflage—remember the Hart Schaffner & Marx bow ties that we wore with Oxford cloth shirts and mannish suits?

As we sought to minimize our femaleness, we also avoided organizing with other women lawyers around issues of mutual concern. A program on maternity leave and part-time options offered in 1980 to women alums of a prominent law school drew a sparse audience; several alums phoned to say they feared how their firms would react if they attended. A Chicago business started during the late 1970s to promote alternative work schedules for lawyers soon closed down for lack of support. A national conference for women lawyers staged in the mid-70s was a flop.

Although our display of female plumage was far from bold, it kept us undeniably apart. The men knew we were different; and we knew it too.

Abandoning camouflage, we changed our strategies. We began searching for our own identity, one separate from that of male lawyers.

The stories in **The Woman Advocate** are part of that search. As part of our search for identity we began talking about our pasts, as the authors have done here. We began telling our stories to other women, as the authors do here. In these stories, we admit that we have faced sex discrimination, that the discrimination hurt, and that it made a difference in our lives. We acknowledge that, at the same time, the battle has made us tougher. Finally, we delight in the successes we are having, despite the battle.

Women practitioners may not often turn to feminist legal theory to explain their situation, but if they looked, the theories would be there. During the 1970s, feminist scholars generally saw their goal as ensuring that the law made no distinctions between men and women who were similarly situated, a goal that was in keeping with the notion of formal equality adopted by the Supreme Court in 1971. What counted was the similarity between men and women; the aim was to eliminate group-based stereotypes and to gain a status for women equal to that of men. Yet within a decade, the emphasis had shifted from similarities to differences. Some scholars wrote about the differences among women of different races, classes, and sexual orientations. Others discussed the differences between men and women, some of them arguing for the superiority of women's culture over men's.

In **The Woman Advocate**, practitioners wrestle with these issues. Are the differences between male and female lawyers paramount, or do the similarities predominate? If women lawyers behave differently, should they cultivate those differences or try to tame them? Clients, jurors, and judges, the people who count, do they believe that the "man's way" is better? If they do, do women succeed by out-manning the man—or will that technique backfire as the audience senses the attempt at imitation? Suppose the research shows that adopting the attitude of the "good girl" is most likely to please jurors. Should you do this even if it perpetuates unfortunate stereotypes? Should you do it even if you think it may portray you as lacking the assertiveness essential to a successful advocate?

There are also questions about family issues. Should women fight for the right to extended maternity leave or should they hurry back to work? If a woman resumes full-time work quickly she will undoubtedly please her partners; but what about her children? They are not likely to be as effective advocates as her partners; but doesn't their inability make their case more compelling? So, perhaps the solution is to return to work part-time. But if a woman works part-time, what are her rights in relation to full-timers, many of whom are men? And what about the woman whose sexual orientation means that she will never need a maternity leave? Is she entitled to something else in compensation?

Also, women may ask, how do we handle the everyday decisions that these issues raise without losing our sense of humor? And, what is the effect of all these churning thoughts about our sexuality? In striving to resolve these issues, are we unwittingly succumbing to second-status thinking: While the men worry about trying the case, we worry about our consciences, our self-esteem, the needs of our families and—oh yes—the needs of the case. Trained in a profession that values the ability to see both sides of an issue, how can a woman become doctrinaire on these subjects? Yet, if she is not doctrinaire, will she be consumed with ambivalence?

Asking and starting to answer these questions is what **The Woman Advocate** is about. It is unusual for a book on professional development to involve such personal questions. It is even more unusual for lawyers to discuss their own self-doubt, their humiliations, and even their failures. Yet that is what the authors do here. The authors also offer strategies for handling self-doubt and failure; the creativity and effectiveness of the strategies make clear how the authors have been able to establish successful careers for themselves.

The Woman Advocate consists of 21 chapters, each by a different person. All but one author is a woman. Most of the authors are practicing lawyers, but the list also includes a judge, a law professor, a psychologist, a sociologist, a legal recruiter, and a legal publisher. The articles by nonpractitioners add to our understanding of the discrimination women lawyers face, and also offer useful advice.

THE SETTING: WHAT WE'RE UP AGAINST

The book is divided into three sections; the first is *The Setting: What We're Up Against*. Drawing from opinion surveys of lawyers and lay people; from findings from social science and litigation research; from studies providing results in graphs, tables, charts, and testimonial evidence; and from personal storytelling, the seven chapters in *The Setting* describe the discrimination that women lawyers face. The chapters show that if the optimism we felt in the 70s about equal treatment was a case of denial about the extent of discrimination, there was—and still is—a lot to deny.

"Gender in the Courts: The Task Force Reports" (Chapter 1), by law professor Judith Resnik, is one of the most extensive analyses of the work of these task forces. According to Resnik, the task forces have consistently reported that state and federal courts are a venue of discrimination, despite their emblem of "equal justice under the law." The studies show that the courts discriminate "against women in general, against people of color in general, against women of color in distinct ways, against not only litigants, but also against court employees, and against the lawyers who come to the courts on behalf of litigants." Yet, the task force studies have sparked some positive change. At least in some jurisdictions, progress can be demonstrated in appointments to the bench, educational programs about discrimination for lawyers and judges, and rule changes. Also, gender bias and women's concerns are now on the agenda of both judges and lawyers. As for the work that remains. Resnik emphasizes the need to go beyond the generic "woman" in the generic "court," and to discover "the distinct experiences of women of different races, ethnicities, classes, ages, and sexual orientation and of women in different kinds and phases of dispute resolution."

"Evolving Attitudes or Confessions of a Male Chauvinist Attorney" (Chapter 2), by lawyer Thomas W. Johnson, Jr., begins, "What you are about to read may upset you."

Johnson is right about that.

With candor, Johnson writes of attitudes and actions so politically incorrect that few will be brave enough to admit to having had them. Johnson tells what he and other men thought about women lawyers in the late 60s and early 70s, when Johnson went to law school and started practicing law. He recalls wishing that the female students had been excused from his criminal law class when the discussion turned to the elements of rape such as "penetration" and "consent." He tells of male attorneys who referred to a female opponent as a "bitch" or a "dyke," or who commented that a woman attorney who looked uptight "needs to be screwed." Presumably, no one makes such crudely discriminatory comments any more. Yet it is important to acknowledge that they once were part of the landscape.

As Johnson's chapter makes the reader uncomfortable, so it does the author. "It bothers me, and I wrote it," Johnson writes. Johnson has matured, however, along with the rest of us. Losing an important argument to a female attorney, arguing motions before female judges, trying a case with a competent woman partner, these experiences have made him see that "a woman could put her femininity on hold as easily as a man could arrest his macho."

Yet the attitudes that Johnson describes have not vanished. Statistical evidence of their continuation is contained in "Survey of Female Litigators: Discrimination by Clients Limits Opportunities" (Chapter 3), by Lynn S. Glasser. Glasser, Co-President of Prentice Hall Law & Business, reports on the results of a recent Prentice Hall survey of women litigators in which the venue emphasized was the office, not the courts. The survey demonstrates entrenched sexist attitudes just as surely as do the gender task force studies. More than half the women polled stated that they had been sexually harrassed by clients over the past five years, that their business opportunities were more limited than those of male litigators, and that they believed that their chances of making partner were not equal to those of men. The situation may not improve, Glasser suggests, until women take over more positions of influence in the client companies that law firms represent.

Statistical evidence of sex-based stereotypes also comes from the first reported study of what lawyers themselves think about how a lawyer's gender affects behavior in court. "Women and Men in the Courtroom: What Trial Lawyers Believe" (Chapter 7), by sociologist Jeanne J. Fleming, suggests that gender shapes the behavior of all lawyers, both men and women, and that gender stereotypes work to the disadvantage of women. Fleming found that male and female lawyers agree that their behavior is shaped by the gender of other courtroom players such as the judge and jurors, that women litigators behave differently from men litigators, and that lawyers of the "other sex" use their masculinity or femininity to sway the jury unfairly. Reports from women themselves show how they are hindered by sex stereotypes. Those responses suggest that acting the "good girl" in court and ignoring hostile remarks is an effective technique for persuading a judge or jury. They also show that women appear to be avoiding somewhat riskier, more overtly attention-getting techniques such as staging dramatic moments, which usually are successful for those who use them.

In "Credibility and Gender in the Courtroom: What Jurors Think" (Chapter 6), psychologist Reiko Hasuike describes the complex attitudes and assumptions that tend to handicap the credibility of women litigators. Using findings from social science and litigation research, Hasuike explains why average jurors assume that male lawyers will be more competent in certain types of cases, and why people often assume a woman's unusual competence is due to luck. Hasuike also shows how a woman can turn these prejudices to her advantage and change the attribution of luck to skill.

The five chapters just described deal with attitudes about what Resnik calls the "generic" woman in the "generic" court. Two chapters in Section I: *The Setting* offer personal observations on distinct experiences. The chapters are "As a Woman of Color" (Chapter 4), by attorney Beverly Nelson Muldrow, and "A Lesbian Lawyer Speaks Out" (Chapter 5), by Gina Briggs. Legal theorists who contend that the concerns of women of color and lesbians may conflict with those of white heterosexual women will find confirmation here for that belief. Muldrow says that the racial differences she has with white women are more significant than the gender connection they share, and she criticizes some white female attorneys who, she says, adopt the views of their white male counterparts in order to fit in. For her part, Briggs writes about seeking out male, not female, lawyers for help in promoting the rights of lesbian lawyers. She says she did this in part because she felt less personal and political affinity with women. Nevertheless, Muldrow and Briggs achieved great success in meeting the challenges they faced. They serve as important role models for those who follow them, and as a caution to others.

THE SKILLS: TEACHING EACH OTHER TO EXCEL

The Skills: Teaching Each Other to Excel is Section II of **The Woman Advocate**. The seven chapters in this Section discuss traditional legal skills such as negotiating, taking a deposition, and trying a case. But the approach is not traditional: the chapters aim to help women take advantage of the pluses of their gender and to minimize the minuses.

Several chapters in Section II: *The Skills* are based on the premise that women advocates are treated by male colleagues as women first and as professionals second. In "Depositions and the Gorilla Adversary" (Chapter 9), lawyers Lorna G. Schofield and Jill A. Lesser tell how to deal with the male lawyer who opens the deposition by saying "Where did you go to law school, little girl?" For Schofield and Lesser, the key is to respond to the aggression and to reestablish your authority while avoiding behavior that might be considered conciliatory. The authors warn that a passive approach is fraught with danger. Therefore, they recommend that if a woman chooses to ignore a hostile remark, she should act disdainful by looking bored, avoiding eye contact, and shuffling documents. Within this framework, the authors offer a variety of practical strategies for taming the male gorilla, whether he is the woman lawyer's opposing lawyer, that lawyer's witness, or her own witness.

Lawyer Janet Kole takes a different approach in "The Woman Lawyer in the Courtroom or We Love Your Hairdo" (Chapter 10). Rather than trying to beat men at their own game, Kole advises women to emphasize the advantages of their femaleness. But she cautions that she does not mean the traditionally conceived female methods of dealing with men such as being flirtatious or acting like daddy's little girl. Instead, she recommends the real advantages that can be drawn from society's positive views of women, such as being perceived as being more trustworthy than men. She also maintains that because both men and women care about how women look, women should take their appearance seriously. To the woman who says that looks shouldn't count on a moral level, Kole responds, "reality shows that looks do count."

In "Bench With a Point of View: How to Create Confidence in the Courtroom" (Chapter 11), Judge Norma L. Shapiro agrees that looks are important. "Simplicity, not imitation of 'masculine' severity, sets the proper tone," she writes. Also important is a professional demeanor and an argument that is fully prepared and delivered confidently. The woman advocate may need this special assistance because of gender bias, which Judge Shapiro believes is endemic in our society. At the same time, she warns that paying too much personal attention to prejudice gives it credence. Her own way of dealing with it is to consider it "a defect of the discriminator—and a sign of insecurity—not mine."

The premise of "Negotiating Skills for Women Lawyers" (Chapter 8), is one that attorney-author Courtenay L. Bass might have drawn from Jeanne Fleming's research reported in "Women and Men in the Courtroom: What Trial Lawyers Believe" (Chapter 7). The premise is that women negotiate differently from men and that they behave differently depending on whether the opposing lawyer is a man or a woman. Women lawyers, Bass says, should draw on their natural skills such as being effective listeners and being able to work toward cooperative resolutions without concern over who gets credit. She also tells women to avoid the traditional male "win/lose" style of negotiation. Women won't feel comfortable with it, she warns.

"Grabbing the Brass Ring: Making Partner At a Large Firm" (Chapter 14), is organized around ten basic principles for making partner that author-lawyer D. Jean Veta has discerned. Veta makes no claim for women having special skills or sex-linked liabilities. While recognizing that a woman's life outside the firm, including family responsibilities, may be a threshold issue in deciding whether she is committed to the task of becoming a partner, Veta's ten principles—all excellent advice—are likely to be as useful for men as for women.

Two chapters in Section II: *The Skills* deal with the issues that affect women lawyers differently from their male counterparts.

In "Making Rain" (Chapter 12), Jean explains that developing business is a special concern for women because the social side of rainmaking often involves what are traditionally men's activities with clients who too typically are men, and because after-hours social activities may overwhelm the schedule of women with husbands and children.

The issue of finding a mentor also affects women differently from men. In particular, recent changes in law firm practice that discourage informal relationships like mentoring affect women disproportionately, writes lawyer Louise A. LaMothe in "Where Have the Mentors Gone?" (Chapter 13). The changes include increased pressure on lawyers to generate new business and the pressure from clients for partners to do the work themselves and not to involve junior associates. What has become a problem for men is a crisis for women, according to LaMothe.

The chapters on mentoring and rainmaking offer lots of practical advice, including checklists to evaluate your progress.

THE PRACTICE: WE'RE ON OUR WAY

Section III of **The Woman Advocate** is titled *The Practice: We're On Our Way*. Here six lawyer-authors discuss their own litigation practices in law firms of several sizes, in a public interest organization, and in a governmental agency. Finally, a legal recruiter explains "What If Your Job Won't Take You Where You Want To Go." In Chapter 21, author Marty Fay Africa offers advice to the woman advocate who can't stand her job: "Don't bolt: assess. Then re-assess," writes Africa. The reason: "Too many lawyers decide to change jobs without first taking the time to understand their internal stop orders, their current workplace, and their prospective employers." These stop orders, Africa explains, are our "customized internal glass ceiling." Africa challenges the reader to eliminate these stop orders as the cause of discontent before exploring outside issues.

The other chapters in Section III: *The Practice*, written by women lawyers at places in their careers where they can look back and reassess, offer views of several styles of litigation practice.

Two of the authors have made rewarding careers out of solo or small firm practice; yet neither one chose this style of practice freely; instead, solo practice offered an escape from the discrimination both women perceived in the larger firms where they had worked previously.

"Canaries in a Coal Mine: Reflections Upon Life in a Large Law Firm" (Chapter 15), is written anonymously under the name Judith

Gracchus. In describing the firm where she practiced for 13 years, Gracchus says:

> The Firm's ethos was predicated on distrust and fear beneath a deceptive veneer of blandness. Each new crop of young associates was hand-picked by those who had just preceded them. Thus each new crop, a replica of the preceding one, was nonetheless a greyer, grimmer, more humorless version thereof. In such manner did the pickers protect themselves from excessive competition from the picked.

Gracchus also describes some of her former partners. One whom she calls The Senior Partner had never tried a case to a jury but was nevertheless assigned to some of The Firm's largest cases. Another, The Firm Wit, issues this warning about The Senior Partner: he is The Titanic in search of an iceberg. Finally, there is The Weather Vane, so named because he could always signal which way the wind was blowing.

While Gracchus looks back at her experience at a large firm, Robin Page West mostly looks to the future. In "Going Solo: The How's and the Why's for Women Litigators" (Chapter 16), West tells the reader how to set up a solo practice if, like West, she finds her progress at a firm hampered by the firm's sexism. West invites the reader to take the same quiz she did to decide whether her firm is harboring sexism. If it is, West says you shouldn't stay around hoping things will get better. She writes, "[l]ike a verbally abusive marital relationship, a sexist relationship in a law firm is often difficult to identify and almost impossible to change."

Priscilla Schwab's approach to a sexist work environment is just the opposite. In "A Godmother Makes Good: Practice in a Government Agency" (Chapter 17), Schwab describes her nine-year effort—finally successful—to make a comfortable place for herself in a sexist environment. The venue of discrimination is ironic: the federal agency charged with the task of eradicating bias from the workplace. How does the sexism show itself? In an application form that asks women, but not men, if they have been married before; by male colleagues who talk over and interrupt women at meetings; by the male supervisor whose praise, "you did fine," is delivered in a manner that silently adds, "for a woman." Yet, Schwab remained. Nine years later, she has gained a private window office, "the ultimate achievement in the federal service," and other measures of success, and she also has preserved her sense of humor, an essential tool for survival.

Like Robin West, Ann Brick made a radical career change because of her experiences as a woman. Brick tells about the change in "When I Grow Up, I Want To Work For the ACLU: On Becoming and Being a Public Interest Lawyer" (Chapter 18). The experience that altered her perspective was becoming a mother after a 14-year marriage. Brick writes: "For the first time in my professional life, the law was no longer the be-all and the end-all of how I wanted to spend my time." After much soul-searching (and the birth of a second child), Brick decided to leave the firm where she had spent 12 happy years to go to work for the ACLU of Northern California. Besides the "gender-neutral" gratification of doing public interest work, some of the pluses at Brick's new job are related to being a woman. For the first time she is working with another woman, who acts like a mentor, and she can take advantage of an office structure that accommodates part-time work schedules.

Even new mothers who do not change careers are likely to find that having a baby alters perceptions about priorities. Certainly that is the experience of the two **The Woman Advocate** authors who write specifically about motherhood. In "The Litigating Mom" (Chapter 19), Andra tells how glad she is to have broken her promise to herself to become a partner at a firm before becoming a mother. For Andra, as for Brick, the experience of becoming a mother confounded her preconceived notions about combining career and family. Nevertheless, she decided to go back to work full-time. Both her roles as mother and as litigator are essential to her identity. Andra writes: "I am who I am because I do both."

What if she were forced to choose only one role? "There is no question but that my family would win in a heartbeat." All the lawyers who write about their careers in Section III also mention their families. It is clear that none would make a choice different from Andra's.

With similar priorities, Catherine Hodgman Helm has chosen to work part-time. "Life As A Mom Who Works Part-Time" (Chapter 20) describes Helm's experience as a part-time litigator and the full-time mother of preschool-age twin daughters. As she writes about her own experience, Helm tells readers how to approach the firm about setting up a part-time arrangement, how to deal with clients and colleagues, and how to establish a daily schedule. Add this to Andra's advice on when to have children, on childcare alternatives, on making the return to full-time work after maternity leave, and on balancing full-time work with parenting, and many questions are answered for those planning to have children.

THE WOMAN ADVOCATE

Publication of **The Woman Advocate** represents the convergence of several good ideas from several good people. It starts with Lynn S. Glasser, for seventeen years Co-President of Prentice Hall Law & Business, and with Louise A. LaMothe, a partner in Riordan & McKinzie in Los Angeles who, in 1992-1993, was the second woman to chair the ABA's Section of Litigation and the first woman to put the agenda of women on the Section's agenda.

Glasser and LaMothe's idea was that these two organizations would sponsor a national conference aimed at litigators who were women. As Dave Weiner describes in the Preface to **The Woman Advocate**, the conferences that grew out of that association have been such a smashing success that they have become an annual event.

The Woman Advocate is a separate project, although it was an outgrowth of the first year's conferences in 1993 (we were co-chairs of those conferences; Andra had the laboring oar for the conferences, as Jean did for the book).

The Woman Advocate could not have been completed without a lot of hard work from a lot of people. Besides our authors, we especially want to thank our editorial board whose members are Lynn Glasser, Louise LaMothe, Miriam Kass, Janet Kole, and D. Jean Veta. Also we want to thank Daniel E. Mangan, Vice President/Editorial at Prentice Hall, whose invaluable work was essential to producing **The Woman Advocate**. Finally, we want to thank you, our readers. We hope that you will read this book and learn, as we did when we wrote it, and we also hope that you will help us continue the storytelling.

Jean Maclean Snyder
Andra Barmash Greene
Editors
The Woman Advocate

Section I

The Setting: What We're Up Against

CHAPTER 1

Gender in the Courts: The Task Force Reports

by
JUDITH RESNIK

JUDITH RESNIK

J udith Resnik is the Orrin B. Evans Professor of Law at the University of Southern California Law Center, where she teaches procedure, federal courts, feminist theory, large scale litigation, and prisoners' rights. Professor Resnik is a graduate of Bryn Mawr College and New York University School of Law, where she held an Arthur Garfield Hays Fellowship.

Professor Resnik was a member of the Ninth Circuit Gender Bias Task Force, the first to report on the effects of gender on the federal court system. She is also a member of the Task Force on Civil Justice Reform of the Litigation Section of the American Bar Association, of the American Law Institute, of the Board of Governors of the Society of American Law Teachers, and of the editorial boards of several journals. She has served as the chair of the Section on Civil Procedure and of the Section on Women in Legal Education of the American Association of Law Schools.

Professor Resnik is the co-author (with Robert Cover and Owen Fiss) of a book, Procedure (Foundation Press, 1988). She has written extensively about judging (see, e.g. "Managerial Judging," 96 Harv. L. Rev. 374 (1982); "Failing Faith: Adjudicatory Procedure in Decline," 53 U. Chi. L. Rev. 494 (1986); and "From Cases to Litigation," 54 Law and Contemporary Problems 5 (1991)), as well as about the relationship between feminist theory and adjudication. See e.g., "On the Bias: Feminist Reconsiderations of the Aspirations for our Judges," 61 So. Calif. L. Rev. 1877 (1988); "Dependent Sovereigns: Indian Tribes, States, and the Federal Courts," 56 U. Chicago L. Rev. 671 (1989); Convergences: Law, Literature and Feminism (with Carolyn Heilbrun), 99 Yale L. J. 1913 (1990);

and "'Naturally' Without Gender: Women, Jurisdiction, and the Federal Courts," 66 N.Y.U. L. Rev. 1682 (1992).

Professor Resnik has testified many times before congressional committees, has served as a court-appointed expert, and has also been active occasionally as a litigator. In 1987, she argued in the United States Supreme Court on behalf of a local Rotary Club's right to admit women; over the past few years, she has participated in cases involving attorney fee disputes and sanctions.

CHAPTER 1

Gender in the Courts: The Task Force Reports

by
JUDITH RESNIK*

Anything may happen when womanhood has ceased to be a protected profession, I thought, opening the door.

Virginia Woolf, A Room Of One's Own 41 (1929).

THE EMERGENCE OF GENDER AS A TOPIC FOR COURTS

The very existence of task forces on bias in the courts is remarkable. At their core, these task forces present a radical innovation that has actually been successful in engendering some change. Radical, because all of these efforts are taken on by court systems themselves, as chief judges and other senior officials of the legal profession actually ask: Do *we* discriminate? How? Against whom? In general? In pervasive and diffuse ways?

Why should such questions be termed "radical"? Recall that the Supreme Court of the United States, when asked in 1987 in *McCleskey v. Kemp*[1] to consider whether Georgia had imposed the death sentence in a generally racially-discriminatory fashion, declined the broad inquiry.[2] The Court said that, while it was prepared to look individually at a particular person's claim that he or she had been sentenced to death because of racial prejudice, the Court could not entertain a claim that the administration of the death penalty as a whole violated the Equal Protection Clause. [3] For the majority, to take on the general issue of racism in death penalties would open the door to challenges of racism in all forms of sentencing.

In this conclusion lurks a "so what?"—why not explore the general issue of racism in all forms of sentencing? The opinion is unembarrassed about why such a fundamental challenge was beyond comprehension. In the words of the Court:

> [I]f we accepted McCleskey's claim that racial bias has impermissibly tainted the capital sentencing decision, we could soon be faced with similar claims as to other types of penalty. Moreover, the claim that his sentence rests on the irrelevant factor of race easily could be extended to apply to claims based on unexplained discrepancies that correlate to membership in other minority groups, and even to gender. [4]

Task forces on gender, racial, and ethnic bias do exactly what the Supreme Court refused to do: They ask the forbidden questions.

Such questions about gender bias have been prompted by women, who have long organized around their participation in legal institutions—via groups such as the National Association of Women Lawyers, [5] the National Conference of Women and the Law, [6] the National Conference of Women Bar Associations, [7] the National Association of Women Judges, [8] and the Section on Women in Legal Education of the American Association of Law Schools, [9] and via several journals that now exist at law schools around the United States. [10]

In the 1960s and 1970s, as women litigated about their rights, they found that some of the pain of discrimination came from the very places to which they brought claims—the courts. In an effort to educate judges about the discrimination that was occurring under their aegis, the Legal Defense and Education Fund of the National Organization of Women founded the "National Judicial

Education Program" (NJEP), which worked in cooperation with the National Association of Women Judges.[11] Women advocates titled this issue "Gender Bias in the Courts," and a principal mechanism for responding became the creation of "Gender Bias Task Forces."[12]

New Jersey led the way in 1982 when Chief Justice Robert N. Wilentz of that state's Supreme Court created the first such Task Force.[13] In 1988, the Chief Justices of all the state courts adopted a resolution calling for study of gender, racial, and ethnic bias.[14] By the spring of 1990, "task force activity at various stages of operation [was] underway in some 30 jurisdictions" in the United States,[15] and in 1993, the Conference of Chief Justices called for implementation of reforms proposed by such task forces. These task forces review an array of topics, including the application of substantive legal doctrine, courtroom interactions, and the role of the court as employer.

From 1982 until 1990, task forces on gender bias in the courts were exclusively the domain of *state* courts. The federal courts (either acting circuit by circuit or as a whole by action of the Judicial Conference of the United States) neither took the lead nor followed suit in forming committees to ask questions about the interaction between gender and the federal court system. However, beginning in 1990, and again prompted in large part by the efforts of women advocates, the federal courts began to take up the question. In 1992, the Ninth Circuit became the first within the federal system to issue a report on this topic.[16] In the same year, the Judicial Conference of the United States called for studies of gender bias.[17] As of the spring of 1994, the District of Columbia's federal courts were at work on a report on gender, racial and ethnic bias in the courts, and the First, Second, Eighth, Tenth, and Eleventh Circuits had formed committees to consider how to address the question of gender.[18]

Thus, from a host of jurisdictions and relying on an array of research methods, people are thinking about the extent to which gender affects the courts and how the allocation of jurisdiction between state and federal courts affects our understanding of gender distinctions. This essay provides a brief overview of this effort to understand the relationship between gender and the courts, the findings reported thus far, how the work of gender bias task forces varies from state to federal court, and the questions yet to be explored.

THE QUESTIONS ASKED AND ANSWERED

Task forces are not only radical in their inquiry, they are also radical in their frequent and consistent answer: That despite their emblems of "equal justice under law," courts *are* a venue of discrimination—against women in general, against people of color in general, against women of color in distinct ways, against not only litigants but also against court employees, and against the lawyers who come to the courts on behalf of litigants.

Task forces have published their results, providing graphs, tables, charts, and testimonial evidence. These materials now form a tall mound, containing serious concerns about many aspects of the legal process across a range of issues. From states as disparate as California, Georgia, Kentucky, Maryland, and Minnesota, one learns that women seeking redress for "domestic" violence are often either blamed, accused of provoking their attacks, treated as if the experiences were trivial, or disbelieved. [19] When the focus is on race and ethnicity, the reports are similarly distressing; findings include that people of color are less likely to be released on bail than are whites for similar offenses[20] and "are more likely to be held in custody following conviction and prior to sentencing." [21] Moreover, there is evidence of sentencing disparity "that can be attributed only to race in the rate of convictions and the types of sentences." [22]

The Many Roles of Women Within Courts

A significant portion of most of the reports detail problems of bias as experienced by litigants, lawyers, court staff, and some-times by judges themselves. Courtroom interactions—on and off the record—are often affected by race, ethnicity, and gender bias, and employment opportunities for lawyers and staff are limited by these forms of bias. More than twenty reports document that women as witnesses face special hurdles; their credibility is readily questioned, their claims of injury undervalued. Almost all of the jurisdictions that have published gender bias task force reports address questions of credibility, as parts of discussions of domestic violence, sexual assault, courtroom interaction, and rights sought by women litigants under employment and federal benefits law. Many of the reports detail the specific problems faced by women testifying about sexual aggression. For the Ninth Circuit Gender Bias Task Force, credibility of women as witnesses emerged as a concern from inquiries in several areas, including federal benefits, immigration, and employment law. The Task Force learned that women's testimony may simply be thought to be complaints about life, rather than as legally cognizable harms, and that, even when believed, women's injuries may be trivialized or viewed as not "worth much" in monetary terms. [23]

Reports also document that the higher echelons of most judiciaries remain filled with white men. [24] One example comes from the federal system. As of June, 1991, four of the 13 federal appellate circuits had no women judges; 60 of the 94 federal trial courts had no life tenured women judges. [25] Four federal districts have no women in any judicial position, including bankruptcy and magistrate judges. While women were a bit better represented in the ranks of bankruptcy judges and magistrate judges (constituting 13 and 16 percent, respectively, as compared with under 7 percent of the Article III judges), of the roughly 1100 administrative law judges in 1991, women constituted five percent. [26] In contrast, more than ninety-eight percent of the legal secretaries in the federal judiciary system are women. [27]

Notice how these data are provided. Only two categories are offered: women and men. Women and men of color are invisible. Unfortunately, until 1993, the Equal Employment Office of the United States Courts, which is a primary resource, had separate categories for gender and then for groups described as: "White, Black, Hispanic, American Indian, [and] handicapped;" [28] no data were given on the intersectionalities of gender, race, and ethnicity within the federal judiciary.

The Parallel Themes

After accumulating the data, gender bias task forces assess what they have found. Although coming from different jurisdictions, the comments are parallel. The conclusions of the Report of the New York Task Force on Women in the Courts are illustrative:

> gender bias against women . . . is a pervasive problem with grave consequences. . . . Cultural stereotypes of women's role in marriage and in society daily distort courts' application of substantive law. Women uniquely, disproportionately and with unacceptable frequency must endure a climate of condescension, indifference and hostility. [29]

Other states echo this theme: "[W]omen are treated differently from men in the justice system and, because of it, many suffer from unfairness, embarrassment, emotional pain, professional deprivation and economic hardship."[30] Task forces on racial and ethnic bias come to parallel conclusions: "[T]he perception [is] that minorities are stripped of their human dignity, their individuality and their identity in their encounters with the court system."[31] "[T]here is evidence that bias does occur with disturbing frequency at every level of the legal profession and court system."[32] While a few reports do note areas in which progress has been made,[33] the fears of the majority in *McCleskey* were well-founded: when willing to consider discrimination by the courts, "unexplained" disparities in treatment correlate with membership in minority groups and "even [with] gender."[34]

Once issued, these reports have not been met with widespread denial of the existence of the problems documented. Rather, in some jurisdictions, the reports have done a good deal more than simply sit. Proposals for change have been considered, legislation passed, and some "progress"—measured in terms of appointments to the bench, integration of court-appointed committees, programs to educate judges and lawyers about their discriminatory patterns, rule changes, and the like—has occurred. Bias is now a topic of judicial conferences, of lawyer meetings, and of private discussions.[35] Sexual harassment policies have

been developed, [36] canons of ethics rewritten, [37] legislation enacted, [38] and training programs on the problems of victims of
violence created. As the five-year summary of efforts in New York
puts it: "Now, inescapably, gender bias and the concerns of
women are on the agenda." [39] Some celebration is in order, for a
measure of success can fairly be claimed.

A STATE-FEDERAL DIALOGUE ON GENDER BIAS

But a question must be asked: what are the "concerns of
women" that are now on the agenda? Thus far, the focus of task
force work has been to look at women as lawyers and judges in
courts and as litigants in particular kinds of cases; much of the
work is about women in families and as victims of violence. This
emphasis stems in part from a 1986 Manual that has been of great
help in assisting state by state efforts and that highlights topics to
be addressed; in addition to courtroom interaction and the court
as employer, the substantive legal issues proposed are "domestic
abuse," "alimony," and "juvenile justice." [40]

State Task Force Reports echo that emphasis. All of the
chapters of Maryland's report (other than those dealing with
courtroom interaction, selection of judges, and treatment of employees) address issues of domestic life and violence. [41] Connecticut's Task Force created subcommittees on courtroom interaction,
women attorneys, public hearings, and court administration; the
areas of law addressed were "family law" and "domestic violence." [42] Utah's Task Force and Nevada's approaches have been
similar. [43] While several state reports (particularly the more re-
cently-published ones) have pushed beyond these parameters, to
consider civil damage awards, [44] employment law, [45] prostitution, [46]
correctional facilities, [47] and court awarded attorneys' fees, [48] even
in those reports the bulk of the discussion remains on domestic
and criminal law. [49]

The entry by federal circuits into gender bias work—occurring
a decade after the state courts began the effort—offers an opportunity for reconsidering the framing of the gender bias inquiry as
well as for reconceptualizing the federal docket itself. The topics

that predominate in the state work—domestic relations and violence—are not perceived to be of primary concern to the federal
courts. Indeed, the federal courts lagged almost a decade behind
the states in taking up the topic of gender bias in part because of
the assumptions that gender was relevant to families and that the
federal courts had little to do with family law.

Illustrative of that view was the 1990 Report of the Federal
Courts Study Committee (FCSC), chartered by Congress to think
about the federal courts in the coming century. [50] While the Report
noted that the many studies of gender bias in the state systems
had found problems of discrimination in judicial proceedings, the
FCSC Report refused to call for a study of gender bias in the
federal system.

> Although we have confidence that the quality of the federal
> bench and the *nature* of federal law keep such problems to
> a minimum, it is unlikely that the federal judiciary is totally
> exempt from instances of this general social problem. [51]

The FCSC concluded that a study of such problems in the federal
system was not needed, but that awareness and education would
be appropriate. The Report's language captured a widely-held
sentiment that something intrinsic in the subject matter of federal
law and of the jurisdiction of the national courts (''the nature of
federal law'') has not much to do with women and the problems
we face. That view was reiterated when the Chief Justice argued
against a civil rights provision for women who were the victims of
gender-based violence on the grounds that the federal courts
should be ''reserved for issues where important national interests
predominate.'' [52]

Two questions thus emerge: What in the ''nature'' of the
workplace, ideology, or jurisdiction of the federal courts might
support a conclusion that discrimination against women is a
pervasive problem in state courts but kept to a minimum in the
federal courts? And what in the ''nature'' of state law, jurisdiction,
and ideology, or the selection of state judges enabled those
judiciaries to be more responsive to concerns of discrimination?

State/Federal Divergences: What Might Explain Them?

Many factors may have influenced the state courts to take the leadership on these issues. State judges may be more open to perceiving themselves in need of education (in general) than are Article III judges. Further, perhaps because many state judges are elected, they may be more concerned about the perceptions of justice in their courts. Because state and local governments include more women and men of color and white women than does the federal system, those voices might have been heard more easily. Law firms, public sector lawyers, law professors, and litigants have played critical roles in urging judiciaries to study these issues, and those advocating such studies may have thought state judiciaries more accessible than the federal courts.

Turning to the federal system, answers about its reluctance to embark on inquiries about gender bias stem in part from an assumption that, aside from equal protection, reproductive rights, and Title VII law, the federal courts do not have much to do with "women's issues," that women are less present in the federal courts, less relevant to their work than to the work of the state courts. Women's presumed absence from the federal courts has a material basis. In several respects, women are in the federal courts in smaller, less visible and less powerful roles than are men. The demographics of that workplace demonstrate dense concentrations of women as staff and a sizable representation of women as litigants but few women as judges and lawyers. Despite the fact that women are a significant percentage of federal litigants[53] and employees, the workplace is dominated by the professionals who populate it daily. These individuals are overwhelmingly male.

In the one completed study as of the winter of 1994 on gender in the federal system, women advocates told the Ninth Circuit's Task Force of their experiences of exclusion at the federal bar. The perceptions of exclusion correlated with the data that, as of 1992, within the Ninth Circuit, women were 16 percent of that bar, as contrasted with 25 percent of major law firms and of the bars of some states.[54] Women lawyers who responded to the Ninth Circuit survey reported their experience of the federal courts as a "club"—and not one much welcoming of them. [55] The Task Force heard repeatedly of what one woman called an "infrastructure of sexism." [56] And the Task Force received other data that filled in the picture; over the last sixty years, the United States Supreme Court has made appointments of special masters more than 80 times; none have been women. [57]

Perceptions of Jurisdiction Over Family Law

But it is not only the professional workplace of the federal courts that supports the image of a less visible relationship between women and the federal courts; that image is also predicated on pervasive ideological, legal, and sociological assumptions and actions about the subject matter of federal law. Women, seen as actors in private rather than public life, are assumed primarily to interact with law as wives, mothers, and victims of violence, some of which occurs inside homes but does not deserve the gloss of the word "domestic." Family, in turn, is assumed *not* to be much a part of federal jurisdiction or a topic of federal jurisprudence. Federal judges repeatedly claim that family law is the "province of the state," and some have lobbied against federal jurisdiction over civil rights claims predicated on gender-based animus. [58]

While the family remains a vehicle for creating distinctions based on gender, [59] both the equation of women with family and the narrow focus of the law of the family as encompassing only matters of marriage, divorce, and custody derive from nineteenth century images. These equations lead to another claim, also grounded in the nineteenth century, about the relationship between federal and state court jurisdiction: that family life is governed by the law of the states, and that the federal courts "ought" not to get involved. But there is no intrinsic "ought" and nothing "natural" about this jurisdictional relationship; indeed, federated systems in other countries—such as Canada—place family law within the national sphere. [60]

Three elements are missing from this ideological construction. First, jurisdictional rules and doctrine to exclude "domestic relations" from federal court authority are not "natural" but chosen to delineate barriers. Second, a wealth of federal law implicitly and explicitly regulates many aspects of family life. Third, women are in fact litigants in a range of disputes unrelated to the family. I will not here catalogue the breadth of federal laws that bring women in as federal litigants, but let me note a few. It is not only the high visibility so-called "women's cases," such as litigation about reproductive freedom, Title VII, and equal protection, but also a host of other kinds of cases, ranging from immigration law to the more than two billion dollar Dalkon Shield case (emerging out of the injuries done to women's bodies) to consumer bankruptcies in which, according to one study, women are 75 percent of the claimants, filing either singly or jointly. [61]

Women are in the federal courts, and the fact of family status does not define women as litigants. Moreover, the federal courts do have a lot to do with family life. Many have written about the constitutionalization of family law. [62] But it is not only constitutional issues that draw the federal courts into family life; a host of federal statutory laws define and structure economic relations among family members. We do not typically call these "family law" but rather tax law, pension law, and federal benefits law. [63] All, however, have direct and specific effects on family life. [64] Federal immigration law judges sometimes have to decide whether wives have been battered; federal bankruptcy judges deal with community property and ownership of assets of divorcing spouses. Moreover, federal courts have authority over members of the military and claim power over members of Indian tribes. It is time to understand and to name the wealth of "federal laws of the family" [65] as well as to understand that women's legal problems stem from a range of interactions of which being in the family is but one.

The belated entry of the federal courts into the work of uncovering gender bias may thus be an occasion to reassess misguided assumptions about the lack of involvement of the federal courts with family life and about the impropriety of cabining women in families. In addition, federal gender bias studies may prompt ongoing state court task forces to revisit their focus on professional interactions and on women in families, in the criminal justice system, and as victims of violence. A dialogue between jurisdictions may prompt new avenues of inquiry into how gender affects adjudication, [66] and how jurisdictional lines are drawn on assumptions about gender roles.

THE QUESTIONS THAT REMAIN

Now, with the luxury of a decade of intensely difficult and genuinely successful work behind, it is time to consider what the shape of the second decade of gender bias task force work might be. Given the energy invested and the considerable accomplishments realized, one might be tempted to end simply with congratulations. But feminist gains need always to be reassessed against changing social and political landscapes. It is not from a lack of appreciation (some of it all too first hand) of how hard it has been but from the strength gained by the success already achieved that one must ask: How might or should the work of this decade be different from that upon which it is built?

Across jurisdictions, studies of gender bias have given sustained attention to women lawyers, the very individuals who are the subject of this volume of essays. The focus on women as professional workers within courts (as well as litigants in familial disputes and as victims of violence) has been based not only on the importance of these issues to women but also on the relative ease of studying such issues. The choice of the phrase "relative ease" needs immediate qualification. Nothing about this work is "easy"—it is labor intensive, often marginalized, and sometimes explicitly unpopular, as feminist work so often is. However, there is "relative ease" in choosing topics in which there may be access to data and less hostility. The study of women as workers in courts—as judges, lawyers, and employees—is relatively easy, in the sense that the number of women in specific positions can be recorded, assessed, and then, after time reassessed. Further, because so many of the task forces are comprised of women judges and lawyers, the members have special interest in the effects of gender on their own professional lives.

Similarly, the focus on specific areas of law, such as family and criminal justice issues, also helps to narrow the wide range of possible avenues of inquiry. Task forces, chronically underfunded and understaffed, must make their projects manageable. Moreover, while gender bias work is never comfortable, focusing on the professions and the family helps to cushion the threat and to mask the radical nature of the inquiry. Because of the view that obtaining court support is so important, that support may come more readily for topics as familiar as women and their children, and for women as lawyers.[67] Indeed, reflective of the effort to cushion the pain of the findings of widespread discrimination, task forces in the United States have chosen titles like "fairness" and "equity."[68] No task force in the United States that has published to date has titled its work "feminist" or explained itself as about the "oppression of women by the patriarchy." In contrast, parallel work in Canada is styled "An Inquiry into Systemic Racism in the Criminal Justice System of Ontario."

The question is whether the coming decade is one in which topics that raise even greater anxiety can be broached. The willingness to increase the disquietude engendered by this enterprise must be based on the view that staying with the current titles and subjects is too limiting. One risk is that we have or will engender a relatively comfortable conversation about enhancing opportunities for professional women. While there is no question that women as lawyers have been subjected to unfair treatment by judges, colleagues, clients, opponents, and court personnel, women professionals are privileged as compared to many women litigants. Another concern is that we will continue to document but not to address the difficulties faced by women as litigants because we have failed to investigate the differences *among* women and to look at the problems that they encounter outside families and in the less visible exchanges of alternative dispute resolution, administrative adjudication, and while on probation or dealing with court personnel. Because so much of the discussion is cast as about the generic "woman" in the generic "court," we will miss the distinct experiences of women of different races, ethnicities, classes, ages, and sexual orientation and of women in different kinds and phases of dispute resolution.

We must acknowledge that some of the bias reports published to date have these limitations, but also that progress is being made in addressing the multiplicity that is "woman." Until recently, much of the data provided were about "women" rather than about groups of women identified by race and ethnicity. However, a few of the gender bias reports do address women of color.[69] Similarly, of the task forces on race and ethnic bias, several do not devote sustained attention to women of color, but again a few do take up this issue.[70] Few reports of either gender, race, or ethnic task forces have discussed the effects of class, age, and sexual orientation.[71] Families themselves are dealt with in traditional terms; and few task force reports have taken on the interdependency of gender bias and of discrimination based on sexual orientation, which often cabins women and men in stereotypical roles.[72] And relatively few have considered how gender affects alternative dispute resolution, processes that courts are sponsoring with increasing frequency.

Thus the questions that remain are whether the ongoing task forces and the implementation committees derived from the completed task forces will be able to look further, harder, and in areas that are the most difficult to study and discuss. Happily, I can conclude not only with comment about the need for such work but also with the report that those engaged in contemporary task force efforts are aware of these concerns and considering how to enable these issues to occupy a more substantial part of the research agenda.[73] Here, of course, is where the woman advocate remains key; the women professionals who shape and create a good deal of this work will have to focus on ways to transform the lives of women litigants—thus genuinely, to borrow Virginia Woolf's words, "opening the door."

ENDNOTES

   * © All rights reserved. Judith Resnik is the Orrin B. Evans Professor of Law at the University of Southern California and a member of the Ninth Circuit Gender Bias Task Force. My thanks to Christine Carr, Dennis Curtis, Andrea Fugate, Veronica Gentilli, Rose-Ellen Heinz, Vicki Jackson, Angela Johnson, Peter Lee, Sheri Porath, Joan Schaffner, Lynn Hecht Schafran, Lee Seltman, and to my colleagues on the Ninth Circuit Gender Bias Task Force, the Honorable John Coughenour, the Honorable Proctor Hug, Jr., the Honorable Marilyn Patel, Deborah Hensler, Margaret McKeown, Terry Bird, Henry Shields, and Mark Mendenhall, who have shared in so much of this work.

1. 481 U.S. 279 (1987).

2. Warren McCleskey's constitutional claim relied in large measure on a statistical study authored by Professors David Baldus, Charles Pulaski, and George Woodworth and reviewed 2000 murder cases in Georgia during the 1970s. The data indicated that "black defendants, such as McCleskey, who kill white victims have the greatest likelihood of receiving the death penalty." McCleskey, 481 U.S. at 287. The Court held that "the Baldus study does not demonstrate a constitutionally significant risk of racial bias affecting the Georgia capital sentencing process." Id. at 313.

The four dissenting Justices—Brennan, Marshall, Blackmun, and Stevens—disagreed. In their view, the data meant that "defendants charged with killing white victims in Georgia are 4.3 times as likely to be sentenced to death as defendants charged with killing blacks. . . . [T]here was a significant chance that race would play a prominent role in determining if [McCleskey] lived or died. Id. at 321 (Brennan, J., dissenting) (citations omitted). On September 25, 1991, after Mr. McCleskey had argued unsuccessfully in subsequent proceedings that his punishment was unconstitutional for other reasons (see McCleskey v. Zant, 111 S.Ct. 1454 (1991)), Georgia authorities executed him. See Peter Applebome, Georgia Inmate Is Executed After 'Chaotic' Legal Move, N.Y. TIMES, Sept. 26, 1991, at A18."

3. Justice Powell's opinion for the Court interpreted the Equal Protection Clause as requiring that a claimant had to show that "decisionmakers in his case acted with discriminatory purpose." McCleskey v. Kemp, 481 U.S. at 292 (emphasis in original). A defendant could not rely on a claim of discrimination that "[i]n its broadest form, . . . extends to every actor in the Georgia capital sentencing process, from the prosecutor who sought the death penalty and the jury that imposed the sentence, to the State itself that enacted the capital punishment statute and allows it to remain in effect despite its allegedly discriminatory application." Id.

4. McCleskey, 481 U.S. at 315-17 (footnotes omitted).

5. In 1899, women formed the National Association of Women's Lawyers. See National Association of Women Lawyers, 75 YEAR HISTORY OF NATIONAL ASSOCIATION OF WOMEN LAWYERS, 1899-1974 at 7 (Mary H. Zimmerman, ed., 1975). Exactly when women first began to practice law in the United States is not known, but scholars place that event around 1870. See KAREN BERGER MORELLO, THE INVISIBLE BAR (1986) at 11.

6. This organization, started in 1977, sponsors annual conferences. See Herma Hill Kay and Christine A. Littleton, Text Note: Feminist Jurisprudence: What is It? When did it Start? Who Does It?, in HERMA HILL KAY, SEX-BASED DISCRIMINATION 884 (3d ed., 1988).

7. Martha Middleton, Women's Bars Form Coalition, 7 Bar Leader 6 (ABA, Sept.Oct. 1981) (started in 1981 to provide "clearinghouse" on information about women's bar associations that then included some 10,000 lawyers).

8. Esther McGuigg Morris is described as the first woman to be a member of a judiciary; although not a lawyer, she was a justice of the peace in South Pass City, Wyoming, in 1870. See Morello, supra note 5, at 219. By 1979, there were enough women judges to inspire the creation of the National Association of Women Judges (NAWJ), formed in response to the "very lonely, very isolated lives of those women judges who may be the only one on their bench in that locale or state." Morello, supra note 5, at

245 (quoting one of the founders, Joan Dempsey Klein). *See also* Gladys Kessler, *Foreword to* 14 GOLDEN GATE U. L. REV. 473, 477-78 (1984) (Symposium on National Association of Women Judges, whose purposes include formulating "solutions" to the "legal, educational, social and ethical problems mutually encountered by women judges.")

9. The Section on Women in Legal Education was founded in 1970. *See* Kay, *supra* note 6, at 880.

10. These journals include: The Women's Rights Law Reporter (Rutgers Law School; founded 1971); Berkeley Women's Law Journal (founded 1983); Women's Law Forum of the Golden Gate Law Review (founded 1979); Harvard Women's Law Journal (founded 1977); Women and Law (Hofstra, founded 1978); Wisconsin's Women's Law Journal (founded 1985); Yale Journal of Law and Feminism (founded 1987); USC Review of Law and Women Studies (founded 1990); Texas Journal of Women and the Law (founded 1990); UCLA Women's Law Journal (founded 1990); Columbia Journal of Gender and Law (founded 1990); American University Journal of Gender and the Law (founded 1991); Law & Sexuality: A Review of Lesbian and Gay Legal Issues (founded 1990, Tulane University School of Law).

11. *See* Norma Juliet Wikler, *On the Judicial Agenda for the 80's: Equal Treatment for Men and Women in the Courts,* 64 Judicature 202 (1980) (as founding director of the NJEP, Dr. Wikler summarized the evidence of gender based stereotypes and of the new project to educate judges); Norma J. Wikler, *Water on Stone: A Perspective on the Movement to Eliminate Gender Bias in the Courts,* 26 COURT REVIEW 6 (Fall, 1989) (history of founding of NJEP).

12. *See* Lynn Hecht Schafran, *Educating the Judiciary about Gender Bias,* 9 WOMEN'S RIGHTS LAW REPORTER 109, 124 (1986) (as Executive Director of the NJEP, describing its "dream" to be "a task force in every state").

13. FIRST YEAR REPORT OF THE NEW JERSEY SUPREME COURT TASK FORCE ON WOMEN IN THE COURTS (June, 1984) at 4 [hereinafter NEW JERSEY GENDER REPORT]; *see also* Lynn Hecht Schafran, *Documenting Gender Bias in the Courts: The Task Force Approach,* 70 JUDICATURE 280, 281 (1987).

14. 26 S. Ct. Rev. 5 (1989).

15. Betty Weinberg Ellerin, Chair of the National Task Force on Gender Bias in the Courts of the National Association of Women Judges, ANNUAL REPORT TO THE BOARD OF DIRECTORS OF THE NATIONAL ASSOCIATION OF WOMEN JUDGES (September 4, 1990) (on file with author). *See generally* Lynn Hecht Schafran, *Gender Bias in the Courts: An Emerging Focus for Judicial Reform,* 21 Ariz. St. L. J. 237 (1989) (reviewing the achievements).

16. *See* the NINTH CIRCUIT GENDER BIAS TASK FORCE, GENDER BIAS IN THE COURTS: DISCUSSION DRAFT (July, 1992) (available from the Circuit Executive's Office) [hereinafter NINTH CIRCUIT GENDER BIAS TASK FORCE PRELIMINARY REPORT]; Ninth Circuit Gender Bias Task Force, *Executive Summary of the Discussion Draft,* 45 Stan. L. Rev. 2153 (1993); Ninth Circuit Gender Bias Task Force, THE EFFECTS OF GENDER IN THE FEDERAL COURTS: FINAL REPORT (July 1993), and its Executive Summary (available from the Circuit Executive's Office) [hereinafter NINTH CIRCUIT GENDER BIAS TASK FORCE FINAL REPORT], 67 S. Cal. L. Rev. 745.

17. *See* REPORT OF THE PROCEEDINGS OF THE JUDICIAL CONFERENCE OF THE UNITED STATES 64 (Sept. 22, 1992) (Bias in the Federal Judiciary).

18. Impetus for this work comes not only from the findings of the Ninth Circuit Task Force but also from resolutions in support of such work, passed in 1992 and 1993 by the Judicial Conference of the United States and from provisions of pending legislation, the Violence Against Women Act, which calls for studies of gender bias. *See* Title V of The Violence Against Women Act of 1993, S. 11 and H.R. 1133, 103rd Cong., 1st Sess. (1993).

19. *See* Judicial Council of California, ACHIEVING EQUAL JUSTICE FOR WOMEN AND MEN IN THE COURTS, THE DRAFT REPORT OF THE JUDICIAL COUNCIL ADVISORY COMM. ON GENDER BIAS IN THE COURTS at 4-5 (1990) [hereinafter CALIFORNIA GENDER BIAS DRAFT REPORT]; GENDER AND JUSTICE IN THE COURTS: A REPORT TO THE SUPREME COURT OF GEORGIA BY THE COMM'N ON GENDER BIAS IN THE JUDICIAL SYSTEM 19-21 (1991) [hereinafter GEORGIA GENDER BIAS REPORT]; EQUAL JUSTICE FOR WOMEN AND MEN, KENTUCKY TASK FORCE ON GENDER FAIRNESS IN THE COURTS 28 (1992) [hereinafter KENTUCKY GENDER FAIRNESS REPORT]; REPORT OF THE SPECIAL JOINT COMM. ON GENDER BIAS IN THE COURTS 2-5 (1989) [hereinafter MARYLAND GENDER BIAS REPORT]; MINNESOTA SUPREME COURT TASK FORCE FOR GENDER FAIRNESS IN THE COURTS, FINAL REPORT, *reprinted in* 15 WM. MITCHELL L. REV. 825, 872-77 (1989) [hereinafter MINNESOTA GENDER FAIRNESS REPORT]. *See also* THE FINAL REPORT OF THE TASK FORCE ON RACIAL AND ETHNIC BIAS AND TASK FORCE ON GENDER BIAS IN THE COURTS 119 (District of Columbia, 1992) ("cross-examination of victims tends to be more hostile in sexual assault cases than in other assault cases.").

20. REPORT OF THE NEW YORK STATE JUDICIAL COMM'N ON MINORITIES, Vol. II, 150-51 (1991) (published in five volumes) [hereinafter NEW YORK REPORT ON MINORITIES]; REPORT AND RECOMMENDATIONS OF THE FLORIDA SUPREME COURT RACIAL AND ETHNIC BIAS STUDY COMM'N: "WHERE THE INJURED FLY FOR JUSTICE," Vol. II, 23 (1991) [hereinafter FLORIDA RACIAL/ETHNIC BIAS STUDY, Vol. II].

21. MINORITY AND JUSTICE TASK FORCE, FINAL REPORT 11 (1990) [hereinafter WASHINGTON MINORITY AND JUSTICE REPORT].

22. NEW YORK REPORT ON MINORITIES, Vol. I, *supra* note 20, at 43; *see also* Alaska Judicial Council, ALASKA FELONY SENTENCING PATTERNS: A MULTIVARIATE STATISTICAL ANALYSIS 27-36 (1974-1976) (Blacks received higher sentences in several categories of cases); INTERIM REPORT OF THE ALASKA JUDICIAL COUNCIL ON FINDINGS OF APPARENT RACIAL DISPARITY IN SENTENCING 54 (1979) (race of Blacks and Native Alaskans a factor in denial of probation).

23. NINTH CIRCUIT GENDER BIAS TASK FORCE PRELIMINARY REPORT, *supra* note 16, at 70-71, 97-103, 110-111. *See also* Lucie E. White, *Subordination, Rhetorical Survival Skills, and Sunday Shoes: Notes on the Hearing of Mrs. G.,* 38 BUFF. L. REV. 1 (1990).

24. *See, e.g.,* REPORT AND RECOMMENDATIONS OF THE FLORIDA SUPREME COURT RACIAL AND ETHNIC BIAS STUDY COMM'N: "WHERE INJURED FLY FOR JUSTICE", Vol. I, 14 (1990) [hereinafter FLORIDA RACIAL/ETHNIC BIAS STUDY, Vol. I] (one percent of the judges are women of color, and none sit at the appellate level); *Executive Summary of the Discussion Draft, supra* note 16,("Eighty-eight percent of Ninth Circuit judicial positions are held by men").

25. THE UNITED STATES COURT DIRECTORY 5, 13, 23-27, 56-338 (August 1992). The Directory, published by the Administrative Office of the United States Courts, provides information on Article III active and senior judges, judges in Article I and Article III specialized courts, bankruptcy judges, and magistrate judges. These data were collected for the Ninth Circuit's Gender

Bias Task Force; the Preliminary Report of the Task Force of the D.C. Circuit, released in June of 1994, provides a more recent summary.

26. John C. Holmes, ALJ *Update, A Review of the Current Role, Status, and Demographics of the Corps of Administrative Law Judges*, 38 FED. B. NEWS & J. 202, 203 (1991) (a "veteran's preference" remains a part of the selection of ALJs).

27. *See, e.g.*, Administrative Office of the U.S. Courts, ANNUAL REPORT OF THE JUDICIARY EQUAL OPPORTUNITY PROGRAM FOR THE TWELVE-MONTH PERIOD ENDED SEPTEMBER 30, 1990 (Preliminary Report), at 14 (1990).

28. Id., Table 1 at 8 (1990). Compare Kimberle Crenshaw, *Demarginalizing the Intersection of Race and Sex: A Black Feminist Critique of Antidiscrimination Doctrine, Feminist Theory and Antiracist Politics*, 1989 U. CHI. L. FORUM 139.

29. REPORT OF THE NEW YORK TASK FORCE ON WOMEN IN THE COURTS 5 (1986) [hereinafter NEW YORK GENDER REPORT], reprinted in 15 FORDHAM URBAN L. J. 11, 17-18 (1986-87).

30. REPORT OF THE CONNECTICUT TASK FORCE ON GENDER, JUSTICE AND THE COURTS 12 (1991) [hereinafter CONNECTICUT GENDER REPORT]; *see also* REPORT OF THE FLORIDA SUPREME COURT GENDER BIAS STUDY COMMISSION 42 (1990) [hereinafter FLORIDA GENDER BIAS REPORT] (finding that "gender bias permeates Florida's legal system today"); The 1990 REPORT OF THE ILLINOIS TASK FORCE ON GENDER BIAS IN THE COURTS 3, 5, 15, 16, 25, 28 (1990) [hereinafter ILLINOIS GENDER BIAS REPORT] (finding that women are "at a disadvantage during divorce settlement negotiations;" rape victims are discouraged from prosecuting "by treatment they receive from the system;" while there are not plentiful examples of "overt discrimination," there is "evidence that more subtle forms of bias persist"); MARYLAND GENDER BIAS REPORT, *supra* note 19, at iii-iv ("women's negative experiences cover the range from the aggravating to the life-threatening"); WASHINGTON STATE TASK FORCE ON GENDER AND JUSTICE IN THE COURTS, GENDER & JUSTICE IN THE COURTS xvi (1989) [hereinafter WASHINGTON GENDER REPORT] ("[G]ender discrimination exists and can negatively impact judicial decision making and affect the outcome of litigation.").

31. NEW YORK REPORT ON MINORITIES, Vol. II, *supra* note 20, at 1; *see also* WASHINGTON MINORITY AND JUSTICE REPORT, *supra* note 21, at xxi-xxii ("minorities . . . [do not] trust the court system to resolve their disputes or administer justice even-handedly"); NEW JERSEY TASK FORCE ON MINORITY CONCERNS, FINAL REPORT, ' NEW J. LAWYER 1225, 1230 (Aug. 10, 1992) [hereinafter NEW JERSEY MINORITY REPORT] ("Minority litigants, minority witnesses, and minority attorneys are subjected to racial and ethnic slights from all levels of court and security personnel—from the bailiff to the bench."); FLORIDA RACIAL/ETHNIC BIAS STUDY, Vol. II, *supra* note 20, at viii ("evidence in Florida suggests that the rights of non-English speaking defendants are systematically being compromised due to the lack of trained, qualified court interpreters.").

32. FINAL REPORT OF THE MICHIGAN SUPREME COURT TASK FORCE ON RACIAL/ ETHNIC ISSUES IN THE COURTS 2 (1989) [hereinafter MICHIGAN RACIAL/ETHNIC REPORT]; *see also* NEW JERSEY MINORITY REPORT, *supra* note 31, at 1238 ("Ample evidence supports a broad perception of insensitivity and indifference exhibited sometimes by judges, court employees, members of the bar . . . and other persons who work in courthouses . . . ").

33. *See, e.g.,* GEORGIA GENDER BIAS REPORT, *supra* note 19, at xi (finding "no widespread or overt gender bias," yet "there is evidence that bias does exist within Georgia's judicial system."); KENTUCKY GENDER FAIRNESS REPORT, *supra* note 19, at 6 (reporting that "experiences in the courts are not as bad as they once were."); FINAL REPORT OF THE NEW MEXICO STATE BAR TASK FORCE ON WOMEN AND THE LEGAL PROFESSION 2 (1988) ("although the law has made significant gains," remedial recommendations were still appropriate); THE FINAL REPORT OF THE TASK FORCE ON RACIAL AND ETHNIC BIAS 9 (1992) [hereinafter D.C. RACIAL/ETHNIC BIAS REPORT] (commenting that because the majority population of the District of Columbia is African-American, that court is a unique environment); THE FINAL REPORT OF THE TASK FORCE ON GENDER BIAS IN THE COURTS (1992) [hereinafter D.C. GENDER BIAS REPORT] 93 (the local courts of Washington D.C. were more hospitable to women because of the presence of many women on the bench and the number of women practitioners).

34. *McCleskey,* 481 U.S. at 316-17.

35. *See, e.g.,* the resolution enacted unanimously by the officers of the Essex County Bar Association of New Jersey, calling for (inter alia) a "permanent task force" on issues of racial/ethnic discrimination in the courts; a revised bail system "free of bias [that] . . . gives minimum weight to economic criteria because such factors generally impact unfairly upon racial minorities;" "cautionary jury instructions relative to . . . cross-racial identification . . . "; the "establishment of a non-discriminatory bar examination;" and a requirement that judges read and post statements "opposing racial and ethnic bias in the courts." Memorandum of Robert D. Lipscher to Hon. Theodore Z. Davis, *Comments on the Final Report of the Supreme Court Task Force on Minority Concerns* 3-4 (Dec. 28, 1992).

36. *See, e.g.,* Western District of Washington, United States District Court and Bankruptcy Courts, Sexual Harassment Policy 1 (adopted February, 1993) (applicable to "a member of the District or Bankruptcy Clerk's Offices, Probation Office, Pretrial Services Office, or judicial staff" as well as to "any non-staff person.").

37. *See, e.g., Mich. Bar Approves Antibias Rules for Codes of Conduct,* 15 BAR LEADER at 4-5 (ABA, Nov.-Dec. 1990) (state bar approves new rules that provide that lawyers and judges not "engage in invidious discrimination on the basis of gender, race, religion, disability, age, sexual orientation, or ethnic origin and shall prohibit staff and agents subject to the lawyer's direction and control from doing so."); American Bar Association, MODEL CODE OF JUDICIAL CONDUCT Canon 2(C) (1990) ("A judge shall not hold membership in any organization that practices invidious discrimination on the basis of race, sex, religion or national origin.").

38. *See, e.g.,* FLA. STAT. ANN., section 43.29 (West Supp. 1993) (requiring that each judicial nominations commission shall be composed of three members, "at least one of whom must be a member of a racial or ethnic minority group or a woman"); Ch. 39 L. 1988, *codified in* N.Y. CRIM. PROC. LAW, section 170.55(4) (McKinney Supp. 1993) (permitting adjournments in contemplation of dismissal conditioned on a defendant attending educational programs on family violence).

39. *See* FIVE YEAR REPORT OF THE NEW YORK JUDICIAL COMMITTEE ON WOMEN IN THE COURTS 27-31, 44 (1991) [hereinafter NEW YORK FIVE YEAR REPORT].

40. Lynn Hecht Schafran and Norma Juliet Wikler, Operating A Task Force On Gender Bias In The Courts: A Manual For Action at 5-7, 24 (1986). The manual provides a wealth of suggestions about how to enlist support, collect data, disseminate findings, and set up a structure for ongoing distribution of information, for implementation of reform, and for monitoring of changes.

41. Maryland Gender Bias Report, *supra* note 19, Table of Contents ("Chapter I. Domestic Violence; Chapter II. Child Custody and Visitation; Chapter III. Child Support; Chapter IV. Alimony; Property Disposition and Litigation Expenses").

42. Connecticut Gender Report, *supra* note 30, (List of Task Force Subcommittees on unnumbered prefatory page).

43. Utah Task Force on Gender and Justice, Report to the Utah Judicial Council at iii. (Again, courtroom interaction and employment were also addressed.); Justice for Women, Nevada Supreme Court Gender Bias Task Force (1988) at i-ii (addresses divorce, domestic violence and courtroom interaction).

44. Report of the Gender Bias Study of the Supreme Judicial Court, Commonwealth of Massachusetts (1989) at 135-139 [hereinafter Massachusetts Gender Bias Report]; New York Gender Report, *supra* note 29, at 81-83; New Jersey Gender Report, *supra* note 13, at 25; Minnesota Gender Fairness Report, *supra* note 19, at 913-917; Gender and Justice in the Colorado Courts, Colorado Supreme Court Task Force on Gender Bias in the Courts (1990) at 104-105; Illinois Gender Bias Report, *supra* note 30, at 177-197; Kentucky Gender Fairness Report, *supra* note 19, at 40-41; Final Report of the Michigan Supreme Court Task Force on Gender Issues in the Courts (1989) at 38 [hereinafter Michigan Gender Report]; Final Report of the Rhode Island Committee on Women in the Courts: Final Report on Gender Bias (1987) at 31; Gender and Justice, Report of the Vermont Task Force on Gender Bias in the Legal System (1991) at 148-154 [hereinafter Vermont Gender Bias Report]; Washington Gender Report, *supra* note 30, at 83-107; Wisconsin Equal Justice Task Force Final Report (1991) at 25-28 [hereinafter Wisconsin Gender Report].

45. Minnesota Gender Fairness Report, *supra* note 19, at 917-922; Washington Gender Report, *supra* note 30, at 100; Wisconsin Gender Report, *supra* note 44, at 34-39.

46. *See, e.g.*, Florida Gender Bias Report, *supra* note 30, at 162-182; Kentucky Gender Fairness Report, *supra* note 19, at 36.

47. California Gender Bias Draft Report, *supra* note 19, at Section 7; Florida Gender Bias Report, *supra* note 30, at 91; Georgia Gender Bias Report, *supra* note 19, at 133-145; Kentucky Gender Fairness Report, *supra* note 19, at 34; Massachusetts Gender Bias Report, *supra* note 44, at 127-132; Minnesota Gender Fairness Report, *supra* note 19, at 906-907.

48. Washington Gender Report, *supra* note 30, at 99-102.

49. *See* Judith Resnik, "Naturally" Without Gender: Women, Jurisdiction, and the Federal Courts, 66 N.Y.U. L. Rev. 1682, 1768 (1991) (table of topics addressed by state gender bias task forces).

50. *See* Judicial Improvements and Access to Justice Act, Pub. L. No. 100-702, 101-109, 102 Stat. 4642, 4644-46 (codified temporarily as 28 U.S.C. § 331 "note" (1988)).

51. Report of the Federal Courts Study Committee (Apr. 2, 1990) at 169 (emphasis added).

52. *See* William H. Rehnquist, *Chief Justice's 1991 Year-End Report on the Federal Judiciary*, 24 THE THIRD BRANCH 1-2 (1992) (commending the then-views of the Judicial Conference, which at that time opposed proposals to confer jurisdiction on federal courts for claims of violence motivated by gender-based animus but which has subsequently modified its views).

53. Judges responding to the Ninth Circuit Gender Bias Task Force surveys reported that in an average month, about ten percent of the criminal and twenty percent of the civil litigants that appear before them are women; bankruptcy judges reported that about thirty percent of the litigants are women. Lawyers in private practice reported that about twenty-five percent of their clients are women. NINTH CIRCUIT GENDER BIAS TASK FORCE FINAL REPORT, *supra* note 16, at 20.

54. NINTH CIRCUIT GENDER BIAS TASK FORCE FINAL REPORT, *supra* note 16 at 14. *See also* Claudia Maclachlan & Rita Henley Jensen, *Progress Glacial for Women, Minorities*, NAT'L L.J., Jan. 27, 1992, at 31 (reporting that a national study found that women attorneys comprised 26 percent of all attorneys at the 250 largest law firms in the country).

Women also constituted 16 percent of the Civil Justice Reform Act Advisory Groups, appointed by district court chief judges pursuant to the Civil Justice Reform Act of 1990. 28 U.S.C. §471 et seq. (1990). Veronica Gentilli, Composition of the Civil Justice Reform Act Advisory Groups, Working Paper, Ninth Circuit Gender Bias Task Force (May 1992). In four districts, no women sat at all. The district with the highest percentage of women, 40 percent, was a district in which a woman was the chief judge and thus in charge of appointments. In all of the districts in which women were chief judges, women constituted 27 percent of those selected to be committee members.

55. *See* NINTH CIRCUIT GENDER BIAS TASK FORCE FINAL REPORT, *supra* note 16, at 22.

56. *Executive Summary of the Discussion Draft, supra* note 16.

57. Lee Seltman, The Appointments of Special Masters: A Demographic Analysis of the Ninth Circuit and The United States Supreme Court, Working Paper, Ninth Circuit Gender Bias Task Force (Feb. 1992).

58. *See, e.g.*, REPORT OF THE JUDICIAL CONFERENCE 1991 AD HOC COMMITTEE ON GENDER-BASED VIOLENCE 6 (Sept. 1991) (opposing the Violence Against Women Act of 1991's jurisdictional provisions and arguing that permitting federal jurisdiction over such civil rights claims would "embroil the federal courts in domestic relations disputes"). In contrast, in 1993, that committee revised its views and recommended that the Conference take no position on the jurisdictional provisions but that it support the provisions of the Violence Against Women Act that call for study of gender bias. *See* Judicial Conference Resolution on Violence Against Women (March 1993).

59. *See* SUSAN MOLLER OKIN, JUSTICE, GENDER, AND THE FAMILY 170-171 (1989) ("The family is the linchpin of gender, reproducing it from one generation to the next . . . .").

60. *See, e.g.* Martha A. Field, *The Differing Federalisms of Canada and the United States*, LAW & CONTEMP. PROB. (forthcoming) (1991 manuscript on file with author) ("marriage and divorce and criminal law . . . are governed by

the central government in Canada but the state governments in the United States . . .").

61. TERESA A. SULLIVAN, ELIZABETH WARREN & JAY LAWRENCE WESTBROOK, AS WE FORGIVE OUR DEBTORS: BANKRUPTCY AND CONSUMER CREDIT IN AMERICA 146-65 (1989).

62. *See, e.g.,* Sylvia A. Law, *Rethinking Sex and the Constitution,* 131 U. PA. L. REV. 955 (1984).

63. *See generally* Edward J. McCaffery, *Taxation and the Family: A Fresh Look at the Behavioral Gender Biases in the Code,* 40 UCLA L. Rev. 983 (1993); Mary E. Becker, *Obscuring the Struggle: Sex Discrimination, Social Security, and Stone, Seidman, Sunstein & Tushnet's Constitutional Law,* 89 COLUM. L. REV. 264 (1989).

64. *See, e.g., Ablamis v. Roper,* 937 F.2d 1450 (9th Cir. 1991) (analyzing effects of state property regimes on federal marital property rules under ERISA).

65. *See* Resnik, *supra* note 49, at 1721-30.

66. For example, the nascent federal court task force work has taken up topics such as the effects of gender on immigration, bankruptcy, federal benefits, and federal Indian law.

67. *See, e.g.,* the reception accorded to feminist theories sometimes labeled "cultural feminism" that consider women's "differences" (*see, e.g.,* Carol Gilligan, *Moral Orientation and Moral Development in* WOMAN AND MORAL THEORY (Eva Feder Kittay & Diana T. Meyers eds., 1987), as compared with those theories labeled "radical feminism" and challenging male "domination." *See, e.g.,* CATHARINE A. MACKINNON, ch. 2 *Difference and Dominance: On Sex Discrimination,* FEMINISM UNMODIFIED (1987).

68. Of thirty titles reviewed of reports on gender, thirteen studies use the words "gender bias" in their titles and ten use one of the following: "fairness;" "equity;" "equality;" "equal justice," or "gender and justice."

69. For example, the Draft California Gender Bias Task Force Report has a section devoted specifically to the distinct issues of women of color. CALIFORNIA GENDER BIAS DRAFT REPORT, *supra* note 19, at Section 10. The report also stressed its concern with its own limited focus and called for the creation of a task force devoted to racial and ethnic discrimination. Id. at 3-4. The Ninth Circuit Gender Bias Task Force's Final Report provides some data on women who are minority members and lawyers and also studies areas, such as immigration and federal Indian law, of specific import to women of color. NINTH CIRCUIT GENDER BIAS TASK FORCE FINAL REPORT, *supra* note 16, at 18; 99-122; 145-156.

A few other reports make references to women of color on occasion. *See, e.g.,* KENTUCKY GENDER FAIRNESS REPORT, *supra* note 19, at 8, 22, 35 which found that "minority women law professors encounter even greater barriers to advancement [than white women professors]", "black women were less likely to receive alimony than white women" and in one study found that while 42 percent of black women apprehended for shoplifting were officially charged, 8.8 percent of white women apprehended were officially charged. The CONNECTICUT GENDER REPORT, *supra* note 30, at 82-83, examined sentencing to determine whether gender and race had any impact and found that "holding constant the relevant control variables, black and latin defendants were more likely than whites to receive a jail sentence to be served" and "black women's average sentence length was 10.5 months longer than white women's." The D.C. GENDER BIAS REPORT, *supra* note 33, at 62-63, found a lack of African-American women in the upper echelons of the court's workforce. Yet other reports, while not exploring the issues of women of color, make note of the problem. *See, e.g.,* ILLINOIS GENDER BIAS REPORT, *supra* note 30, at 224 (testimony received that "this problem [derogatory comments by judges] is even more severe for African-American women, who suffer from the double burden of race and gender bias."); NEW YORK GENDER REPORT, *supra* note 29, at 195-97 (subsection "race and economic status as affecting credibility"); *id.* at 250-59 (discussion of distinctive issues of minority women as court employees); MARYLAND GENDER BIAS REPORT, *supra* note 19, at 1 ("while the Committee's mandate was to investigate gender bias, evidence of racial bias also came to the attention of the Committee."); MICHIGAN GENDER REPORT, *supra* note 44, at 21 (analyzing data based on "race and gender" profiles and distinguishing responses based on majority and minority males and females and also discussing the problem of "category blending.").

Michigan and Washington had Task Forces, operating at the same time, on gender bias and on race/ethnic bias. *See* MICHIGAN GENDER FORCE REPORT, *supra* note 44, at 1; WASHINGTON GENDER REPORT, *supra* note 30, at 3.

70. Florida's report on racial and ethnic bias devotes a chapter to issues of women of color; the specific focus is on "minority women employees and attorneys." FLORIDA RACIAL/ETHNIC BIAS STUDY, Vol. II, *supra* note 20, at 49-60. The recently issued report from Minnesota states its intention to consider the distinct experiences of women of color. *See* the Honorable Rosalie Wahl, Preface, MINNESOTA SUPREME COURT TASK FORCE ON RACIAL BIAS IN THE JUDICIAL SYSTEM, "We have focused in our study on how the law and our whole court system impacts on four communities of color—Hispanic, Native American, African American and Asian/Pacific Islander—in all our substantive and administrative areas of study. We have focused also on women of color, a group not specifically covered in our gender bias study, and on victims." The report thus considers racial bias in the "criminal process, e.g. arrest and sentencing, interpreters, juvenile and family law, access to representation and interaction, and general civil process, and building cultural diversity in the justice system." *Id.* at iii.

Other reports occasionally mention women of color. *See, e.g,* D.C. RACIAL/ETHNIC BIAS REPORT, *supra* note 33, at 18 (discussing the differences in hiring patterns of Black and White females); MICHIGAN RACIAL/ETHNIC REPORT, *supra* note 32, at 40, 42, 62, 64 (reporting data delineating majority males and females from minority males and females); NEW YORK REPORT ON MINORITIES, Vol. I., *supra* note 20, at 22 (noting that "[r]acial bias against litigants is sometimes compounded by gender bias."); WASHINGTON MINORITY AND JUSTICE REPORT, *supra* note 21, at 65-66, 68-69, 76 (noting "how the combined effects of race, ethnicity and gender are related to law practices and incomes" and to legal education), *id.* at 110-115 (data on representation of people of color in court employment); NEW JERSEY MINORITY REPORT, *supra* note 31, at 1231 (female "minority prisoners" affected by "multiple factors,"); at 1245 (discussion by president of Black Women Lawyers' association); at 1266 (workforce data by color and gender).

71. Five reports mention lesbians and gays. *See* CALIFORNIA GENDER BIAS DRAFT REPORT, *supra* note 19, at Section 4, 33, 62 (proposing rules of judicial

conduct to prevent discrimination based on sexual orientation, as well as race, gender, and ethnicity); GEORGIA GENDER BIAS REPORT, *supra* note 19, at 185 (citing a newspaper article that judges took "sexual lifestyle of custodial parent" into account and tended to deny custody to gay women regardless of parently skills . . . ."); MASSACHUSETTS GENDER BIAS REPORT, *supra* note 44, at 65 and 76, n. 56 (sexual activity of women less relevant in child custody than it used to be but one fifth of lawyers answering questions reported that judges discriminated against "lesbian or gay parents"), and at 81, 90, 98 (finding that victims of domestic violence "are still confronted with treatment reflecting racial and ethnic bias, as well as bias against homosexuals" and recommending education against such stereotyping); VERMONT GENDER BIAS REPORT, *supra* note 44, at 45 (recommending that the Code of Judicial Conduct be amended to prohibit judges from discriminating based on "race, sex, religion, national origin, disability, age, sexual orientation, or socio-economic status" and noting that the House of Delegates of the American Bar Association Adopted a model code with these provisions); WISCONSIN GENDER REPORT, *supra* note 44, at 156 (Domestic Abuse Subcommittee Report stated that "[c]are must be taken to treat [litigants] who are gay or lesbian with the same courtesy and professionalism as other parties. Wisconsin statutes do not differentiate between opposite-gender and same gender parties."). *See also* Susan H. Russell and Cynthia L. Williamson, Demographic Survey of the State Bar of California (August, 1991) at 6-7 (membership survey, undertaken by the California Bar in the spring of 1991, which asked: "Do you consider yourself to be a member of the gay, lesbian, or bisexual community?"; 3 percent of the respondents answered affirmatively).

72. *See generally*, Sylvia A. Law, *Homosexuality and the Social Meaning of Gender*, 1988 Wis. L. Rev. 187 (roots of discrimination against lesbians and gays is based on patriarchal attitudes towards women and insistence on gender-specific roles). The ongoing practice of gender and class stereotyping by dress codes that prohibit women lawyers from wearing pants (or "pant suits") has also not been discussed by state reports. While one might debate the importance of ceremonial dress in courts, it is difficult to make a claim that women must remain in nineteenth century garb to be appropriately dressed "for" court. In 1991, the Committee on Professional Ethics of the New York County Lawyers' Association concluded that a woman who wears "an appropriately tailored pants suit" has not violated the Code of Professional Responsibility. *See* Martin Fox, *Bar Panel Tackles Sticky Issue of Appropriate Garb for Women*, NEW YORK LAW J., Dec. 23, 1991, at 1. In the 1970s, Florynce Kennedy, expelled by a judge because she wore a pants suit to court, is claimed to have said: "What makes that man in drag think he can tell me what to wear?"

73. At least one ongoing task force on gender and racial bias, that of the federal courts for the District of Columbia, has divided into one group focusing on race and one on gender; the gender group in turn has a subcommittee devoted to Class, Race, and Gender issues. Task Force of the District of Columbia Circuit on Gender, Race and Ethnic Bias. At the Second National Conference on Gender Bias in the Courts, held in 1993 and co-sponsored by the National Center for State Courts, the National Association of Women Judges, and the Women's Fund for Justice, a panel discussion

was held on women of color; similarly, at the 1993 meeting of the National Consortium of Task Force and Commissions on Racial and Ethnic Bias in the Courts, discussion was also had on the need to pay attention to women of color.

APPENDICES

APPENDIX I: Reports on Gender, Racial, and Ethnic Bias in the Courts (as of April, 1993)

I. Race and Ethnic Bias Task Force Reports

FINAL REPORT OF THE TASK FORCE ON RACIAL AND ETHNIC BIAS AND TASK FORCE ON GENDER BIAS IN THE COURTS (District of Columbia, 1992)

REPORT AND RECOMMENDATIONS OF THE FLORIDA SUPREME COURT RACIAL AND ETHNIC BIAS STUDY COMMISSION, "WHERE THE INJURED FLY FOR JUSTICE," Volume One (Florida, 1990)

REPORT AND RECOMMENDATIONS OF THE FLORIDA SUPREME COURT RACIAL AND ETHNIC BIAS STUDY COMMISSION, "WHERE THE INJURED FLY FOR JUSTICE," Volume Two (Florida, 1991)

FINAL REPORT OF THE MICHIGAN SUPREME COURT TASK FORCE ON RACIAL/ETHNIC ISSUES IN THE COURT (Michigan, 1989)

TASK FORCE ON RACIAL BIAS IN THE JUDICIAL SYSTEM: FINAL REPORT, MINNESOTA SUPREME COURT (May, 1993)

NEW JERSEY SUPREME COURT TASK FORCE ON MINORITY CONCERNS, INTERIM REPORT (New Jersey, 1989)

NEW JERSEY SUPREME COURT TASK FORCE ON MINORITY CONCERNS, FINAL REPORT (New Jersey, 1992)

REPORT OF THE NEW YORK STATE JUDICIAL COMMISSION ON MINORITIES (New York, 1991):
    Volume One: Executive Summary
    Volume Two: The Public and the Courts
    Volume Three: Legal Education
    Volume Four: Legal Profession, Nonjudicial Officers, Employees and Minority Contractors
    Volume Five: Appendix—Staff Reports and Working Papers

MINORITY AND JUSTICE TASK FORCE, STATE OF WASHINGTON: FINAL REPORT (Washington, 1990)

II. Gender Bias Task Force Reports

A. *Federal Reports*

NINTH CIRCUIT GENDER BIAS TASK FORCE, PRELIMINARY REPORT: DISCUSSION DRAFT (1992)

NINTH CIRCUIT GENDER BIAS TASK FORCE, PRELIMINARY REPORT: EXECUTIVE SUMMARY (1992)

THE EFFECTS OF GENDER IN THE FEDERAL COURTS, THE FINAL REPORT OF THE NINTH CIRCUIT GENDER BIAS TASK FORCE (July, 1993)

THE EFFECTS OF GENDER IN THE FEDERAL COURTS, THE EXECUTIVE SUMMARY OF THE FINAL REPORT OF THE NINTH CIRCUIT GENDER BIAS TASK FORCE (July, 1993) B. State Reports

ACHIEVING EQUAL JUSTICE FOR WOMEN AND MEN IN THE COURTS, THE DRAFT REPORT OF THE JUDICIAL COUNCIL ADVISORY COMMITTEE ON GENDER BIAS IN THE COURTS (California, 1990)

COLORADO SUPREME COURT TASK FORCE ON GENDER BIAS IN THE COURTS, GENDER & JUSTICE IN THE COLORADO COURTS (Colorado, 1990)

REPORT OF THE CONNECTICUT TASK FORCE, GENDER, JUSTICE AND THE COURTS (Connecticut, 1991)

FINAL REPORT OF THE TASK FORCE ON RACIAL AND ETHNIC BIAS AND TASK FORCE ON GENDER BIAS IN THE COURTS (District of Columbia, 1992)

REPORT OF THE FLORIDA SUPREME COURT GENDER BIAS STUDY COMMISSION (Florida, 1990)

GENDER AND JUSTICE IN THE COURTS, A REPORT TO THE SUPREME COURT OF GEORGIA BY THE COMMISSION ON GENDER BIAS IN THE JUDICIAL SYSTEM (Georgia, 1991)

ACHIEVING GENDER FAIRNESS: DESIGNING A PLAN TO ADDRESS GENDER BIAS IN HAWAII'S LEGAL SYSTEM, A REPORT OF THE AD HOC COMMITTEE ON GENDER BIAS (Hawaii, 1989)

REPORT OF THE FAIRNESS AND EQUALITY COMMITTEE OF THE SUPREME COURT OF IDAHO (Idaho, 1992).

THE 1990 REPORT OF THE ILLINOIS TASK FORCE ON GENDER BIAS IN THE COURTS (Illinois, 1990).

REPORT OF THE INDIANA STATE BAR ASSOCIATION COMMISSION ON WOMEN IN THE PROFESSION (Indiana, 1990).

REPORT OF THE KANSAS BAR ASSOCIATION TASK FORCE ON THE STATUS OF WOMEN IN THE PROFESSION (Kansas, 1992).

KENTUCKY TASK FORCE ON GENDER FAIRNESS AND THE COURTS, EQUAL JUSTICE FOR WOMEN AND MEN (Kentucky, 1992)

LOUISIANA TASK FORCE ON WOMEN IN THE COURTS, FINAL REPORT (Louisiana, 1992)

REPORT OF THE SPECIAL JOINT COMMITTEE ON GENDER BIAS IN THE COURTS (Maryland, 1989)

REPORT OF THE GENDER BIAS STUDY OF THE SUPREME JUDICIAL COURT (Massachusetts, 1989)

FINAL REPORT OF THE MICHIGAN SUPREME COURT TASK FORCE ON GENDER ISSUES IN THE COURTS (Michigan, 1989)

REPORT OF THE MINNESOTA SUPREME COURT TASK FORCE ON GENDER FAIRNESS IN THE COURTS (Minnesota, 1989)

JUSTICE FOR WOMEN: FIRST REPORT OF NEVADA SUPREME COURT TASK FORCE ON GENDER BIAS IN THE COURTS (Nevada, 1989).

REPORT OF THE NEW HAMPSHIRE BAR ASSOCIATION TASK FORCE ON WOMEN IN THE BAR (New Hampshire, 1988)

THE FIRST YEAR REPORT OF THE NEW JERSEY SUPREME COURT TASK FORCE ON WOMEN IN THE COURTS (New Jersey, 1984)

THE SECOND REPORT OF THE NEW JERSEY SUPREME COURT TASK FORCE ON WOMEN IN THE COURTS (New Jersey, 1986)

FINAL REPORT OF THE NEW MEXICO STATE BAR TASK FORCE ON WOMEN AND THE LEGAL PROFESSION (New Mexico, 1990)

REPORT OF THE NEW YORK TASK FORCE ON WOMEN IN THE COURTS (New York, 1986)

FINAL REPORT OF THE RHODE ISLAND COMMITTEE ON WOMEN IN THE COURTS: FINAL REPORT ON GENDER BIAS (Rhode Island, 1987)

UTAH TASK FORCE ON GENDER AND JUSTICE, REPORT TO THE UTAH JUDICIAL COUNCIL (Utah, 1990)

GENDER AND JUSTICE, REPORT OF THE VERMONT TASK FORCE ON GENDER BIAS IN THE LEGAL SYSTEM (Vermont, 1991)

FINAL REPORT OF THE WASHINGTON STATE TASK FORCE ON GENDER AND JUSTICE IN THE COURTS (Washington, 1989)

WISCONSIN EQUAL JUSTICE TASK FORCE: FINAL REPORT (Wisconsin, 1991)

CHAPTER 2

Evolving Attitudes or Confessions of a Male Chauvinist Attorney

by
THOMAS W. JOHNSON, JR.

THOMAS W. JOHNSON, JR.

Thomas W. Johnson, Jr., was born and educated in Indianapolis, Indiana. He moved to California after graduating from law school in 1969. Mr. Johnson now lives in Fountain Valley, California, with his wife, Barbara, and three stepsons, ages 14, 12, and 6.

Mr. Johnson joined his present firm, Irell & Manella, as a corporate associate in 1969. He worked on a number of corporate acquisitions and public offerings. He then became interested in the U.S. income tax aspects of international transactions and represented several clients in international investments and licensing transactions. Almost by accident, at least at first, Mr. Johnson became involved as a litigation associate in a six-month trial representing Doris Day against her former attorney and business manager. The trial resulted in a $26 million judgment for Doris Day and forever changed Mr. Johnson's career.

Today, Mr. Johnson is a business litigator and specializes in transactions and disputes involving complex commercial insurance. He counsels clients on insurance, identifies potential insurance coverage for property and casualty losses incurred by business clients, and represents policyholders in insurance coverage litigation.

Mr. Johnson's article chronicles his first brief career as a junior high school English and science teacher. He still enjoys teaching and does so regularly for the American Bar Association, the State Bar of California, the California Continuing Education of the Bar, The Rutter Group, the Association of Business Trial Lawyers, and a whole host of local bar and professional organizations.

41

Many of his lectures on how to read and interpret insurance policies are available on CLE videotapes.

Mr. Johnson's views on the role of women in the legal profession have evolved dramatically (as evidenced by his article). He believes that his initial resistance, 25 years ago, to the entry of women into the legal profession was relatively typical among his less outspoken male colleagues. He also suspects that his own gradual "enlightenment" parallels the increasing sensitivity of his entire generation, women included, toward women in the workplace. Mr. Johnson insists that he agreed to write this article only because his partner, Andra Greene, pressured him to do so. He admits that he never expected to publish such a personal article and hopes that his revelations will produce a "positive benefit rather than negative sentiment toward the author."

CHAPTER 2

Evolving Attitudes or Confessions of a Male Chauvinist Attorney

by
THOMAS W. JOHNSON, JR.

What you are about to read may upset you. It bothers me, and I wrote it. I am about to recount conduct which reflects my past prejudices toward women in the legal profession. This is an abbreviated autobiography that reveals some of the misconceptions I have had about women during my legal career. I have tried to present my thinking (as best as I could recall it) at the time of each incident I relate. I had hoped that the article would present some record of my progress, but I confess that it reads more like the confession of a male chauvinist. I assure you that I do not present these episodes with pride, but rather to explain what I was thinking when they occurred. I hope and believe that my attitude has changed significantly over the last three decades. So much for the caveats and qualifications; now let me regress thirty-some years ago.

I attended college in the early 1960's. I changed my undergraduate major six times. I finally worked myself into a position where the only degree I could obtain with my diversified curriculum was a Bachelor of Science from the School of Education. I decided to become a seventh grade science and English teacher, primarily because I had obtained a teaching degree and a provisional license to teach school, and I really wasn't trained or qualified to do much else. So, almost by accident, I entered a profession long characterized by a lack of any discernible gender bias—at least at the entry level. When I interviewed for that first teaching position, I was competing against male and female applicants, and it never occurred to me that any of us had any unfair advantage over the others.

My Early Job as a Teacher

I got the job. The faculty was equally divided between men and women, but all of the administrators were men. At the time, it seemed logical and customary for men to run the school. After all, in 1963 the business world was dominated by men. I was the first to acknowledge that women were well suited to teaching, particularly the elementary grades. Moms are women, and the younger students seemed to find comfort with female teachers. The percentage of male teachers increased in the upper grades as the subject matters became more intellectually challenging. That made sense; the men had taken all those math and science courses in college while the women enrolled in the sociology and art classes. I didn't perceive any gender bias at the time. What I thought I saw were men and women doing what they each did best.

We had a career day at the junior high school. Each student was to pick a particular career and write an essay about it. I distinctly recall one precocious seventh grade girl who wrote an essay about becoming a lawyer. I thought it was a curious choice, but I gave her an ''A'' on the essay. It didn't surprise me to learn that her mother owned and operated a small business. ''Like mother, like daughter,'' I said to myself. I felt certain that as my student matured and separated from her mother's influence, she would probably come to realize that a legal career might be difficult for a woman. Thank goodness I didn't counsel her on this subject. I wonder if she became a lawyer.

After I taught school for two years, I met the father of one of my students at a parent-teacher conference. I assumed that he had scheduled the meeting to discuss his son's progress; but he surprised me by asking whether I had ever considered becoming a lawyer. He invited me to see his firm and attend a lunch meeting at the local bar association. I accepted the invitation and accompanied the father and his seven law partners to the local bar association for lunch. At least seventy lawyers were having lunch in the dining room. As I recall, the only women present were the waitresses. This situation did not seem unusual or disturbing; I don't believe that I had ever met or seen or heard of a female attorney before entering law school.

I Decide to Go to Law School

Impressed by my one-day introduction to the practice of law, I decided to go to law school. I was already married and self-supporting, so the most suitable opportunity was the local night law school.

I can still remember the very first class. The Dean of the law school taught Constitutional law, a mandatory course for all first year law students. Of the approximately one hundred students in my class, four or five were women. At the time I thought to myself that only one of the four or five looked like a woman, and I wasn't surprised when she dropped out of school at the end of the first semester.

The Dean taught Constitutional law by the traditional Socratic method. The students were called upon to give cases and to answer questions. I dreaded my turn, but it went well. It did not go well for one of the female students. Nervous and out of place, she stumbled over her answers. I felt sorry for her. I remember thinking that watching that female law student try to respond to the Dean's barrage of questions was as painful as watching an anemic boy in a physical education class trying to learn to play football. I also thought the Dean was being inconsiderate by making the female students perform in front of the rest of us and I wondered why these women had chosen such a difficult career path. Only later did it occur to me that perhaps the Dean knew what he was doing. These women had to learn how to get along in the male-dominated legal profession characterized by competitive challenges and an adversarial process. They had to learn to compete with men. What a challenge!

I remember the embarrassment I felt for the women in my criminal law class when we discussed the elements of the crime of rape. When we got to the cases that defined "penetration" and "consent," I thought that the female students should have been excused from the discussion. Instead, the professor actually called on a woman to present one of the cases. "What an unwarranted humiliation," I thought. After all, a woman may become an attorney, but surely she wouldn't be asked to prosecute or defend a rape case. On the other hand, I couldn't help but notice that the female student handled the situation well, even doing a good job of briefing the case. In fact, the women seemed to be less bothered about their participation in sexual or violent subject matter than I was. Could it be that I was being overprotective?

I Saw Women Taking Men's Places

On a purely personal level, I was pleased that the female students were able to survive the Socratic method. Only a mean-spirited person enjoys witnessing a defeat. But on another level, I was perplexed and even annoyed by the increasing numbers of female students who were enrolling in my law school. To my way of thinking, these women were taking places away from male applicants who needed the education to pursue a dream or earn a better living to support their families. One male applicant rejected from my law school was a close friend. He had always wanted to be an attorney, and his undergraduate grades were acceptable, but his LSAT score missed the cut-off by less than a percentage point. I pictured each woman in our class sitting in my friend's seat. To make matters worse, one of my female classmates became pregnant and dropped out of school. I asked myself how many of the women in law school would go on to practice law.

My male classmates often made derogatory remarks about the female law students. The perceived lack of femininity was a favorite topic. We convinced ourselves that the terms "lady" and "lawyer" were antonyms. We joked that female sexuality and legal training did not seem compatible.

How to Protect a Female Attorney Who Is My Adversary

Some will say we were threatened by this invasion of female law students. I don't think so, at least not on the level that we feared the women might take our future jobs. Deciding how to interact with the female law students was the problem, just as it is my problem with the entire women's movement and the changing role of women in today's society. I was taught to respect and protect women. How do I protect a female attorney if it's also my job to be her adversary? I remember being reprimanded for attempting to open a door for a female classmate. "Don't you think I'm capable of opening my own doors?" seemed a harsh reaction to such a well-intentioned act. The old ways were better, I thought, and I hoped that these Amazons would not become the prototype for all women.

There were no women on my law review or in the moot court competition, programs reserved for the students with the highest academic averages. Women never participated in these activities.

I graduated from law school in 1969 and served a one-year term as a law clerk for the Chief Justice of the Indiana Supreme Court. All of the justices and all of the law clerks were men. I never saw a woman argue a case before the Indiana Supreme Court and I never wondered why that was so. After all, as a general rule, only senior litigators appeared before the high court.

How Things Looked Upon Joining My Law Firm

When I joined my law firm twenty-four years ago, there were thirty-six lawyers in the firm. One of them was a woman, an associate in the estate planning department. She was a timid creature who apparently had been hired to draft wills and trusts, although I was once told that she did not have much client contact because her timidity did not inspire confidence in her work product. She left the firm during my first year as an associate. I remember commending the partner who had hired her for at least attempting to find a place for a female lawyer.

In the early 1970's, I began to see articles about the increase in the number of women applying to prestigious law schools. I wondered when my firm would try again; but I did not have to wonder long. We soon began to interview female law students and, although we did not develop any formal affirmative action plan, we did make a concerted effort to hire women. As a member of our firm's recruiting committee, I interviewed most of the female applicants. At each interview, I asked the applicant whether she really intended to pursue a lifelong full-time legal career or whether motherhood would ultimately disrupt her full-time position with our firm. Somehow, twenty years ago, that question seemed fair and relevant. Each applicant had the same answer; she would do her best to juggle her conflicting responsibilities. Some of them asked me if I had children (which I did not) or how I handled my family responsibilities. I thought these responses were at best argumentative and perhaps even inane, since it was common knowledge that the principal responsibility for the "man of the family" was to earn a decent living. At that time in our society, the principal responsibility for childcare fell to the female spouse.

Childcare Is Not for Women Only

Today I no longer assume that childcare is the exclusive responsibility of the mother. Nevertheless, I can't help but wonder about the emotional development of children who spend a significant percentage of time in childcare centers or at home alone or with the housekeeper while both parents pursue full-time careers. I grew up four decades ago in a middle-class midwestern society where mothers were available to take their children to cub scouts and piano lessons. Today we live in a different society, and circumstances often compel both parents to hold full-time jobs. I appreciate that these parents do the best they can, but I also wonder whether many behavioral problems are linked to parents who have little time to spend with their children. I do not discredit the work or the worth of a female attorney because she appears to spend less time with her children than my mother spent with me, but it would be disingenuous of me not to say that I still am concerned for the children of hard-working parents.

Despite these concerns, I have learned not to ask gender-based questions of female applicants. Not so in the 1970's.

Questions That Were Asked in the 70's

I remember other questions that I frequently asked female law students in the 1970's. Did she really think that she could muster the necessary demeanor and tenacity to be an effective trial lawyer? Could she put aside emotions and impatience to negotiate the best result for our clients? Wouldn't the very sensitivity that we identify with femininity get in the way? Often the responses proved my point. The applicants became agitated or overemotional, even though doing so obviously hurt their cause. After all, I was judging their potential ability to practice law while they were reacting emotionally to questions I considered fair and logical. Wouldn't it stand to reason that they might do the same thing in court or with an important client?

I considered sex-based humor to be entertaining. When our firm hired a recruiting coordinator—a woman—she turned out to have a fine sense of humor, and I thought I did too. More than once, when she asked me if I had time to interview a female law student, I replied by asking whether the recruit was well built. Now, of course, my response was intended to be funny and often was met with an equally outrageous reply by the recruiting coordinator. On occasion, we would engage in this ridiculous banter in the presence of my secretary or another attorney in the office. It never occurred to me that anyone would be offended by my silliness.

Working with Female Associates

Despite my interviews, we managed to hire several female associates. I worked with two of them in my first big trial. One of them accused me of being a racist and a sexist, telling the partner in charge of the account that the firm was simply not big enough for both of us. She was right. She left the firm when the trial ended.

One day the other female associate came to our courtroom to bring me some files. She had just appeared on a motion in another case. Before I could ask for the files, she started telling me about what had happened to her in the other courtroom.

She had been presenting a routine motion to a judge who was well along in years. In the middle of her argument, the judge interrupted to say that she had the "prettiest legs" of anyone in his courtroom. The associate looked to me for a response, and I asked whether she had won the motion. Annoyed, she said that the judge had given her only part of what she had sought. "But what about his comment?" she asked.

What did she want from me, a confirmation of the compliment? Married at the time, I decided the safest course would be to make light of the situation. "He shouldn't have interrupted your argument, but I have to agree with his judgment on the underlying issue," I joked. I expected her to laugh or at least smile. Instead she looked as if she were going to cry. She turned around and walked away without saying anything. I knew I had said the wrong thing, but I couldn't figure out what I should have said or how I could have made things better.

I Understood for the First Time

Even though I did not handle this situation with distinction, I remember feeling ashamed of what the judge had said. His remarks were clearly inappropriate. Perhaps for the first time, I could understand how difficult it is for a female attorney who is not taken seriously. Of course, it did not occur to me that at times my own conduct had been as insensitive and as sexist as the judge's. But, perhaps my ability to perceive and disapprove of a male colleague's sexist misbehavior was a harbinger of a shift in my own attitude.

As time went by, some female associates became my partners. I also argued motions before female judges. One day I lost an important argument to a female attorney. Slowly at first, my misgivings about women's ability to separate emotion from logic began to fade. I saw that a woman could put her femininity on hold as easily as a man could arrest his macho. I saw that a woman was as adept at presenting or resisting an argument as was her male counterpart. In fact, women's sensitivity to the feelings of others, particularly of judges and juries, had not been a deterrent; at times it had proved to be an asset.

Trying a Case with a Female Partner

Just last year, I tried a case with a female partner in our firm for the first time. She and I took turns putting on the five-week trial. If I had any lingering doubts about whether a woman could be an effective trial lawyer, her performance erased them forever. Her examinations of witnesses were among the best I have ever seen.

During the trial, I popped a button on my coat. Almost instinctively, my partner offered to sew the button for me using a sewing kit she kept in her purse. Equally instinctively, I accepted her offer.

The female associate with the firm representing our adversary was horrified. "How could you do his sewing for him?" she asked.

A Lawyer Who Is Also a Mom

"I'm also a mom," my partner replied with a smile. I thought to myself that I had just witnessed the best sense of balance I had ever seen from a female attorney. An experienced trial lawyer, my partner also has the courage to own her separate role as a woman. There is no discernible doubt in her mind about the compatibility of these roles, and her self-assurance and competence inspire confidence in others.

I could relate many more incidents to illustrate the point I am about to make, but enough is enough. I was what I was because of what I had been taught to be. I am what I am today because those same teachings have been modified by my personal experience and observation. I will never be rid of the prejudice of the early teachings unless my errors are brought to my attention specifically and convincingly.

When I was asked to write this article, I was asked to explain why my attitude toward my female colleagues had changed. At first, I focused on my positive professional experiences with female attorneys. But on further reflection, I realized that the obnoxious behavior of some male colleagues also was important.

Recognizing Your Own Prejudice

It is much easier to recognize prejudice in another person than it is to see it in yourself. I was offended when a judge told a female lawyer that she had pretty legs even though I probably have done the same thing. Still, what I remember is not my own conduct, but that of male colleagues.

And what I remember was crude and offensive. For example, I have heard many a male attorney refer to his adversary as a "bitch" or a "dyke." I am a seasoned litigator, much too thick-skinned to be bothered by profanity. Even today, I do not object to the use of a profane term such as "bitch" or "dyke" which can only be applied to a woman if the woman has earned the metaphor by abusive tactics or obnoxious conduct. Male attorneys often refer to each other as "sons of bitches" or "pricks;" the mere use of profanity should not be confused with sexism. But I do find profanity offensive when it is used unfairly. On occasion, a female attorney is called a "bitch" only because she is an effective advocate. Her male adversary has been disappointed or embittered by his defeat, so he resorts to a form of unfair revenge. "She may look like a woman, but she's really a bitch." If the same attorney had been a man, the comment might have been "he is a tough trial lawyer" or even "he's a son of a bitch," which for most of us male litigators, an inexplicable form of compliment.

Calling a Woman a Bitch

But that's not the case when a woman is called a bitch. The use of the term "bitch" in this instance is gender bias at its worst. It is used by a male attorney who feels insecure about his own performance and resorts to sexist attacks on his more effective female adversary. Every time I witness patent deliberate prejudice against a female colleague (or a minority), I want to distance myself from it. Yes, there are bigots in the legal profession, and I don't want to be one of them or to be associated with them. Yet my revulsion at deliberate prejudice has undoubtedly caused me to question my own conduct. Surely, I say, my transgressions don't make me look as bad to others as these bigots look to me. I hope not; maybe I ought to be more careful about how others are reacting to my comments.

Incidently, since I am spilling all the trade secrets, I might as well let you in on some of the other nasty comments made about female attorneys. If a female colleague appears particularly impatient or overly anxious, some of my more backward colleagues are apt to comment that "she needs to be screwed." The meaning is evident. If a female attorney loses her temper easily, someone is likely to speculate that she must be "on her period." And, if she's too fat or too skinny, it is sometimes said that her behavior can be attributed to her inability to attract men. Most men, I can assure you, are offended by these remarks. The bigots who regularly resort to them lose respect. Most men do not wish to be associated with these sentiments, and our rejection of this extreme display of gender bias probably causes all of us to examine our own conduct.

At no time in my life would I have ever admitted to "gender bias." I was taught to respect and protect women. I never set out to be vicious or deliberately hurtful to anyone. I tried to be fair, and the term "prejudiced" still seems much too extreme to describe my attitude toward women. I was just misinformed. My "family values" were misapplied.

Change is always difficult. Change now seems to be occurring at an ever increasing pace. Just about the time that I take pride in my enlightenment, I am made to recognize that another of my prejudgments constitutes unfounded "gender bias." I have always enjoyed learning new ideas. But unlearning old beliefs is not pleasant.

I am still bothered by the hostility of the women's movement. The transgressions cited by the angry spokeswomen were not committed by me with malice aforethought. As I try to understand the injustices caused by my prejudices, shouldn't I be entitled to be understood rather than vilified?

This has been a difficult article to write. Maybe it will help someone else understand the depth and the extent of the problem we must all now try to resolve.

CHAPTER 3

Survey of Female Litigators: Discrimination by Clients Limits Opportunities

by
LYNN S. GLASSER

Lynn S. Glasser

Lynn S. Glasser is Co-President and Publisher of Prentice Hall Law & Business (Englewood Cliffs, NJ), a division of Simon & Schuster. The company publishes services, books, directories, journals, newsletters, and other materials for lawyers, tax advisors and business executives. The company also sponsors seminars and issues audiotapes and videotapes on timely topics.

While at Simon & Schuster, Ms. Glasser also has run other divisions of the company, including Prentice Hall Information Services and Tax & Professional Practice Newsletters.

Ms. Glasser, along with her husband, Stephen A. Glasser, started the Law & Business publishing program in 1978 as a joint venture with Harcourt Brace Jovanovich, Inc. In 1986, HBJ and the Glassers sold Law & Business to Paramount Communications, Inc. (formerly Gulf + Western)/Simon & Schuster. In a separate transaction in 1986, Legal Times, a Washington, D.C. national weekly newspaper for the legal profession founded by the Glassers in 1978, was sold by Law & Business to Am Law Newspapers Corp.

Ms. Glasser has organized over 1,000 seminars and conferences on topical legal and business subjects ranging from corporate-securities-business law and finance to environmental, intellectual property, personal injury and business litigation. She is widely regarded as the premier developer and innovator of seminars in the field. Over 100,000 people have attended meetings she devised.

Prior to co-founding Law & Business in 1978, Ms. Glasser and her husband started the Law Journal Press and Law Journal Seminars, subsidiaries of The

New York Law Journal. She directed their activities for six and one-half years as Vice President and Chief Operating Officer. From 1968 to 1971 she was the Assistant to the Director of the Practising Law Institute, New York City, and from 1966 to 1968 she was the Publications Editor of the Institute of Continuing Legal Education at the University of Michigan Law School.

Ms. Glasser has served as a consultant on legal education and publishing to a number of groups, including the Harvard Law School and American Trial Lawyers Association.

Ms. Glasser has addressed many legal groups, including the American Bar Association, Association of Legal Administrators, National Association of Legal Vendors and the Association of Continuing Legal Education Administrators. In 1994 she served as co-chair of "The Woman Business Lawyer" Conference. She has also given presentations to numerous law firms including Baker & Hostetler, Morgan Lewis & Bockius, and Pettit & Martin.

She is a graduate of Chatham College and is listed in "Who's Who in America" (49th Edition).

Ms. Glasser and her husband have four children (Susan, Laura, Jeffrey, and Jennifer) and live in Montclair, NJ. Ms. Glasser has served on the fund-raising board of D.E.B.R.A. (a foundation aiding children with E.B.). She is a member of the Board of Trustees of the New Jersey Chamber Music Society. She has served as committee chair and committee member for numerous fund-raising benefits for various organizations including Mountainside Hospital, the Montclair Public Library, Montclair Kimberley Academy, NJ Chamber Music Society and Montclair Art Museum. Mr. & Ms. Glasser have established Stephen A. Glasser and Lynn S. Glasser Scholarship Funds at Colgate University and Bloomfield College.

CHAPTER 3

Survey of Female Litigators: Discrimination by Clients Limits Opportunities

by
LYNN S. GLASSER

A survey of women litigators conducted by Prentice Hall Law & Business reveals that women trial lawyers' opportunities in the profession are as much limited by discrimination from clients as from colleagues, judges, and others. The responses describe an environment in which some male clients refuse to be represented by female attorneys because of their gender. And, in some cases, senior male colleagues also are reluctant to fully support female subordinates for fear of losing important clients. This situation is exacerbated by a "client entertainment culture" which caters to men and men's activities.

Among the survey highlights:

- Women identified the "absence of women at client companies" as by far the most significant factor in limiting business development opportunities.

- More than one-half of women litigators polled and 30.8 percent of partners in large law firms stated that they had been sexually harassed by clients over the past five years.

- More than three-quarters of the women surveyed believed that they are held to a higher standard of performance in court than male litigators.

- While a majority of all respondents said that women at their firms had an equal opportunity for advancement, only 41.7 percent of women associates at large firms believed that their chances were equal to those of men.

The survey also confirmed notions that have been the subject of more traditional media interest concerning gender bias. For example, two-thirds of the respondents stated that women litigators with young children receive less desirable case assignments than those without children. Overall, substantial percentages of women stated that opposing counsel and law firm colleagues were sources of sexual harassment in the past five years.

However, the survey also reveals that the majority of women litigators believe that discrimination and harassment are not overwhelming problems for them. It rejects the notion that a large majority of women litigators feel that there is pervasive and systematic discrimination within the legal profession. Less than half of the respondents report that sexual harassment or gender discrimination is a large or pervasive problem. More than 80 percent say they are satisfied with the level of responsibility they have been given on cases. And a majority report that women in their firms have roughly equal opportunity for advancement with men.

METHODOLOGY

This is how the survey was conducted. Prentice Hall Law & Business sent questionnaires to 5,000 women litigators around the country. More than 570 were returned. Preliminary results were printed in **Inside Litigation** (Feb. 1993) and **Of Counsel** (March 15, 1993), two newsletters published by Prentice Hall Law & Business. In addition, survey forms were distributed to attendees at the 1993 seminar programs on "The Woman Advocate," co-sponsored by Prentice Hall Law & Business and the ABA Section of Litigation. More than 270 people filled out those questionnaires.

The vast majority of the respondents work at private law firms. Prentice Hall divided these into small, midsize, and large firms. A small firm was defined as one containing one to 10 lawyers; a midsize firm, 11 to 50 lawyers; and a large firm, 51 or more lawyers. Attorneys were broken down into categories of partners and associates. (Attorneys designated "of counsel" were included as associates.) Attorneys not in private practice were grouped in a separate category of non-law firm persons, primarily those employed in government or by corporations.

BUSINESS DEVELOPMENT OPPORTUNITIES

By far, the most dissatisfaction was expressed concerning business development opportunities. Only 6.8 percent of the respondents believe that such opportunities for women litigators are equal to those of male litigators. And more than a third say that these opportunities are "severely limited."

As former Section of Litigation Chair Louise LaMothe has pointed out, men have learned to subtly limit access to power by limiting access to new business. "The people at law firms aren't stupid," says LaMothe, a partner at Los Angeles' Riordan & McKinzie. They know how to conceal their resistance, she says, but the resistance is "tremendous." At the same time, LaMothe agrees with the overwhelming majority of respondents who say that a primary reason for their limited business development opportunities is the absence of women in positions of power at client companies. As in so many areas, lawyers are generally content to follow the lead of their clients.

As Compared to Those of Male Litigators

In the survey, respondents were asked to complete the statement:

In my experience, business development opportunities for women litigators, compared to those male litigators enjoy, are: (1) severely limited; (2) somewhat limited; or (3) equal in number.

Overall, the largest percentage of respondents, 57.0 percent, said that such opportunities were "somewhat limited." An additional 36.2 percent answered "severely limited," and only 6.8 percent responded "equal in number."

Reasons for Limited Opportunities

To find out just what factors were responsible for limiting these opportunities, a follow-up question asked women litigators:

If limitations exist, which of the following are significant factors in this lack of business opportunities: (1) the absence of women in influential positions in client companies; (2) restrictions on membership in private clubs; (3) unwillingness of male partners to act as mentors; (4) employer-imposed limitations on formal business development opportunities; or (5) other?

An overwhelming 77.0 percent of the overall number of women litigators responding to the question selected "the absence of women in influential positions at client companies" as a significant factor in limiting business development opportunities. This answer was also chosen by the highest percentages of partners and associates in small, medium, and large firms, the figures ranging from 86.8 to 98.1 percent.

Another factor cited by more than half of the respondents involved was "unwillingness of male partners to act as mentors," chosen by 52.2 percent. Interestingly, it is in the larger firms (more than 50 lawyers) that the lack of mentoring is cited as an extremely important factor, with 68.7 percent of the respondents noting this as a significant limiting factor. "Private-club restrictions and employer-imposed limitations" were cited much less frequently by our respondents.

These answers indicate that overwhelming numbers of women litigators believe the absence of women at client companies is the most important factor in limiting their business development opportunities. Logically, more female clients or women in positions of influence in companies would increase the chances of a female litigator being asked to represent the client.

The description by women litigators of "other" factors that limit their business development opportunities provided an even clearer picture of the role clients play. Many women pointed out that the whole client entertainment culture was dominated by men and geared toward male activities such as golf, basketball, and even attending "strip bars." Many women said they were understandably uncomfortable in these environments and therefore did not feel it was as easy for them to attract clients as it was for men.

Women litigators' responses also suggest that male client perceptions of them in a social context play an important role in limiting their opportunities. Many women said they found it difficult to discuss business with potential male clients over drinks. Some said this was because male clients often misconstrue female attorneys' efforts as "come-ons." As one woman put it, "some men are uncomfortable with women making business development overtures and perceive social involvement to mean sexual involvement."

A few survey respondents stated that even clients' spouses can play a role in the dynamic. One said that some male lawyers can be cautious about drinking or participating in sports such as skiing with a female lawyer when their spouses aren't present. Another attorney said, "Wives don't appreciate husbands attending sporting events, dinners, or theater performances with a woman. But they have no objection to them attending with a male attorney."

A second limitation on business development opportunities that women litigators described in the "other" category was time restrictions due to family obligations. Many respondents stated that client entertainment after hours is difficult to engage in when their families need them at home.

GENERAL BUSINESS DEVELOPMENT ISSUES

Prentice Hall Law & Business also asked the respondents for some general information about business development. The survey asked women litigators:

Have you brought in new business for your firm, and if so, how?

Overall, 74.1 percent of those responding to the question stated that they had brought in new business. The most common response to the question of how such business was acquired was doing good work for current clients, which in turn caused satisfied clients to return and also resulted in numerous referrals.

Given the fact that women litigators indicated current clients were a major source for acquiring new business, the survey followed with the question:

What percentage of your time do you spend on client development?

Overall, 56.0 percent of respondents who answered the question said they spent 0-5 percent of their time on client development. Of the total number of partners, 41.0 percent said they spent "0-5 percent" of their time on client development, and 32.0 percent answered "6-10 percent." The answer "0-5 percent" was chosen by the highest percentages of respondents in each category according to status and law firm size.

In small firms, however, 27 percent of the partners reported spending more than 20 percent of their time on client development; overall, only 8 percent of the respondents reported spending that much time on rainmaking.

One factor that would assist women litigators in developing and maintaining a client base would be firms' inclusion of them in formal business development opportunities. Participants were asked:

Are you included in client presentations or other formal business development opportunities?

In response, 35.7 percent answered "no," compared to 64.3 percent who answered "yes." Several respondents gave answers of "sometimes" or "a limited number of times," which were counted as "yes" answers. Responses of "rarely" were counted as "no" answers. The percentage breakdown of overall responses was about the same in response to the question:

Are you included in less formal business opportunities?

Overall, 29.9 percent answered "no" and 70.1 percent answered "yes." Among the less formal business development opportunities described were a variety of activities, including keeping in close touch with current clients through informal lunches, dinners, and other social activities.

MANAGEMENT OPPORTUNITIES

Limitations on business development opportunities for women litigators might also be expected to limit how many women make partner. This, in turn, could limit the numbers of women who have a hand in law firm management, since only partners elect firm managers. Responses to a survey question on management opportunities confirmed these relationships. The survey asked each respondent:

Are you involved in law firm management in any way?

Overall, a slight majority, 50.1 percent, answered "yes." Of the total number of partners responding to the question, 81.3 percent answered "yes." Not surprisingly, the highest percentage of those answering "yes" in the individual categories came from partners in small firms (94.2 percent).

To determine what accounts for the substantial percentage of women not involved in firm management, we asked:

What obstacles do you find to women becoming involved in law firm management?

The answer most often given was "lack of female partners." Another closely-related obstacle was the fact that there are few women with seniority in law firms. According to several women, the "good old boy" network operates to limit women's advancement as men with more things in common tend to have more power. Some women stated that female lawyers are perceived by many male superiors as "lightweights" who are less organized and less capable of management responsibility in general.

Another frequently mentioned obstacle was that women are just not the big sources of revenue in law firms in that they have narrower client bases. These limited rainmaking opportunities have many sources, including discriminatory treatment by clients who prefer male counsel. Some women said family responsibilities contributed to their limited ability to put in hours and thereby generate more revenue.

Thus, respondents described a "multi-layered" series of obstacles that play a role in preventing women litigators from taking part in management. Family obligations often limit the number of hours women put in, reducing revenue-producing ability, which negatively affects partnership consideration and effectively locks women litigators out of management positions. Discriminatory attitudes and offensive stereotypes about women's abilities pervade some law firms and also limit their opportunities.

SEXUAL HARASSMENT

By Colleagues

In the aftermath of the Anita Hill/Clarence Thomas hearings, the issue of sexual harassment has come to the forefront in the legal profession. Prentice Hall asked a three-part question on sexual harassment in the survey. Parts one and two asked:

> **Have you experienced sexual harassment in the past five years? If so, please indicate whether such harassment came from: (1) clients; (2) law firm colleagues; (3) judges; (4) opposing counsel; (5) courtroom personnel; or (5) other.**

In response to the first part of the question, a considerable 55.2 percent of women litigators overall indicated they had experienced sexual harassment. By category, the highest percentages of "yes" answers came from associates generally, with the greatest percentage of these answers coming from associates in small law firms (68.2 percent). However, 63.6 percent of small law firm partners also reported being harassed in the past five years.

Comparisons of partners' and associates' responses were consistent with the overall results. Among partners in medium and small law firms, the answers chosen by the highest percentages were "opposing counsel," with 63.6 and 67.3 percent respectively. However, associates in large and midsize law firms chose "firm colleagues" by the highest percentages as the sources of sexual harassment. For associates, particularly in large firms, 42.6 percent of all respondents report sexual harassment by colleagues. These differences may in part reflect the increased vulnerability of associates, who have not had as much time or opportunity to establish themselves, to harassment by colleagues within the firm. The results suggest that women litigators who have made partner have more of a problem with harassment from opposing counsel.

By Clients

The survey results showing that many women litigators have experienced sexual harassment, while troubling, are perhaps not surprising, given the attention gender bias has received in the media in the past two years. However, little attention has been devoted to the issue of client harassment of women litigators. An astonishing 62.1 percent of respondents claiming that they had been sexually harassed said that clients were the source. For partners at large law firms, the percentage was 61.5 percent. This harassment can take many forms, ranging from disparaging or inappropriate remarks to actual physical or emotional abuse.

Scope of Problem

The third part of the question asked respondents to complete this sentence:

In my experience, sexual harassment is: (1) no problem; (2) somewhat of a problem; (3) a large problem; or (4) a pervasive problem, for women litigators today.

The highest percentage of respondents felt that sexual harassment in their experience was "somewhat of a problem" (66.4 percent). This was also the answer selected by the highest percentage of partners and associates in small, medium, and large law firms. Of the overall number of large, midsize, and small firm respondents, the largest percentages also answered "somewhat of a problem" (73.3 percent for large firms, 73.4 percent for midsize firms, and 53 percent for small firms).

The responses indicating that 55.2 percent of women litigators have been harassed in the past five years are comparable to responses to similar questions included in two recent studies of sexual harassment in the profession. A recent 9th Circuit study found that 60 percent of female lawyers had been harassed in the past five years. Also, in a **National Law Journal** study, 60 percent of respondents said they had experienced unwanted sexual attention of some kind.

Our figures vary somewhat from the 9th Circuit study. In that survey, the largest percentage of female lawyers said they had been the subject of harassment by clients (39 percent) as opposed to 34 percent reporting sexual harassment by opposing counsel and 32 percent by colleagues. The **National Law Journal** survey did not ask a comparable question.

GENDER DISCRIMINATION

Closely related to the sexual harassment question in the survey was one which asked respondents to complete the following statement for each source indicated:

In my experience, gender discrimination from (colleagues, clients, opposing counsel, judges, and court personnel) is: (1) no problem; (2) somewhat of a problem; (3) a large problem; or (4) a pervasive problem.

The largest percentages of partners and associates in large, midsize, and small firms described gender discrimination from colleagues, clients, opposing counsel, and judges as "somewhat of a problem" and from courtroom personnel as "no problem."

Older White Men

But more significant than these answers were the explanations offered by survey respondents. Clients again came in for much criticism, especially older, white men, many of whom were said to be reluctant to deal with female litigators because of the "white, male, macho image." Several survey respondents stated that these male clients act differently with female attorneys than they do with male lawyers. One noted that these men believe that "if a woman is not rude and aggressive, she can't be tough." According to some women litigators, these male clients will insist on a male attorney to represent them because they want a "strong person in their corner."

These attitudes by some clients can also influence senior male partners, who may choose not to assign a case to a woman attorney for fear of losing the client. One woman said that the reluctance of some partners to risk offending a client who prefers a man creates an environment where only the "superstar women" get choice assignments. The sense from many women was that most of those colleagues who act in a discriminatory way are also older, white men, who are in the larger, older, and more conservative law firms. One woman stated that these male colleagues still "labor under the misapprehension that women are lightweights and less productive."

Colleagues' Ingrained Stereotypes

Some women said that discrimination by colleagues still results in part from the "good old boy" system in law firms, where women aren't invited to participate in non-work activities, with or without clients. One woman said that the worst gender discrimination she had experienced came from her own colleagues, "whose wives don't work and who have no understanding or respect for career women.'' Several respondents said that blatant discrimination in law firms is rare, and one said that while colleagues may think sexist thoughts, they are too ''politically correct'' to express them. Rather, female litigators described an environment where women are subtly treated in accordance with ingrained stereotypes.

Male Litigators

With regard to discrimination by opposing counsel, women litigators said that male attorneys use sexual discrimination as a tool to gain an edge in court. In one woman's experience, opposing attorneys have tried intimidation tactics such as using foul language, cute names, or ''sex talk.'' Another said that she was called a ''bitch'' when she stuck to her guns in arguing her position on a case. But a few women stated that they have found ways to use discriminatory treatment by opposing counsel to their advantage.

Judges

Most of the discriminatory conduct engaged in by judges was described as involving use of terms such as ''honey,'' ''baby,'' and ''little girl'' to refer to women lawyers, as opposed to ''sir,'' or ''Mr.'' for male attorneys. Respondents stated that the judges who do this most often are older, white males. But several litigators said that judges have improved their behavior, particularly in certain areas of the country. Geography was mentioned by a few women as another important factor that influences the likelihood of discriminatory treatment of women litigators. One woman said that the cities afforded women litigators better treatment generally than the suburbs and small towns.

HOW GENDER DRIVES PRACTICE FIELDS AND CASE ASSIGNMENTS

The survey results also show that women litigators are not only limited in their advancement by the above-described factors, but they are often guided into particular fields because of their gender. The survey asked:

Do you believe you have ever been steered to particular work because of your gender?

Overall, 36.1 percent of women litigators answering the question stated that they believed they had. By category, 48.5 percent of partners in small firms who responded answered that they had been steered. This was the highest percentage answering "yes" among all categories of partners or associates. Running second were associates in midsize firms, 40.1 percent of whom answered "yes."

Of those attorneys who answered "yes," the area that was most often referred to as the one to which women are steered was domestic relations law. In some cases, respondents indicated that they were pressured by male partners from the time they were first hired to "specialize" in family law, whether or not they were interested in the field. Another type of work that respondents repeatedly said they had been steered to was research and writing. Other areas frequently mentioned were sexual harassment/discrimination defense litigation, breast implant cases (representing defendants), insurance defense litigation, toxic shock cases, and estate and probate work. At the same time, several respondents stated they were subtly steered away from litigation and courtroom work and from such areas as medical malpractice, product liability, and complex litigation. One woman described these areas as the "power groups," where more male litigators are encouraged to work.

Such steering was described by respondents as being done not only by senior male partners, but also by clients themselves. A few women litigators indicated that clients often dictate that they want a female attorney to represent them in a particular kind of case to create a certain impression for a jury. Some women stated that the decision is often described as a "strategic" one, where the client and the law firm believe that the case stands a better chance of succeeding if a woman litigator handles it. For example, several women mentioned that they had been assigned sexual harassment defense cases for this reason so the defendant would not appear "insensitive" to women.

The Mommy Track

While a substantial minority of the survey respondents believed that they have been steered away from glamour areas, a majority believes that the 'mommy track' hinders the professional lives of women with children. The survey addressed this issue by asking whether respondents agreed or disagreed with this statement:

Women litigators who have young children receive less desirable case assignments.

Overall, 63.8 percent of women litigators stated that they either "somewhat agreed" or "strongly agreed" with the statement. By firm size and individual status, 76.4 percent of partners from small firms responding to the question agreed that women with children received less desirable cases. This was the category with the highest percentage of respondents agreeing with the statement. In every category, those who agreed with the statement outnumbered those who did not.

OPPORTUNITIES FOR ADVANCEMENT

Even with such perceived disadvantages facing women litigators with young children, the survey respondents feel more positively about opportunity for advancement generally. The survey asked respondents to indicate whether and to what extent they agreed with this statement:

Realistically speaking, women at my law firm have equal opportunity for advancement with men in the firm.

Overall, 57.6 percent of respondents stated that they "somewhat" or "strongly agreed," compared to 38.1 percent who disagreed.

A closer look at the statistics by category reveal a stark difference between the way partners and associates reacted to the question. While 72.8 percent of all partners responding to the question "somewhat" or "strongly agreed," only 53.4 percent of associates agreed. At big firms, only 41.7 percent of associates agreed that women have an equal opportunity for advancement. Perhaps this disparity is in part due to the fact that partners are nearer the top of the firm career ladder and have already been promoted through the ranks compared to associates who may have less evidence of advancement opportunity.

A separate survey conducted as part of Prentice Hall's yearly **Of Counsel 500** directory of law firms indicates that women aren't being promoted to partner at the rate that they are entering law firms. Even though women have been entering law firms at about a 40 percent rate over the past 10 years, only 23.7 percent of the partners named at 340 large law firms in 1992 were women.

STANDARD OF COURTROOM PERFORMANCE

But as tough as the law firm environment is for women, particularly those with young children, the courtroom may be even tougher. The survey asked women litigators whether they agreed or disagreed with this statement:

Female litigators are held to a higher standard of performance in court than male litigators.

Overall, a whopping 78.5 percent of those who responded to the question "somewhat" or "strongly" agreed. By category, the percentage breakdown was remarkably consistent, with those agreeing outnumbering those disagreeing by about three to one across the board.

Level of Responsibility

But while many women litigators perceive that the standard for them in the courtroom is tougher, they are generally satisfied with the level of responsibility they have been given on cases. The survey asked respondents:

Are you satisfied with the level of responsibility you have been given on cases?

Overall, 82.4 percent of women litigators answered "yes." There was a significant variance between partners and associates—33 percent of associates from large law firms who responded to the question answered "no," the largest such response from any category. Many dissatisfied women litigators stated that they were kept out of court and depositions more than male attorneys. Others specifically mentioned they were too often made second chair on trials, with the first chair nearly always going to a male attorney. This pressure to second chair or serve in a backup capacity was described as coming from both colleagues and clients in certain kinds of cases, for example, in "high-profile" matters. A few respondents also stated that male attorneys often engaged in excessive second-guessing and micromanagement of their work.

EARNINGS

One of the most difficult factors for the survey to measure was whether women litigators' earnings are comparable to male litigators. Few attorneys are privy to the salaries of their colleagues. Participants were asked:

Are your earnings comparable to male litigators at your firm?

Of all respondents, 64 percent believed their earnings were comparable to those of male litigators. However, only 14.7 percent answered "no" because 21.2 percent were unsure.

By category, the largest percentage of affirmative responses came from partners in small size firms, 80.4 percent of whom answered "yes." Running second were associates from large firms, 71.9 percent of whom stated that their earnings were comparable. But only 45.8 percent of associates from small firms felt their earnings were comparable. Of those respondents who believed that their earnings were not comparable to those of male litigators, several lawyers stated they believed that male litigators get higher bonuses than female litigators. Another important factor, according to women respondents, was family responsibilities. A few women stated that their compensation fell or suffered compared to that of male attorneys when they took maternity leave or devoted increased attention to their families.

The survey also asked some general questions about billable hours and time spent in trials and other litigation activities. 57.3 percent of the respondents working full-time schedules reported billing in excess of 1900 hours, with 9.0 percent reporting "workaholic numbers"—more than 2400 hours billed per year. Only 20.6 percent of the respondents said they billed less than 1800 hours per year.

Nearly half of the respondents (44.0 percent) reported that they had not served as lead counsel on any trials over the past five years. The disparity between associates and partners on this topic was palpable. While only 10 percent of the partners participating in the survey reported not having served as lead trial counsel during this time period, 75.6 percent of associates reported no lead trial experience—even in pro bono or minor trial matters.

Respondents reported spending the largest percentage of time on discovery and motion preparation. 74.3 percent reported spending more than 20 percent of their time on discovery, while 44.8 percent reported spending a similar percentage of time preparing motions. Only a small percentage of all respondents reported spending as much as 20 percent of their time on settlement negotiation (14.7 percent) or trial (9.7 percent).

CHAPTER 4

As a Woman of Color

by
BEVERLY NELSON MULDROW

BEVERLY NELSON MULDROW

Beverly Nelson Muldrow has been employed by Waste Management, Inc., a subsidiary of WMX Technologies, Inc. in two capacities since January of 1993. As environmental counsel, she advises company operations on issues related to the lawful disposal of refuse, clean water, and clean air. Ms. Muldrow also heads the Minority Outreach Task Force for the Waste Management, Inc. Mid-Atlantic Group Office in Pennsylvania and is a member of WMX Technologies, Inc. Diversity and Environmental Justice Task Forces. The goals of that Task Force are to increase minority employment and minority contracts and improve relations with communities, government and media.

Prior to joining Waste Management, Inc., Ms. Muldrow was a Senior Assistant Regional Counsel at the United States Environmental Protection Agency - Region III in Philadelphia, where she was responsible for the enforcement actions pursuant to the Toxic Substances Control Act, the Clean Air Act and the Comprehensive Environmental Response, Compensation and Liability Act ("CER-CLA" or "Superfund"). During this time, she assisted EPA Headquarters by partic-ipating as an instructor in EPA's Trial Advocacy Institution given for EPA attorneys and as a facilitator in EPA's Negotiation Course. Before Ms. Muldrow became an environmental attorney, she practiced criminal law as an Assistant District Attorney with the Philadelphia District Attorneys Office from 1979 to 1989. In that capacity she prosecuted major felony cases, including child abuse crimes. From 1976 to 1979, Ms. Muldrow was Associate Counsel at Temple University Legal Aid Office where she supervised law students in their legal representation of indigent clients in all types of civil matters. Ms. Muldrow began her legal practice in 1974 as a Deputy Attorney General with the Pennsylvania Justice Department.

Ms. Muldrow has participated on panel discussions on the topic of Environmental Justice with the NAACP and the Congressional Black Caucus. She is a member of the Philadelphia Barristers, the National Bar Association Woman Lawyers Division, the Federal Bar Association, and the Pennsylvania and New Jersey, and Philadelphia Bar Association. She received her B.A. from Franklin and Marshall College and her J.D. from Ohio State University College of Law.

CHAPTER 4

As a Woman of Color

by
BEVERLY NELSON MULDROW

My concern, as I began writing about practicing law as an African-American attorney, was that many of my experiences may just be particular to me. In other words, I have a distinct personal history that undoubtedly affects my perceptions of ''my experiences.'' If other female attorneys of color who read what I have written can understand how I felt during some of these events, my writing will have meaning beyond myself.

The bulk of my legal experience has been as a trial attorney. I have developed some skill in telling the whole story of the case in such a way as to educate and persuade. I will attempt to do that here. I want those minority female lawyers who are dealing with adversity to know what I have learned: that we can create some light for ourselves at the end of the tunnel. We do have power and opportunity, which may come to us in unidentifiable forms. We have to recognize that power and opportunity, seize it, and use it to spur ourselves on to the next level. We cannot let ourselves become inhibited by the narrow minded individuals with whom we will come in contact. As my mother would have put it, ''you have to become skillful at taking lemons and making lemonade.''

I am the fifth child in a family of six children, four girls and two boys. Having a lot of siblings did not make my environment, during my early years, a stable or secure one. As I recall, my father, who worked for an automotive and machinery parts company, was often laid off. My mother, like many black women of that time, worked constantly as a domestic, but made little money. We were poor. Often there was not enough food to eat. The Polish grocer who had a small convenience store on the corner would come by sometimes and leave his day-old baked goods for us. I was taught early on to be grateful for what people gave you.

MY EARLY YEARS

Despite my parents' financial status, they had mortgages on a row home in the city and a house in disrepair on a couple of acres in a rural area about an hour away. We were raised with an appreciation for the outdoors. My father taught my older brothers how to hunt and fish. During the lean times, dinner would include fish or animals that my father and brothers had killed.

When I was five years old, my mother had a heart attack and died. Over the years, people who knew my mother would remark about what a sweet personality she had. I remember my mother as being passive and long-suffering. I knew that my own personality was not like hers. I was always viewed as being aggressive and mouthy. I used to feel that my mother's gentle being was something I wanted to adopt for myself. And this was a source of conflict, for I also realized that being passive often means relegating yourself to being someone's door mat.

I was never very close to my father, emotionally or otherwise. A year and nine days after my mother death, he fatally wounded himself in a hunting accident. My brothers and sisters and I were left orphaned. As orphans, we had less protection than children with parents. All six of us were divided up to live with relatives. Since my father had been in the military, our caretakers, mainly blood relatives, received his veterans' and social security benefits. Nevertheless, they treated us like stepchildren even though our federal benefits helped them to financially move up to the middle-class.

I entered school having already been taught the alphabet and the spelling of my name. That fact combined with my talkative and assertive personality may have caused my teachers to credit me early on with some intelligence. Their acknowledgment of my ability gave me confidence that helped me do well in school. My relatives told me that I was going to be a teacher someday and I believed that I probably would go to college and do just that. In the Baptist Church I attended there were some recent college graduates who taught in the Sunday school. They were encouraging and they helped me to believe that I could do what they had done—get a college education.

I grew up in a working class community, mainly white and ethnic. From my relationships with my friends and the many books which I literally devoured I realized that there are things people share that transcend race and gender—things that are part of the total human experience. Yet, by the time I was 15 or 16 I still felt a need to connect with my racial and cultural background in order to develop a better understanding of myself.

READING ABOUT THE 'BLACK EXPERIENCE'

It became an ongoing process. I try to read all of the authors who write about the "Black Experience." Over the years, the topics I focus on have expanded. But even now, I spend a significant portion of my time on books authored by African-American females. My interest in my racial history is crucial to my present day survival. It is from this reading that I have learned of the many black people who came before and did phenomenal things for our society as a whole. By reflecting on their experiences, I gain insight into my own possibilities.

I have worked since I was a teenager, and I was also involved in the national honor society, the school paper, the choir, the National Conference of Christians and Jews, and my church youth group in high school. I did not plan to become an attorney. The idea was presented to me, along with going into medicine as a viable option for black students in the early 1970's, when I was about to graduate from college. I entered law school with a limited goal: to develop an understanding of the law so I would be empowered to effect social change. After all, I had grown up watching the civil rights and anti-Vietnam War movements on the nightly news. The turmoil of social change was a welcomed sight to me. I knew that historically black people had little power. I had observed this fact up close in the actions of my older family members when they encountered whites in certain social situations. The brutality blacks faced when they attempted to execute their constitutional rights was evident almost everywhere. Because the tone of the times was rapid change, I thought that I could be part of that process.

LEARNING ABOUT LAWYERS

Prior to entering law school, I did not know any attorneys—male or female, black or white. Once I entered law school, the relevance of law school studies to my goals was not always clear to me. I graduated with the desire to be an effective attorney but with no idea how to go about it. In the mid-1970's, there were few female attorneys and even fewer female minority attorneys.

Moreover, I had to fight a perception problem right off the bat. Having received academic scholarships, I benefitted from the affirmative-action efforts of colleges and universities in the late 1960's and 1970's. We (black attorneys) took and passed the same tests and the same bar exams as white attorneys did. If we received any consideration, it was in getting the opportunity to attend certain schools and to receive financial aid where it had been previously denied. Nevertheless I viewed affirmative action as a double-edged sword. Those who want to perpetuate our lack of equal professional status used the existence of affirmative action as a way of justifying their characterization of us as being less than qualified. This barrier became glaringly apparent when I began working as an attorney.

THE STATE ATTORNEY GENERAL OFFICE CAME FIRST

I started my legal practice at a state attorney general office. I was hired with several other law school graduates to do civil litigation. My colleagues were too liberal to use the discriminatory terminology of the past. Instead, they used buzz words like "competent" or "incompetent." As a young lawyer, I was anxious to prove that I was among the competent—a part of the in-group.

There were more experienced lawyers there who could have assisted me in developing a more workable understanding of how to analyze legal issues and take charge of legal representation. But I noticed that their help was often replete with a lack of trust in or respect for my capabilities as an attorney. Instead of being able to focus on the positive aspects of my work, I felt that I had to spend a lot of time invalidating what appeared to be the immediate assumption on the part of my white colleagues that I was incompetent. This lack of trust and respect was manifested by the fact that my work was often subjected to extra scrutiny.

Some of my understanding of how I was perceived as an African-American attorney was derived from the comments I heard about the black male attorneys who worked at the same office. They were viewed as never being quite up to par. As I recall, they did their jobs as well as anyone else and yet, they were perceived as inadequate.

BEING FRIENDS WITH WHITE WOMEN

Of course, there were white female attorneys in that office and I was friendly with many of them. They, too, were new to the profession. They would often, in their interest to fit in, adopt the views of their white male counterparts and be equally as willing to equate whiteness with competency. This was particularly difficult for me to accept because I believed that the issue of equal rights for women got its major legal support in the 1964 Civil Rights Bill (legislation that resulted from the intense struggle of many black people). We should have been close allies. My sense was that the racial difference I had with white women was more significant than the gender connection we shared.

As I reflect now on my time at the attorney general's office, I can only say that it was painful. I could not grow professionally in such a negative environment; I left the job feeling less confident as an attorney than I did when I had arrived. I had few opportunities there to enhance my status and reputation. The chance to do that would come some years later during other employment when I would make legal arguments before juries.

Today I'd like to think that the social environment at the office has improved, but that does not appear to be the case. Recently I spoke with a friend who is female, African-American and an experienced attorney with Ivy-League credentials. She also happens to work for the state government. She explained that when she attended her first meeting with one of her clients, another government employee, and advised him that she represents the state in certain legal matters, his disbelief was such that he called her office, before she returned, to check on her professional qualifications. I would like to have seen his reaction when he heard what impressive credentials she has. Upon learning what he had done, my friend was angry at the fact that he did not presume her to be qualified.

AN URBAN LAW SCHOOL SETTING

After leaving state government, I took a position that allowed me to regroup. I worked in a portion of an urban law school which doubled as a legal aid office and a law student clinical program. I worked with two young male attorneys—one African-American and one white. This job allowed me to do things that were consistent with my pre-law school goals. I was in a position to help those who were in some instances disenfranchised because of their poverty. I had the opportunity to get my feet wet as a trial attorney and I began to stretch professionally.

The office handled divorce, custody, support, workmen compensation, social security, unemployment compensation, and small claims cases—all on a shoestring budget. It was an empowering experience because we did it all, from serving the subpoena on the defendant to representing the client in court.

FRIENDSHIPS IN THE TRENCHES

The atmosphere there was special. It is clear that gender and racial indentification can become almost irrelevant when you're working in the trenches and your goals are to survive and win. My co-workers and students were mutually supportive, and I formed friendships with them that have lasted for years. If the judges I appeared before had difficulty relating to my female, black self, I don't recall it. I was able to focus on overcoming the fear inherent in representing a client in court.

Sometimes I won the cases I handled and sometimes I lost. Nonetheless, I began to learn how to represent clients. I saw that one often had to bridge racial, language, and economic differences in communication to ascertain the facts, apply those facts to the law, anticipate your adversary's arguments, and direct the actual litigation of the case. The more difficult my assignments became, the more my self confidence grew. The first time a court officer who observed me handle a custody case referred another such cases to me to handle, I took it as a vote of confidence.

GETTING HANDS-ON TRIAL EXPERIENCE

I left this job after three years to become an assistant district attorney. By moving to the prosecutor's office, I embarked on an intensive hands-on trial practice experience. I had no plan except to try to meet a new challenge. As an African-American woman and an attorney, I had no difficulty making the decision to prosecute. Having worked in an urban area, I knew that more often than not the victims of crime were minority group members. The system needed to treat their demands for a safe community and their cries for justice with the same concern as those of any other group.

The district attorney's office had a "take no prisoners" environment. It was almost totally dominated by men, even though there were some women ADAs there when I arrived. You learned in the lower units of the office that your competency was equated with your toughness. Early in my employment there, I was told that if I wanted to be a good prosecutor, I had to perform like a female attorney in one of the upper units who had a reputation for being extremely determined and tough. But I wanted to learn to utilize my own personality in such a way as to become a successful prosecutor.

PLANNING DIDN'T HELP

Initially, there was no time to plan and strategize about professional growth. Our ability developed whether we planned for it or not. Almost all new ADA's were assigned to preliminary hearings—the prima facie hearing in felony cases. The prosecutor's job was to establish that a crime had occurred and that the defendant was the person responsible. To accomplish this the prosecutor would have to present testimony to establish the elements of the alleged crime. If you were successful, the court would bound the defendant over for trial.

I was assigned thirty-eight cases the first day I did preliminary hearings by myself. This was customary. The prosecutor and the public defender would arrive sometime before 8:30 A.M. at a designated police station where the hearing was to take place. Court opened with the call of the list and remained in session until every ready matter was heard. Continuances were frowned upon. It was rare for the court to adjourn before lunch. This meant that I usually would not get back to the office until late afternoon. I then had to prepare my statistics (a summary of what had occurred in court) and, if I had time, start calling my witnesses for the next day's court appearance.

THE MOTHER'S JUGGLING ACT

I had a four month old daughter when I started in the district attorney's office. Juggling my responsibilities as a prosecutor and as a mother made my job extremely challenging. I would have to leave the office by 5:45 P.M. to have enough time to get to the day care center before six o'clock. I knew that if I was late picking up my daughter, I would have to pay a substantial fee. To meet my obligations at work and manage my responsibilities as a mother I had to take a lot of work home. Whether my daughter was asleep or not, I began calling witnesses at 8:00 P.M. Sometimes I would still be making calls after 10:00 P.M. Nevertheless, some of the unmarried male assistants complained that I was lazy because I left work earlier than they did. Some of these men did not understand my situation until years later when they became fathers. Some of them never understood.

Usually our first visual contact with our witness took place when the case was called at the preliminary hearing. I learned, as did all ADAs, to assess the quality of a witness and to reassure that witness in a matter of minutes. Regardless of the witness's race or gender, my concern was getting the case held for court and the defendant bound over for trial. The victim of the crime, my witness, and I were working together towards that one goal. I learned to set a professional tone and the victim would usually follow my lead.

UNCERTAINTY WAS THE ONLY CERTAINTY

You could never be certain of what would occur in court. As a young prosecutor, you took things the way they came and tried to let any annoyance roll off your back. On several occasions the witness standing right next to me called the defendant a "Nigger" or some other racial name. While it offended me, I learned to focus on my goal of having the defendant held for court. As a minority attorney, your statistics (the number of cases held for court) were of particular significance. If you were given a number of what turned out to be unprovable cases or, in the upper units, if your case went to trial and was not given a disposition favorable to the State, your competency would sometimes be questioned. On one occasion another attorney in my unit called up a complainant in a matter I had handled to find out what I had said when the case was not held for trial. He refused to wait for the notes of testimony or to believe what I had said about the quality of the evidence.

I observed that African-Americans in the office who were viewed by whites as less threatening were often given supervisory positions. Once promoted they wielded little power and commanded even less respect. My first supervisor in preliminary hearings was an African-American woman. She had been there for approximately five years and had risen to the level of Chief of Preliminary Hearings. She did not seem to have a lot of support from her colleagues or supervisors. She left four months after I started working for her. Her replacement was an African-American male who had an outstanding reputation as a trial attorney in one of the upper units.

AN OUTSTANDING SUPERVISOR IS REMOVED

Besides preparing us for court appearances, he held weekly meetings in which he taught us how to take control of the trial of a case. He was also an advocate for his staff. I learned from the office grapevine that when he thought some of us were ready for advancement, he would go to the district attorney's chiefs' meeting and get us moved on to the next unit. Nevertheless, while he was on his honeymoon, the district attorney removed him from his position as Chief of Preliminary Hearings, and gave the position to someone else, despite the fact that the District Attorney and my boss were said to be personal friends. This was further evidence to me that strong blacks with leadership ability can be quashed.

Within the district attorney's office, assistants had very little power and, if they were minority attorneys, they had even less. We were simply given our assignments. Rarely were we even asked for input on the kinds of cases we wanted to handle. For many years black women never got beyond the child abuse or rape units, while white women, white men and African-American men were allowed to work in what was viewed as the highest unit, homicide.

A SUPERVISOR WHO HINDERS LEARNING

When I was in the unit above preliminary hearings, Municipal Court, my supervisor, a white male, would require that almost all of the minority attorneys, including myself, receive closer supervision. He would meet with us individually regarding certain cases as if he did not trust us to handle them ourselves. I learned very little under his instruction. I suspect he set us apart so that he could feel superior to us and thereby counteract his own insecurity. After about six months of working under his supervision, I was reassigned to the Juvenile Court Unit which was one of the least desirable units of the office. Most of the minority assistants went through that unit at one time or another.

At first I feared that this assignment would thwart my professional growth, but I ended up benefitting from the three years I spent there. The supervisor left us alone to try our cases and I found mentors within my unit and among one or two of the juvenile judges. I learned to do full trials without having to deal with the speedy trial requirements. There was an older African-American woman judge to whom I was often assigned. She taught me how to apply our criminal laws to children in a helpful way. Kids appeared before her who were charged with all kinds of crimes. Some of these children had gotten into fights because someone had called them "Nigger." She would take the time to tell these children that she had often been called that name and that she ignored it and did not let it stop her. She would also lecture the parents about their obligations and admonish the child defendant about breaking the law. Her sentences were fair, and the juveniles who appeared before her both feared and respected her.

NICKNAMES FOR BLACK DEFENDANTS

Many of the ADAs had nicknames for those who came to the attention of the criminal justice system. The blacks were called "critters" and the whites "dirtballs." The assistants using these terms were usually white and seemed to recognize a distinction between those whites who committed crimes and those who did not. But I always felt that the term "critter" was intended as an all inclusive term for blacks. Indeed, some of the assistants took particular interest in the prosecution of a black defendant if his victim had been white. I heard some co-workers verbalize this sentiment.

Part of my assignment in juvenile was to represent the State in the pretial conference courtroom. Many of the children who were charged with offenses were black and poor. They would appear with or without parents. If a child was already in custody, the judge decided whether he would remain there or be released, and whether he would be placed in a diversionary program or sent to trial. Working this courtroom was often extremely sad for me. Most of these children would have to overcome serious obstacles to become productive members of society. Their parents were inept and often disinterested in fulfilling their responsibilities. There were very few community facilities with space for children who were in need of care, guidance and support.

THE HOPELESSNESS IS OVERWHELMING

One day the hopelessness I encountered in this courtroom overwhelmed me and the tears began to flow. I looked over at the public defender, my adversary, who was also an African-American woman, and saw that she, too, was wiping tears away. I did my job there. But the feelings I experienced would motivate me to work with the court in future situations to come up with a disposition that provided for rehabilitation as well as punishment for offenders whenever possible.

Once when I was in the Juvenile Unit, I was called to the main office for not trying a case when the victim, who was white, asked me to handle it. I had represented the victim at a previous listing but the case was continued to another date for trial. At that second listing, the other ADA in court with me divided up the assignments, putting the victim's case on his sheet. He eventually tried the case against a private defense attorney, a black female, and lost. I was reprimanded by the first deputy even though I had been told many times that the victim does not get to pick the ADA who handles his case. Thus, I came to understand that a white victim may indeed get to direct a black ADA to handle his case.

MOVING TO THE JURY TRIAL UNIT

After three years in the Juvenile and two merit salary increases, I met with the district attorney and was told that I would be moved to the Jury Trial Unit. This was a true advancement, and I was excited about the prospect of doing jury trials. As part of my reassignment, I was teamed with a black male from North Carolina who had taught school before becoming an attorney. We appeared before an African-American judge who was highly respected by the hierarchy of the district attorney's office. My co-counsel knew a great deal about the practical application of criminal law, having begun his tenure in the office in the motions unit, and later moving up through the ranks to juries. Having come from the Juvenile Unit, I benefitted from his knowledge because he was an excellent teacher.

It was apparent that our judge preferred dealing with me more than my co-counsel. Our judge was from the old school and very knowledgeable. The fact that my co-counsel was a dark-complected black male from the South did not endear him to the judge, who was a member of the local northern Negro elite. I, at least, was from the North and was lighter in complexion.

We were undoubtedly assigned to the African-American judge because our white supervisors thought it would help us to win in court. We did not know how to tell them that they were dead wrong. Some of the minority judges resented being assigned fellow minorities as prosecutors or public defenders. In some instances, it seemed as though they viewed it as a slight of some sort. Those of us who appeared before them literally received no respect.

HOW THEY TREATED WOMEN

As a female, I found their approach to me doubly distasteful. Either they thought I was a child and they must teach me, or they found me attractive and felt they must control me. When my co-counsel went to another unit for six months, a white female was assigned to work with me before the same African-American judge. It was clear that as far as he was concerned she could do no wrong. He bragged about her background and her performance in court. Despite his apparent preference, I learned how to try cases to a jury. I won many cases in his room because, for me, the jury was the great equalizer.

When I began doing jury trials, I was concerned about how to express myself to the jury. I wanted to find a way to develop a rapport with the members of the jury so they would follow my lead. Since the victims of crimes were often from poor backgrounds, I had to convince jurors from middle-class environments that they should have equal concern about the rights of the less fortunate. I found that in this way you could bring them around to share your beliefs.

ALL THE COURT'S A STAGE

Representing the State in a jury trial took a great deal of work and concentration. When I was not in court, I would keep trying the case mentally by assessing the evidence. When I was in court, I was on stage. The trial was never over until the jury returned a verdict. An attorney could appear to lose the case during testimony and then win it with the closing argument. I learned that no matter how nervous I felt, I had to appear confident and in control throughout the process. I eventually understood how to apply my true personality to my legal representation. Often I would return from court and search out a friend to discuss some surprising testimony that had been presented that day. I came to realize that there was an argument to be made in closing to further my position no matter what the testimony had been.

When you were on trial, help came from just about anyone in the office. On one occasion, I was given several cases to try in front of a woman judge. One of them was a drunk driving and aggravated assault. Although the victim was not expected to appear, he showed up in court and I had to go forward with a non-jury trial. After hearing how the victim had lost his leg, the judge took the case under advisement and gave the state four days to come up with case law supporting the concept that a drunk driver's conduct in running over someone's leg constituted an aggravated assault. I did legal research and I talked to the homicide, jury and appeals ADAs. Once I told them the facts of the case, they took time from their schedules to assist me in my research. Thanks to their help, I was able to make a convincing argument before the court and the defendant was convicted of aggravated assault. Sometime later the case established legal precedent when the judge's decision was sustained on appeal. Within months other assistants confronted with similar issues came to me for help.

COLLEAGUES TO TALK TO

As part of my survival in the office, I developed my own group of colleagues to confer with during a trial. They were knowledgeable and encouraging. These friends came from all races and genders. I could be on trial and an unanticipated issue of appellate significance requiring legal research would arise. The judge would give me a few minutes to decide on the next course of action. I could make a phone call to one of them and within minutes I would have an answer. The appellate attorneys were often anxious to assist the guys doing the trials. I found, as I had when I did legal services before, that in the trenches there is no time for prejudice.

Another time I had to do a six month detail to the Charging Unit where we worked twelve hour shifts around the clock preparing complaints and authorizing search warrants. My daughter was six years old at the time. The assignment required some juggling of my personal schedule but I managed. However, I did feel some resentment when I discovered that I was the first mother to be given such an assignment.

Within a year of my return to juries, I was called in by the district attorney and asked if I wanted to go to the Domestic Violence Unit. He told me that the head of the unit, whom he failed to identify, but whom I knew to be a white female, did not have the jury trial experience that I had. I declined. This was the only time I was asked about an assignment before it was given to me. It was not unusual in such a political office for supervisors, who often had political connections, to have less legal or trial experience than their staff.

LAWYERS GET PINK SLIPS

Within a year a new district attorney was elected. Soon after the election, several ADAs received pink slips. Prior to the change in administration there were approximately twenty-three black attorneys in the office. A majority of the attorneys who received pink slips were black. Many of the remaining African-American attorneys were moved from the jury trial unit and put in other units. I was told that I would be sent to child abuse. The unit was small and there were no other black attorneys there at the time. I was not happy about the move. I felt that they needed a minority attorney and I was the unlucky choice.

TRANSFER TO THE CHILD ABUSE UNIT

My change of assignment to the Child Abuse Unit eventually became a tremendous opportunity. Probably because I had done more trials than my twenty-something year old supervisor, I was assigned major felony jury trials involving potential sentences of at least a mandatory five year prison term. Unlike some of the robbery, burglary and aggravated assault trials I handled in the Jury Unit, I was presented with cases about which I had very strong feelings. It was in the Child Abuse Unit that I came to realize that one of the things minorities and women can bring to the practice of law is creativity. Child abuse litigation was a hot area to be involved in because the law was changing. Issues such as the competency of the child witness, and the admissibility of prior statements by the child witness were still developing.

The first day care center child abuse case I prosecuted took several months of preparation. The children were four and five years old. I met with each child and the parents several times. I took the children to the courtroom and had someone who looked like the assigned judge sit on the bench. I did not want the children to be afraid during the trial. Once the case began I had to take their testimony the way it came. I had them demonstrate what happened by using anotomically correct dolls. I had to put this evidence into a closing argument and try to win. When the jury found the defendant guilty after a little over two hours of deliberation, I was as as surprised as anyone. My supervisor had told me that the day care center case would be the most difficult trial I would ever handle. Yet, after I won that conviction, many equally difficult cases were sent my way. I enjoyed the challenge as well as the recognition I received when I won.

LYING IN WAIT FOR YOUR FOE

Opposing counsel (white males) would underestimate my ability in court. But I perceived their sense of superiority as something I could use against them. I would intentionally try my case in a laid-back but confident fashion. I would be respectful to the victim, the defendant, and everyone else in the courtroom. Then, in closing argument, I would try to put the facts in the case together with a blend of moral and legal philosophy that would compel the jury to convict. I loved the children that I represented, and I found ways to convey this to the jury. This strategy worked well until I developed a reputation for winning.

After three years in the Child Abuse Unit, I was confronted with the glass ceiling that existed at that time for African-American female assistants in the district attorney's office. I asked to be assigned to the Homicide Unit because I could not do child abuse cases any longer. My supervisor had told me confidentially that I was rated number one in the Child Abuse Unit. From the grapevine I heard that other supervisors, all of them white males, were recommending this move for me. Eventually, I was told by my supervisor's boss that I would be reassigned in January or February. When April came and I had not yet been moved to homicide, I left the district attorney's office. A couple of black women who were assistants in the lower units observed what was taking place with my advancement. They, too, left the district attorney's office, right around the time I did.

BECOMING A PROSECUTOR DID NOT MAKE ME MALE OR WHITE

I had learned a great deal as a prosecutor, but ultimately it did not make me male or white. I took a new job as an assistant regional counsel with a federal agency. Initially, I had a great deal of respect for the regional counsel, my new boss, who was a southern white woman, until it became clear that she, too, underestimated the capabilities of minority attorneys. During a diversity training meeting that was held for technical and legal supervisors, she stated that she had instructed her staff that minority attorneys do not write as well as others. In an apparent act of liberalism, she had told her supervisory staff not to hold it against the minority attorneys in their evaluations. When the agency's EEO officer challenged this statement, the regional counsel countered by observing that the minority attorneys even dressed differently. It was hard to respect someone who had such a distorted perception of minority attorneys.

Because of my background, I was asked to be an adjunct instructor in the agency's trial advocacy institute, which was given for agency attorneys who had little or no trial experience. I agreed and ended up attending the institute three weeks after I started work. I had to earn my acceptance into the group of instructors, who were all white. I opted to do the closing argument demonstration against someone who later became my supervisor. When I finished, the other staff members came forward and shook my hand one at a time. Doing the presentation was challenging because I had never done a closing argument in front of forty attorneys.

HEADQUARTERS PAYS THE COSTS

My work as part of the trial advocacy institute staff helped me to gain some recognition at agency headquarters. After participating in the institute for a subsequent year, I was asked to do negotiation training at various regional offices around the country. My immediate supervisor, a white female, expressed her displeasure to me directly about my having this opportunity. When I requested the permission to make these visits, she would come to me and demand to know in the rudest tone whether our regional office was paying for the travel costs. Each time I told her that the agency's headquarters office was paying the costs.

During my employment with this agency, I was in a position to increase my knowledge of federal civil procedure and regulatory and administrative practice. Having been a prosecutor, it was difficult for me to adjust to the lack of autonomy that agency attorneys were given. Without the authority to make decisions and exercise judgment, I felt as though I had lost part of my ability in certain situations.

LIFE AT A FEDERAL AGENCY

Life for minority attorneys at the federal agency was no different than what I had experienced at other times in my past employment. At one point, I was assigned an administrative case involving an African-American university. The technical support person assigned to me for this case was also an African-American female. Neither of us had attended this particular university. I had no interests other than making sure the university complied with agency policy and the applicable regulations. Yet when the technical support supervisor learned that the two of us were working on the case, he removed the original technical person and assigned a white male in her place. I settled the case for a small amount but more than my new technical person recommended. The settlement was not approved by the law division until I let my hierarchy know who my technical person was and that he had endorsed the low settlement figure.

BECOMING AN IN-HOUSE COUNSEL

I left this job after three and a half years to take a job with a major corporation as in-house counsel. My current office atmosphere is friendly and my work presents me with many challenges. Part of the TQM training offered by the company includes a discussion of the need for more minority and female hiring. We have endorsed efforts by the local bar association to have corporations such as ours hire law firms that have minority attorneys on staff. This is a significant start because when I attend negotiations on behalf of my client with many attorneys representing various corporations, I may see one minority attorney once in a while.

My first concern, as an in-house counsel, is doing a professional job in servicing my client. By my very actions, I try to educate and persuade my colleagues that our success as a company will be found in the inclusion and involvment of people from all groups. I try to emphasize our common strengths as people when I interact with other employees while giving legal advice or socializing.

In the early years of my legal practice, it often seemed as though, by becoming an attorney, I had entered no man's land. I had a difficult time establishing meaningful connections with people who could help me enhance my professional growth or increase my sense of acceptance. It took me several years before I learned how to build bridges that go over negativity and around racism and sexism. Admittedly, this is something that requires continual effort. And yes, I do get weary.

RECOGNIZING WHAT IS CRITICAL

I came to realize that it is crucial for me to create my own criteria for measuring my success, criteria that consist of achievable goals. Reaching my personal objectives always has the additional effect of increasing my professional self-confidence. This is a never ending internal process in which I strive to grow professionally by setting higher and higher standards. When I was growing up, the older folks in my family would say that whatever work you choose to do, be the best. There is no limit to what we can do, if we believe in ourselves.

I have found it important to associate with positive people who believe in my ability. When I can't find such individuals at work, I seek them out elsewhere and socialize with them outside of work. There are six women of various professional backgrounds who I try to get together with every couple of months. Invariably, I leave these meetings feeling stronger and encouraged.

I make time to network. The larger my circle of friends and supporters, the more clout I can bring to my legal position. I try to associate with a diverse group of individuals because, put simply, assistance may come from a variety of sources. Minority women attorneys cannot afford to be prejudiced. I believe racism and sexism to be a manifestation of ignorance and fear. When I am confronted with either of these attitudes, I try to keep my eye on my goals and keep moving forward.

Our nation fails to acknowledge the extent of present-day racism and sexism. I have and continue to experience both. Other African-American women I know agree that such attitudes are still going strong. To distrust individuals because they are different from ourselves and to belittle their intellect and capabilities is detrimental to all of us. It undermines the talents of our people.

I have told you my "experiences" in an effort to say to other minority women attorneys that no one can stop us unless we let them. I have read about Harriet Tubman, Mary Macleod Bethune, Barbara Jordan, Mother Hale, Dr. Marian Wright Edelman and many others. We are strong and powerful because we are connected by history to women such as these. No matter what anyone throws in our path, we can step over it and move forward. I am determined, as I know others are, to keep on rising. We can do it all.

CHAPTER 5

A Lesbian Lawyer Speaks Out

by
GINA BRIGGS

GINA BRIGGS

Gina Briggs is a 1990 graduate of Temple Law School, Philadelphia, Pennsylvania. Upon graduation, she joined Stradley, Ronon, Stevens & Young, a medium to large Philadelphia law firm, as a litigation associate, where her practice emphasized antitrust, franchise and surety law. She left Stradley for a position in the Professional Liability Section of the Resolution Trust Corporation, where she supervised the investigation of failed savings and loan associations and directed the litigation against former directors and officers and the professionals who provided services to the institutions. She is currently a candidate for an LL.M. in Taxation at NYU School of Law.

Gina Briggs remains active with the Philadelphia Bar Association and Gay and Lesbian Lawyers of Philadelphia ("GALLOP"), formerly Philadelphia Attorneys for Human Rights ("PAHR"). During her tenure as PAHR's liaison to the Philadlephia Bar Association Young Lawyers Division Executive Committee, she petitioned to have the Young Lawyers Division bylaws amended to provide for a designated voting seat on the Executive Committee for a representative of gay and lesbian young lawyers. The Young Lawyers Division overwhelmingly voted to confer full committee member status to a representative of the gay and lesbian legal community. In addition, Ms Briggs is a co-founder and volunteer with Vote With Pride, a non-partisan gay and lesbian voter registration project.

CHAPTER 5

A Lesbian Lawyer Speaks Out

by
GINA BRIGGS

I realized I was different when I was about 8 years old. I didn't know what it was called or what it meant, but I knew to keep my mouth shut.

In high school, I tried not to give it much thought. I certainly didn't forget that I was different, but I kept it to myself and tried not to think about it.

In my early twenties, I actively suppressed my feelings. My Catholic upbringing taught me the virtue of martyrdom: martyrs suffer, die, and then, once dead, are adored. I feared the shame I might bring to my family—the people I loved the most—if I acted on my feelings. So, I reluctantly became a martyr-in-training and lived in the deepest regions of my closet, trying not to think about "it," consciously deciding that I would spend the rest of my life focusing on work, family, and friends. I thought that if I kept myself busy, maybe I would not miss romantic companionship. I quickly learned that I could never be too busy.

In my mid-twenties I finally realized that my family loved me as much as I loved them and that they would accept me for who and what I am. It was my uncle who inadvertently led me out of the closet.

My uncle helped raise me. He was handsome and bright, fluent in four languages. He traveled the world, changed careers with seemingly little effort, and charmed virtually everyone he met. He was adored by everyone in my extended family, by great aunts and third cousins, by anyone half-way related by blood or marriage. No one ever talked about his sexuality; like many other families, we knew but did not discuss it.

One day my uncle started coughing and the cough didn't go away. When he and my cousin developed the flu, she got better in a week, but he was still sick a month later. I drove my uncle to the doctor's office for his examinations, convincing myself that he would get better. When he finally entered the hospital three months later and was placed in intensive care, I wanted to believe that he would be released soon. When he said he had AIDS, I told him that I knew. And when he died, I missed him so badly I thought the pain would never go away.

SHAME ABOUT WHO YOU ARE

Shortly after my uncle died, I learned that he purposely postponed hospitalization until it was too late. Simply put, he was afraid that if he recovered and continued to return to the hospital, people would find out that he had AIDS, and they would suspect that he was gay. He wanted to die quickly because he didn't want to bring shame to the family.

I cannot describe the anger and hate I felt when I learned of my uncle's decision. I wanted to tell those responsible that they were evil—that my uncle died with the fear that they would hate or shun him if they knew he was gay. I now know that I was mad at my uncle for being afraid, for giving in. I wanted him to fight, to say that it didn't matter if he was gay or straight and that instead what mattered was that he was dying. I wanted him to fight for himself and for me. But he didn't fight. And, as he wished, we lied about his cause of death. That made me even angrier, and, briefly, I hated my family for being relieved that he told no one and wanted no one to know.

I knew that I must do something constructive or I would be consumed by bitterness, anger, and hatred. So I made some promises. I promised that I would not surrender a day of life to conceal that I am gay. I promised to get involved in gay causes— to fight back. And, most important, I promised that I would no longer keep my mouth shut.

I came out the year after my uncle's death. I had just finished my first year at Temple Law School. Coming out there was realitively easy. Most of my school friends were straight, but gay and straight students mixed socially. A group of us would get together for dinner or happy hour after classes. Usually, we went to straight bars or restaurants, but occasionally everyone would go to a gay bar or club. And if someone was having a party, I was encouraged and expected to bring whomever I was dating.

HOW SCHOOL DAYS ARE HEAVENLY

I knew that I was having more fun than anyone should ever have in law schol. As I passed my final days at Temple, I suspected that it was not only law school that would end.

After my first day as a litigation associate at a large Philadelphia firm, no one had to tell me that I wasn't at Temple anymore.

I was introduced to the firm as a summer clerk. I wasn't the only gay person at the firm, but I was the only lesbian lawyer. Social events were enjoyable, and I exhibited ''appropriate social behavior''—having fun but tailoring my comments to the company I kept. I avoided talking about relationships, although that is probably wise for summer clerks regardless of whether they are gay. As one summer program director was fond of telling new clerks, ''Remember, they (the firm's attorneys) are not your friends.''

During my summer clerkship and my first year at the firm, I considered myself open, but discrete. I neither hid my sexual orientation nor expressly disclosed it; instead I camouflaged it with gender-neutral language. I did not engage in such affirmative cover as bringing men to functions and using masculine gender to describe past or present romantic interests and I believe I was healthier for not trying to hide. Using gender-neutral language consumed enough energy: I cannot imagine the energy I would have spent creating a parallel heterosexual universe.

WHAT DO THEY SUSPECT?

The only people at the firm who knew I was gay were other self-identified gays and one straight female senior associate with good "gaydar" (the ability to spot gays and lesbians). When I started at the firm, however, I believed that the partners at least suspected. A straight male classmate had told me that they were likely to pick up on it—presumably because he did. I hoped that he was right, because that would mean that my sexual orientation was not an issue. But he was wrong.

I received indirect confirmation that at least the younger partners were unsuspecting when I learned of a rumor that I was having an affair with a straight male associate who was my closest friend at the firm. He, too, had thought that the firm attorneys suspected I was gay, and he was aghast at the rumor of our affair. Initially, I found it amusing because it was so off base. Then it struck me that the rumor undercut my hope that my sexual orientation had become a non-issue. I realized that "open, but discrete" actually concealed the truth. And, open, but discrete was hardly satisfying. I often felt left out. I could not participate spontaneously when other associates talked about relationships or complained about their single status. It was particularly difficult because many of the associates were people I liked and respected.

WHAT TO DO ABOUT OTHER ASSOCIATES

And the anguish and mental energy wasted on if, how, and when to come out can be phenomenal. For example, there was the problem of who to invite to a party I decided to give soon after I began working at the firm. I wanted to invite one of my fellow first-year associates whom I will call "Mary." Unfortunately, Mary did not know I was gay, and I did not feel comfortable coming out to her before the party. I liked Mary; she was smart and appeared open-minded. But she was straight-laced and a devout Catholic. Of course, I could simply invite her and say nothing, but surely at some point she would realize that at least half the guests were gay men and lesbians. It seemed unfair not to tell her in advance.

So I didn't invite Mary to my party. And I felt especially terrible, because it turned out that an old friend of hers—a straight associate at another big firm—came to the party as a guest of a friend of mine from law school. Over the next few weeks whenever I saw Mary I felt like a coward, and I went out of my way to avoid discussing the party because I didn't want to hurt her feelings.

I gathered that Mary and I were supposed to bond as we both climbed the ladder to partnership, but bonding was hardly possible when I felt that I couldn't develop an honest friendship with her. I don't mean to say that I expected to have life-long friendships with every fellow associate; indeed, there were some associates I preferred to avoid. However, I also distanced myself from a few associates I liked because I didn't know how they would react if I came out to them. Simply put, I felt as if I were lying by not sharing an important part of my life with the other associates; not sharing did not seem very different from faking a straight life.

DESTROYING THE FACADE OF DISHONESTY

It eventually became clear to me that I had to destroy what I had created. If I felt left out, it was because I did not join in. In the beginning of my second year I decided to come out at work and to get involved in gay organizations and issues. I found that coming out served a purpose beyond friendship with other associates. It also saved me the time, energy, and angst of analyzing every comment for evidence that "they know."

Here is an example of the way things can get out of proportion: I was told informally during the firm's review process that there had been comments about my physical appearance and a suggestion that perhaps I should get more suits. I was offended and embarrassed when I heard this from someone who, I believe, was telling me for my own good. Friends and fellow associates with whom I discussed the comment agreed that, though I was not the most fashionable associate, I dressed appropriately and with reasonable variety. I counted my suits and discovered that I had more than many of my straight male co-workers. The only real difference between my taste in clothes and that of other female litigation associates was that I generally wore dark suits and they occasionally wore dresses and preferred brighter colors.

IS IT PARANOIA OR REALITY?

I began to obsess about my appearance, more embarrassed than angry. Finally, a straight male friend asked, "Gina, do you think that they suspect that you are gay?" Then I became angry—and scared. In turn, I worried that I might become overly sensitive. Before the comment about my personal appearance, when I expressed concerns to friends about some comment a partner made or the significance of its timing, I was told I was being paranoid. Yet a little paranoia may be a good thing, because the truth is that partners do talk about you—and they are rarely direct or candid about these private comments.

The fashion incident taught me that I was not paranoid. But I was tired of worrying about what would happen if the partners knew. I was ready to find out for myself.

The process of my coming out began at home. Although my brother and sister-in-law knew I was gay, I had not told my mother. She had to be first because I intended to address the concerns of gays and lesbians through the Philadelphia Bar Association; she deserved to be informed before I told my co-workers and members of the legal community. Mother was not surprised.

Then I began to sound out a few partners I felt would be supportive. I asked Andre Dennis, then the chancellor-elect of the Philadelphia Bar Association, whether any of the association's committees were focusing on the concerns of gays and lesbians. He did not know, but he gave me the names of two openly gay attorneys and promised to be accessible and to keep me informed.

FINDING MEN WHO WILL HELP

Other partners I approached, straight men like Andre, were helpful, interested, and supportive. Of course, I chose them carefully and had no illusion that they were representative of the partnership as a whole. I did not seek out women partners for several reasons. First, there were far fewer women partners than men. Second, I had more personal and political affinity with the male partners I approached than with the women partners at the firm. Third, I did not want to put a woman partner on the spot to support me about an issue that did not interest her. None of the women partners was a lesbian.

I also tried to get involved in the local gay law association, Philadelphia Attorneys for Human Rights (PAHR). PAHR was looking for a liaison to the Young Lawyers Section (YLS) Executive Committee. I volunteered for the position, obtaining a non-voting seat established for education and advocacy.

At my first YLS meeting I was introduced simply as PAHR's representative. Shortly thereafter, I had a conversation with John Savoth, the YLS Chair, in which we agreed that many committee members probably had no idea what PAHR stood for or whom it served. At the meeting that followed, I was again introduced as PAHR's representative, but this time PAHR was described. After the second introduction, no one could not know. Immediately before John began the introduction I was nervous, but as he spoke, I felt a tremendous sense of relief.

YOU CAN'T TURN BACK

Every lesbian and gay man I know who has come out cannot imagine returning to the closet. The tremendous benefits—greater confidence and self-esteem—permeate your life. Before coming out, I lived in Philadelphia approximately six blocks away from my office—a five-minute walk. At night when I would step out to pick up the *Au Courant*, a local gay newspaper, I would glance furtively over my shoulder. So, too, when I entered the only lesbian bar in town. True, most folks at the firm probably had never heard of the *Au Courant* and would not know that Hepburn's was a lesbian bar. But the fear was still there—fear that someone would see me, someone I might not see, and that that someone might be homophobic and might say things that could hurt me and my career. I felt as if I were in hiding or were being stalked. Finally, I could not stand it any more.

After I sounded out partners and joined the YLS committee as a self-identified "out" lesbian, I felt stronger and surer of myself. By the time I left the firm, I would walk back from lunch and pick up a copy of the *Au Courant* to bring back to work. I freely entered gay bookstores, bars, clubs, and restaurants. I didn't care who saw me or what he or she might say.

STAYING BRAVE AND HEALTHY

Some people said they thought I was brave for coming out. That was nice, but I knew I was just trying to stay healthy. Fairly soon I began to see that I reacted in healthier ways when confronted with insensitivity or homophobia. When I submitted a pro bono memorandum requesting credit for my involvement with the YLS Executive Committee, I used the stronger words "gay" and "lesbian" rather than the less threatening "sexual minority." When "Bob," the partner who initially reviewed the memo, refused to sign off on it because it made him uncomfortable, I got angry—not embarrassed, not scared. Bob's job was simply to review the pro bono request to make sure that the project would not interfere with my work (it wouldn't) and that it was legal work (it was).

A second partner ("Rick") was responsible for making sure that the project fell within the definition of pro bono as outlined in the firm handbook. Rick said that my work on the YLS committee was a bar association activity which did not qualify for pro bono status. Although I think he defined pro bono narrowly, I know that he tried to be fair and just. Shortly before I left the firm, I was told that Rick spoke to the firm management committee about Bob's reaction to my memo because he thought that the reaction was troublesome.

"SHOCK VALUE" AS A MOTIVE

Rick was also the partner who handled the next "gay problem" when he was asked to calm down another partner who ran to tell him that "gay associates are going to bring dates to the prom (firm ball) for 'shock value'." Rick first checked to see if any of the gay associates intended to bring dates. No one did, but I had thought about it and had told some associates that I might bring the woman I was seeing if she wanted to go (she didn't). One of the other gay associates and I were outraged by the assertion that we would bring dates for "shock value." We realized that the frantic partner probably thought our very existence was shocking. Before I left the firm, I learned that Rick had told his frantic partner that the invitation was addressed to "attorney and guest" and that gay attorneys were entitled to bring whomever they wanted. Rick handled the matter well, which felt good, but not knowing the identity of the frantic partner was unsettling.

Overall, my experience at the firm was mixed. Once I came out, I felt ridiculous for making a big deal out of it—coming out can be quite a production number. I was relieved that I could finally speak freely around more people. Despite enduring some pettiness and the occasional homophobic transgression, I did not look back. Without question, coming out was the best thing I have done for myself. I know that I could not have written this chapter before that.

MUST YOU FIGHT FOR YOURSELF?

One day, I was explaining to a friend at the firm the difficulties in getting gay and lesbian attorneys to come out. My friend asked, "How can gay and lesbian lawyers be effective advocates for others if they cannot or will not fight for themselves?" My answer was, "Maybe not fighting for yourself allows you to advocate on behalf of others." But I did not really believe this. I think that my friend was right—fear is not something a lawyer needs. Lawyers are supposed to be gutsy, adversarial, and brave. Being afraid of how my peers would react if and when they found out I was gay undermined my confidence. But I knew that, even if I did a first class job, there would always be someone who might think I wasn't good enough because of who and what I was.

This was written some time ago. I left the firm and started a new job. And I came out to a new group of co-workers. Now I am in school and will be looking for a new position after graduation. And I will have to come out to a new group of co-workers, but I already know how to do it. I've already started. And it is likely that coming out will never stop.

CHAPTER 6

Credibility and Gender in the Courtroom: What Jurors Think

by
REIKO HASUIKE

REIKO HASUIKE

Reiko Hasuike, is a psychologist who specializes in assisting attorneys with trial strategies.

Ms. Hasuike is President of DecisionQuest, Inc. in Los Angeles, which is a trial consulting firm founded in 1991 by former principals of Litigation Sciences, Inc. She was former Managing Director of Litigation Sciences, Inc. and worked in its Los Angeles, Chicago, and New York offices before leaving the company in April, 1991.

Ms. Hasuike was born in Tokyo, Japan and came to the United States when she was a junior in college. She says her parents are very traditional and allowed her to come to the States to study only because they believed such an experience would be a good training ground for a future "diplomat's wife." After doing graduate work in theoretical linguistics and teaching at California State University and Princeton University, Ms. Hasuike ended up going back to graduate school in social and cognitive psychology at Princeton University.

Ms. Hasuike's interest in psychology began as a natural extension of her own adaptation to living in a foreign country and trying to understand how Americans think and feel about things. Although she has been living in the States for 23 years (which is longer than the years she spent in Japan), she feels that her different cultural background is an important asset as a trial consultant. She has many years of practice in figuring out the patterns and rules of behaviors of Americans, and she has an outsider's observations and perspectives, which are helpful in analyzing juror behavior.

Ms. Hasuike designs empirical studies (such as mock trials and surveys), writes questionnaires, analyzes and interprets data, interviews jurors, and works with witnesses. She warns that what people write in questionnaires or what they say during interviews are often conscious or unconscious rationalizations, not the real reasons for their decisions or feelings. She says what she enjoys the most is trying to figure out what truly motivates people to make certain decisions or judgments.

Ms. Hasuike plays the piano, but she regrets not having the talent to be a singer because that is what she really wanted (and still wants) to be.

CHAPTER 6

Credibility and Gender in the Courtroom: What Jurors Think

by
REIKO HASUIKE

How does the fact that you are a woman affect your credibility in the courtroom? To answer that question you must look at the five roles people play in the courtroom: judges, lawyers, witnesses, litigants, and jurors. Do jurors react differently to the performances of men and women in these roles? I will answer this question by discussing what we can learn from social science and litigation research about the relationship between credibility and gender.

First, let me list the major findings relating to the issue of credibility and gender:

- People (both men and women) think that men generally are more competent than women.

- The areas of expertise for men are seen as being more favorable than the areas of expertise for women, just as masculine traits include more positive characteristics than do feminine traits.

- When a woman shows competence in areas of expertise considered to be masculine, people may believe that her high performance is caused by luck not skill.

- Women who show competence in "masculine" areas are

often seen as being more competent than men who perform at the same level.

- Women benefit tremendously when they perform competently in "masculine" ways, so long as these ways are seen as being positive and so long as the women do not challenge traditionally female values such as motherhood.

- Women jurors do not necessarily like women advocates more than male advocates.

- Women jurors with more progressive views on women's role in society tend to like women advocates who deviate from traditional roles; but male jurors with progressive views do not share this view.

Women advocates will be more effective if they keep these in mind. In preparing for trial, each woman must analyze (1) the content of the case—does the subject matter strike jurors as being masculine or feminine?; (2) her own style—does she tend to be aggressive, friendly, or confident?; and (3) the attitudes of the jurors whom she has to persuade—what are their views on women's role in society?

WHAT ABOUT NONTRADITIONAL TRAITS?

If a woman advocate displays traits other than traditional feminine ones—either naturally or by conscious choice—she must make sure to establish her competence early. One way to do this is to have someone with authority acknowledge her competent performance in front of the jurors.

By now, it should be clear that credibility is not so much an objective characteristic as it is a perception on the part of the observer. What matters is what the juror or judge perceives about the believability of an attorney or witness.

Using a statistical procedure called "factor analysis,*" psychologists and communication specialists have studied the factors that

---

* First, people are asked to rate the communicator on many attributes such as whether they are honest, articulate, deceptive, likable, understandable, attractive, confusing, interesting, or believable. The factor analysis

affect the perceived credibility of a communicator. In his recent book, *Persuasion: Theory and Research*, Daniel O'Keefe, Professor of Speech Communications at the University of Illinois, concludes that the research points to two underlying factors that affect the receiver's perception of a communicator's credibility: competence and trustworthiness. According to Prof. O'Keefe, competence (also called "expertise" or "qualifications") is the assessment that the communicator is in a position to know the truth, while trustworthiness (called "personal integrity" or "character") is the assessment that the communicator is likely to tell the truth when it is known.

THE KEYS ARE COMPETENCE AND TRUSTWORTHINESS

Prof. O'Keefe reports that competence is represented by attributes such as having expertise or being experienced, informed, or qualified. In other words, people's ratings of these attributes are highly correlated with one another, and factor analysis has identified the underlying factor for these attributes as "competence." Also, people's ratings of the communicator's tendency to be honest, just and fair identified trustworthiness as an underlying factor. For example, in an intellectual property case involving computer software technology, an experienced programmer is seen as being more competent than a computer software salesman because of their respective qualifications. In a product liability case involving a drug, an outside medical expert is assumed to be more trustworthy than a medical researcher employed by the defendant-company. The reasoning is that a communicator who is biased or has a vested interest in the outcome of the trial is not as trustworthy as an expert who has no stake in the outcome. This result is also related to the issue of bias perceived in the communicator.

---

method groups these attributes on the basis of their correlation. For example, the attributes such as "honesty," "believability," and "trustworthy" typically are highly correlated with each other. Attributes that are highly correlated are grouped together, and factor analysis is used to identify the underlying factor that affects people's perception of the communicator.

The communicator who is seen as being more competent and trustworthy than others is perceived as being more credible. This finding is not news to those who are familiar with trial techniques and courtroom psychology. In an essay in the book *Psychology of the Courtroom*, G.R. Miller and J.K. Burgoon point out that impeachment of a witness is commonly based on the witness' incompetence to testify about the issue or the witness' possible self-interest and bias.

PERCEPTIONS ABOUT MEN AND WOMEN

Do people perceive the competence of men and women differently? In fact, both men and women tend to rate a man's performance more favorably than a woman's when their performance is identical. This is the conclusion of Kay Deaux, a leading scholar in the field of psychology and gender research. In her book *The Behavior of Women and Men*, Ms. Deaux explains that she reached this conclusion after reviewing various psychological studies on gender-related issues. Such studies also have shown that women are seen as being more competent than men in what are viewed as women's areas of expertise such as domestic tasks, child-rearing, and interpersonal tasks oriented around feelings. In the litigation context, jurors tend to find a male advocate more competent when the litigation is technical, abstract, and complex. A woman advocate, on the other hand, is perceived as being more competent when the litigation involves family issues and other so-called women's issues.

Sometimes, however, women have the edge, because of a perceptual phenomenon called contrast effect and a psychological model called equity theory.

WHEN WOMEN HAVE THE EDGE

Contrast effect is a perceptual distortion that occurs when people experience something that is outside their expectations. When that happens, the difference between what was expected and what actually occurs is magnified. Here is how it works. At 5 feet 6 inches in height, I am tall for a Japanese woman (we are 5 feet 2 inches tall, on the average). Because of the contrast effect, people think of me as being taller than I really am. So, if a woman advocate is seen as being more competent than expected, she will also be considered more competent than she actually is, because her perceived competence is outside of the expected range.

This is where equity theory comes in. Equity theory holds that people like to compensate others fairly based on their efforts and on their level of performance. In their essay "Locus of Cause and Equity Motivation as Determinants of Reward Allocation," psychologists Gerald Leventhal and James Michaels have suggested, for example, that people who perform well in spite of a handicap will be rewarded out of proportion to their performance. Kay Deaux and Janet Taynor, also a psychologist, studied whether this would happen when a woman performs unusually well in a situation where only men are thought to excel. They reported on their studies in an essay, "When Women Are More Deserving Than Men: Equity Attribution and Perceived Sex Differences." As expected, the researchers found that, in this circumstance, people were more willing to reward a woman than a man.

A SUBJECT OFF LIMITS TO WOMEN

Recently, I observed a trial involving complex financial transactions in which the main trial lawyers included a woman. Jurors typically consider complex financial transactions to be a masculine subject, so they are likely to expect a woman to be less competent dealing with those issues. Yet in this case, post-trial interviews revealed that the jurors thought the woman lawyer was much more competent in the area of financial transactions than her male counterparts. In fact, they gave the woman advocate rave reviews, while they were indifferent to the performances of the men. This perceived difference in the lawyers' competence held true despite the fact that financial experts observing the trial found the woman lawyer to be no more (and no less) competent than the men.

Findings related to contrast effect and the equity theory suggest that if a woman lawyer establishes her competence in an area where she is not expected to excel, her skill will be seen as being greater than a man's for doing exactly the same job. What happens is that the jurors' expectation (that the woman will not be competent) is betrayed, and the betrayed expectation enhances the perceived competence of the woman, causing jurors (and judges) to want to reward the woman for performing well despite her perceived handicap.

WHEN A WOMAN'S GOOD LUCK ISN'T LUCKY

Two obstacles can affect this result, however. First, jurors cannot always assess a lawyer's performance correctly. Second, if they do conclude that a woman is doing a good job, they are likely to attribute her good performance to luck.

Jurors cannot evaluate the significance of a lawyer's performance because they do not have a legal background. For example, a devastating cross-examination of a witness often goes unnoticed by jurors, partly because the witness may not show embarrassment or discomfort and partly because jurors do not appreciate the significance of the testimony the lawyer has been able to elicit.

The second obstacle to getting full credit is the tendency of jurors to attribute a woman's competence in an unexpected area to luck rather than a skill. As an example, in one study by Kay Deaux and researcher Tim Emswiller titled "Explanations of Successful Performance of Sex-Linked Tasks: What is Skill for the Male is Luck for the Female," people judging the equally competent performance of a man and a woman of a masculine task (such as car repair), attributed the man's performance to skill and the woman's to luck. When a feminine task (such as cooking) was at stake, the woman was seen as being more skillful than the man; but the difference is much smaller. Why is that so? Deaux concludes that people are more likely to invoke "ability" for a man and "luck" for a woman.

SUCCEEDING BY SUCCESSIVE SUCCESSES

How can a woman change the attribution of luck to skill? The best way to attack the problem directly is by repeated good performances. But since jurors may not understand that they have seen a good performance, the first task is to convince them of that. You can do that by providing a signal from someone else saying "that was great."

Two sources of authority are in the best position to give this signal: the expert witness and the trial judge. When you select and prepare an expert witness, keep in mind that you want the expert to admire you. Look for this attitude during the hiring process; the expert's opinion of you, whether high or low, will certainly be communicated to the jurors. Also avoid hiring experts who need to show that they are smarter than anyone else, including their own lawyer.

When the time comes to examine the expert at trial, plan to ask a few questions that clearly display your knowledge and competence. If you have chosen wisely, the witness will communicate respect for you right from the beginning.

CAN YOU PLEASE THE JUDGE?

Getting the judge to signal approval is more of a hit and miss proposition. Often you do not have a choice of judges, and some judges will never be impressed no matter what you do. Yet even these judges are human. They do form an impression of you while reading your legal briefs and listening to your arguments, and they will not forget what they read or hear. Ask yourself whether you are paying enough attention to the impression your legal writings and oral arguments make. Ask whether your arguments reveal your "unexpected" competence, even if the relevation has no bearing on winning the motion. First focus on what "competence" you want to establish with the judge, and then write or argue with that in mind.

Establishing your competence when you are trying a complex or technical matter is especially important. You need to establish your competence at the beginning of the trial and repeat your performance throughout. In your opening argument, tackle a seemingly difficult concept and explain it simply. Nobody likes to feel stupid, and jurors are no exception. If you simply show that you know something and the jurors don't, they may conclude that you are showing off. But if you help them understand a difficult subject, they will appreciate it. They will perceive you as being competent because you helped them learn something difficult that you understood well enough to explain to them.

TRUSTWORTHINESS COUNTS TOO

Besides competence, a person's perceived trustworthiness affects credibility. Research on the relationship between gender and trustworthiness is scant, however, partly because studies on gender stereotyping have not shown a relationship between gender and perceived trustworthiness.

Many factors that affect jurors' perceptions of an advocate's trustworthiness also affect their perception of competence. However, there is an important exception: likability. Liking a person affects judgments of the person's trustworthiness without affecting judgments about competence. Jurors tend to find the likable advocate to be trustworthy; but they do not necessarily find an advocate competent on the basis of likability alone.

DO JURORS LIKE WOMEN ADVOCATES?

Do women jurors like a woman advocate more than male jurors do? Do they like a woman advocate more than they like a male advocate? The answers to these questions are No and No. Researcher Ellen Berscheid reviewed the literature on interpersonal attraction in an essay that appeared in Handbook of Social Psychology and in the book "Interpersonal Attraction" that she edited with Walster. Berscheid concluded that, while perceived attitudinal similarity creates greater liking, similarity of gender by itself does not. In fact, women jurors often give especially critical evaluations of women advocates. The criticism is not caused by dislike, however. Instead, women tend to notice more things about other women than men do (just as men notice more things about other men than women do), and this comparatively intense observation often leads to critical evalutions.

Women jurors do tend to like a woman advocate more than a man if they believe the woman advocate is similar to them in terms of attitudes, beliefs, and values. Here is one way to use that knowledge. When you are questioning a woman with traditional values during voir dire, ask questions about the woman's children and show your appreciation of what the woman has accomplished in the home. You also can validate traditional values of jurors during oral argument by using examples or analogies involving children (or parenting).

Of course, being a trial lawyer was not a traditional role for a woman in the past; nor was it customary for women to be aggressive or assertive in an adversarial setting. Has that changed? Do women jurors who have played a more traditional role in their lives dislike women advocates? And, conversely, do women jurors who have deviated from a traditional role relate better to a woman advocate?

WHEN IT'S OK WITH JURORS TO DEPART FROM TRADITION

Answers to these questions were developed by Janet Spence, Robert Helmreich, and Joy Stapp, social psychologists at the University of Texas and published in their essay, "Likability, Sex-Role Conference of Interest and Competence: It All Depends on How You Ask." Their initial results showed that both men and women like women who deviate from the stereotyped role more than women who do not, so long as (1) the women are competent in the nontraditional (masculine) activities; (2) they do not express opinions that are counter to values traditionally considered important to women, such as motherhood and family; and (3) their deviation from the stereotypical role is toward an attribute or characteristic that is viewed as being positive. The psychologists found that striking out on even one of these factors is dangerous.

Their studies showed that women who attempt masculine activities without being competent at them are strongly disliked. For example, a woman sportscaster is disliked if she fails to show that she is knowledgeable about the statistics relevant to the game and its players. The studies also showed that women who express opinions counter to traditional women's values are not liked as much as more traditional women. For example, a woman advocate who argues against the emotional distress experienced by the mother of a child disabled by a defective pharmaceutical product will be seen as expressing values that are counter to those of traditional women and will be disliked for doing so.

JURORS TRY TO BE FAIR

The studies also suggest that people feel they should evaluate a nontraditional woman fairly, even if they hold conservative views on women's roles. Unfortunately, that impartiality is not always achieved. In fact, the researcher's initial conclusion that nontraditional women lawyers would be favored if they were competent and did not challenge traditional values turned out to have some exceptions.

Further studies revealed that men, whether conservative or progressive, prefer competent women in traditional roles to competent women in nontraditional roles. In other words, even male jurors who have progressive views on women's roles prefer a woman advocate who is seen to excel in traditional ways. Women, on the other hand, have different reactions depending on their view of women's roles. Conservative women react the way men do; they like a woman advocate who symbolizes traditional values and who excels in a traditional role. But women who hold progressive views toward sex roles prefer competent women in nontraditional roles to competent women in traditional roles.

What can a woman advocate do if faced with jurors who prefer traditional women? Voir dire is where you can show an interest in these jurors' lives by asking questions about children, hobbies, and social and religious activities. Make sure you communicate genuine interest. When examining witnesses, bring out aspects of their lives (such as family and childhood) that will interest traditional jurors. These little things can make a difference.

DOES IT HELP TO BE PRETTY?

To no one's surprise, research also shows that greater physical attractiveness leads to greater likability. Despite this, many researchers have found that attractiveness does not significantly influence the communicator's perceived competence or trustworthiness. Here is what *is* surprising: the way people handle their attractiveness can influence people's reaction to them. If people perceive that someone is taking advantage of his or her attractiveness, their liking of that person drops substantially. In the context of jury trials, criminal defendants who are seen to have used their attractiveness to help commit a crime receive more severe punishment than do unattractive defendants. Jurors also are sensitive to being manipulated. If they feel that a person is trying to manipulate them by means of physical attractiveness, they have a strong negative reaction to that person.

DOES IT MATTER IF THEY LIKE YOU?

If likability does not relate directly to trustworthiness or competence, what role does it have for lawyers? For one thing, likability becomes more important when jurors are not naturally involved with the content of the case. Jurors tend to be more involved with cases that have some relationship to their daily lives. For example, a products liability lawsuit usually is more interesting to jurors than a complex antitrust case. Likewise, jurors can connect more easily when a case obviously suggests some general principle, and a skillful advocate will work to find a principle to make a case more than the mere sum of legal theories and facts.

Likability, therefore, is more important for a case that is not close to home and one that does not obviously suggest a working principle. The lawyer who seems likable will have an easier time making the jurors understand the case and care about the verdict.

Here is another interesting finding about likability and persuasion. When jurors freely choose to listen to an advocate they dislike, the advocate becomes more persuasive. This can happen when jurors want to side with a litigant who is represented by a lawyer they dislike. Since they want to find for the side represented by the disliked lawyer, the jurors choose to listen to the disliked advocate. When they do, the advocate becomes more persuasive. But when jurors are forced to listen, the opposite occurs: the advocate who is liked becomes more persuasive than the disliked advocate. This can happen when a juror does not want to find for the side represented by the advocate, but is forced to listen as a matter of obligation.

Sometimes jurors form strong likes and dislikes about the lawyers, especially strong dislikes. You need to remember that jurors watch and notice the kind of things that lawyers do. Whenever jurors are bored, they look at the lawyers; whenever they get together, they talk about the lawyers.

HABITS TO AVOID

Here are some habits to watch out for. Some women jurors have told me they are offended when a male lawyer treats his female assistant rudely. One woman developed a strong dislike for a lawyer who became irritated and snapped at his female assistant when she brought him the wrong document. In fact, the issues of treatment of female subordinates is so sensitive that I counsel my clients who are male to use another man to help with exhibits and documents. Rudeness to underlings is not a danger for men only, however. When a woman is perceived as being abusive toward her assistant, you can be sure that the incident will be noticed and will contribute to the jurors' feelings about the lawyer.

Another pet peeve? Lawyers who cough on jurors or show insensitivity for jurors who are not feeling well. One irate juror who was pregnant told me she had come to hate a lawyer who had coughed on her; he could not know that her pregnancy prohibited her from taking regular medication and made her worry about getting sick. Another juror told me that a coughing fit she had during the plaintiff witness's testimony had triggered a dirty look from the plaintiff's lawyer. The juror told me about this incident three months after it happened, and she was still upset. The message should be clear: pay attention to jurors' feelings.

WHO IS EASIER TO PERSUADE?

Are women easier to persuade than men? Studies collected in B.J. Becker's *The Psychology of Gender* have shown that they are; but the studies also show that the differences are small, and some researchers have questioned whether sex-linked differences exist at all. It turns out that male researchers tend to find sex differences in persuadability more frequently than female researchers do. Perhaps the difference is a function of expectation. Male researchers tend to expect women to be more persuadable, so they subtly influence the research process and obtain the results they expected. If this is true, it is interesting to ask, Do male lawyers expect women jurors to be more persuadable than male jurors? We do not know enough to answer this question, but the topic is worth exploring.

Whether women are more easily persuaded than men is debatable; but there is no debate that male and female jurors behave differently during deliberation. For one thing, men are significantly overrepresented as leaders of the jury (we still call the job foreman). In one venue where we have statistics, approximately half the jurors who served over the last ten years were male, but three-quarters of the foremen were men.

MORE ISSUES SEPARATING THE SEXES

The other issues that separates the sexes is the question of who emerges as an "expert" during deliberation. Women jurors tend to become experts in litigation dealing with what are seen as women's issues or women's products (such as women's contraceptive devices). In fact, male jurors may be pressured not to behave in a "sexist" manner by asserting that they know more than women about women's issues.

Knowing how men and women behave during deliberations suggests certain strategies for jury selection and for choosing jurors to focus your argument on. Here, as elsewhere, knowledge is the key.

No one is going to say that the research described here is good news for the woman advocate. Clearly it is not. Instead, it confirms that women must work hard to have full credibility in the courtroom. But exposing and describing that challenge is the first step toward meeting it. In this chapter, I have suggested strategies for dealing with and changing the handicap the woman advocate faces. I hope the chapter challenges you to use these strategies and also to create strategies of your own.

References

Becker, B.J. (1986) Influence again: an examination of reviews and studies of gender differences in social influence. In J.S. Hyde & M.C. Linn (Eds) *The Psychology of Gender: Advances Through Meta-analysis*. Englewood Cliffs, N.J.: Prentice Hall.

Berscheid, E. (1983) Interpersonal attraction. In G. Lindszey and E. Aronson (Eds.) *Handbook of Social Psychology* (3rd ed.).

Berscheid, E. & Walster, Ed. (1978) *Interpersonal Attraction*. Mass: Addison-Wesley.

Deaux, K. (1976) The Behavior of Women and Men. Brooks/Cole Publishing Company. Monterey, Calif.

Deaux, K., & Emswiller, T. (1974) Explanations of Successful Performance of Sex-Linked Tasks: What is Skill for the Male is Luck for the Female. *Journal of Personality and Social Psychology*.

Leventhal, G.S. & Michaels, J.W. (1971) Locus of Cause and Equity Motivation as Determinants of Reward Allocation. *Journal of Personality and Social Psychology*.

Miller, G.R., & Burgoon, J.K. (1982) Factors affecting assessments of witness credibility. In N.L. Kerr & R.M. Bray (Eds.) *Psychology of the Courtroom*. New York: Academic Press.

O'Keefe, D.J. (1990) *Persuasion: Theory and Research*. Newsbury Park, CA: Sage Publications.

Spence, J.T., Helmreich, R., & Stapp, J. (1976) Likability, sex-role congruence of interest, and competence: It all depends on how you ask. *Journal of Applied Social Psychology*.

Taynor J. & Deaux, K. (1973) When women are more deserving than men: equity attribution and perceived sex differences. *Journal of Personality and Social Psychology*.

CHAPTER 7

Women and Men in the Courtroom: What Trial Lawyers Believe

by
JEANNE J. FLEMING, Ph.D.

JEANNE J. FLEMING

Dr. Jeanne Fleming is a Principal of Metricus, Inc., a jury research firm in Palo Alto, California. She has worked on cases involving fraud, securities fraud, product liability, patent infringement, copyright infringement, misappropriation of trade secrets, antitrust, libel, age discrimination, and breach of contract. Dr. Fleming's articles on jury-related topics have appeared in a variety of publications, including *Inside Litigation, Trial Lawyers Forum*, and the *Texas Bar Journal*. In addition to directing the ABA Section of Litigation survey described in her chapter of this volume, she directed the Metricus National Juror Opinion Survey, a study of the attitudes toward attorneys and litigants that jury-eligible Americans bring with them to court. The results of both surveys received considerable attention both in the legal press (e.g., *Litigation News, The ABA Journal*) and in the business press (e.g., *The Wall Street Journal*). Dr. Fleming holds a Ph.D. in sociology from Stanford University.

CHAPTER 7

Women and Men in the Courtroom: What Trial Lawyers Believe

by
JEANNE J. FLEMING, Ph.D.

Gender matters in the courtroom. That is certainly the simplest and clearest finding of Metricus' recent survey done in conjunction with the first conference on *The Woman Advocate*.

Male and female litigators believe that the gender of other courtroom players such as the judge and jurors shapes their own behavior. They also believe that women litigators' behavior and men litigators' behavior differ. And they believe that the "other sex" uses some aspect of masculinity or femininity to unfairly sway the judge.

At the end of 1992, Metricus surveyed 737 randomly selected members of the American Bar Association Section of Litigation regarding their courtroom behavior. Approximately half of the survey respondents were men and half were women. The survey, which has a sampling error of four percent, was designed to determine whether there are systematic differences in the way male and female trial lawyers behave in the courtroom, and which techniques of persuasion female trial attorneys report as being most and least effective.

One result from the study—troubling because it is consistent with sterotypes of women and inconsistent with stereotypes of successful advocates—is that, in general, the experiences of

women litigators suggest that being a "good girl" in the courtroom—ignoring hostile remarks, for example, and acting respectful toward the opposing party—is effective when it comes to
persuading a jury or a judge. While men also report that courteous
behavior works for them, they do not report this style of behavior
to be as effective as women report it to be.

WOMEN DON'T SHOUT

Moreover, some women appear to be avoiding somewhat
riskier, more overtly attention-getting techniques such as staging
dramatic moments—techniques with which just about everyone
who uses them reports success. And, compared to men, women
are avoiding overt displays of hostility such as shouting or using
sarcasm—techniques that most litigators find to be ineffective, but
with which some litigators do, in fact, report success.

In short, the results of the survey suggest that women litigators'
repertory of courtroom persuasion techniques may be somewhat
smaller than the repertory of male litigators, and that the women's
repertory may be weighted toward low risk (i.e., not overtly
attention-getting), respect-oriented and courtesy-oriented behavior.

What accounts for this apparent difference? One likely explanation is that women feel that the risks associated with highly
aggressive techniques—techniques that may include overt displays of hostility—are greater for them than they are for men.
Hence women avoid using them.

The data support their concern. Specifically, women litigators
who have used techniques that involve displaying hostility report
greater failure with them than do the male attorneys who have
used the same techniques. Female attorneys who have used non-
hostile, good-natured modes of behavior report greater rewards
from them than men do. In other words, what female attorneys,
on average, perceive to be true is that both judges and juries are
most responsive to them when they tread softly in court.

At the same time, many women litigators are concerned that
they are perceived as being less aggressive than their male

counterparts. The fact that a substantial minority of men litigators—about one in five—sees women as behaving in an overly aggressive manner in the courtroom only adds fuel to the fire.

THE DOUBLE BIND FOR WOMEN

This particular situation has all of the earmarks of the double bind that women in many traditionally male-dominated professions report, namely: if women behave aggressively, they believe they run a high risk of being perceived as harsh, unpleasant and unwomanly, but if they are not aggressive, they believe they run a high risk of being perceived as lacking in the forcefulness and self-confidence that the job requires. In other words, many women feel they must choose between being perceived as wimps or as preoccupied with proving that they are not wimps.

Interestingly, the survey results suggest that a comparable double bind may exist for men. Specifically, at least some male litigators appear to believe that if, in court, they treat women attorneys with a show of courtesy, the women will perceive their behavior as patronizing and condescending. And they also believe that if they behave aggressively toward a female opponent, they will be perceived as being rude and bullying. In other words, for men, the choice may seem to be between being too much or too little the gentleman.

Perhaps the most unsettling finding of the survey, however, is the fact that women appear more reluctant to use attention-getting, non-hostile techniques of persuasion—techniques that *all* the litigators who have used them agree are effective. We can only speculate that this reluctance is rooted in their sense that being a judge-pleasing or jury-pleasing "good girl" might be compromised by more theatrical behavior. Indeed, the comments of one survey respondent, a woman litigator in Massachusetts, capture the pressure felt by a great many of her peers: "Women are much more careful to be polite and to do nothing that makes them appear as anything but a nice person."

MOST LITIGATORS THINK THAT MEN AND WOMEN TRIAL ATTORNEYS ACT DIFFERENTLY

Most litigators—roughly six out of ten—believe that men and women trial attorneys behave differently before juries and judges. (See Table One.) Perhaps surprisingly, it is women more than men who are convinced that the sexes' courtroom behavior differs. Specifically, among those attorneys who have an opinion on this issue, 77 percent of female litigators believe that women and men behave at least somewhat differently before a jury, compared to 61 percent of male litigators. Sixty-nine percent of female litigators believe that women and men behave at least somewhat differently before a judge, compared to 52 percent of male litigators.

We asked survey respondents to tell us in what ways they believe men and women behave differently. As Table Two reveals, certain differences were cited with considerable frequency. For example, women are significantly more likely than men to believe that women are behaving less aggressively than their male counterparts. As a female trial attorney in Florida commented, "Women speak softly and appear feminine and kind." A woman in California noted: "Women tend to be more deferential. . . . They speak softer and their voices carry less."

The comments of other female litigators suggest that this softness and deference may, in part, be rooted in a fear of being

---

TABLE ONE

Litigators' Responses to the Question: "In your experience, do women trial attorneys and men trial attorneys usually behave the same way toward a jury or toward a judge, or do they usually behave differently?"

(n = 737)

| | Percent Saying Women and Men Behave: | | | |
	The Same	Somewhat Differently	Very Differently	Don't Know
Toward a Jury	29%	51%	10%	10%
Toward a Judge	38%	46%	10%	6%

TABLE TWO

**Most Frequently Cited Differences
Between the Behavior of Male and Female Litigators**

Perceived Differences in the Sexes' Behavior Toward a Jury:	Frequency Cited by:	
	Men	**Women**
Women are less aggressive than men.	22%	47%
Women use their femininity with the jury.	19%	3%
Women are harsher than men.	16%	3%
Perceived Differences in the Sexes' Behavior Toward a Judge:	**Frequency Cited by:**	
	Men	**Women**
Women are less aggressive than men.	23%	38%
Men "buddy up" to a male judge.	1%	22%
Women use their femininity with the judge.	16%	4%
Women are harsher than men.	18%	2%

---

perceived as harsh and aggressive. For example, a woman from California observed: "Women seem a little more formal than men. . . . They have to be careful not to alienate." A woman in North Carolina noted: "Women have to be careful not to appear to be too aggressive."

Other female attorneys, however, prefer what they see as women's "softer" style to the style they see as typical of male litigators. For example, a female attorney from Tennessee commented that "Women are more down-to-earth and able to make contact with jurors with less B.S."

While many female litigators are either concerned or well-pleased that, in their view, women behave *less* aggressively in the courtroom than men do, a substantial minority of male litigators describe the behavior of their female counterparts as being *more* aggressive than their own. For example, a male attorney from Florida commented that "Female attorneys spend more time trying to prove they are tough." A man in Massachusetts observed that "Women attorneys overcompensate in 'toughness'—or the appearance thereof."

HOW WOMEN THINK MEN TREAT THE JUDGE

Women are also significantly more likely than men to say that they perceive another difference in the behavior of the sexes, namely: that men approach the judge in different ways than women do. A woman from Pennsylvania, for example, noted that "Men often try to be more familiar with the judge, as though they are just one of the boys." A woman from New York said that "Men act more like peers [of the judge], like they have an inside track." And a woman from Florida complained that "Men try to act like the teacher's pet if it's a female judge, and like a good friend if it is a male."

In short, a substantial minority, just under one-quarter, of women litigators believes that male litigators' behavior toward judges—especially toward male judges—tends to exclude women. And they view this difference in behavior as a problem.

On the other hand, what many male attorneys perceive to be happening in the courtroom is that women are "using their femininity," both with the judge and with the jury. And these men do not like what they see. For example, a male attorney from Massachusetts said that "Some women attorneys act 'feminine' when they are talking to male judges. Older male judges are taken in by this little-girlish approach." A male attorney from Ohio commented that "Women sometimes flirt [with the judge]"; and a male attorney from the District of Columbia said, disparagingly, that women tend to "sex up the old bird [i.e., the judge]."

As Table Three shows, a large number of both male and female litigators say that they modify their behavior in response to the gender of the judge, a result that is consistent with women saying men "buddy up" to a male judge *and* with men saying women flirt with a male judge. Moreover, a majority of litigators, male and female, report that they modify their behavior to respond to the genders of all of the important players in the courtroom.

What techniques of persuasion are men and women using in the courtroom? And are they equally effective for both sexes?

We asked the litigators we surveyed to tell us how well each of a series of courtroom communication techniques has worked for

TABLE THREE

Litigators' Responses to the Question:

"Generally speaking, would you say that you modify the way you behave in the courtroom based on: the gender of your opponent, the gender composition of the jury, the gender of the judge, the gender of the witness or the gender of the party (an individual)?"

(n = 737)

Percent of Litigators, by Gender, Saying that They Modify their Behavior In Response to the Gender of:

	Women	Men
Witnesses	73%	81%
Jury	67%	71%
Party (Individual)	61%	68%
Opponent	53%	56%
Judge	40%	42%

them, personally, in jury trials and in bench trials. The techniques included, for example, "showing anger," "using literary allusions" and "staging dramatic moments."

Our results indicate that there are some significant differences between the success women litigators and male litigators report experiencing with various means of persuasion. Specifically, female attorneys report greater success than their male counterparts with non-hostile, good-natured courtroom techniques such as: 1) acting respectful toward the opposing party; 2) ignoring hostile remarks; 3) smiling at jurors; 4) using humor; and 5) demonstrating intellectual prowess. (On average, both men and women agree that these techniques have worked well for them. Women, however, report them as being significantly more effective than men do.)

Women litigators and men litigators both rate as effective and assign comparable scores to somewhat riskier, yet still non-hostile techniques—i.e., techniques that are overtly attention-getting, such as staging a dramatic moment or moving around a great deal

TABLE FOUR

**Male and Female Litigators' Use of
Different Courtroom Techniques**

(n = 737)

Techniques	Percent Saying They Have Used Technique:	
	Women	Men
Using allusions to popular culture	70%	100%
Covering a lot of territory in the courtroom	62%	82%
Staging dramatic moments	61%	77%
Telling a story to make a point	77%	88%
Playing to selected jurors	73%	82%

while speaking. Nevertheless, women are significantly less likely to have used them. (Table Four shows the frequency with which both genders have tried these techniques. All of the differences reported are statistically significant.)

Since more women than men are relatively new to trial practice, one question we had was whether women simply have not yet had time or occasion to try out these techniques that are so uniformly endorsed by their peers. We found, however, that— even taking age into account—women litigators simply are much less likely to have experimented with overtly attention-getting techniques such as those listed in Table Four.

WOMEN AVOID RISKY TACTICS

Women litigators are also significantly less likely than men to have tried even higher risk, more overtly aggressive behavior, such as embarrassing or upsetting a witness, interrupting a witness, getting personal in attacking the opposing party, shouting, using sarcasm and directly criticizing opposing counsel. When they do use these techniques, women report experiencing less success with them than do men. For example, while men, on average, assign a score of −2.9 to "getting personal in attacking the opposing party," women, on average, assign the same technique a score of − 3.3. (These scores are on a scale that runs from − 5, for a technique that the user has found to have had a "very negative effect," to +5, for a technique with a "very positive effect.")

FEMININE CHARM SEEMS TO SUCCEED

One technique with which women do report having particular success is "emphasizing their femininity." While many women— 39 percent—say that they have never, at least consciously, emphasized their femininity in the courtroom, those women who have done so report, on average, that it has been effective for them. On the other hand, men, on average, say that "emphasizing their masculinity" tends to backfire.

A final caveat may be in order. The survey measured what trial attorneys believe their behavior is like in the courtroom and what techniques of persuasion they believe are effective in that arena. Perceptions of reality and reality are not always the same, and it may be that systematic observation of the in-court behavior of 737 randomly-selected male and female trial attorneys—and of the reactions of juries and judges to that behavior—would yield somewhat different results.

Section II

The Skills: Teaching Each Other to Excel

CHAPTER 8

Negotiating Skills for Women Lawyers

by
COURTENAY L. BASS

COURTENAY L. BASS

Courtenay L. Bass was born in 1959 in Dallas, Texas. She received her Bachelor of Arts degree in Business Administration, magna cum laude, from Baylor University in 1979. In 1982, she received her Juris Doctor degree, cum laude, from Baylor University School of Law.

Ms. Bass began her legal practice in the broad area of insurance defense with a medium-sized firm. Her practice included litigation in a variety of areas, including personal injury, products liability, professional malpractice, and worker's compensation. In 1983, Ms. Bass joined a large business firm and concentrated her practice in commercial litigation, including representation of financial institutions, real estate developers, contractors and corporations. Her practice expanded into a wide variety of areas incuding contracts, consumer protection, lender liability, employment law, foreclosure, real estate, construction/surety, partnership and shareholder disputes and bankruptcy litigation. She also continued her work in personal injury and products liability.

In 1989, Ms. Bass began her career as a solo practitioner concentrating in Alternative Dispute Resolution, primarily focused on mediation. Since 1989, Ms. Bass has mediated over six hundred and fifty disputes in a wide variety of areas including commercial litigation, contracts, personal injury, worker's compensation, products liability, professional malpractice, insurance, employment, construction/surety, partnership dissolutions, securities, governmental entities, trade secrets, covenants not to compete, and consumer protection. Ms. Bass also represents clients in ADR processes and serves as a consultant for preparing and presenting cases effectively in ADR procedures. She is a co-founder of ADR

Solutions, Inc. ("ADRS"), a consulting firm which provides training in dispute resolution techniques to corporations and other consulting services in the area of ADR.

In addition to her mediation practice, Ms. Bass is actively involved in teaching trial advocacy, mediation, and negotiation. She serves as an Adjunct Professor at Southern Methodist University School of Law in the Trial Advocacy Program. She is a faculty member for the National Institute for Trial Advocacy and has taught at the NITA National Program, Southern Regional, Gulf Coast Regional, Southwestern Regional, Pacific Regional and the Bankruptcy and Negotiation and Mediation Advocacy Programs. She has also taught at the ABA National Institute on Jury Persuasion and the Dallas Bar Association Trial Skills Program.

Ms. Bass is a co-founder of the American Academy of Attorney-Mediators, Inc. ("THE ACADEMY"), a training organization which conducts mediation trainings for attorneys at all levels of expertise. She is also a faculty member for the Dallas Bar Association Mediator Training Program and was a founding faculty member for the NITA Mediation/ADR Skills Program. Ms. Bass has participated in numerous mediation trainings for bar associations, insurance companies and corporations, as well as the Texas College for Advanced Judicial Studies. She was also a founding faculty member for the Attorney-Mediators Institute, Inc. ("AMI").

Ms. Bass is a charter member of the Association of Attorney-Mediators, Inc. ("AAM"), for which she has served as Secretary, chaired the Programs and Training Committee, and served as a member of the Ethics and Standards Committee. She is also a member of the Society of Professionals in Dispute Resolution ("SPIDR"). Ms. Bass is licensed by the State Bar of Texas, the Northern, Southern, Eastern and Western Districts of Texas, the Fifth Circuit, and the United States Supreme Court. She is a member of the American Bar Association, the Dallas Bar Association, the Dallas Association of Young Lawyers, the Texas Young Lawyers' Association, Texas Bar Foundation, and the College of the State Bar of Texas.

CHAPTER 8

Negotiating Skills for Women Lawyers[1]

by
COURTENAY L. BASS

Do women negotiate[2] differently? Yes, based upon both their family and their educational backgrounds. Women typically negotiate differently depending on whether their opponent is another woman or a man. Women negotiating with women adopt a cooperative, problem-solving mode, while women negotiating with men typically take a more competitive approach. Men change negotiating techniques even more drastically when negotiating with women, especially when the relative ages of the negotiators are far apart. For example, older men negotiating with younger women tend to be condescending, although they would describe themselves as being "fatherly."

Women have many natural traits which can make them more effective negotiators. Women lawyers frequently err by adopting a more aggressive and dominant negotiating style, which is traditionally associated with men. This approach usually fails for two reasons. First, if you are not being natural, the people will sense your insincerity and distrust you. Secondly, by adopting an unnatural style, you are throwing away your natural talents in a self-defeating effort. Why should Streisand want to sing like Pavorotti? Remember, the first rule of successful negotiation is to be yourself.

It is easy to understand why so many women lawyers mimic masculine negotiating styles. As late as the early and mid-1980's, women lawyers were trained primarily by male professors and mentors. The natural result of this male-dominated education was that women learned professional communication styles and skills from men. Their mentor's styles were formed in an almost exclusively male legal world with a natural bent toward an aggressive "win/lose" style of negotiation. This style typically does not work well for women.

RAMBO TACTICS THE NORM

Ironically, the emergence of women in the ranks of lawyers overlapped with (but was unrelated to) what is frequently described as a loss of civility in the legal profession. "Rambo" tactics became the norm as opposed to the exception, and everyone had to "get tough or die." The norm meant that men were trying to act tougher, so the pressure on younger women was intense.

Some women lawyers, however, discerned a new and challenging possibility, namely that women could be devastatingly effective simply by acting like women. While some women became successful by taking the hard line, most succeeded simply by working harder and following their instincts. As time went on, we determined not only that women could play on the same field, but could, indeed, beat men at their own game. This is especially true in negotiation.

WOMEN'S NATURAL SKILLS

Many women naturally possess certain skills that are very beneficial in negotiating. These skills are: (1) being effective listeners, (2) being able to work toward a cooperative resolution without concern over who gets the credit, (3) being able to keep their cool when baited, (4) being able to listen politely without interrupting, and (5) being naturally inquisitive. Unfortunately, many of these skills can be misunderstood, especially when you are negotiating with men.

The most basic and essential skill for good negotiation is listening. The ability to listen patiently to the other party and to let him know that he has been heard and understood can truly alter the entire course of a negotiation. This principle has been framed by Stephen Covey as "Seek First to Understand, Then to be Understood."[3] In the male dominated culture in which we were raised, people often feel they must speak first to establish their status. Even if men[4] do allow you to speak first, they usually do not listen to what you say because they are thinking of what they are going to say as soon as you finish.

Men are frequently observed "responding" to points that either have not been raised or have been appropriately conceded by the other side. This occurs because they are focused on what they are going to say instead of listening to what is being said. Much of this is behavior based upon an upbringing demanding leadership, toughness, and a need to be right. In the quest to prove they are right, men will frequently miss important things that would allow their interests, and those of their clients, to be better served.

LETTING THE MAN HAVE THE FIRST WORD

One approach to getting men to hear what you believe is most important is to let them speak first. Let your opponent give his speech without interruption, and let him know that you have heard and understood. You can do this by reframing and restating the high points until it is clear you understand them. Then confirm that there is nothing else your opponent needs to say at that point. Then, and only then, proceed with your presentation. You have heard the other side out, so they can clear their heads to listen to you. You may also use your natural inquisitiveness to ask additional questions to clarify or draw out more information, demonstrating that you are truly interested and are listening to what they have to say.

Sometimes it is inappropriate for your opponent to speak first (for example, when you represent the plaintiff and have yet to make a demand). Begin your presentation by noting points of agreement between the two sides. Construct your presentation so that the "hot points" that are going to draw an argumentative response are toward the end. If appropriate, appeal to the ego of your opponent by acknowledging his expertise, the work he has done preparing the case, and so on. See if you can defuse some of his strong points and reframe them so that they are your strong points, much as you would do on voir dire with a jury panel. Herbert Stern, a former judge and an excellent teacher of trial advocacy, described this tactic as "let them hear the explanation before they hear the problem."

Women lawyers must also guard against making the same mistake that men frequently make. In an adversarial situation, we are taught to be quick with our responses. Inevitably, this leads to thinking about what we will say in response to what the other party is saying, instead of listening carefully to what is being said (and what is not being said). This kind of thinking will destroy your prospects for succeeding in negotiation. First, your opponent will understand that you are not listening to him and are only concerned about what you have to say and what you want. As a result, he will also focus internally on his own positions and interests, ignoring yours. The result will be a series of monologues in an ever escalating cycle of conflict with no true communication between the parties. To win the negotiation, you need to understand what your opponent is saying. This can only be accomplished in one way: by listening.

WHY WOMEN ARE ON EDGE

Not only do women tend to be better listeners, women more naturally take a cooperative approach to problem solving. Groups of girls who have been studied from early childhood have been observed to work in a cooperative effort to accomplish a mutually desired result, as opposed to forming a hierarchical structure in which a leader determines what others will do to accomplish the leader's desired result, a style more typical of men.[5] Women act cooperatively by emphasizing points of agreement, acknowledging points of disagreement, and focusing on the real problem to be solved, even if it does not serve their own egocentric best interests. So long as an appropriate result is reached, women can more easily take their egos out of the process and derive personal satisfaction from reaching an acceptable conclusion. This shows a natural "win-win" approach to resolving conflicts.

Women also tend to be better at taking personality conflicts out of a negotiation and focusing on the issues. I once served as a mediator in a dispute involving two attorneys—one male and one female, both of whom I had worked with and liked. The attorneys could agree on virtually nothing and genuinely did not like each other. (Indeed, the fact that I got along with each made the other a little suspicious of me!) Having me serve as mediator was the only thing that they had agreed upon during the pendency of the litigation. During our first joint session, when the tension was thick, I asked the female attorney to explain the basic facts of liability and damages of her case. To her credit, she began by saying, in a direct, yet not apologetic tone, that it was no secret that she and the other attorney did not get along, but that the purpose of our meeting was to focus on resolving the clients' disputes, not the attorneys'. By this simple statement, she graciously acknowledged the obvious, released the tension, and refocused everyone on the problem at hand. She also set aside her own self-interest and avoided getting into a cycle of conflict about which attorney had been the bigger jerk. The case was quickly resolved.

THE EGO BATTLE ABOUT SPEAKING FIRST

Who speaks first, loudest, and last can become an ego battle in an adversarial relationship. For men, this is frequently a matter of status or control. Men feel that in order to be perceived as being at the ''top of the heap,'' they have to establish themselves as the leader, the dominant presence, and then hold on to that dominance at all costs—even if it means being rude or irrational. This posture is frequently advanced by ignoring the opponent whenever the opponent speaks, as if to signal that the other person has nothing of significance to say. This baiting can take many forms, from allowing phone calls and other business to interrupt the negotiation when someone else is speaking, to reading files or the newspaper. I have actually seen lawyers work on crossword puzzles while their opponents were speaking!

DON'T RANT AND RAVE

When confronted with this kind of ploy, it is important to react appropriately. Ranting and raving or responding in kind will only push the negotiation into a hostile environment which will not assist you in accomplishing your goals. Worse, it will make you appear irrational and will seem to justify your opponent's refusal to negotiate with you. In other words, if you play the game, you will lose. So what should you do? There are a variety of responses that work well: they establish your right to be heard but preserve your opponent's ego. One option is a direct, polite request to be listened to, along with a subtle stroke or graceful exit, if necessary. For example, "I understand you are very busy, but I showed you respect in listening to what you had to say without interruption and would appreciate your doing the same," or, "I'm sorry, I thought we had arranged this at a convenient time. If this is a bad time for you, let's reschedule." The message should be sent in a strong, sincere way and not with a sarcastic tone. How you say it is as important as what you say. Always take the high road. If clients are present, avoid directly embarrassing your opponent— he will feel that he has no choice but to defend himself and attack you. A polite and clear message will be more effective in accomplishing your long-term goals.

If several other parties are involved in the negotiation, another effective response is to direct your comments and questions to the others. Eventually, the person who is ignoring you will enter back into the discussions when he sees that the tactic is having no effect on you.

GOING TO THE BALCONY

Keeping your cool is also an invaluable negotiation tool. William Ury refers to this as "going to the balcony."[6] Nothing signifies success more completely to your opponent than to know that he has gotten to you. In the long run it is better to keep your cool, whether your opponent's attack is personal or professional. However, staying cool does *not* mean that you do not respond if you feel a response is absolutely necessary. Consider *carefully* whether a response is needed or justified. If an attack must be countered, your response should be cool, rational, and dignified. If you do lose your temper, apologize.

Another key point to remember is that different behaviors are construed differently by different people, and by people of different genders. What you perceive as a supportive communication style may be offensive or threatening to your opponent. For example, women tend to finish sentences for the other person in the conversation. They consider this approach to be a show of understanding and support. When they finish sentences for other women, it is typically understood in this way. However, men find it belittling, interruptive and intrusive. [7]

Similarly, cultural differences may affect how you negotiate. Many cultures predicate a social superiority of men over women. In such cultures, women are to be seen, but not heard. Trying to negotiate with a man whose basic belief system was formed in such a culture can be difficult, if not impossible. For you, as a woman, to address this man directly may constitute an insult. Simply to disagree with him may be regarded as an affront. While it may be rare to find an attorney with such cultural limitations, in today's international legal marketplace it is not unusual to face an opposing client with such beliefs about women.

If you find yourself in this situation, there are two options. First, set up a preliminary meeting in order to get acquainted and develop a framework of trust and respect in which to conduct the negotiation. If appropriate, address your concerns with opposing counsel to insure that gender will not become a barrier. Secondly, consider using a male colleague to handle the negotiations as the primary player. While this may be personally frustrating, your goal is to reach a negotiated agreement, not to reform someone's cultural heritage.

Not only are there differences between genders and cultures, there arc differences in how people express themselves and process information. What you may perceive as a negative reaction (for example, silence) may only be a difference in how another person processes information (perhaps the person thinks carefully before responding). Do not bargain against yourself by misconstruing a procedural, stylistic or personal difference as a substantive difference. People frequently say the same thing in different ways and come to the mistaken conclusion that they have a dispute. The contrary is also true: people who are not listening carefully incorrectly concluded that a point of agreement has been reached when they had not reached agreement.

Personality Differences Count

Personality differences also affect negotiations. A basic understanding of personality styles can be critical in sizing up your opponent. The Myers-Briggs Type Indicator ("MBTI") can be consulted as a quick reference. The MBTI evaluates personalities on four scales:

(1)   Extraversion v. Introversion

(2)   Sensing v. Intuition

(3)   Thinking v. Feeling and

(4)   Judging v. Perceiving.

Each of these factors operates on a continuum with persons falling somewhere between the two extremes. If you assume everyone communicates in the way you do, you will misconstrue much information.

How Lawyers Stack Up

In the July 1993 ABA Journal, Larry Richard contributed an excellent article based upon the MBTI entitled, "The Lawyer Types: How Your Personality Affects Your Practice." Mr. Richard tracks not only the differences in gender on each of the four scales, but also the gender differences among attorneys compared to the public in general. Perhaps the most significant finding, if not the most surprising, is that among attorneys, the gender percentages are fairly close on all four scales with one notable exception: the Thinkers v. the Feelers. Men tend toward the "thinker" side, making decisions using objective, logical, and detached reasoning. Thinkers do not take conflict personally and, quite frequently, enjoy a good argument, especially if it involves an intellectual challenge. By contrast, "feelers" have a more subjective, value-based approach to decision-making. Feelers want to help people and tend toward approaches that feel right, even if they are not totally logical. Negotiations between a male "thinker" and a female "feeler" can be frustrating for both: the thinker believes the feeler's argument is non-persuasive because it is not entirely logical, while the feeler feels that the thinker is insensitive and caught up in technicalities that prevent him from effectively evaluating the overall case.

Women negotiating with other women are more apt to behave like a community of feelers working on a problem to be solved. Such negotiations can be very enjoyable because they focus on the problem and take personalities out of the mix. If two women are negotiating and one has taken on the more aggressive thinker style, the thinker will accuse the feeler of being emotional and soft and the feeler will think the thinker is a shrew. The important thing to remember, whether negotiating with a man or a woman, is to adjust your style and presentation to accommodate the listener. If your opponent is a thinker, approach him from a logical, objective view. If he is a feeler, go for a value-driven result.

A CHECKLIST TO STUDY

Effective negotiation is something that requires study and practice. You need to study not only the legal and factual aspects of your case, but also the human factors that will affect, perhaps even control, your negotiations. You should also study negotiation techniques and strategies. This is relatively easy to do. Every day we are confronted with many mini-negotiations at home or at work. Use these opportunities to practice basic communication and negotiation skills. Know your own communication and negotiation styles and learn to adjust them to more effectively deal with your opponent. When it comes to negotiating, follow this checklist to be more effective.

1. *Prepare your case.* Whether you are negotiating the settlement of a lawsuit, the purchase of a building, or any other matter, it is essential that you have all the necessary information at your disposal before entering into the negotiation. Think of negotiation as something like serving up a dinner: if you put in the time and energy to shop, prepare, and cook, you have a big advantage in controlling what shows up on the table as compared to those who simply come to eat. Have a planning session[8] with everyone who will be present at the negotiation on behalf of your client. Discuss facts and strategy fully so that your efforts at the actual negotiation will be coordinated. Devise responses for new information you might obtain during the session identifying the potential variables and determining their effect on various parts of your negotiating strategy. Build flexibility into your approach. Don't miss a good opportunity simply because it was unexpected.

2. *Be reasonable.* Always have a supportable basis for your positions, demands, and offers. Do not be satisfied with the brand of negotiation that says, "Here's my story and I'm sticking to it." Be willing to concede points you cannot win and let the other side have the things you know they will ultimately get. Be generous with issues that may have little value to you, but great value to the other side.

3. *Pace Yourself.* Negotiating is a process that moves at different speeds depending on the people and the issues involved. Plan how you will make your moves and support your demands or offers. Decide in advance how you will disperse information sought by the other side, and how you will go about getting the information you need. Be careful of demanding or giving too much or too little, of moving too fast or too slow—either mistake can jeopardize your ultimate goals. If the negotiating session is likely to involve "down time," prepare by taking other work along. If your client will be with you, make sure she does the same.

4. *Know Your Opponent.* Find out all you can about everyone on the other side. Who are the decision makers? What are their responsibilities over the subject matter of the negotiation and the negotiating process itself? What are their negotiating styles and personalities? Perhaps the easiest way to get this information is to offer some of it yourself. Let your opponent know who you will be bringing and their respective roles, and request that the same information be provided to you. Be sensitive to any internal negotiations occurring on the other side, and decide whether they are based on substance or personality.

5. *To Give is to Get.* One of the most frequent mistakes people make in negotiations is holding cards too close to the vest. Unless certain information is being exchanged, it is almost impossible to have a successful negotiation. If possible, use a cooperative approach to acquiring this information: work with your opponent to get the relevant information exchanged informally, rather than through formal discovery requests. This approach serves two purposes: it will establish an ongoing dialogue with your opponent and will set a problem-solving, cooperative tone for doing the deal. By demonstrating in this fashion that you are trustworthy, you'll have a better shot at defusing the ego of your male opponent or taming the female shrew.

6. *Listen Carefully.* Understanding where your opponent is coming from does not imply that you agree with him: it is simply an acknowledgment that you know where he stands. Be sure to let your opponent have his say. Avoid "supportive" listening techniques such as finishing sentences or interrupting with consistent thoughts. Many men consider this an attack and it diminishes their willingness to listen to you.

7. *Hear Positions, Focus on Interests.* Listen carefully for what is NOT said by your opponent. Beyond the positions articulated by the other side lie deeper, but unexpressed

interests those positions are designed to serve. Even when you and your opponent take directly conflicting positions, your interests may still overlap to a surprising degree. To be successful, you need not so much to validate your opponent's position, but to meet his interest. Make it hard for him to say no. [9]

8. *Keep Substance Over Form.* Focus on the substantive goals to be accomplished and do not let procedural or personality matters interfere. In other words, keep your eye on the ball. Recognize that people have different ways of communicating and negotiating. Be sensitive to those differences and avoid overreacting to them. Remember: You're probably driving your opponents crazy, too!

9. *Keep Your Cool.* Count to ten, take a break, do whatever you must to calm down. The easiest way to defeat a negotiation is to lose your objectivity. Representing your client to your maximum ability means doing what is in the client's best interest. If you want to negotiate, never let your temper flare and never let your pride or ego interfere with the negotiation process.

10. *Be Yourself.* Everyone wants to negotiate with someone trustworthy. Nothing sacrifices trust more quickly than insincerity. Be the best you can be—and be yourself.

ENDNOTES

1. This article is based on informal research obtained through conducting approximately 600 mediation sessions, most of which have had women participants. It is also based on approximately ten years of teaching advocacy and five years of teaching mediation and negotiation skills. For a more scholastically researched book on communication styles of men and women, I highly recommend *You Just Don't Understand,* by Deborah Tannen, Ph.D. New York, NY.: William Morrow and Company, Inc., 1990. For an excellent, detailed guide to different negotiation skills, I highly

recommend *Getting Past No*, by William Ury. New York, N.Y.: Bantam Books, 1991.

2. Negotiation is the art and science of working with another to reach a mutually satisfactory goal. There are three basic types of negotiation—(1) Win/Lose—I get what I want and you don't; (2) Lose/Win—I defeat my goals and allow you to accomplish yours; and (3) Win/Win—all parties interests are met through effective negotiation. Fisher, Roger and Vry, William, *Getting to Yes*. Boston: Houghton Mifflin, 1981.

3. Covey, Stephen R., *The 7 Habits of Highly Effective People*, pp. 236-260. New York, N.Y.: Simon & Schuster, 1989.

4. While these traits are typically associated with men, there is a significant gender crossover. For simplicity's sake, this article will address these traits along gender lines. However, what is most important is that the traits and patterns be recognized for what they are and dealt with appropriately, regardless of the gender of the person exhibiting them.

5. *You Just Don't Understand, supra* at pp. 188-214.

6. *Getting Past No, supra* at pp. 11-33.

7. *You Just Don't Understand, supra* at pp. 188-214.

8. For more information on negotiation planning, *see*, Schoenfield, Mark K. and Schoenfield, Rick M., *The McGraw-Hill 36-Hour Negotiating Course*, pp. 269–329. McGraw-Hill, 1991.

9. For a thorough discussion of positional v. interest based negotiation, *see Getting Past No, supra*, and its predecessor, *Getting to Yes*, by Roger Fisher and William Ury, 1981. Boston: Houghton Mifflin.

CHAPTER 9

Depositions and the Gorilla Adversary

by
LORNA G. SCHOFIELD AND JILL A. LESSER

LORNA G. SCHOFIELD

Lorna G. Schofield graduated from law school in 1981 and is a partner with the law firm of Debevoise & Plimpton in its New York office. She represents clients in commercial civil litigation, including securities, professional liability, tax and other matters. She also represents clients in internal, regulatory and criminal grand jury investigations.

From 1984 to 1988 Ms. Schofield was an Assistant United States Attorney in the Criminal Division of the U.S. Attorney's Office in the Southern District of New York. There she prosecuted criminal cases including white collar fraud, tax evasion, international arms sales and domestic terrorism.

In 1978 when she was in college, a boyfriend who was a law student advised Ms. Schofield not to go to law school because she was "too emotional" to be a lawyer. In 1983, while in private practice, a very senior lawyer asked her, "What's a little girl like you doing with a big book like that?" The tone changed in the mid-80's. In 1988, one of 10 defendants she prosecuted for arms dealing described her as his "main adversary" and "tormentor" in a book entitled *Broker of Death: An Insider's Story of the Iran Arms Deals*. The judge in the same case described her as "unflappable."

In 1990 Ms. Schofield achieved an unusual settlement in a pro bono case involving a court-ordered involuntary cesarean section on a terminally ill patient who was 26 weeks pregnant. The hospital not only paid a monetary settlement, but also revised its policies and procedures so that similar events would not occur at the hospital again.

Ms. Schofield is a member of the American Bar Association and is Co-Chair of the Class Action and Derivative Action Committee in the Section of Litigation. She was Co-Chair for the Conference on the Woman Advocate held in 1994, and was on the Planning Committee for the 1993 Conference. She is also a member of the Association of the Bar of the City of New York and the New York Council of Defense Lawyers.

Ms. Schofield is married to Gabriel S. Zatlin, a doctor, and has one daughter, Sarah, a second-grader.

JILL ANN LESSER

J ill Lesser is currently the Director of the Civic Media Project, a joint project of People For the American Way and the Media Access Project, in Washington, D.C. The Civic Media Project was established earlier this year to protect the First Amendment rights and liberties of all Americans in the emerging media environment. The Civic Media Project was formed by two organizations well known for their First Amendment advocacy. People For the American Way is a 300,000 member constitutional liberties organization committed to protecting the mandate of the First Amendment and confronting intolerance in our society. The Media Access Project is a twenty-year-old public interest law firm dedicated to protecting the First Amendment rights of all Americans in the media. As Director of the Civic Media Project, Ms. Lesser analyzes policy and legal issues as they relate to the information superhighway, drafts congressional testimony on behalf of People For the American Way and Media Access Project, lobbies Congress and engages in education and outreach to the public interest community and the general public about the potential of new telecommunications technology to unite our society, reinvigorate democratic participation and strengthen our civic infrastructure.

Prior to moving to Washington, Ms. Lesser was an associate at the law firm of Debevoise & Plimpton in New York, where she practiced general litigation for more than three years. At Debevoise she gained considerable experience in pretrial discovery, taking and defending depositions, drafting interrogatories and their responses and leading settlement negotiations in several cases. Ms. Lesser joined Debevoise in 1990 upon her graduation from Boston University

School of Law, where she was an Article Editor of the Boston University Law Review. She did her undergraduate work at the University of Michigan, from which she graduated with honors in 1987.

CHAPTER 9

Depositions and the Gorilla Adversary

by
LORNA G. SCHOFIELD AND JILL A. LESSER

A male gorilla asserting authority over his territory typically breaks tree branches, pounds his chest and makes hooting noises. This behavior is a show of strength and a warning to any intruders that he is in control. As *Gorillas in the Mist* has taught us, an adversary or interloper can respond in kind as a challenge or can adopt a "tail-up" submissive posture (the female gorilla sexual posture), conceding the first gorilla's authority and relinquishing any hope of gaining control over the situation.

What female litigator has not encountered a tree breaking, chest pounding, hooting male adversary? And what female litigator has not wondered how best to send the message back that she will not go "tail up," that such tactics will in no way deter her from effectively and forcefully representing her client?

While facing an antagonistic and aggressive adversary is not uniquely a woman's problem, it does pose special difficulties for women. Women may elicit more challenges than men because women are perceived as being weak. Women may have more difficulty responding effectively than men because women have been socialized to mollify aggressors. Men often begin to hone their fighting skills playing war games as little boys. Women, on the other hand, are usually not as extensively practiced in the art of combat.

This is all the more reason to train seriously now. In learning to deal with difficult adversaries, some overriding principles are useful:

First, a woman lawyer must remember that her primary objective is to advance her client's interests. Staying focused on this objective is hard to do when you feel angry, demeaned or threatened. However, staying focused is crucial to determining how best to react.

Second, she must remember that the most effective way to advance her client's interests is to assert her authority in her own style in response to a challenge. Once she makes clear that she is at least as forceful and competent as her male challenger, she can get on with litigating. If, instead, she reacts submissively, she alters the balance of power against her client and invites further challenges.

Finally, women lawyers should strive to be significantly better prepared than their male adversaries. Many women lack the height, weight, deep voice, grey hair and other physical attributes that convey authority and experience in our society. Moreover, the prejudice persists that women are neither smart nor forceful, and therefore do not make worthwhile opponents. Mastering the facts, law and procedural rules will help to neutralize these disadvantages. It will also serve to arm and fortify you when your brute strength fails and you are tempted to retreat. Keeping these several admonitions in mind, let's start with taking a deposition.

OPEN WITH AUTHORITY

The primary purpose of taking a deposition is to obtain responsive, truthful—and with luck—even helpful answers from the witness. To this end, it is important to control the deposition and establish authority over the witness. A woman lawyer taking a deposition opens in a position of authority. She has called the deposition, she is in her own conference room, she has hired the court reporter, she has chosen the documents that will be discussed, and she will ask the questions. But what tends to happen when the witness is represented by counsel who happens to be a man?

Frequently, the male lawyer will attempt to bully and intimidate his female colleague. This is done in a number of ways. He will interrupt her continually or attempt to engage her in interminable colloquy or argumentation. He will try to undermine her confidence by objecting to every question she puts forth, or by suggesting that she does not know how to ask a proper question, or by instructing his client not to answer. SOB adversaries often make gender an overt issue with comments like: "Where did you go to law school, little girl?" or "Speak up, the witness can't hear you if you act so timid." or "Can you believe that this pretty little thing is opposing counsel?"

These tactics not only break the stride of the woman lawyer who is conducting the deposition. They can also delay, and even prevent, her from obtaining the information she needs. What's worse, a witness who hears his attorney speaking to the interrogating lawyer without respect may himself become uncooperative.

HOW TO APPROACH AN ADVERSARY

There are several ways to combat intimidating or inappropriate behavior of this kind. The most passive approach is to ignore the abusive adversary and be calm, persistent and respectful with the witness. For example, a particularly aggressive male lawyer might want to distract the female interrogator by making her angry. If the woman resists and is calm yet persistent, the adversary may give up his bullying.

Nevertheless, the passive approach is fraught with danger. If the female interrogator is simply trying to avoid confrontation, she should understand that her behavior may have the opposite effect. There is a fine line between being hopelessly submissive and being quietly effective. Furthermore, the witness may be the kind of person who won't cooperate with the woman lawyer who is deposing him unless he sees her as a victim. However, this is not to say that projecting an image of weakness is always desirable in such an instance. It's a tactic that can easily backfire where the witness is likely to be encountered again during the litigation or settlement negotiations.

A safer approach is to respond to the aggression and reassert authority. The deposing lawyer may still choose to ignore the bully, but she can do so more affirmatively, perhaps by being disdainful. She can, for example, look bored and avoid eye contact, shuffle documents, or have a cup of coffee. She can inquire whether the reporter has recorded every word, and then ask the windbag if he has finished; or she can ask whether he has instructed his witness not to answer, and if not, she can ask the witness to answer.

A more aggressive response would be for the woman to tell the male adversary that she is entitled to the information under the applicable discovery rule, that she intends to get it, and that she is prepared to ask questions all night or all week, if necessary. This statement is a direct challenge to the obstructive behavior. It also might motivate the witness to be more cooperative, notwithstanding his attorney.

Inappropriate gestures or body language should be described for the record. Obscene speech can be emphasized on the record by asking the offending adversary to repeat his comments. Demanding that such behavior be stopped is likely to be more effective than asking for the adversary's forbearance, which may sound more like a plea.

WHEN THINGS GET OUT OF HAND

If an adversary is being caustic, a quick, caustic and clever response can be very effective, although this is usually difficult to pull off. Before matters get out of hand, the female lawyer can emphasize her authority by standing up. This will make her taller than her seated male adversary and place him in the position of having to look *up* at her, a posture that will almost certainly make him uncomfortable. A word of warning, however: this tactic can result in everyone except the court reporter standing up.

Such outrageous scenarios are less likely possibilities where a problem witness is encountered. In fact, handling a problem witness at depositions is sometimes easier for the woman lawyer than dealing with an obstructive adversary, because the deposition process puts the witness in the lawyer's control. She has required his presence, she is asking the questions he must answer, she probably knows more about the facts than he does, and she is playing by lawyers' rules, which he probably does not understand.

Even so, this imbalance of power may so threaten a male witness that he will become aggressive. In such a case, the lawyer may want to cede some of her authority—for example, by displaying a warm and solicitous demeanor or by first asking questions about non-contentious matters to put the witness at ease. Some lawyers have the ability, with greater or lesser consistency, to extract helpful testimony with their charm. Yet many lawyers overestimate their talent in this area. A woman lawyer will almost certainly have a greater problem regaining control if her ''soft'' demeanor turns out to be ineffective.

MAINTAINING AUTHORITY

The better approach is for the woman lawyer to reassert her authority when challenged by an offensive witness and to avoid any behavior that might be interpreted as conciliatory. If a male witness makes rude remarks or personal comments, the woman lawyer deposing him should admonish him directly. If the witness is merely being uncooperative, for example, by refusing to answer questions, the lawyer should explain that she is entitled to ask her questions and he is obligated to answer them, and that, if necessary, she will seek a judicial order compelling his answers. She might also invite the witness to consult with his attorney for confirmation of these points. If the witness still refuses and his attorney is unhelpful, the deposing lawyer should threaten to adjourn the proceeding so that the deposition can be continued on videotape, and make good on her threats if necessary. (But check the court's rules on videotaping.)

If the witness's answers are problematic—for example, embellished in a way that is harmful to the woman's client, or lacking recollection whenever convenient—the lawyer should try to discipline the witness with documents that discredit the testimony. Obviously, preparation and organization are key. The lawyer also should ask narrow questions designed to elicit brief answers and ask the reporter to strike testimony that is non-responsive.

Giving in to an uncooperative witness in deposition skirmishes usually encourages the witness to become even more difficult. If documents are not available to discredit his testimony, the deposing lawyer should still attempt to challenge or dilute it. If the witness claims, for example, that he had a damning conversation with the deposing lawyer's client, his statements can be assailed as follows: "Did you take notes? Did you make a record of the conversation? That's your general recollection of the conversation? That's not verbatim what was said?" The witness can also be asked if he is aware of contradictory evidence in the record, and whether his position depends on his version of the facts. If necessary, the lawyer should then consider shifting from her planned course to a line of questioning where the facts are well supported by documents and she can better control the witness.

WITNESSES WHO FLIRT

Another potential problem is presented by the flirtatious witness. While this witness may provide useful testimony, the woman lawyer deposing this witness must be on her guard. If she smiles back at the witness to make him feel more secure and cooperative, he may misconstrue the response and shift the focus of his attention and testimony in ways that ultimately undermine her authority. A better alternative would be simply to ignore the innuendo and exhibit an attitude of control and professionalism. Or you can show you mean business by delving into potentially unnerving subject areas.

DEFENDING A DEPOSITION

The male gorilla can also pose a problem when you are defending a deposition.

The primary objective in defending a deposition is to protect the witness. A witness questioned by an aggressive or abusive attorney must believe that his own lawyer has the situation under control. The defending attorney should intercede if the adversary is harassing or mistreating her client. If necessary, she can also direct the witness not to answer.

One of the most effective ways to combat this kind of abusive behavior is to prepare the witness for the problem before the deposition. Try to learn your adversary's style ahead of time, and brief your witness accordingly. In addition, explain that it is your job to ensure that the questions are proper and, that any reaction on your part is simply an effort to control the adversary. Finally, you should instruct the witness to listen to your objections and to comply with your instructions not to answer.

THE PROBLEM CLIENT

But what happens if the lawyer's own client is the problem?

Dealing with a difficult client or witness is somewhat different from dealing with an adversary. A witness who lacks confidence in his woman lawyer will likely manifest his negative feeling in some way well in advance of the deposition. The relationship must then be restored so as not to divulge any tensions to opposing counsel while the deposition is under way. For example, in preparing the witness, the woman should take every opportunity to display her knowledge of the law and facts. Even if she is somewhat reluctant to engage in self-aggrandizing behavior, she should feel free to tell war stories of her prior victories. If the witness disagrees about the need to pursue certain subjects, she should demonstrate her skill by showing him how the adversary might work up a devastating cross-examination on these very points. If he disagrees with her strategy, she should explain her approach.

Once again, winning over a mistrustful male client can and often should be accomplished with charm. This approach, however, must be mixed with a display of the woman lawyer's knowledge and skills that will impress the client. For example, the client must be made to understand that a hard-ball adversary is likely to ignore her attempts to halt aggressive behavior and will probably try to intimidate him into answering dangerous or improper questions. If the witness disregards instructions from his woman lawyer, she should adjourn the deposition as soon as possible and have a hallway conference with him. She should explain that her instructions are proper and that they are designed to help him. She should then tell him as forcefully as necessary to follow her direction.

If the client says to his woman lawyer that he wants her to be more aggressive in objecting and dealing with the other attorney, she should reassure him that her function at the deposition is to protect his interest, and she should explain how she is doing that. She might also point out that no one will read arguments by counsel in the transcript, and that what counts on her part are objections, instructions, and if she chooses, her own coaching.

SEEKING HELP FROM THE JUDGE

Occasionally, however, it will be impossible to deal with an abusive witness or adversary without judicial intervention. The courts have now become increasingly willing to sanction inappropriate behavior during discovery, especially obstreperous behavior of lawyers.

When deciding whether to seek judicial intervention, a female attorney must evaluate the strategy carefully. Judges generally do not favor motions for sanctions and, because women are often accused of being overly sensitive, particular caution should be exercised.

Rule 30(d) of the Federal Rules of Civil Procedure provides remedies for abusive conduct toward a witness during a deposition. Rule 30(d) states:

> At any time during the taking of the deposition, on motion of a party or of the deponent and upon a showing that the examination is being conducted in bad faith or in such manner as unreasonably to annoy, embarrass, or oppress the deponent or party, the court in which the action is pending or the court in the district where the deposition is being taken may order the officer conducting the examination to cease forthwith from taking deposition, or may limit the scope and manner of the taking of the deposition as provided in Rule 26(c).

If an adversary persists in abusing a witness at a deposition and makes it impossible to proceed with questioning, opposing counsel should adjourn the deposition and seek judicial intervention.

RULE 30(d) MOTIONS

Rule 30(d) motions are often made by attorneys whose adversaries are seeking the disclosure of privileged information. Although motions for protective orders are not generally based directly on discriminatory behavior, it is easy to imagine a situation in which sexist conduct results in a situation that calls for a protective order. In such cases, the deposition should be adjourned before the female lawyer's legitimacy in the eyes of her own witness is threatened, and the witness begins to ignore her instructions.

Motions to compel witnesses to answer may be made where an attorney defending a deposition violates Rule 30(c) and improperly and continuously directs the witness not to answer based on objections other than privilege. As a general rule, it is improper for an attorney to direct a witness not to answer based upon objections such as relevance. Often, however, when an attorney wants to play hard-ball, he will direct his witness not to answer to see how far his adversary can be pushed.

Many courts have also awarded sanctions for pervasive misconduct at depositions. Sanctions in this context are usually awarded in federal courts pursuant to Rule 37 of the Federal Rules of Civil Procedure. State courts usually cite similar local rules as the basis for sanction awards. Although courts generally are reluctant to award sanctions, recent case law suggests that inappropriate and abusive conduct will not be tolerated.

BEHAVIOR THAT IS SANCTIONABLE

One New York state court recently imposed sanctions for the very type of behavior discussed throughout this chapter. *Principe v. Assay Partners*, 586 N.Y.S.2d 182 (Sup. Ct. N.Y. Cty. 1992). The problem in *Principe* arose during the deposition of a fourth-party defendant who was represented at the deposition by a female attorney. Quoting from the deposition transcript, the court cited the following comments made by plaintiff's counsel:

"I don't have to talk to you little lady";

"Tell that little mouse over there to pipe down";

"What do you know, young girl";

"Be quiet, little girl";

"Go away, little girl."

Id. at 184. In addition, the woman attorney testified that these comments "were accompanied by disparaging gestures . . . dismissively flicking his fingers and waving a back hand at me." *Id.*

In finding that the above behavior was sanctionable, the court commented that "the words used here are a paradigm of rudeness, and condescend, disparage, and degrade a colleague on the basis that she is female." *Id.* The court further noted that "[t]he condemnation of such improper remarks springs from a growing recognition of the seriousness of gender bias and that bias of any kind cannot be permitted to find a safe haven in the practice of law . . . ." *Id.* at 183. In finding that the behavior in this case was inappropriate, the New York court relied on several cases in which Judges had been publicly disciplined or removed from the bench for sexually discriminatory conduct. *Id.*

We have found no other cases in which sanctions were imposed for abusive behavior during depositions based solely upon gender discrimination. There are, however, several recent decisions that indicate an increased willingness on the part of the judiciary to impose sanctions for unreasonable behavior at depositions.

SANCTIONS ON THE RISE

In VMP *International Corp. v. Yushkevich*, 92 Civ. 7573 (LJF), N.Y.L.J., Dec. 24, 1992, P.1 Col.4 [hereinafter VMP I], Judge Freeh of the United States District Court for the Southern District of

New York imposed sanctions against both litigants and attorneys on two separate occasions. In December 1992, Judge Freeh imposed sanctions on the lawyer for the plaintiff for "unjustified" and "outrageous" stalling tactics that were used at a November deposition of the plaintiff. VMP I at 1. Apparently unmoved by the December sanctions, the attorneys and litigants continued to engage in unreasonable tactics during discovery. On February 3, 1993, Judge Freeh issued a second order, this time sanctioning both the plaintiff and the defendant's counsel for unreasonable conduct during a deposition. VMP *International Corp. v. Yushkevich*, 1993 WL 33463 (S.D.N.Y. February 3, 1993) [hereinafter VMP II]. In imposing these sanctions, Judge Freeh stated that he "would not hesitate to impose additional sanctions, including dismissal of the action or other penalties, if the parties continue to disrupt this case with unnecessary and unreasonable discovery disputes." Id.

SANCTIONS FOR BAD FAITH

Courts have also invoked 28 U.S.C. § 1927, which imposes liability for excess costs caused by counsel acting in bad faith, as the basis for sanctions for discovery abuse. In *Unique Concepts, Inc. v. Brown*, 115 F.R.D. 292 (S.D.N.Y. 1987), the court imposed sanctions and awarded costs because the case was "marred from its inception by incivility and a consistent lack of cooperation between counsel." Id. at 293.

The motion that ultimately led to the imposition of sanctions involved a deposition at which plaintiffs' counsel directed several personal attacks at the deposing counsel:

> "You are being an obnoxious little twit. Keep your mouth shut." and "You are a very rude and impertinent young man."

Id. When deposing counsel suggested that sanctions might be appropriate, plaintiffs' counsel went on to say:

> "If you want to go down to Judge Pollack and ask for sanctions because of that, go ahead. I would almost agree

to make a contribution of cash to you if you would promise to use it to take a course in how to ask questions in a deposition.''

Id. In invoking Section 1927, Judge Pollack stated that the purpose of the section is to deter unnecessary delays in litigation. Id. at 293 (citing Oliveri v. Thompson, 803 F.2d 1265, 1273 (2d Cir. 1986)). He also noted that the court retains inherent power to supervise and control proceedings and to impose attorney's fees and costs for ''continuing an action in bad faith, vexatiously, wantonly or for oppressive reasons.'' Id.

HELP FROM BAR ASSOCIATIONS

In addition to making motions for the imposition of sanctions, female attorneys who encounter discriminatory behavior during discovery may take their complaints to their local boards of bar grievances or local bar associations. In fact, a woman might very well find that a male adversary who is reprimanded by a body of his peers will be more responsive the next time around.

Recently, grievance boards have reprimanded and courts have suspended attorneys for unconscionable conduct based on the violation of state codes of professional responsibility. In Office of Disciplinary Counsel v. Levin, 35 Ohio St. 3d 4, 517 N.E.2d 892 (1988), an attorney deponent who repeatedly threatened counsel taking his deposition and addressed him with a variety of obscene expletives was brought before the state Board of Commissioners on Grievances and Discipline for violating several disciplinary rules of the Code of Professional Responsibility. Id. at 4, 517 N.E.2d at 892. The Board recommended that he be publicly reprimanded, and the Ohio court agreed. Id. at 6, 517 N.E.2d at 845.

An increasing number of state bar associations and state and federal courts have firmly stated that inappropriate and discourteous conduct will not be tolerated among members of the bar. Many state and federal courts have promulgated individual rules aimed at ending abusive or outrageous conduct during litigation. Although most of the standards being promulgated are not specifically addressed to conduct during discovery, or to discrimination based upon sex, such standards illustrate an increased awareness within both state and federal bars of the importance of professional and respectful conduct.

STANDARDS TO REGULATE CONDUCT

For example, in *Dondi Properties Corp. v. Commerce Savings & Loan Assoc.,* 121 F.R.D. 284 (N.D. Tex. 1988) (per curiam), the court adopted "Guidelines of Professional Courtesy" which had recently been accepted by the Dallas Bar Association. Among the standards adopted were the following:

"(C) A lawyer owes, to opposing counsel, a duty of courtesy and cooperation, . . .

(E) Lawyers should treat each other, the opposing party, the court, and members of the court staff with courtesy civility and conduct themselves in a professional manner at all times.

(K) Effective advocacy *does not require antagonistic or obnoxious behavior* and members of the Bar will adhere to the higher standard of conduct which judges, lawyers, clients and the public may rightfully expect."

Id. at 288 (emphasis added). The willingness of the Federal District Court of the Northern District of Texas to recognize the need for the promulgation of standards to regulate professional conduct helps give credibility to complaints about behavior during litigation discovery. With any luck, similar standards will be adopted by courts throughout the country and the importance of courteous and respectful litigation will become more widely recognized.

HELP FROM A NEW RULE

Offering some help in that direction are amendments to Rule 30 of the Federal Rules of Civil Procedure that attempt to clarify inappropriate behavior by counsel and witnesses at depositions. The new rule essentially integrates into the Federal Rules standards of conduct that have been developed judicially over the past several years by mandating a heightened standard for acceptable deposition conduct.

The old version of Rule 30(d) provided for judicial intervention only when a deposition was being *conducted* ''in bad faith or in such manner as unreasonably to annoy, embarrass or oppress the deponent or party . . . .'' Rule 30(d) did not, however, specifically address the problems encountered by lawyers taking depositions when faced with problematic witnesses or defending counsel. Amended Rule 30(d), however, specifically attempts to alleviate these problems as well.

Amended Rule 30(d) mandates that objections ''shall be stated concisely and in a non-argumentative and non-suggestive manner.'' At the very least, this supplies a lawyer faced with inappropriate conduct at a deposition with a specific standard as a reference when trying to combat the behavior as it occurs. The Amended Rule also incorporates the many cases holding that a lawyer is not permitted to instruct a witness not to answer unless the objection is primarily one based on privilege. Most importantly, Amended Rule 30 makes specific provision for sanctions if the Rule's directives are violated. In other words, a deposing lawyer faced with an SOB adversary will not be required to make a Rule 37(a) motion before seeking sanctions for inappropriate behavior.

This is another weapon for the female attorney who needs to cope with offensive behavior during a deposition.

Over the past twenty years, women have made significant strides in the fight to close the gender gap in the legal profession. Unfortunately, we cannot yet claim complete victory. The more we learn to deal effectively with confrontation—whether it be sexist or not—the more authority and respect we will command.

CHAPTER 10

The Woman Lawyer In the Courtroom or "We Love Your Hairdo"

by
JANET S. KOLE

JANET S. KOLE

J anet S. Kole, spends most of her professional time litigating environmental and toxic tort claims, for both plaintiffs and defendants. She is a partner at a major law firm in Philadelphia.

Ms. Kole graduated from law school at the age of 33, after four years of night classes and a full time job. In her previous lives, she was a fledgling literary scholar, a newspaper reporter, a trade book editor for a major publishing house and finally a photojournalist for Harper's Bazaar and Vogue. She believes her visual skills translate into an ability to think out the "look" of a courtroom presentation in addition to thinking about the words she should use.

As a new lawyer, Ms. Kole was lucky to have as her mentor the chairman of the litigation section of the national law firm where she started her career. She knew she had "graduated" when she changed firms, litigated against him, and won a million dollar-plus judgment.

Her recent personal bests as a litigator include (1) winning, after a four-week jury trial, a more than $2 million verdict for her real estate developer clients, who had sued the sellers of contaminated property for misrepresentation and breach of contract, and for cleanup under state and federal environmental statutes; and (2) having a Court of Appeals reverse a $13 million default judgment against her defendant clients, Spanish national corporations that are international film distributors, on the grounds of insufficient service of process abroad.

Ms. Kole is the tired but proud mother of a two-year old boy. She loves mystery novels and boating, but feels as though she has little time to do anything anymore. Even so, she is active in the ABA's Section of Litigation, as a member of the Council, its governing body.

Ms. Kole graduated from Bryn Mawr College (A.B. cum laude), NYU School of Arts and Science (M.A.), and Temple University School of Law (J.D. magna cum laude).

She fully intends to write a mystery novel about the murderous passions generated by the practice of law in today's economy, when she finds the time.

She lives in Philadelphia, Pa. and Earleville, Md. with her son, her partner, and two Siamese cats, Sylvan and Simon.

CHAPTER 10

The Woman Lawyer In the Courtroom or "We Love Your Hairdo"

by
JANET S. KOLE

The jury was out, deliberating. I sat in the courtroom with both the associate who had second-chaired me and my client, a 38-year-old female nurse who was being sued for malpractice. I also represented the prestigious hospital where the nurse worked.

The plaintiff, an elderly woman who had been badly hurt by the alleged malpractice, had died two weeks before trial. Fearing that this might happen, her lawyer had videotaped her trial deposition three years earlier. As I watched myself on videotape during the trial, I had been pleased with my cross-examination of the witness. I had been respectful but tough, eliciting testimony that exonerated my clients. My only discomfort was a twinge of regret at seeing my three-year-old hair style.

Awaiting the jury's return, our team was not calm. Five days earlier, we had rejected the judge's recommendation to settle by paying the plaintiff $1.3 million.

Finally the court crier let us know the jury was ready to render a verdict. The judge and the court reporter, both male, entered the courtroom. My opponent, a successful plaintiff's attorney many years my senior, strolled nonchalantly to his seat. The jury entered. The foreman rose.

"We find against the plaintiff and for the defendants on all counts."

The judge thanked the jury, and they were escorted out of the courtroom.

The defendant nurse burst into tears of relief and gratitude. We hugged. I began to breathe normally again.

The judge signalled to those of us remaining that he had something to say. We arranged ourselves decorously. "My crier, my court reporter, and I all want you to know something," he said. "We had time to discuss this while the jury was out. We reached a verdict: Ms. Kole—we love your new hairdo."

I blanched momentarily, and the judge moved on to another topic.

He proceeded to congratulate the lawyers for both sides, saying we had done a fine job. He said the cases had been well presented, and he sounded like he meant it. Still, it sobered me to realize that, for the man in charge, I was a woman first and a lawyer second.

All women litigators are in the same boat. In the view of our male colleagues and superiors we are, even today, women first and professionals second.

ADVANTAGES FOR A WOMEN

For women professionals, what are the advantages of being born female? They are *not* the traditionally-conceived female methods of dealing with men in a man's world, things like playing sexy, being flirtatious, or acting like daddy's little girl. Instead, the real advantages can be drawn from the positive views our society has of women, as mothers, sisters and teachers. Many of us who were activist feminists in the sixties and seventies saw these traditional female roles as confining and disabling. And yet, para-doxically, these roles have given women lawyers a benign legacy: juries are more likely to believe women lawyers than men.

Indeed, in a 1989 survey of how juries view lawyers, Starr & Associates, Inc. found that 60 percent of the three hundred respondents believed women lawyers are or may be more ethical than male lawyers. This result is consistent with an earlier study about women in the population as a whole conducted by James

Patterson and Peter Kim, who found that most of the more than 2,000 people they contacted believed that women lie less than men, and that men are more likely to tell serious lies.

In a sense, every good advocate, male or female, is a teacher, educating the factfinder about the facts and about how to view them. But the teaching can't work if the students believe the teacher is lying. A woman advocate plays to a receptive audience, one that wants to learn and wants to believe her. With regard to the perception of trustworthiness, the female litigator is one up on her male counterpart.

DISADVANTAGES IN THE COURTROOM

That's the good news. The bad news is that there are many more things that are clearly, for most women, disadvantages in the courtroom, things like our smaller stature and higher-pitched voices, and the audience's heightened interest in our looks and clothes. Obviously, some men are also short; however, their voices usually aren't high pitched and they are not required to be fashion plates. This combination of typically female physical characteristics and the social emphasis on looks can destroy women's "believability" advantage by rendering us "beneath notice."

In one of my recent jury trials, for example, the male federal court judge sat high on a raised bench, and the opposing lawyers, all male, were five foot nine inches, six-one, and six-seven. I am 5'3", and so it was easy for all of them to overlook me—literally. To make sure that the jury noticed me, I wore a bright red suit on the first day of the trial. As the case went on, I was also careful to wear clothing that provided a bright spot in the wood panelled courtroom as a means of focusing the jury's attention. The alternative to this strategic choice of clothes would have been for me to stand on stilts. (Yes, my client won.)

How did I find ways to counteract my shortness? I learned about being overlooked early in my career. At one trial, the male judge and the other lawyers—all male—began a sidebar conference before my legs could carry me to the bench. I was furious and embarrassed—my client and the jury had seen me be ignored by the other players. What I did to counteract the situation was to shout in a deep voice as I walked from counsel table to the bench: "Gentlemen, it takes twice as many steps for my shorter legs to get me there. Don't start without me." The remark was as inoffensive as I could make it. By addressing them collectively as "gentlemen," I included the judge (who looked embarrassed at his lapse in having the sidebar begin without me). By not calling out, "Your Honor", I avoided pointing a finger at the judge as the thoughtless party. My regret about that remark (and it rankles me to this day) is that by explicitly referring to my own short stature, I diminished myself in the eyes of the jury.

TURNING MINUSES INTO PLUSES

As this anecdote shows, even some negative aspects of being a woman such as the overemphasis on appearance can be turned to our advantage. I am able to use clothes to get the attention I deserve but might not otherwise get because of my height and voice.

Nevertheless, the issue of looks and clothes is fraught with danger. It can have negative aspects, as I have described above. Or it can be relatively benign, as it was in the story that began this chapter. I know that the judge who praised my new hairdo didn't mean anything by his comment. It was delivered at the end of a trial in which he exhibited no discernible gender bias. It was not said in front of the jury. I wasn't being harassed, at least by my standards. But, clearly, my looks were on his mind. He didn't make any personal comment to my male opponent about his looks or attire, even though he wore expensive, well-tailored, and attractive suits every day.

HOW WOMEN LOOK

Both men and women care more about how women look than how men look. Women attorneys can ignore this gender difference or they can try to use it to their advantage. Both schools have their proponents. My bias is strong: use the difference.

Some female lawyer friends violently disagree. They say I am politically incorrect, and that I am perpetuating stereotypes and gender bias. Many say that I shouldn't write about dress and looks in this chapter, because it will give people "the wrong idea." These women, all close friends, tell me that professionals should be judged on their abilities, not their looks, and that focusing on looks in a "how to" book will allow social attitudes to remain static.

It bears noting, however, that all these women are attractive professionals who dress well, in their own distinctive styles. While they may prefer that dress and looks remain unspoken issues, they have clearly decided to use their attractiveness instead of ignoring it.

To a certain extent, I agree with their fear that discussing looks perpetuates unfortunate distinctions between female and male professionals. Any discussion of courtroom tactics, however, must go beyond words and legal arguments, and focus on how things look to the factfinder. A trial is theater. You, as a litigator, are one of the leads on stage.

CLOTHES AND LOOKS DO COUNT

Clothes and looks are part of your advocacy style. If you believe you should wear a severe pin-stripe suit beause it makes you feel powerful, do it. If you believe, as did one lawyer I once saw, that wearing a buckskin vest and skirt with fringes and cowboy boots makes you a better advocate, do it.

If you think looks shouldn't count, on a moral level, you're right. But reality shows that looks do count—not necessarily good looks, but neatness, visual appeal, something that says to a factfinder "I am trustworthy, believable, and right." It was no mere accident that the first three panelists at The Woman Advocate Conference (1993)—all women—wore bright red suits. Red is power. Red draws attention. Dressed in red, the three panelists held our attention.

If it makes some women litigators mad to think that women must pay so much attention to their looks, remember this: men, too, must meet minimum levels of acceptable dress. When I was a new lawyer in a large national law firm, a young man in my incoming class was told that his clothing was inappropriate and was given a salary advance to buy new suits. At least women have some choice in dress; unlike men, they are not reduced to thinking about whether the red stripe in their tie is too wide.

Because women can play with their appearance, they can turn an aspect of gender bias into a courtroom advantage. And, again, everyone has her own style. The "Annie Oakley" lawyer I mentioned earlier even appeared in buckskin at oral argument in a state Supreme Court. Whether this was her habitual style, or whether she was pitching her persona to one justice who had an eccentric style of his own, it did not matter; she won the argument.

I know a woman partner in a boutique litigation firm who overemphasizes her femininity in the Dolly Parton manner, wearing very high heels, teased bleached-platinum hair, and tight short skirts, in part to offset her towering six-foot height. This works for her because she completely disarms male adversaries, who do not expect to confront her razor-sharp, Harvard-educated brain. For her, the look is a game; her manner is no-nonsense.

TOOLS TO HELP YOU GET NOTICED

Your clothes, your voice, your manner, the language you use—all of these are tools that help show that you should be noticed, that you are trustworthy, and that you have an important story to tell.

As I said before, studies of jury attitudes have brought good news for women. But studies of lawyer attitudes, by contrast, bring some bad news—male lawyers attribute stereotypical female coping mechanisms to female litigators. That means that as far as male lawyers and judges are concerned, we do not have the advantage of seeming trustworthy. Instead, our every action is viewed with the suspicion that we may be attempting to use feminine wiles. When that is the assumption, we can expect resistance to what we have to say.

For example, in the Metricus survey of male and female litigators described elsewhere in this book, six times more men than women said they believed that women use their femininity with the jury, and four times more men than women thought women use their femininity with the judge. According to the Metricus survey respondents, "using femininity" means anything from "flirting" to "sex[ing] up" the judge.

A LOW-KEY MANNER HELPS

It is undoubtedly for this reason that most successful female trial lawyers try to be low-key, competent, and controlled—a conclusion that was confirmed in the Metricus survey. A low-key manner (should we call this "reasonable woman" behavior?) certainly helps defuse the preconceptions of male colleagues. For example, despite provocative behavior of male opponents, I have purposely held my temper in check so that no one could accuse me of being overly sensitive, or being an hysterical woman.

But being unwaveringly courteous and calm has a drawback. You run the risk of appearing weak. It is important to have some tricks up your sleeve, something to vary the pace, surprise your opponent, and wake up the factfinder. It may be a flash of anger, the ability to talk loudly, or a withering sarcastic joke. These little bombs can be extremely effective, particularly when they are unexpected. Here are two examples from a case I tried recently. They involve the use of sarcasm and anger.

In this lawsuit, our complaint alleged that the defendants had concealed the burial of toxic chemicals on their farm and then sold the property to my clients, residential developers. The male lawyer representing the defendants took on the persona of a defender of innocent victims of a conspiracy. His strategy was to convince the jury that my clients had conspired with a bank to injure the defendants financially and physically—pretending to find chemicals on the property that either weren't there or that, while present, were not harmful. Since no such conspiracy existed, the lawyer attempted to create the appearance of one.

TIME FOR A CHERRY BOMB

I objected courteously and persistently to his cross-examination techniques, which included misstating earlier testimony and asking the witness to explain the supposed inconsistency. The judge refused to sustain most of my objections, "letting it all in" for the jury to decide. The jury was doggedly listening to all the testimony, looking grim but otherwise unreadable. Not a joke had been told, not a smile cracked. Finally, after eight days of trial, with the jury beginning to realize just how long my opponent was planning to drag out the case, it was time for a small cherry bomb. I was examining my expert about TCE, a common degreaser and pollutant, which had been found in a well downstream of the property my clients had bought from the defendants, called the Omera well. Then the following occurred. (I have edited the transcript for clarity and added stage directions):

> MS. KOLE: Does the NUS report state where the water sample containing TCE was found?
>
> OPPONENT: Your Honor, I would stipulate that it was found in 2.6 parts per billion in that particular well, *if that would move things along.* (His tone is condescending.)
>
> MS. KOLE: Will you stipulate that it was found in the Omera well? (I register surprise.)
>
> OPPONENT: (The condescension deepens.) I believe that's what you're referring to. If that will move things along, that a sampling taken on June of 1990 found 2.6 parts per billion in the Omera well. That's in the report, I will stipulate to that if it will move it along. (He looks at the jury and smiles.)
>
> MS. KOLE: (Sarcastically) I'm thrilled to hear that you would like to move things along, Mr. Opponent.

The jury burst out laughing.

GIVING THE JURY A BREAK

Now, that was not a witticism. It was garden variety sarcasm. But it was a break for the jury, and left Mr. Opponent looking smarmy and untrustworthy. The jury knew he really didn't want to move things along, even though he said he wanted to—three times!

Another combative exchange occurred during closing arguments. After four weeks of grueling trial, I thought it was time to take off the gloves. My opponent had spent hours trying to wear down every witness on cross-examination. He even resorted to claiming that my clients were lying, and that there was a hidden witness who could exonerate the defendants if my clients would only produce him (we did just that, to prove he knew nothing). I thought the jury had had its fill of my adversary and that they were ready for me to get mad. My opponent gave me the perfect opportunity in his closing argument.

> MR. OPPONENT: The plaintiffs make their own rules, and take the law into their own hands. This isn't a land of vigilante justice. This isn't a place where we settle our disputes outside the courtroom, with threats of intimidation and violence. . . .
>
> There is something terribly wrong when banks and builders can make themselves both the judges and the juries and the executioners and not allow the court system to take its way, its course. . . .
>
> The plaintiffs' actions are like a steamroller. Because that gentleman there [pointing to my client] sat on the stand and very calmly, without any emotion, gave testimony that was not true, was false. You saw no human emotion from an individual who was being put on the stand and having a finger pointed at him for what he said. No emotion at all.

I knew my client was steamed at the characterization of him as an emotionless liar, and I was sure the jury was waiting to see if I'd fight back. Here's what I said when the judge allowed rebuttal:

> MS. KOLE: Thank you, your Honor. Remember yesterday I told you that Mr. Opponent was going to throw a lot of

red herrings at you. Well, the red herrings were so numerous that I'm not even going to attempt to address all of them because we'd be here for another two hours. . . .

I take very seriously Mr. Opponent's attempts to mislead all of us by taking statements out of context, or in some cases out of the recesses of his own mind. . . .

Now, this is not, this is not a red herring, this is something different. [I raise my voice.] It is offensive that Mr. Opponent used the term vigilante justice and attempted to link it up to my clients. That's the phrase he used. He used that yesterday, he suggested it again today. There is no evidence, no testimony, no document, to prove or even suggest that my clients ever threatened anyone with physical violence or ever used physical violence on anybody. . .

Mr. Opponent's portrayal of Steve Client as a monster with no emotion is equally offensive and equally untrue. If Mr. Client had jumped out of the witness box and strangled Mr. Opponent for the combination of mischaracterization, half truths and innuendos, then Mr. Opponent would have something to complain about. The fact that Mr. Client acted like a gentleman can hardly be held against him.

My client thanked me, of course, for rehabilitating his character, but my main reward was watching the jury sit up straighter when I delivered my diatribe. My opponent, finally rendered speechless, declined the judge's offer of surrebuttal. The jury returned a verdict for my clients.

TREADING SOFTLY

It is certain that juries, and judges too, are more receptive to women who act reasonably and who only explode when pushed beyond endurance. This conclusion is borne out by the Metricus study, which found that both male and female litigators believe that factfinders respond best to women who tread softly in court.

The important thing to remember, though, is that even those who tread softly must carry a big stick and must be prepared to use that stick at the appropriate moment.

Anger and sarcasm are useful tools. Neither requires a great wit, a great sense of humor, or quickness of thought. Both depend more on tone of voice than on substance. And the appropriate time to use these tools is usually obvious. Sarcasm is usually appropriate when your opponent is condescending, snide, or overly ingratiating and you sense the jury has had enough. Anger is usually appropriate when your opponent has finally gone too far and you sense the jury is waiting for him to get slapped. Anger and sarcasm are the two most important tools of aggression for the woman litigator. For women, as for men, they should be used sparingly to be most effective.

CARRYING A BIG STICK

By rising to your opponent's bait only on rare but telling occasions, you convey an attitude that reinforces the jury's desire to trust you. You are saying, in essence: "I know my facts and my case, inside and out. I know that my client is right. By the time we're done here, you'll know that, too. Nothing this gorilla tries is going to worry me or fool you."

To the greatest extent possible, you should deal with a condescending or impossible opponent yourself. You want the jury and the judge to respect your ability to handle him. Sometimes, though, you cannot do it alone. When you ask the judge for help, be low-key, direct, and clear. Do the asking, if possible, at sidebar, out of the jury's hearing. And let the judge know in as few words as possible what your opponent is doing and how the judge can fix it.

For example, most of us have met real life litigators who decide the best way to get your goat is to object to your every question, or better yet, to object in the middle of a question, with the goal of breaking your rhythm and making the factfinder lose the thread of the witness's story. This kind of harassment can severely affect your case, and you must curb it as soon as possible. When the objections are phrased condescendingly, as they often are (''I object, your honor. This little girl is asking irrelevant questions''), your anger may get in the way of your expression of legitimate concern, so it's important to think about this possibility ahead of time and prepare a short speech. The scenario should go something like this.

HAVE A SPEECH READY

You ask a question. Your opponent objects. You explain why the objection is frivolous. (I assume that you, like any good litigator of either sex, know the evidence rules inside and out.) The judge overrules the objection. Your witness answers. The situation repeats itself, time after time. Finally, you realize the witness's testimony is so chopped up that no one can follow it. You request a sidebar. This is what you say:

> Your honor, Mr. Opposing Counsel has now objected to every question I have asked this witness. You have overruled every objection. Mr. Opposing Counsel is clearly trying to undermine the trial process, not to offer legitimate objections. My witness can't get a straight story out. It is rude to me, rude to the jury, and disrespectful of this Court. If Mr. Opposing Counsel truly believes he needs to build a record, let him have a standing objection to every question.

Most judges will agree to intervene when a request is phrased this way. One judge I appeared before went further; he picked up my rudeness theme and admonished my opponent for his discourtesy.

If the judge is the problem, or part of the problem, help may have to come from a higher court. Gender bias studies have shown, however, that only the most egregious examples of bias by trial judges are redressed by appellate courts. That means that if your judge is more subtle, letting slip an occasional ''dear'' or stressing ''Ms.'' every time he addresses you (''Your witness, Ms. Kole''), you cannot count on getting relief from a higher court.

This is especially true if the bias does not appear in the transcript (stressing "Ms." or giving you a wink are prime examples).

SCOPE OUT THE JUDGE

Often this means that the only one who can help you, at least at trial, is you. All good trial lawyers will try to scope out their judge before trial, although in some jurisdictions this is impossible because the trial judge is not assigned ahead of time. If you can, determine if the judge is sexist and, if he is, how the sexism manifests itself. Is he intrusive, eroding a female litigator's control of the case by questioning her witnesses himself? If you discover his technique, prepare ahead of time to defuse it. Remember, though: there is only so much you can do. With a piggy and wily judge, you just can't win for trying. Don't berate yourself; it has happened to all of us.

TRY ROLE-PLAYING

Role playing with colleagues is one way to perfect defusing techniques. Assigned the problem of an intrusive, take-over judge, five experienced litigators played out alternative scenarios at The 1993 Woman Advocate Conference in New York. They came up with the following suggestions, in order of increasing chutzpah and danger.

1. Use words to show the judge you are happy he's helping, while in fact wresting control away from him. For example: "That was a good question, your honor. I'd like to follow up on that line of questioning with the witness." Then go back to your own scenario and ask your planned questions.

2. Disagree politely but firmly. "I appreciate the reason you asked that question, your honor, but that's not the line of questioning I'm pursuing now. We will be getting to that question."

3. Be firm and confrontational. "Your honor, I appreciate your degree of interest. But my client has the right to have his case presented as his counsel sees fit, so with all due respect I'd like to proceed."

Thankfully, the really objectionable judges are retiring or dying, and fewer are being appointed or elected. And, of course, as more appellate courts reverse and sanction the really disgraceful cases of judicial gender bias, fewer biased judges will allow themselves the luxury of acting out.

HELP FROM FEMALE JUDGES

In my experience, most are neutral, even-handed, and non-sexist. They can be a godsend when your opponent has a major case of gender bias. Yet I have heard male colleagues complain about woman judges, labelling them "erratic," "irrational," and "menopausal." When I have polled female colleagues about these "erratic" judges, they found the female judges to be fair, competent, and calm. Since the poll was unscientific, I can't check for variables, such as "the judge ruled against me" or "the judge agreed with my legal argument."

Another factor may be at work, however. Because women judges were women lawyers once, they know the problem of condescension by male opponents and judges. By making clear to all litigants that gender-biased behavior will not be tolerated, these female judges may give female litigators a sense of well-being while making male litigators wary. Perhaps that accounts for the differing perceptions of these judges' demeanor and behavior.

Once I tried a case where the only man in the courtroom was a witness. My female opponent was well-prepared and no-nonsense; the judge was fair, competent and no-nonsense. (There was no jury.) We were all courteous and "reasonable women." After the trial, the male witness (*my* witness, by the way), remarked that he's never been "in that situation" before, and he found it a little weird. He looked glazed, but that could be because he'd been skillfully cross-examined by my female opponent.

A FEMALE LAWYER AS ADVERSARY

My experience with female opposing counsel is similar to my experience with women judges. They have been fair and reasonable, and the good ones have been tough adversaries. My male partners tell of completely different experiences with the same women. For example, one woman I have crossed swords with has a reputation among male lawyers as being "the bitch." There is no question that she is a tough adversary. When I opposed her in a major lawsuit, she played by the book and knew her case inside out. As plaintiff's counsel, she moved the case along, refusing to allow me, the defense counsel, to drag things out. But she was never a "bitch"—never mean, hystrionic, hysterical, or unfair.

Was my experience with this female litigator aberrant, or were my male partners responding to her mental toughness when they called her "the bitch"? Lynn Hecht Schafran, Director of the National Judicial Education Program to Promote Equality for Women and Men in Courts (a NOW project), says: "If a woman litigator presents herself in a very strong, straightforward style, she risks being put down as a pushy bitch." I believe that Schafran is right, and that my female opponent got her appellation from her mental toughness.

Treading the line between wimpiness and bitchiness is no fun, and it adds a layer of dissatisfaction and stress to the lives of female litigators. Developing an advocacy style that is both effective and comfortable isn't easy when you know the other actors are viewing you with preconceptions that can undermine your success. Nevertheless, the thrill of doing it right in spite of the additional burdens is unique. It makes the struggle worthwhile.

Let me sum up with this story, which I've heard a lot recently. Three litigators die and go to heaven. When they get there, they discover one more trial awaits them. St. Peter takes each one aside.

"You must do one more thing to get into heaven," St. Peter whispers to the first candidate—a man. "Spell 'God'."

With alacrity, the lawyer spells "G-O-D," and is whisked into heaven.

The same thing happens to lawyer number two, also a man. He spells "God," and he's part of the heavenly multitudes.

Then St. Peter comes to the woman advocate. "To enter heaven, you must do just one more thing."

"One more thing! They always wanted one more thing from me, just to get to the same level of success as my male colleagues. I can't believe it's the same here."

"Calm down," says St. Peter. "All you need to do is spell a word."

"Okay, I guess I overreacted," says the woman. "What's the word?"

"Czechoslovakia," says St. Peter.

The audience always laughs at this joke, because it is painfully true. But the real punchline is this: she got in.

CHAPTER 11

Bench With A Point Of View: How To Create Confidence in the Courtroom

by
HON. NORMA L. SHAPIRO

HON. NORMA L. SHAPIRO

J udge Norma L. Shapiro has served as a U.S. District Court judge since her appointment to the bench by President Jimmy Carter in 1978; she was the first woman judge to sit in the Third Circuit. Judge Shapiro received a B.A. degree with honors in Political Theory from the University of Michigan in 1948, and a J.D. degree Magna Cum Laude in 1951 from the University of Pennsylvania. She then served as a law clerk to Justice Horace Stern, Supreme Court of Pennsylvania. Prior to her nomination to the bench, Judge Shapiro was associated with the law firm of Dechert, Price & Rhoads from 1956-58 and 1967-73 and became a partner from 1973-1978. She also served on the Dechert, Price & Rhoads Policy Committee.

While in private practice, Judge Shapiro was active in the Philadelphia Bar Association as Chair of the Women's Rights Committee and first chair of the Board of Governors, and was also active in the Pennsylvania Bar Association Commission on Women in the Profession and the American Bar Association. Since becoming a federal judge, she has served as Chair of the ABA Conference of Federal Trial Judges and its delegate in the House of Delegates. She is a member of the House as delegate of the Judicial Administration Division.

Judge Shapiro is a member of the Board of Directors of the NAWJ Women Judges' Fund for Justice and for many years has been an active participant in professional and community service organizations, including service as vice-president of the Jewish Publication Society, the Philadelphia Jewish Community

Relations Council, and as a member of the University of Pennsylvania Board of Overseers and the American Law Institute.

Judge Shapiro formerly served as a member and president of the Lower Merion Board of School Directors; a member of the Pennsylvania Governor's Commission on the Status of Women, Lawyer's Advisory Committee; Task Force on Mental Health of Children and Youth; and a reviewing member of the Supreme Court of Pennsylvania Disciplinary Board. She was a member of the Committee on Court Administration of the Judicial Conference of the United States from 1984-87.

In 1993, Judge Shapiro received the first Sandra Day O'Connor Award from the Philadelphia Bar Association. In 1992, Judge Shapiro was honored by the National Council of Jewish Women with the Hannah G. Solomon Award. The Federal Bar Association Bill of Rights Award was presented to her in 1991. In 1979 she was the Oxford Circle Jewish Community Center Woman of the Year and the Golden Slipper Club honored her as their Woman of Distinction.

Judge Shapiro is married to Bernard Shapiro and has three children and one grandchild.

CHAPTER 11

Bench With A Point Of View: How To Create Confidence in the Courtroom

by
HON. NORMA L. SHAPIRO

Now when I enter the courtroom no one mistakes me for the court clerk, or a client. I like to think it's my commanding, confident manner, but more likely than not it's appearing in the front of the courtroom wearing a black judicial robe that leads to the conclusion the lady is indeed a judge. The lady lawyer has no such luck. In the courtroom, she must establish her role as woman advocate by the confidence created by her argument, demeanor, and appearance. Unfortunately, in the courtroom cosmos, these factors impact in reverse order of real importance; but they do matter and must be considered by any aspiring advocate.

Implicit in my comments is the view that there is such a thing as a woman advocate, that is, that neither our courtrooms nor our communities are yet sex blind or sex neutral. It should be no surprise that psychological studies show that less credence is given to women protagonists than to their male counterparts and suggest that less credence is given to women witnesses, and to women experts in particular. For the result-oriented client, the problem is whether to choose a woman counsellor; fortunately, the excellent results achieved by exceptionally able women advocates make that decision easier and easier. For the result-oriented woman counsellor, the problem may be whether to engage a woman expert for use at trial. My anecdotal evidence, unsupported by scientific study, but confirmed by a series of gender bias studies culminating in the impressive 9th Circuit Gender Bias Task Force Report (*see* 45 Stan. L. Rev. 2153 (1993)), convinces me that the woman must still be wiser and warier, but when she is, she is exceptionally effective.

It follows from my belief that gender bias remains endemic in our society, that special advice to the woman advocate may be of assistance. But before I address argument, demeanor, and appearance, a word of warning. Paying too much personal attention to prejudice gives it credence. Excusing or explaining problems purely as manifestations of bias may mask weaknesses not fairly attributable to womanhood, and so retard the remedying of bias. In that spirit, here are suggestions for accentuating the positive, eliminating the negative, and creating confidence in the courtroom.

SIGNS OF A LAWYER

I have never learned how you "look like a lawyer," but until recently no sex stereotype suggested any young woman fit the mold. Sign carrying is not in vogue but briefcases are: they help. So do glasses; they suggest seriousness. Simplicity, not imitation of "masculine" severity, sets the proper tone. The able advocate will want to call attention to her message, not make a fashion statement. Clothes should fit and complement the person. Be conservative, not avant garde; jewelry will be pleasing if neither obviously expensive nor clearly distracting. Studies have shown, rightly or wrongly, that appearance aids in acceptance. There is nothing wrong with aiming to have a pleasant appearance, rather than one that offends. Good grooming is as important for a woman advocate as for a male attorney. Unkempt hair or a dishevelled appearance suggest similar sloppiness of thought and hurt the client's case.

Professional demeanor in the courtroom is as hard to define as obscenity, but just as easy to know when you see it. Courtesy to the court and courtesy to counsel are its hallmarks; insecurity creates its antithesis. Self-confidence enables an advocate to state a position with authority, answer questions with insight, and accept favorable rulings with equanimity and adverse rulings with restraint. It is fair to inquire how a fledgling lawyer acquires that confidence without the depth of experience that male lawyers have found easier to obtain.

One cannot deny that some aspiring advocates come to law school with more confident personalities than others; many (almost half in some law schools) come to their legal studies as a second career and their previous successes serve them well. But one reported study has shown that students lose self-confidence between the beginning and end of law school and that this loss of confidence disproportionately affects female students. The cause is beyond the scope of these comments, but the effect is not.

BUILDING CONFIDENCE

Creating confidence is a challenge for any advocate but is perhaps the chief concern of the woman advocate. Experience, especially successful experience, builds confidence that is readily conveyed to others. In the absence of experience, try pretense. That is, even if you don't feel confident (in fact, especially when you are nervous beyond reason), act as if you are confident in yourself and your position. Insecurity is displayed at home, in the office, or the club house, but never in the courtroom. By acting confident, you may actually feel confident, especially when opposing counsel concedes the strength of your argument or the court rules in your favor!

Be sure to stand straight when you are erect and sit straight when you are sedentary. A slump is not a sign of security. Most important of all, speak up, loudly and clearly. If you swallow your words, there are two distinct disadvantages: no one will understand you and no one will think you wish to be understood. If what you say is important, it's important enough to be heard. Don't worry about your voice being high pitched and feminine; worry about being heard at all. It always amazes me to have attorneys come to court and mutter to themselves when I thought they were supposed to convince the jury or me. While this problem is hardly unique to female attorneys, it is a problem for many. If you are afraid of your own voice, you won't sound, act, or be confident.

Be prepared. Hardly anything adds to self-confidence as much as pretrial preparation. Complete command of the facts and the case law commands respect of the court. It also prevents the kind of panic that can come from the sudden feeling that you haven't the vaguest notion of what you are doing or why you're at the courthouse instead of somewhere else.

Be punctual, but if you are unfortunately late, at least be properly apologetic. Lateness tries the patience of the judge because of the pressure of the court calendar. It's nice to notify chambers if you are unavoidably detained, but notice is not the equivalent of an expression of genuine regret at the earliest possible moment. Common courtesy suggests an awareness of the pressures on others as well as those on one's self. (That's good advice for the judge too, but that's another chapter!)

POLITENESS HELPS

Be polite to the court, to counsel, to the citizens who serve on our juries, and to the supporting staff. Court clerks, not diamonds, are a girl lawyer's best friend, or they can be. If treated with courtesy and respect, court personnel will have helpful information and occasional invaluable advice; if ignored or worse yet, insulted, they will not go out of their way to ease your way.

As a general rule, rudeness never pays and should never be used as a ploy, by man or woman. But it is my observation that it works less well for a woman. In short, lady lawyers are expected to be lady-like. You may ask, how then does a woman deal with the macho man who uses ridicule and rudeness as a trial tactic? Obviously, there are many responses, but responding in kind is not one of them; self-respect helps. You realize that this is in a way not your problem but that of your denigrator.

CONSIDER THE CAUSE OF DISCRIMINATION

As a woman who began practice in 1956, it would be nonsense to announce that I never suffered acts of discrimination or sexual harassment. But I can say that I coped satisfactorily by never assuming that the mistreatment resulted from the fact that I was a woman or, indeed, because of anything I said or did. Discrimination and anti-female prejudice I considered a defect of the discriminator and a sign of insecurity—not mine, but his. It was a sign that he feared me and had something to learn. In other words, I used it to support my own sense of security. Such an attitude seems to work; at least it did for me.

Humor, indeed good humor, helps. Machoism rarely survives when it is not taken seriously. Just take yourself seriously. The courtroom is a serious place where serious people come with serious problems. Informality of dress or address have no place there. Be formal rather than familiar. You should introduce yourself by surname not nickname and address others likewise— whether witness, attorney, or court employee. Usually, people will respond in kind and afford you the dignity you deserve.

Women judges seem to have peculiar problems regarding appropriate forms of address. Even after I became judge, my fellow judges devoted a significant part of a judges' meeting to a well intended consideration of how to address holiday cards to a female, but married, member of the judiciary; it seems Emily Post had no precedent! Similarly when I attended the first sitting of the first female member of an appellate court, counsel for the appellant awkwardly inquired of her, "Would you prefer me to address you as Mrs. Justice, Madame Justice, Justice or Judge?" Her terse reply was, "Have you considered simply addressing me as, "Your Honor?"

However, the most amusing of the embarrassing incidents in my career involved an able but inexperienced male Assistant U.S. Attorney who persisted in addressing me as "Sir" for at least a year. He responded "Yes, Sir" to almost everything I said. I would patiently remind him, outside the presence of the jury, that I was not a "Sir," as, indeed, one could plainly see. But his slip of the lip persisted. Finally, after a day of repeated misspeaking, of which the members of the jury were increasingly aware, I responded in kind. After some submission of his, I sweetly replied. "Thank you, Mrs. X." The result was rewarding; the jury laughed but Mr. X blushed a deep scarlet. More important, he never addressed me as "Sir" again. My friends in the U.S. Attorney's office tell me that until he left for private practice, every one of his files assigned to my docket had "Madam" in large print on the cover!

Don't patronize non-lawyers or appear to do so in using legal lingo to show your superiority. Of course, it is not polite or correct to be condescending, but beyond that, it won't work. Jurors are intelligent, considerate, and fair, but they don't respond well to legal code language and there's no need to use it. Simplicity and directness convey sincerity and are convincing; an attempt at pomposity is always preposterous and self-defeating.

DO WOMEN ACT DIFFERENTLY?

At this point, it's fair to ask whether, from a judge's perspective, the fair sex performs differently in court. My candid answer must be, not really. Of course, there are differences in dress and demeanor, but, in the end, it is argument not demeanor nor appearance that is the mark of the able advocate. And it is preparation and practice that not only build self-confidence but enable effective performance. Oral presentation can be enhanced by rehearsal and a critical review by a friend or videotape. Seeing yourself as others see you can be surprising, if not comforting, but the experience is invaluable in advocacy training.

Adverting to mastery of the facts and the law might seem unnecessary because it is so fundamental. But in my experience, advocates seem not always to understand this principle. Consequently, no discussion of advocacy, whether directed to male or female lawyers, can fail to mention this simple proposition: Just as nothing succeeds like success, no one is prepared without preparation.

THE DANGERS OF PERCEIVED BIAS

It would be wrong to assume that being a woman is always a disadvantage to be overcome. On occasion there is a sympathy factor or jury dynamic favoring the perceived underdog. In an important civil case tried before me, lead counsel for both plaintiff and defendant had trial associates, one male and the other female. Plaintiff's counsel allowed his male associate to examine a few relatively minor witnesses. Defense counsel confined his female associate to displaying numerous charts to the jury. There was a substantial verdict for plaintiff, following which a juror volunteered a comment to counsel that the jury was offended by the subordinate role of the only female attorney. No one present for the entire trial could conclude that this was the only consideration upon which the verdict turned, but it was a remarkable instance where the perception of bias backfired.

As a judicial officer I am sworn to be neutral and objective. To the best of my ability, I treat all parties, and all advocates, alike and equal before the law, whether female or male, poor or rich, plaintiff or defendant, young or old, and regardless of race, nationality, alienage, citizenship, or political persuasion. Having acknowledged that, it would not be candid to say that I have not been more sensitive to women lawyers, not more helpful as some improperly expect, but more hopeful, certainly. I take more personal pleasure in the ability of a young woman advocate, just as I feel more personal pain in one poorly prepared.

Having been a young woman lawyer in the 1950's when we were 3% of the legal population and I knew every woman practicing in Philadelphia, it warms my heart to see so many able young women representing plaintiffs, defendants, and our government effectively. There have been many precious moments in my career as the first female judge on the bench of the Eastern District of Pennsylvania, but none so rare as the criminal trial of a man indicted for perjury when both the Assistant U.S. Attorney and the defense attorney were able and effective young women attorneys. The defendant said he felt like Alice in Wonderland, or perhaps Alex! And it was a joy to observe the jury.

The day will come when observations about women lawyers will be obsolete. Until then, unfortunately, the successful woman advocate must be more able than her male counterpart. Fortunately, for many of them, it's not too difficult.

CHAPTER 12

Making Rain

by
JEAN MACLEAN SNYDER

JEAN MACLEAN SNYDER

Jean Maclean Snyder, concentrates her practice in media, arts, and entertainment law and business litigation.

Ms. Snyder is a sole practitioner in Chicago.

Before going to law school, Ms. Snyder was a free-lance writer and did administrative work for not-for-profit agencies. She went to law school at age 33 while believing, she says, that law was a man's world that nevertheless would open easily for her. At the University of Chicago Law School, her first doubt came during orientation. This was when the director of admissions gave a welcoming talk while wielding several sets of Illinois Reporters in his arms, Reporters he eventually would open so he could read aloud the descriptions of rape and sodomy from various cases involving sex crimes. The next warning sign came when she learned that all her teachers for her first quarter were white males who were younger than she was.

Thus Ms. Snyder felt an especially keen sense of enjoyment several years later when, as a practitioner, she found herself facing a former law school professor as a pro se adversary in a post-decree child support case. Before the day was over, Ms. Snyder had succeeded in getting the professor held in contempt of court and sentenced to one week in jail on a work release program. After the teacher had spent several hours in prison, Ms. Snyder offered to settle the case on terms favorable to her client, and the recalcitrant professor settled quickly.

Other of Ms. Snyder's recent accomplishments:

☐ She won more than $1 million for her clients, individual shareholders in a publicly traded company, who sold their holdings to a buyer who had misrepresented and concealed its intentions to make a tender offer for the balance of the company's shares.

☐ She has won numerous injunction trials involving First Amendment issues, trademark infringement, unfair competition, consumer fraud and deceptive practices, and non-competition covenants.

☐ On behalf of one client who claimed trademark rights in an industry where free copying is the norm, she succeeded on three separate occasions—twice through informal negotiations and once through litigation—in causing her client's competitors to discontinue or to make substantial changes to product lines viewed as confusingly similar to those of the client.

Ms. Snyder also served as a consultant on the movie, "A River Runs Through It," and is an associate producer on "Young Men And Fire," in preproduction at Warner Bros. Both movies are based on stories written by her father, Norman Maclean.

Ms. Snyder is co-chair of the First Amendment and Media Litigation Committee of the American Bar Association Section of Litigation. From 1986 to 1987, she was the first woman editor-in-chief of *Litigation*, the Section's quarterly journal. She is vice president and a member of the board of directors of Independent Feature Project/Midwest, a member of the board of directors of Lawyers for the Creative Arts, and a member of the Board of Governors of the University of Chicago Alumni Association. She is a graduate of the University of Chicago and the University of Chicago Law School.

Ms. Snyder lives in Chicago with her husband Joel, their dog Shasta and cat Mischa and, on vacations, their sons Jacob, 22, and Noah, 19.

As to her initial belief that law was a man's world she easily would enter, Ms. Snyder says she was wrong on both counts and that the task turned out to be more difficult and more interesting than she had anticipated.

CHAPTER 12

Making Rain

by
JEAN MACLEAN SNYDER

A trial lawyer I know—let's call him Arnie—has a touch of magic. When Arnie enters a room, even strangers sense that Arnie is a lawyer. A conversation about politics quickly turns to the subject of law, and before Arnie has finished his first war story, people are telling him their legal problems. One or two may ask if he would represent them in some matter. Not just as a litigator; they also want help setting up a business or doing their estate planning.

Will reading this chapter make that happen to you?

Probably not.

But it will tell you what to do if you don't already have Arnie's touch.

You see, there are two theories about rainmaking. According to one theory, it's all magic; you either are a rainmaker or you're not. The other theory holds that rainmaking is a skill. Innate abilities are important, but so are learning, practice, and hard work.

Arnie is proof that the theory based on magic is at least partly true. He also is proof that the other theory is legitimate. Even Arnie could not be a successful rainmaker without planning his contacts and following through successfully.

My premise is that rainmaking skills can be learned. I reject the idea that rainmaking can be done only by certain select people, most of whom are men. If you need encouragement in accepting my premise, you should say this to yourself: at one time the generally accepted wisdom was that some people, namely women, weren't meant to be aviators, mathematicians, or even trial lawyers. That's an idea we scorn today; it has been disproved thanks to women who refused to believe it.

So too with rainmaking.

WHAT IS RAINMAKING?

Before we get any farther, let's say what we mean by rainmaking. The quick answer is that rainmaking means generating new legal business. At least that's the narrow sense of the term. But the concept really is broader. Rainmaking means believing you deserve a client's business, so much so that you have the drive to get it. It means feeling confident about your career because you like what you do and you think you are good at it. It means looking ahead at your career and ensuring that you get all that is coming to you.

You can tell that rainmaking is an important topic. At some stages in a lawyer's career, it may seem like the only topic.

Women face different issues from men when it comes to rainmaking. For one thing, women perceive business development opportunities as being limited for them, as compared to opportunities for men. When Prentice Hall Law & Business recently surveyed women across the country, more than 90 percent of the women respondents believed that to be true. (The survey is described in detail in Chapter 3.)

It may be true that opportunities are limited, but it is also the case that women do not take full advantage of those that exist. In part this is so because women may not understand the importance of rainmaking. Instead, too many women assume that simply being good at your job is all that is needed. Too, women may find rainmaking distasteful. Because it depends in part on bartering favors, women may balk. We prefer being loved for ourselves alone to being part of a negotiated relationship. This lack of interest or outright dislike of rainmaking means that, as a rule, women do not put the energy or time into rainmaking activities that men do.

That conclusion is borne out by objective evidence. In the Prentice Hall survey, more than half the respondents said they spent only five percent of their time—at most—on client development; three-quarters of the women who were partners in law firms spent ten percent or less of their time.

That is not enough!

Even if you're as much of a magician as my friend Arnie, you can't develop business simply by thinking about the process.

WHEN TO BEGIN

A question that young lawyers often ask is "When should I begin to think about rainmaking?" The answer is, now. The next question is, "How do I get started?" The answer to that question is not so short. Here are some ideas to get going.

It's never too early to work on developing and building relationships, which are the basis of successful rainmaking. The starting associate can meet lawyers from other local firms and from other cities at continuing legal education meetings and bar association activities. She can maintain contact with law school classmates. She can cultivate the firm's existing clients while working on assigned matters. Expanding the work a client brings to the firm only can help. In fact, of the respondents to the Prentice Hall survey who had said they had brought new business to their firm, the most common route was to do good work for the firm's current clients, which caused the satisfied client to return and also resulted in referrals.

Building relationships happen slowly, often over a period of years, so you must not get discouraged if there is no quick payoff. Just for this reason, though, it is important to get started.

A WARNING TO ASSOCIATES

For the associate beginning to develop business, some words of warning are in order. Here are the general admonitions presented to the audience at the 1993 Woman Advocate Conference

by Louise LaMothe, a partner at Riordan & McKinzie in Los
Angeles and 1993 Chair of the ABA Section of Litigation:

> Your first job is to do very well the work that is on your
> desk.
>
> If you don't like that work, talk to the management of
> your litigation group about it. If you don't like any litigation
> work, get moved into another practice area.
>
> Also, get yourself the training needed to develop your
> career. If you're not getting training in taking depositions,
> for example, ask for it.
>
> Finally, keep in mind that achieving these goals is up to
> you. You are the person who cares most about your career.
> If you won't value yourself, why should anyone else?

These are important words of advice. Following them will help
get your career in order and help build character. Strong character
will be important for facing another challenge you didn't get
answers for in law school: balancing a family life with your legal
career, including developing business.

JUGGLING ISN'T EASY

Juggling a family life and the task of rainmaking seems daunting.
It is. For many women, time spent on the practice of law seems
like job enough; adding rainmaking to the agenda seems impossible. Or worse than that, irrelevant.

What can women do about this dilemma? First, women need
to acknowledge that the act of juggling is a job in itself, one that is
especially difficult for women who have small children. For these
women, the act of juggling may take more energy than the
individual tasks of parenting (along with being a wife) and lawyering (along with rainmaking), which are the metaphorical balls that
the juggler must keep in the air. The difficulty is determining the
proper balance. Each person needs to make a decision about that
balance and then feel secure about the decision. That doesn't

mean you won't revisit your decision; reassessing is what juggling is all about. But it does mean that once you have set your priorities you should let yourself alone for a while. And it also means that you should keep in mind that babies are not babies forever; not so long from now, the juggling will be easier.

Moreover, even while immersed in parenting, you can be on the lookout for rainmaking opportunities. After all, carpooling, attending parents' night at school, watching your child at the tot lot all involve meeting new people, many of whom are over the age of 21. Just like you, these people have lives besides being parents; learn what those lives are, for little Billy's mommy or daddy may be a potential client. One young mother I know carries business cards to school and playtime gatherings. She tells me the practice has paid off and that she has gained two important clients through playground chats.

Rainmaking is especially hard on family life because socializing is part of rainmaking, and social time is exactly the time we want with our families. But not all rainmaking activities are after-hours (see chart at the end of this chapter for suggestions); the trick is to concentrate on office-hour activities while your family duties are heaviest.

THE SOCIAL SIDE OF RAINMAKING

The social aspect of rainmaking is another reason why rainmaking is different for women. Until recently, the social world of business has truly been a man's world. For years social activities have been for men only or for male professionals and their wives, who played the second sex as their only role.

Faced with this dilemma, how can we change things?

What we cannot do is to ignore the problem. One woman lawyer I know, who I'll call Lisa, learned this a few weeks after she went to work at a corporation. That's when her boss came into her office, hemmed and hawed, and then broke the news. He said, "Lisa, there's something you need to know. This is a golfing company. Golfing is what we do for personal relaxation, it's the way we share our time together, and it's the way we get our clients." Lisa's boss knew that Lisa had never picked up a golf club in her life. But those days were over if she wanted to keep this job. Lisa decided she did want it. She took up golf, and soon she began enjoying her time on all 19 holes of the course.

That's one solution, but it's not the only one Lisa could have chosen.

RESOLVE TO DO SOMETHING

Lisa could have decided that golfing was something she simply did not want to do. But if that was her decision, she would have needed to change jobs and find a company whose social activities suited her, or a company that expected employees to find their own ways of meeting people outside the office.

So, if you don't like golf, pick something else. The particular activity does not matter; what matters is the resolution to do something. Certainly you can do lunches, drinks after work, or breakfasts. Maybe you can find a cultural activity you enjoy that will make clients and partners comfortable—a concert, a play, the ballet.

Then again, maybe you can give golf a second look.

Not so long ago sports became part of my business life. Here is how. When I worked at a 70-lawyer firm, much of my partners' social life centered around sports—playing sports games or watching them. Our Chicago firm had season tickets to the Bulls games and the Cubs games and to the games of a soccer team I'd never ever heard of.

AN INVITATION TO JOIN

Every Fall a group of my litigation partners went off for a weekend of pheasant hunting in Wisconsin. Being the only woman partner in the Litigation Group, I had not been invited, and so eventually I complained.

One autumn day, a long shiny pheasant feather appeared on my desk, a silent invitation from my partners. I knew that this feather was an offer I couldn't refuse. Together my partners and I made the trip to Wisconsin. We had a wonderful dinner the night before and breakfast the morning of (and I successfully restrained my instinct to jump up and do the dishes). There we spent the day shooting at pheasants. The technique was for all five of us to wait until a bird rose from the field of wheat and snow and then for all five of us to shoot. After several hours we had 17 birds to our credit. Coming home in the car, one of my partners—the one who slipped occasionally and called me "honey"—asked a question that clearly had been on his mind all morning. "So, did it bother you to shoot the birds?" he asked. Truthfully I answered, "Not a bit." What I didn't admit was my certainty that not one of those 17 birds had lost so much as a feather at my hands—the simultaneous shots of my more skilled partners had saved me from the disclosure that my aim was way off the mark. Despite the lack of kill, or maybe because of it, my hunting excursion was enjoyable. I hadn't expected to like it, but I did, and I look forward to going again.

FOR MEN-ONLY ACTIVITIES

There are other business-getting activities that women have been shut out of for reasons unrelated to their own lack of interest. Luncheon and athletic clubs of many cities are by invitation only, and for a long time those invitations went only to men. In most cities that is no longer true—here in Chicago the issue was resolved when clubs that refused to admit women were denied liquor licenses.

The question is, are women taking advantage of these newly opened doors? If not, we should be. When official barriers are broken down, women need to take the initiative to make sure the barriers do not become de facto.

USING YOUR MONEY

There's something else that women can do to generate business contacts—they can use their money. Donating to charities or political candidates opens the way to meet people in business, and to meet them by doing a favor that may bring a favor in return. Why women have shied away from charitable giving as a spring board for business development is hard to say. It's not that we don't have the money—women in the private practice of law certainly can make contributions that will be noticed. It may trace back to the notion that women do not like to barter for favors. If so, women need to save that attitude for their private life or admit that bartering is part of most relationships, although we call it by a kinder name.

Besides providing potentially valuable contacts, being involved in charitable and political activities can provide a venue for socializing with clients. Inviting a client to a gala dinner for 200 people may be easier than dinner alone at a restaurant.

SOCIALIZING WITH CLIENTS

These smaller dinners can be comical in planning and execution. If the woman lawyer is married, does she make the dinner a foursome including spouses? While she and her male client-to-be talk about business, what does her husband talk to the client's wife about? If the woman lawyer is single and the dinner is a twosome, how does she navigate through the unspoken questions of whether the eagerness she is showing is for his business or for his body? Far easier to arrange a table for ten at the Annual Dinner for the Friends of Lincoln Park Zoo.

All this talk about socializing with clients may seem silly. But don't be fooled. These activities provide a forum for building strong, successful relationships, which are the bedrock of successful business development.

Social activities are the first issue discussed here because they are the first issue on women's minds when it comes to rainmaking. That does not mean that rainmaking is all (or primarily) socializing, or that lawyering is all rainmaking. The first job, always, is to develop your skills as a lawyer. Oddly, those skills have implications for rainmaking too.

Here is why.

A LIST TO FOLLOW

At the session on rainmaking at first conference on The Woman Advocate, John Subak, who was group vice president and general counsel of Rohm and Haas Company, a specialty chemical company in Philadelphia, presented a list of qualities that make a good rainmaker.

Here is Subak's list.

First, absolute loyalty. The lawyer should think of the client first, second, and always.

Second, expertise and competence. At the end of the day, every day, the client wants to feel that his (or her) lawyer is tops.

Third, efficiency or cost effectiveness. Doing the job efficiently does more than save the client money; it demonstrates your ability and respect for the client.

Fourth, understand the client's business and needs.

Asking what the client wants is not a strength of litigators, according to Subak. Instead, litigators often give the impression that they are the only ones who know the rules and, therefore, the only ones who can play. Subak warns that clients want to be more than a passive audience. If you aren't good at listening, the client likely will find someone else who is.

As general counsel of Rohm and Haas, Subak was a client every lawyer would like to have. Yet the qualities that Subak praises are not magical qualities attainable by only a few. Nor are they skills to defer acquiring until you become a partner. Instead, they are traits that all of us should be developing throughout our careers. They are the traits that will attract clients and keep them happy.

SHARPER COMMUNICATIONS SKILLS

As litigators, we should ask how clients judge our expertise and competence. After all, they do not see much of what we do.

We take depositions, write legal briefs, and conduct trials, but clients see only snatches of these events. Still, they know that we make a living by communicating, both orally and in writing, and they see us using our communication skills all the time. If you feel hesitant about your skills, do something about it. Courses are available teaching trial advocacy and oral communication as well as legal writing, business writing, and general writing. Taking courses can make you a better lawyer and also a better rainmaker.

ADDING A SPECIALTY

For litigators, there is another aspect to expertise, namely developing a substantive specialty. This too is helpful both for rainmaking and for reasons of professional competence. Today, the practice of law almost demands a specialty, especially if you want to work with larger clients. As far as rainmaking goes, often what you have to sell is your ability to give good advice. An area of expertise give you something to advise about. It also provides a subject to write and speak about, thus giving you the kind of exposure that helps draw clients.

In my own case, outside circumstances helped shape my specialty. In 1988, I began working as a consultant on the movie, "A River Runs Through It," which was based on a story of the same name written by my father, Norman Maclean. Before I worked on "River," intellectual property litigation, including media and First Amendment issues, had been a strong interest of mine. Seeing intellectual property in action, especially the kind of action you see on the set of a movie made by top flight professionals, was enough to convince me that I had tried my last ERISA case.

Since then, I have left the 70-lawyer firm where I worked and set up my own practice. Besides intellectual property litigation, I am doing litigation and transactional work for clients involved in arts, entertainment, and the creative industries. Connecting with these clients has been easier thanks to my work on "River," since that work prompted me to become involved with arts and creative industries groups.

The lesson here is not to wait, poised to jump, until Robert Redford falls in love with a story your father wrote. The lesson is to seize opportunities however they arise.

Besides speaking and writing about a substantive area, there are other ways to use your skills to develop business. You can join bar associations or other legal groups, or nonlegal groups in an industry you are targeting for business development. More specific suggestions are listed in the chart at the end of this chapter. Look over the chart and begin planning what to do.

DECIDING WHAT TO DO

Planning what you will do to develop business is critical. Lists of activities are not a guarantee to success, any more than a kitchen full of ingredients promises a good meal. You need to pick and choose, deciding what works for you. Is speaking to professional groups one of your strengths, or should you focus on your writing? Are you better off joining several groups, or should you join only one where you can work your way to the top? Will you target one particular industry for potential clients, or will you focus on a substantive area applicable to many industries?

It is as important to say "no" to some activities as it is to say "yes" to others. As you begin making choices, you will be developing your own business plan. When you are secure doing that, you are on your way to becoming a successful rainmaker.

Success will arrive when you find your own niche and feel comfortable with it. Along the way you will read articles like this one, and they will help. You will also enlist the aid of people who have been there before you. The traditional rainmakers are men, so watch what they do and ask for their assistance. If they are your law partners, remind them that it is in their interest to include women in their rainmaking efforts such as presentations the firm makes to potential clients.

GETTING MEN INVOLVED

Hold on a minute, you say, these guys are part of the old boy network. Yes, they are; that is exactly the point. It's called co-

opting the enemy (not that other verb you were thinking of). Get
your partners to help you use the old boys network. And when
you have their attention, solicit their help with making contacts
and learning about whatever issues are on your mind.

Of course getting men involved is not as easy; in the Prentice
Hall survey, 50 percent of the respondents to a question about
limitations on business development opportunities said that the
"unwillingness of male partners to act as mentors" limited their
opportunities. Overcoming this reluctance depends on flexibility
and persistence. Do not insist that the man be a mentor with
general jurisdiction; seek out advice on specific issues. Ask and
keep on asking.

The benefits of having men involved in our success are immense, both on a personal level and in the larger sense. Above
all, we want to avoid dividing into armed enemy camps.

WOMEN HELPING WOMEN

Making sure that women help each other needs attention too.
It's easy to get caught up with our own agendas and forget to
think about what we can do for each other. Women lawyers can
help other women lawyers by serving as formal or informal
mentors and by acting as sympathetic colleagues. More to the
point, or to the bottom line, they can make referrals to each other.

It helps, too, that the number of women's faces in the boardroom is gradually increasing. True, the change isn't fast enough.
In fact, in the Prentice Hall survey, 90 percent of the women
answering the question said that the absence of women in influential positions at client companies limited their business development opportunities. Even so, there are more women in business
than there were ten years ago, and progress continues. Those
women in business who have arrived will be glad to see a female
face across the table.

And don't overlook the women at client companies who are
still in the trenches. Some of them play a role in hiring; those that
don't now may move to hiring positions later.

You can tell by now that there are no precise answers to
the question of how to become an effective rainmaker. Watch

successful rainmakers and seek advice from them, read articles and discuss them. Try out techniques until you learn what is best for you. Trial and error can be frustrating, but it is a type of frustration that litigators should be used to. Litigation, after all, is not an exact science. For most litigators, that is part of the fun. It is what enables us to use our intuition, canniness and, dare we say, wisdom. Keep this in mind the next time you think about rainmaking. You wouldn't want it any other way, would you?

SUGGESTIONS FOR RAINMAKING

What can women do to become better rainmakers? Here are some specific ideas.

Navigating the Social Scene.

1. Join men at their activities; learn to play golf or take some of your firm's season tickets to the Bears games.

2. Instead of joining men's activities, find some "sex neutral" activities you like which provide a social scene for business—consider cultural events, charitable events, political activities.

3. Find a midpoint between joining and not joining. Do socialize with clients or potential clients, but substitute breakfast or lunch for one-on-one or two-on-two social evenings.

4. Take advantage of the breakdown of traditional barriers to women that has occurred over recent years. Help keep former legal barriers from becoming de facto barriers. For example, join a luncheon or athletic club—the kind that previously asked you to enter through the back door. Take advantage of the opening up of business to women professionals. Cultivate women business executives as clients, women accountants or bankers as sources of referral; cultivate them as individuals or in a group.

5. Make your money work for you. Men have always established some business relationships by donating to charitable, cultural, or political causes. Women should do this too.

6. Try flying first class. This is not a metaphor; I'm talking about the real thing. You are likely to be one of the few women there, and chances of meeting a potential client are very good.

7. Stuck at PTA meetings instead of on the golf course? You should still be on the lookout for clients. Some men do child care too. And some of the women may have a career on the side as you do.

(Continued)

Getting The Most Out Of Your Professional Life.

1. Become an expert on something. Becoming an expert enables you to get exposure through writing and public speaking. It also gives you something to talk about when the men talk about the Bears game.

2. Join lawyer groups such as bar associations or specialty groups—these organizations may be especially open to accepting women on their own merits. The group activity and public speaking can help build confidence. The contacts may result in referrals.

3. Do some writing. Not just for CLE meetings; write for the firm newsletter, the city's law bulletin, or magazines of trade groups.

4. Cultivate nonlawyer groups. Instead of looking for lawyer referrals, go where the clients are. Your lawyer skills and long-term contact with potential clients (via a professional group, for example) will give you the opportunity to build up trust and respect.

5. Be on top of current trends. For example, learn how to compete in a beauty contest and learn about alternative billing options. A science is developing around beauty contests—contests where several law firms make presentations to a company for its business. There are even courses available about beauty contests and alternative billing. Get ahead of the group—or at least even with it—by taking the appropriate courses.

6. Develop your oral communication skills. Whether in court or at a presentation for the client, oral communication is the number one skill for litigators. Take advantage of the wonderful oral advocacy training now available, especially if you were not on the debating team in school.

CHAPTER 13

Where Have the Mentors Gone?

by
LOUISE A. LAMOTHE

LOUISE A. LAMOTHE

L ouise LaMothe, the Chair of the Section of Litigation in 1992-93, began her involvement with the Section in 1980 as Co-Chair of the National Institutes Committee. During the 80's, she served as Co-Director for the Programs Division, a member of the Section's Council, Chair of the Section's Programs at the 1989 Annual Meeting in Honolulu and Director of Divisions in 1989-90. In 1990 she was elected to Vice Chair, and became Chair-Elect in 1991. After graduating from Stanford University, Ms. LaMothe taught law at the University of Kansas and directed its legal aid clinic. Three years later she moved on to private practice in Los Angeles at Irell & Manella where she felt she would get the high caliber of training she needed to "develop into the best lawyer I could be." She has recently moved her practice to the firm of Riordan & McKinzie. Through her involvement with the ABA Section of Litigation, Ms. LaMothe continues to use her skills to help the administration of justice and the public interest. "I would not be happy if I could not have that public-service element in my legal work. I have to have that in significant doses."

CHAPTER 13

Where Have the Mentors Gone?

by
LOUISE A. LAMOTHE

Regrettably, in recent years, significant changes have occurred in the way law is practiced, and the way in which junior lawyers learn the values of the profession. These changes have had a disproportionate impact on women. Although new obstacles to mentoring have become part of the profession for all attorneys, women face special challenges due to their inherent "differences," to societal stereotyping, and to many other factors that tend to inhibit an informal mentoring relationship.

The legal profession is faced as never before with the challenge of training its young. The *Interim Report of the Committee on Civility of the Seventh Federal Judicial Circuit*, for example, noted a 75% increase in the number of licensed attorneys between 1980 and 1990. Historically, young lawyers were trained in the skills and values of their profession through more senior lawyers for whom they worked, or with whom they came in contact.

Now we are in danger of becoming a "revolving door" profession—thousands of attorneys report they are dissatisfied with the profession, and women lawyers in particular are leaving large law firm practice. Yet when explaining why lawyers leave law firms, managing partners frequently say "it's for personal reasons." Others say "she never should have become a lawyer in the first place." While that assessment may be accurate in any individual case, the firm that often finds itself using that rationale should analyze whether it is simply an excuse. In my experience, junior lawyers leave law firms because no one is paying attention to their needs, because they feel isolated. And this feeling of isolation is understandably intensified in the case of women lawyers. In short, many women lawyers have missed out on the mentoring process.

WHAT MENTORING CAN DO

By mentoring I mean the complex relationship which a junior lawyer forms with one or more senior lawyers. The relationship usually begins and progresses so naturally that the two people may not even recognize the many facets of their connection. It is begun in the working environment, usually by handling a project together. It is cemented by social contact—lunch, a drink after work, dinner while working late, out of town trips, golf or tennis games. Personal information is shared and a relationship forged. I even know of more than one instance in which the mentee named the mentor as godfather of the mentee's child.

The more senior lawyer gives feedback, guidance, and advice, perhaps unaware that his (or her) actions are being absorbed as lessons for future use by the younger lawyer. The younger lawyer sees from the more senior how to behave in a whole host of situations—with judges, clients, opponents, peers, staff, and so forth. The younger lawyer has a role model—a way to behave in the myriad of situations that will confront her in her professional life. Such relationships, while particularly important for young lawyers, can last long into middle age, with the junior though now experienced lawyer still seeking advice and support from her more senior colleague. It could be persuasively argued that no one ever succeeded without a mentor.

In my own case, I never met a woman attorney before I went to law school; I never studied with a woman law professor nor counted a woman as my mentor. My most important early mentor was a man with whom I never practiced; indeed, we never even worked in the same city. Prentice Marshall (now a Senior District Court Judge in the Northern District of Illinois) encouraged me as a young lawyer at National Institute for Trial Advocacy in 1972, gave me my first opportunity to teach at NITA as his assistant in 1973, and took an interest in my career. From him I learned not just how to try a case, but how to act as a lawyer; he supported my efforts, corrected my errors, reinforced many of my ideas, and gave impetus to unformed expressions. And from him I saw how admirable a lawyer could be as a person, how much having a sense of humor matters, how satisfying it can be to teach others new skills, and how much we can all learn from each other. I was lucky to find him; I'm only sorry that our paths did not cross long enough for me to learn more from him.

WHY MENTORING IS IN DECLINE

If this describes a relationship you have had in the legal profession, count yourself fortunate, for this system of one-on-one training is floundering. One reason no doubt is the increased pressure on all lawyers to meet client demands and seek new business, particularly in times of economic decline or stagnation. In the absence of business growth, more senior lawyers are hoarding work rather than delegating it to younger lawyers and training them along the way. Another aspect of the problem is the pressure from clients for partners to do the work themselves and not to involve junior associates. Some clients do not see the value of less experienced lawyers and refuse to pay for their time.

A further reason may be the pressure to clock billable hours, thereby decreasing the time spent in nonbillable activities, including internal firm relationships. Moreover, partners and associates (particularly women) with families do not have the luxury of staying late to socialize at the office. They inevitably miss out on much informal contact simply by being engaged elsewhere. Finally, with decreasing institutional loyalty among all lawyers, some partners now view associates as leverage, as dispensable workers instead of colleagues and future partners. They delegate work simply to get it off their desks with no training component for the associates.

The decline of mentoring as a factor in the socializing of young lawyers has had a ripple effect—it contributes to the decline in civility and the rise in ''hardball'' litigation tactics, to the feeling of disconnectedness and lack of ease that many lawyers, young and not so young, now feel with their profession.

Central to the notion of mentoring is that training young lawyers is the responsibility—indeed the pleasure and satisfaction—of more senior members of the bar. Now we hear around us instead comments of law firm managing partners that "we had to let those junior associates go because clients no longer wanted to pay for training them." This statement amazes me.

A CRISIS FOR YOUNG WOMEN

These days, what is a problem for young male lawyers is a crisis for young women. For them, the informal mentoring system—the "old boy" network—never functioned. Efforts to recruit women traditionally stop when hiring goals are met. Once hired, women feel abandoned, left to fend for themselves in developing their careers. As one young African-American woman lawyer described the situation at the firm she left: "The biggest problem was that there was a free market in terms of how work was assigned, which allowed biases to come in. You got work by a partner knocking on your door. If you hooked up correctly, great; but, if not, you got the dregs." Advancement for women and minorities was largely determined by the biases and stereotyped thinking of white male partners and business executives, whether the stereotyping was conscious or unconscious.

Several factors create the special difficulties women lawyers face in finding mentors. While it would be a positive experience for junior women lawyers to have women mentors, women partners have been scarce. Though the percentage of women partners recently has been growing by about one percent per year, there are still not nearly enough women mentors to go around. The situation for minority partners is even worse. Realistically speaking, most women and minority lawyers will have white male mentors or none at all.

THE HAZARDS OF INFORMAL MENTORING

A senior lawyer begins a mentor relationship based on liking a younger lawyer enough to decide to spend time helping the junior.

It is natural for the senior lawyer to choose someone who reminds him of himself at a younger age. Moreover, informal mentoring is often based on a self-fulfilling prophecy. The senior lawyer is putting his own prestige on the line for the junior lawyer by becoming his mentor. The senior lawyer does not want to risk being closely involved with a person who will fail. Indeed, such closeness will mean that the mentor will have to deliver the inevitable termination message. This problem virtually ensures that associates perceived as "poor risks" are ignored; only the winners get mentored. These factors may explain why it is especially difficult to mentor someone who looks different from you—a young woman, for example—or someone who comes from a different racial or ethnic background.

Since the arrival of more and more women in law schools, overt sexist attitudes have become unfashionable. But sexist attitudes are very much alive in the world of law practice, as substantiated in the numerous recent studies on gender bias in the courts and the legal profession. Gender bias infects decisions about hiring and, to an even greater extent, about promotion, in a manner the subtlety of which makes it difficult to detect and root out. Gender bias takes its toll on the mentoring process too; the most obvious consequence is that some men avoid mentoring women.

Moreover, even non-sexist senior men face both societal disincentives and personal conflicts in mentoring young women. Well-publicized instances of office romances cause some men to believe they will face suspicion from spouses or co-workers if they take an interest in a young woman's career. Other men fear romantic entanglement or worry about charges of sexual harassment. The result is that young women have dramatically reduced opportunities to be mentored by more senior men.

Law firms' problems mirror those of other business organizations. In 1991, the U.S. Department of Labor studied the promotion of management-level women and minorities at nine randomly-picked *Fortune* 500 government contractors. The survey results, published in A *Report on the Glass Ceiling Initiative*, found that the lack of mentors was one of the chief impediments to women and minorities progressing into top management. Women and minorities did not receive the same opportunity as white men to participate in corporate developmental experiences—serving as deputies to senior managers, for example. The report concluded that the importance of equal opportunity goals needed reaffirmation and that executive accountability for meeting these goals had to be increased.

CREATING MENTORS

Is there a way to recapture the lost habit of mentoring? Is there a way consciously to promote mentoring for women who have been historically left out of the process? I think so. Effective mentoring programs can ensure better work product, and act as a built-in check against malpractice. When a junior woman lawyer is in a supportive relationship, she can ask for help, admit mistakes, and seek assistance before problems become crises. A mentor helps a junior lawyer negotiate the shoals of practice—showing how to behave in a deposition when opposing counsel is an SOB, or offering support when the associate is the only woman in a negotiating session and her older male opponent makes a suggestive remark.

The time-honored way to learn is to work on a case together. Handling a *pro bono* case can be a particularly rewarding experience. The senior lawyer oversees the matter and can give the junior lawyer responsibility for significant aspects of it. The experience also demonstrates to the junior lawyer the importance of *pro bono* work to the firm.

One problem is that those who get to the top of corporate law firms are not selected for their nurturing qualities. People without those qualities may not value mentoring and may not encourage others to do so. Just as in business, if the CEO is not involved, a major change in attitude will not take place. We must strengthen firm cultures to encourage mentoring.

THE GLASS CEILING

Firms attempting to establish or revive mentoring find that the lack of women attorneys in upper echelon positions is a negative factor that feeds on itself. Fewer women in the partner ranks of law firms means that fewer women will choose law firm practice, and that retention rates for those who do will continue to be depressingly low. Therefore, one important way to provide mentoring is to fully develop the talents of existing women lawyers.

Since women still bear the responsibility for childrearing, the firm's employment policies have a dramatic impact. The path to partnership is arduous enough, but when family responsibilities are added to it, many women not accustomed to doing any task less than wholeheartedly will simply give up.

In order to retain women attorneys, law firms must revise the system for making partner to accommodate family responsibilities. Instead, the increased acceptance of permanent associates and contract attorneys makes the road more difficult. Such policies exemplify the shortsighted view that investing in the career of a woman attorney is not worthwhile because the woman will quit or lose interest in her practice when she becomes a mother. Those words are not necessarily spoken, but the attitude is there.

FACTORING IN FAMILY LIFE

On the contrary, women with family responsibilities need support for their many roles. It is natural that women in their prime child-bearing years will work fewer hours; the problem is that the lost time is always held against them. The early evidence is that if a woman takes a leave, or chooses part-time work for awhile, her advancement thereafter is permanently affected by attitudes among her co-workers about her perceived lack of commitment.

Women need not be dropouts. Law firms must learn to accommodate family responsibilities, not by relegating women to second class citizenship on the "mommy track," but by allowing realistic work schedules and advancement opportunities for parents who want to take leaves or cut back their hours for a time. Studies have shown that when support is provided, women will be just as productive as men once their children reach 10 years of age.

The evidence is telling: the firm that says it advances women with children but has no such women in its partnership ranks is indulging in empty rhetoric. Similarly, if the firm says it has a paternity policy, it should examine how many male partners have actually taken advantage of it, and how many of those male attorneys who have taken such leaves remain at the firm.

Sound employment practices prove that the firm knows that the investment in its human capital is its most important asset. Sound practices encourage loyalty, diminish costly turnover, and provide the base for future firm growth. The forward-looking firm will establish policies for part-time work and parental leave and will ensure that the policies are implemented.

A POLICY ON SEXUAL HARASSMENT

One aspect of employment practices that has received significant attention recently is sexual harassment, and for good reason. While sexual harassment can rise to illegality, objectionable conduct need not amount to a "hostile environment" actionable under Title VII of the 1964 Civil Rights Act in order to be bad management. Simply put, many women feel unwelcome in the locker-room atmosphere of many law firms. Camaraderie built on that type of interaction excludes women.

Therefore, a well-managed firm must have a written sexual harassment policy with an adequate complaint and investigation procedure. The firm must ensure that the policy is publicized and enforced, and must train its attorneys and its staff to recognize sexual harassment and report it no matter who the perpetrator.

Many firms, recognizing that it is easier to mentor people who look like those already in the organization, are now striving to change their past employment practices in order consciously to develop women and minority lawyers. These firms have begun formal mentoring programs, patterned on those established in industry. Management trainers who specialize in diversity training also are available.

WOMEN AS MENTORS

Law firm leaders should be aware that women will need special support to function effectively as mentors. In order to be a good mentor, it helps to have been well mentored, yet many women have not been. Tips from others about effective strategies are imperative. Moreover, some strategies must be changed. For example, what works when a man is the mentor may not apply when a woman has the superior position. While men are predisposed to respect other men in the hierarchy, women do not fit into that hierarchy. Women in all areas of the profession—from the bench to the classroom to the courtroom—report that respect from younger men is not automatic; they have to earn it.

If law firms really mean to include women in mentoring, they must recognize that diversity is a strength. Indeed, in order to have a truly collaborative practice, a firm needs to have diverse viewpoints. Firms must develop programs to encourage women and to show them in a positive light. Firms must also ensure that women are involved in law firm management—not just as window dressing but as full-fledged participants.

As more women enter the practice, firm cultures will inevitably change, but the process will take many years. In the meantime, if you are a woman in a law firm or a law department, remember to look out for the woman who is your junior. If you had a mentor, you know how important it was; if you did not, you can rectify that problem for others.

Creating a growing pool of women lawyers will also rectify the burnout that many "first" lawyers feel; they have been asked to do so much that they need to be able to turn over the responsibilities for awhile to others who are fresher.

FINDING A MENTOR

A young woman lawyer seeking a mentor needs to evaluate carefully the firms she considers. If you are interviewing, ask questions designed to learn whether mentoring is valued. Do lawyers record time spent in mentoring or training? Does mentoring count positively for the partners who do it? How is work distributed to associates and how is their work evaluated? Are reviews conducted without a "paper trail?" Find out who is in charge of the firm's training program—what is taught and by whom.

Ask also how many women partners there are; how senior they are; whether any of them serves on the management committee; how many have children; and whether the firm's policies accommodate parenting. Then ask the women lawyers how they help each other to advance; are there formal programs or a buddy system? Find out how many women have left the firm over the last few years. Contact a few and see why they left.

Don't be overly influenced by starting salaries. Higher salaries encourage firms to expect young associates to perform at 100% efficiency immediately with no allowance for learning time. There is no such thing as a free lunch—high starting salaries drive the firm's overhead, requiring all lawyers to work harder so the partners will make the same profits as before. You may have to give up something to get an atmosphere where training is important.

Once you decide to join a firm, make it your business to get as much as you can out of every experience. Learn how to be a self starter and to take responsibility for developing your career. Don't wait for partners and senior associates to offer you projects or assign you to cases; seek out those who are reputedly good trainers and ask for work. Don't be too afraid or too proud to ask for help. Besides, phrased the right way, it can be flattering to the person you ask. Develop some special skills and offer them to other lawyers—become the office expert on federal court removal, for example. And once you have accumulated some experience, remember to help others behind you.

If you find yourself shut out of interesting law firm practice, consider joining the district attorney or public defender's office. You can gain valuable trial experience that is unavailable in most private law firms, and later use the experience to come into a firm at a higher level if you wish.

If you begin in solo practice, there are mentors available. Join a bar association in your practice area. If you don't know what you want to specialize in, become active in the young lawyers section of the local bar, the ABA's Young Lawyers' Division, or one of the American Inns of Court. Many specialty bar associations have set up mentor programs. If your bar association does not have one, help set one up.

THE MESSAGE TO EMPLOYERS

We must revive mentoring for the long-term health of our law firms and the legal profession. The values of our profession are passed down by the more senior members to the junior. A firm's leaders must demonstrate that mentoring is important to them and to the firm. They must reward firm loyalty and those who take the long view.

Moreover, firms must broaden the mentoring networks to reach those who have been historically excluded, not only because it is just, but also because both private and public clients are themselves becoming more diverse and becoming likely to seek out firms that have diverse ranks. Firms must recognize the inequities they have allowed to exist and deal with them honestly. This examination in turn will force the comprehensive alteration of attitudes and policies concerning the composition of the firm. A salutary end product would be greater openness to diversity and recognition of the asset it represents.

Mentoring will not only ensure that our lawyers are well trained, but will restore to our practice much of the enjoyment which has been disappearing. We owe it to the future generations of lawyers, and to ourselves.

HOW TO BE A MENTOR

Some Helpful Steps:

- set aside time and be available; it takes time to be a good mentor

- be honest; talk about the bad as well as the good, but praise in public and criticize in private, as the saying goes

- be nonjudgmental and accepting; encourage people to ask for help and to bring up their concerns and mistakes; it's okay not to know the answers; we all make mistakes; it's how we handle them that counts

- work on a case together

- take your mentee along to the oral argument, the deposition, the trial and let her bill her time; write it off if necessary or develop a special time billing category for junior lawyers to use when accompanying a more senior lawyer

- don't hoard your work; delegate the work you can, then follow up to make sure it's done properly

- give recognition to junior lawyers who help you in your cases and in your bar work

- reach out to mentor someone who doesn't look like you

- choose a mentee based on who needs you, not on who is likely to succeed

- play together; do things together out of the office

- pass on what you know

- pass on your business, social, and bar contacts

(Continued)

- it is more helpful to teach problem solving than it is to give the answer—teach a person to fish instead of fishing for her

- being a mentor is an act of generosity—it can cure your feelings of dissatisfaction about your law practice

- you can change the culture of your office to make mentoring a valued activity by setting up systems to encourage and reward mentoring

- you can't be all things to all people. Some men won't feel comfortable enough with you to allow you to mentor them and some women won't want you—or any other woman—as a mentor; face the fact that there are some people who are better off being mentored by others; just help the ones you can

- you can't do it all. The mentee must take responsibility for her own development and career path

- don't give up. Take the long view; people will leave your firm and even leave the practice of law; nevertheless, their experience can be enriched by having had you as a mentor

HOW TO BE A "GOOD" MENTEE

- offer to work on cases that sound interesting to you

- learn how work is passed out in your office; what informal networks are there?

- learn how and whom to ask for help

- offer to help a more senior lawyer—that person will be pleased to get assistance

- develop special skills; become the office expert in something

(Continued)

- take responsibility for the development of your own career; pay attention to the practical experience that others are getting and ask to get it if you are not

- attend as many CLE programs as you can

- develop a specialty in a growing area of the practice; become known for something

- make yourself as available to work on projects as you can

- say "thank you," particularly by being a mentor to someone behind you

- it helps to get a mentor in your office, but if you can't, then look outside it

- don't just look for one person; many mentors is even better.

CHAPTER 14

Grabbing the Brass Ring: Making Partner At a Large Firm

by
D. JEAN VETA

D. JEAN VETA

D. Jean Veta, is a partner at Covington & Burling in Washington, DC. Her practice focuses on the representation of financial institutions and their officers and directors in litigation and regulatory enforcement matters. Most recently, Ms. Veta has represented financial institutions in lending discrimination cases brought by the Department of Justice and/or the bank regulatory agencies. She also represents financial institutions and their officers and directors in formal regulatory investigations, civil enforcement actions, criminal investigations, grand jury proceedings, and related civil and governmental litigation.

Born and raised in Cheyenne, Wyoming, Ms. Veta was graduated from Tulane Law School, Magna Cum Laude and Order of the Coif. While at Tulane, Ms. Veta was elected the first woman Editor-in-Chief, since World War II, of the *Tulane Law Review*. (She was informed that all of the "real" students were off fighting the war when her predecessor in the 1940s was elected.) Following law school, Ms. Veta served as a law clerk to the Honorable Harold H. Greene of the United States District Court for the District of Columbia. She then joined Covington & Burling and became a partner in 1989.

When asked about the role of women in the legal profession, Ms. Veta noted that although great progress has been made, there is still work to be done. "Having gained entry into the profession," she said, "we must now focus on helping women advance — within their law firms, in representing major clients, and in increasing our numbers on the bench."

In addition to her regular practice, Ms. Veta has been active, on a *pro bono* basis, in litigating women's rights issues. She now serves as the partner in charge (representing the National Organization for Women, Planned Parenthood of Metropolitan Washington, D.C., Inc., and others) in three separate clinic access cases, including *Bray v. Alexandria Women's Health Clinic*. Ms. Veta also has been active in litigating domestic violence cases, including seeking to establish new tort remedies for victims of domestic abuse.

Ms. Veta has a long history of involvement in the American Bar Association Litigation Section. In addition to serving as Co-Chair of the Second Annual Conference on the Woman Advocate, she serves as the Litigation Section's Director of Division VI (The Profession). Ms. Veta is a frequent speaker in continuing education seminars on topics related to litigation and financial institutions regulatory issues. She also serves on the Board of Directors of Beth El House, Inc., a not-for-profit organization providing transitional housing for formerly single-parent, homeless families.

As to the future role of women in the profession, Ms. Veta is optimistic and looks forward to the day when women, as often as men, are able to grab the brass ring.

CHAPTER 14

Grabbing the Brass Ring: Making Partner At a Large Firm

by
D. JEAN VETA

Some might say that making partner in a large firm is like grabbing the brass ring on an old carnival merry-go-round: each involves a long shot. But there is an important distinction between the two: grabbing the brass ring entails a little skill and a lot of luck, while making partner requires a lot of skill and as much luck as you can muster. Because of the skill involved in making partner, there are some things a lawyer can do to enhance her chances.

This chapter describes what I call the ten basic principles for making partner. Because each lawyer and each law firm is different, you will need to customize my ten principles (and perhaps add some of your own). Nevertheless, the following principles represent most of the elements that are essential to a successful run at partnership.

A word of warning: even if some of these principles appear simplistic or self-evident, do not overlook them. As in many situations, people tend to get tripped up by worrying about the fine points and forgetting the basics.

1. PERFORM A SELF-ASSESSMENT

First and foremost, make sure you understand yourself. As you consider whether to embark on the long road to partnership

265

it is critical to engage in an honest self-assessment. As part of this self-assessment, evaluate your intellectual capabilities and determine whether they are well suited to the work you will be asked to perform in a large law firm. Ask yourself whether you are interested in doing this kind of work. If your goal in life is to assist criminal defendants in state court cases, you probably shouldn't be practicing law in a big corporate law firm. Also, ask if you have the disposition to work in a large law firm. If you are essentially a free spirit who is happiest working in isolation and on her own schedule, a large firm may not be for you.

Finally, ask whether you have the determination that it takes to run the partnership race. Making partner is a long process. In most big firms, it takes between six and eight years, and sometimes even longer. Moreover, a single flash of brilliance is rarely enough. Instead, you need to be committed to the long haul and to producing first-rate work on a consistent basis. I cannot think of a single partner in a large corporate firm who would describe her road to partnership as an easy one. Even in the most progressive and supportive of such firms, making partner is no picnic; it takes a lot of hard work and the determination to weather the rough times. Along the way, you will also need to demonstrate that you bring energy and a sense of engagement to the practice.

This is not to say that you cannot become a partner if you devote some time to a life outside the firm. Many large firms are becoming increasingly sensitive to family responsibilities or other outside pursuits. Yet you must be prepared to be flexible, to be highly disciplined in allocating your time, and to show a high level of commitment during your working day. In these situations, it is even more important to start out with lots of interest and determination about a long-term law firm career.

If you conclude that you are suited to large firm practice, it is important to develop a professional style that is comfortable for you. Each of us is different. What works for me, or even for most women lawyers, may not work for you. While you may need to alter your personal style in some respects to enhance your effectiveness as a lawyer, most women partners agree that, in order to succeed, you must be yourself. As soon as you try to fit into some pre-set mold, you're setting yourself up for disaster; it is difficult to be someone you're not, and you lose the unique strengths that are the essence of you.

In all events, you should reassess your situation from time to time to determine whether your professional style is working and whether your interest in a large firm practice and in making partner remains strong.

2. UNDERSTAND YOUR FIRM

Equally important is an assessment of the firm in which you are trying to become a partner. Each firm is different. What is standard operating procedure in one firm may be viewed as an outrage in another. If thoughtful analysis and considered judgment are your strengths, you may not fit well in a firm that places a high value on speed and adaptability.

Most large firms are reasonable places, and, if you are a first-rate lawyer, you are likely to become a partner. That is generally true if for no other reason than because it is in the firm's interest to keep its best lawyers. But this general rule, like all general rules, has some exceptions. For example, if the firm has decided not to continue to develop a certain practice area, and that happens to be your area of expertise, your chances of making partner are likely to be significantly reduced unless you do some substantial retooling. If you find yourself in such a situation, you need to assess realistically how likely it is that you will make partner in your current practice area, or, alternatively, whether you have the time or the inclination to establish yourself in another legal specialty before you come up for partner. Of course, if your entire firm is undergoing a major retrenchment, you may need to think about switching firms to enhance your prospects.

A second exception to the rule that "if you're good, you'll make partner" may come into play when an associate has failed irreparably in the eyes of some influential partner. It is a rare lawyer—of either gender—who can make it all the way to partnership without some misstep. Nevertheless, the seriousness of your mistakes and whether you can recover from them to preserve your partnership prospects must be realistically assessed.

If you have decided to divide your energies between the law firm and family responsibilities or other interests, be sure that your firm is receptive and is prepared to award partnership to lawyers who make that choice. Some firms are more receptive than others, although most are showing greater flexibility as time goes on.

3. DO GOOD WORK

One of the most important principles is to do good work, and to do it on every assignment. Even if the assignment appears small or inconsequential, some partner is likely to review your work product or hear about it from a senior associate. And while producing an excellent memorandum on a narrow point of law as a second year associate may not carry much weight by the time you are up for partner, you can be sure that the opposite is true: a partner will rarely forget it if you blow an assignment, even a small one.

Similarly, if a partner says "take a look at this problem and just give me something 'quick and dirty' "—don't take that instruction literally. Obviously, you cannot research and write a treatise on every issue. But you do need to spend enough time on each matter to feel comfortable that you understand the major issues involved. If you do not have enough time to look at all the issues, make sure you point this out. In providing the partner with the oral or written summary of your analysis, describe the materials you reviewed, the issues you considered, and the tentative conclusions you reached. Also it is equally, if not more, important to discuss what other sources should be reviewed and to describe any other issues that must be considered before a more definite conclusion can be reached.

Another key aspect of doing good work is to pay attention to the appearance of your work product. Again, within whatever time frame is allowed, make sure that your work product—even if it is a draft—is as polished and professional as possible.

4. DELIVER ON YOUR COMMITMENTS

Once you say you will take on a project, someone is depending on you to follow through. If you are overcommitted, it is better to say no at the outset than to agree and produce something that is less than your best. Similarly, if you encounter unexpected issues or are starting to run out of time, it is crucial to let the partner know as promptly as possible. Although no one likes to deliver bad news (especially an associate delivering such news to a partner), it is best to provide the partner with as much notice as possible.

5. FIND A GOOD SUBSTANTIVE NICHE

Some firms are still looking for generalists—someone who can do tax and real estate transactions and litigation. Other firms may make someone a partner if she has done well in several different substantive areas even though she has never found a home in any of them.

But most firms are looking for someone who is developing expertise in one or two areas and who can one day take responsibility for existing clients in that area and perhaps attract new clients as well.

In order to be one of those people, you need to find your own practice niche. If you are like most of us, you won't know what it is the minute you walk through the firm's door. For this reason, try to spend some time in a few different practice areas, assuming this is consistent with your firm's organization and expectations.

Once you have sampled several substantive areas, settle on one that is suited to you and to the firm. Because people tend to do their best while working on something they like, be sure to choose a subject that interests you.

For many lawyers, liking the people with whom they work is as important as their substantive area of practice. If this is true for you, seek out lawyers whom you enjoy and with whom you are compatible.

Finally, try to choose an area of your firm's practice that is stable or growing. The reason is obvious: you do not want to devote your energies to a specialty that will be languishing or overstaffed by the time you're up for partner.

6. TAKE RESPONSIBILITY

One of the most important criteria for making partner in most large firms is a demonstrated ability to assume responsibility. As a partner, the lawyer will be expected to manage major client matters and to do so in a way that does not create professional liability exposure for other partners in the firm. Because of this, a key mission for an associate is to increase her level of responsibility as she becomes more experienced.

There are several ways to demonstrate one's willingness and ability to assume responsibility. We have already discussed one of the best ways: doing a good job on each assignment. Producing a well-reasoned, polished work product on time is likely to increase the partner's confidence in you, and that will result in more challenging assignments.

Another way to increase your level of responsibility is to anticipate the next step in an assignment. Although you don't want to charge ahead and rack up countless hours unnecessarily, you will be surprised how often it helps to look ahead.

For example, assume you have been asked to draft a memorandum of points and authorities in support of a motion. If you are likely to be asked later to do the accompanying motion and certificate of service, don't wait to be asked. Simply draw up the accompanying papers and turn them in with your draft brief. Or, if you are unsure whether you should draw up the accompanying papers, at least volunteer to prepare them when you turn in the brief.

By using this technique, you can demonstrate that you do not need to be spoon-fed. This approach has another advantage: an associate who does only the bare minimum is unlikely to stand out; it is the associate who takes that next step who is likely to be remembered.

7. SHAPE YOUR OWN DESTINY

No one is as interested in your own success as you are. Thus, it is a mistake for an associate simply to wait in her office until a partner knocks on her door offering to groom her for partnership. Indeed, as any former associate/current partner knows, the associate who sits in her office will probably wait for a long time.

Most partners do not deliberately refrain from helping an associate in order to determine whether she can navigate the maze to partnership on her own. Rather, they are usually too engrossed in their own practices to spend much time thinking about an associate's professional development. That said, it is equally true that most partners, if approached by an associate, are more than willing to help.

For these reasons, the associate must seize the initiative in planning her career development. On a macro level, this involves a three-part process: identifying the area for which the associate is best suited based on her assessment of herself and the firm's needs (see Principles 1, 2, and 5, above); mapping out a plan for professional training and development; and, soliciting help in revising and implementing the plan from the appropriate partners, such as the partner in charge of associate assignments, the relevant department head, the partners with whom the associate works, or an informal mentor.

This macro planning is not a static, one-shot event. To the contrary, the process is ongoing, and each of these three components must be reevaluated throughout the associate's career.

An associate also can shape her own destiny on a micro level. First, solicit feedback on a regular basis. Do not wait for annual evaluations; rather, periodically ask the partners for whom you are working how you can improve, pressing for details where appropriate. If a partner suggests that you need to work on writing or oral skills, don't get defensive. Work on the area and ask for feedback along the way. Partners may be uncomfortable criticizing your work, but most will provide feedback if you ask for it.

Another way to shape your destiny is to make sure you are exposed to all of the basic elements in your practice area. For example, if you are in litigation and have spent all your time writing memos and briefs but have never taken a deposition, try to do something about it. Perhaps the easiest solution is to talk to the partner in charge of the case on which you are working. The partner may not realize that you lack deposition experience or that you are interested in taking depositions. Simply raising the issue in a forthright manner may be enough to show that you have what it takes to stand up to an opponent in a deposition. On the other hand, if the partner is unwilling or unable to give you deposition experience, don't give up! Talking to the litigation department head or the assignment partner often can lead to a new assignment where you can gain this experience. These other partners also can help by putting pressure on your direct supervisor or by giving you feedback about what you need to do to prepare yourself for your next professional step.

You also should position yourself to take on new responsibility when the opportunity presents itself. In addition to looking for assignments that offer new challenges, sign up for as many different training courses as you can. Thus, the associate who is a terrific brief writer but has no deposition experience may want to take a deposition training course. A partner is more likely to give her a shot at her first deposition if she shows her interest in doing depositions and has made the extra effort to get some training.

Similarly, volunteering for public speaking assignments—both inside and outside the firm—can better position you for oral advocacy opportunities. Among other things, speaking to groups will assist you in developing confidence and learning to think on your feet. In addition, making presentations within the firm will provide opportunities to demonstrate your skills to your colleagues, including the firm's partners.

8. CULTIVATE CLIENT CONTACTS

Every law firm depends on keeping existing clients happy and attracting new ones. Thus, a key to every associate's success is the ability to inspire confidence in the clients for whom she works and, ideally, to attract additional work to the firm.

Obviously, an associate in a large firm is unlikely to spend her days advising the chief executive officer of a Fortune 500 company on the litigation strategy for a major lawsuit. But she may be working on an assignment that requires regular contact with one of the in-house lawyers of that company. By doing good work and by developing some rapport with the in-house lawyer, the associate has created the opportunity for several positive payoffs: the in-house lawyer may report the associate's good work to the company's general counsel, who, in turn, may pass on this compliment to the supervising partner; the in-house lawyer either directly, or through the general counsel, may seek to work with the same associate on other projects; and, as both the in-house lawyer and the associate become more senior, the in-house lawyer (who has now become the general counsel of the existing client or some other company) is likely to call on the associate who created the favorable impression.

Similarly, it is never too early to begin thinking about attracting new clients. Although most large law firms do not expect their associates to be major rainmakers on day one, it is definitely a plus for any lawyer, at any level, to bring in business. Early on, each associate should consider engaging in at least some client development activities. Involvement in bar associations, writing articles for trade magazines and journals, and speaking at continuing legal education seminars are just some of the ways a lawyer can make herself known. Again, you shouldn't expect to start out as the biggest name in your field—but if you become active on a bar association committee or write an article for a legal publication, one success is likely to build on another.

9. RUN THROUGH THE FINISH LINE

Perhaps the best advice I ever received came from two newly-made partners in a New York law firm when I was just months away from being considered for partnership. They said, "Make sure you run through the finish line."

After years of hard work, dedication, and commitment, you may find yourself fairly well situated for becoming a partner. If this is the case, don't slow down! There are too many horror stories of promising senior associates who self-destruct in the year or two before the partnership decision. The most common reasons are that the associate gets too cocky, gets sloppy on an assignment, stops making that extra effort, or stops developing in important areas.

No one can guarantee against a disaster, but you can minimize the risks. When you are a senior associate in a relatively strong position for partnership, by definition, you have found a strategy that works for you. Make sure you stick to your strategy, continuing to demonstrate and enhance the qualities that have gotten you this far. (In fact, continuing to demonstrate these qualities is important for a partner, too, but that is the subject of another chapter.)

10. KEEP YOUR PERSPECTIVE

Making partner in a large law firm is one of most satisfying moments in a lawyer's professional life. That said, keep in mind that this is only one of a number of roads to success. Countless lawyers, including some who began their careers at big firms, now are general counsels of successful corporations, highly respected legal scholars, or key players in government. If you don't make partner, keep it in perspective: being a partner in a large law firm is certainly an attractive career path (and it beats the heck out of being an associate), but it is only one of many roads to professional success.

* * *

A final word to those of you who are still interested in making partner at a large firm: if you keep these ten principles in mind (and are blessed with a little luck), perhaps you, too, will be able to grab the brass ring.

Section III

The Practice:
We're On Our Way

CHAPTER 15

Canaries in a Coal Mine or Reflections Upon Life in a Large Law Firm

by
JUDITH GRACCHUS

JUDITH GRACCHUS

As her name suggests, Judith Gracchus is a literary creation. Her name alludes to the biblical heroine who beheaded her male enemy and to the figure who sought to establish democratic reforms in ancient Rome. To bring the message of her story home, Judith has been given a particularized background: she is Jewish, middle-aged, a Holocaust survivor, a graduate of leading schools, a wife, and the mother of three children.

Her career path has also been sketched with specific details: after earning her J.D., Judith worked in a district attorney's office, and then accepted an offer to join a large law firm. In both positions, Judith was a path breaker, one of the first women to appear on the scene. Her experience at both jobs is disturbingly typical. She suffers insult, condescension, ridicule, and a variety of professional slights from many of the male lawyers she encounters, as well as betrayal by a female colleague with political motives.

Judith's tale is written from the heart. Her candid account of what happened to her is certain to outrage readers; but it is just as certain to teach and to inspire. For Judith is an intrepid survivor, a person of passion and of faith in the American process and in the ideal of lawyer as gadfly and righter of wrongs. She takes solace in poetry and in the domestic pleasures that only a loving family life can provide.

Judith's narrative has an archytypal thrust, and this is by design. For Judith might have had a number of different backgrounds and could have proceeded through a variety of legal career tracks, without any significant change in her spiritual turmoil and professional struggle. The men she encounters at work, "The Master of the Universe," " The Firm Wit," " The Weather Vane" and others, will all ring familiar in the memory and experience of her readers who are woman lawyers.

Judith, in sum, is a bit of every woman lawyer, those whose real-life tales are told in the other chapters of this book, and those who continue to grapple with sexism and discrimination in law offices throughout the country on a daily basis. Judith brings honor to our struggle; so do they.

CHAPTER 15

Canaries in a Coal Mine or Reflections Upon Life in a Large Law Firm

by
JUDITH GRACCHUS

Five years ago, as I approached my fiftieth birthday, the national law firm where I had spent the last 13 years, 6 years as an associate and 7 as a litigation partner, suggested an amicable and uncontested divorce.

For years I had fretted: "I feel like Cinderella's wicked stepsisters in the Grimm's version of the fairy tale. I have cut off my toes to fit the glass slipper. My feet are sore and bleeding. But the bloody slipper still doesn't fit."

My friends, tired of my complaints, would skeptically predict: "You'll never leave, Judith."

For years they were right. The seeming security of the steady income and the prestige which, hypocritically, I complained of, were powerful inducements to inertia.

As I brushed my teeth in the mornings I would hiss at my reflection: "Coward! Before you know it, you will be 55, 60, 65. Then it will be too late, too late, too late."

"You sure are tense," I would hear from my husband of 28 years or my 17-year-old-daughter, the only child of our three still at home.

---

1. Any resemblance to persons, living or dead, is purely coincidental.

''I'm not tense!'' I would snap back between tightly clenched teeth.

In early February of 1989, on the occasion of partners' annual reviews, the Management Committee told me that The Firm was prepared to be generous if I were to leave quickly and quietly. ''Take all the time you need to find something else,'' I was told, ''But the sooner you leave, the more you'll get.''

THE DIVORCE IS FINAL

Two months later I was gone. I rented space from a plaintiff's class action law firm and began to practice law in my own name. My ''divorce'' from The Firm, although unusual at the time, was a harbinger of things to come. The Ponzi scheme premise upon which the large national/international law firms had boomed in the 1970's and 1980's could not and did not persist into the 1990's. Women and minorities were but canaries in the coal mine. They died of the noxious fumes first. But they would not be the only ones to go.

Based on the untenable premise of ever-expanding legal work and an ever-enlarging base of young associates and mid-level partners actively discouraged from independence, the expansion could not continue in the exponential way it had in the past. When the inevitable contraction came, it would crush most with it. The only survivors would be those who had managed to clamber to the top, from which vantage point they could greedily and quickly rake in the high-six and low-seven figure salaries. For they knew full well that one day, all too soon, they would be as expendable as those who they had ''expended'' in their climb.

''They'll have to compensate for your leaving by appointing the first woman partner to the Executive Committee,'' a friend in The Firm accurately predicted. Never married, childless, and responsible for the legal work done for a client with substantial annual billings, the first woman partner was in fact appointed to the Executive Committee within a month of my departure. It was a signal to the other canaries. ''No need to fear. No noxious gas here. Keep on chirping.''

My partnership in The Firm was the envy of all who knew me casually. Yet within two weeks of joining The Firm as an associate out of the District Attorney's Office, I had said to myself: ''This was a big mistake.''

What was it about me that made the relationship between me and The Firm so improbable? Everything. A survivor from the Holocaust, I was an intellectual and a populist. Educated in the most prestigious of schools, I had a Ph.D before I went on to get a J.D. Upon getting my law degree, I did the then unthinkable by joining the DA's Office, a macho bastion if there ever was one. In the early 1970's I was one of the smallest of the handful of women in The Office. Occasionally a police officer would take me for Italian and would ask: ''What's a nice girl like you doing married to a Jew?''

AN ETHOS BASED ON DISINTEREST AND FEAR

The Firm had so quickly become painful, and yet tolerably painful. It was a hierarchical structure. Glacially cold. It maintained a social order where each person seemed to fear every other. The Firm's ethos was predicated on distrust and fear beneath a deceptive veneer of blandness. Each new crop of young associates was hand picked by those who had just preceded them. Thus each new crop, a replica of the preceding one, was nonetheless a greyer, grimmer, more humorless version thereof. In such manner did the pickers protect themselves from excessive competition from the picked.

The Firm's ethos was not exactly my cup of tea. Nor was defending large corporations my idea of a life well spent, regardless of the financial rewards. As for jokes about gas ovens, with which one old geezer actually greeted my arrival at The Firm, these were not my idea of what was funny. Nonetheless, stupidly tenacious, I had stayed on for 13 years. ''Was it for this that I went to law school?'' I would ask myself in perplexity and disbelief, unable to imagine better alternatives. Was it for this that I sought out training as a jury trial lawyer in the DA's office?

The Firm's recruitment call came one day when I, then a district attorney, was sitting at my windowless desk in the big, ornate

Criminal Court building whose courtrooms have 20-foot ceilings, old wooden furniture and, in those days, no air conditioning during the sweltering summers. Trying a criminal case in that old building was the purest of theater on the grandest of stages. The masters would roll off cadences from Shakespeare and the bible when they addressed a jury. It was hardly an apprenticeship for which The Firm had any respect or use. But for the prestigious schools I had been to and superlative grades I had earned there (only in The Law does one's pedigree continue to matter years later), The Firm would never have dreamt of hiring me.

"Well are you ready to stop playing games and join the real legal world?" I was asked.

AN OFFER I COULDN'T REFUSE

After weeks of agonizing over the decision and perversely discounting other options as no better, I accepted The Firm's offer. The street smarts and the sense of what persuades a fact finder that I had gained in the DA's office would stand me in good stead when I finally went on my own. In my naivete, I assumed that they would be recognized at The Firm and therefore put to good use. It was not to be.

Far from seeking out those with proven trial ability, The Firm assigned some of its largest cases to a senior partner who had handled rate cases had never tried any case to a jury, not even a fender bender or a misdemeanor. Such paltry matters were far beneath his soaring intellect. His intellectual arrogance was known to me from my days in the DA's Office. He once caused a brief to be filed in the supreme court of the state. It argued that since the state had a monopoly on divorce, it was obliged to provide the indigent with free counsel in such matters. I caused the case to be dismissed on the grounds that the lawyer handling it—that same senior partner—had forgotten to demonstrate in the trial court that his client was in fact indigent.

This lawyer extraordinaire went on to make jurisprudential history when the jury in a case he was trying for The Firm handed down against his client the largest civil judgment ever awarded at that time. The Firm Wit had concluded long before: "He is the Titanic in search of an iceberg."

We wondered why the client had tolerated The Titanic as its lead trial counsel. The explanation was that The Titanic's mentor, The Senior Partner, had become General Counsel for the client while retaining his position in The Firm. How the conflict was tolerated we wondered with no answer.

The Titanic's arrogance, which was as boundless as his trial courtroom inexperience was bottomless, had many manifestations. One was his newly decorated office. It was a study in green marble and mirrors. "It's a bloody bordello," the Firm Wit would proclaim, his disdain echoing down The Firm's conservative white halls edged in dark wood trim.

SHRIMP AND FRENCH WINE AT $100 A BOTTLE

Even the Titanic's arrogance, although seemingly boundless, was not as great as his insatiable gluttony. He had a taste for large bowls of shrimp at midnight, eaten as he quaffed French wines at $100 plus a bottle—on the client's tab—in hotel suites where he and his legal "team" would hole up to work.

We didn't know the Titanic's income—the draws of the partners were a well-kept secret—but we surmised that he had become a very wealthy man. All his living expenses went on the client's tab, since he worked away from home base. Nor were we surprised when the report would go through The Firm that he could not be reached for a few weeks because he was going on his annual pilgrimage to a fat farm.

One of the Titanic's lieutenants who picked up the out-of-town habit developed it into a fine art form. His home base office secretary would say he was in an outpost office. His outpost office secretary said he was in the home base office. Neither was permitted to give out his telephone number.

As for the Titanic, he would gather his team, referred to as The God Squad, for what were dubbed "strategy sessions" held away from the home base office to work on The Big Case. No work was ever done, as twenty men shot the breeze for a day or two or three to the tune of say $75,000 for each such session. A mere trifle were such numbers for the client.

PENETRATING THE INNER SANCTUM

Once I was invited into the inner sanctum. I flew to a distant city where the boys were holed up, a packet of pre-trial motions which I had prepared single-handedly in my brief case. These I handed to The Titanic with a proud flourish. The uncomfortable surprise on The Titanic's face informed me that the assignment had been made not with any expectation that I would be able to fulfill it. The work was never read. The motions were never used. Instead the work was divided among The God Squad to be redone.

As the meeting progressed, I found myself increasingly disgusted. Never a poker player, my face showed my distaste. I pulled my chair further and further back from the inner circle, arms akimbo. Syncophantically, the boys flattered their leader.

"Anything you say . . ."

"Whatever you think best . . ."

"You are so smart . . ."

Small wonder I was never invited back to join the boys in their ritual adoration of The Titanic in his role of Master of the Universe. Small wonder no woman lasted on that team for long. A female presence ever exposed that male bonding ritual, to the men's discomfort.

As the trial date for The Big Case neared, I became fast friends with an in-house lawyer from the client's legal department, assigned to the trial team as a Two-Fer—she was both a female and an Afro-American—and thus was supposed to pacify the prospective jury.

CONFRONTING THE MASTER OF THE UNIVERSE

One Sunday we resolved to beard the Master of the Universe in his den, a nearby hotel. Apparently he found it unacceptable to work at the office despite the avilable conference rooms. Was it because no room service was available—at least not a service that would provide bowls of shrimp and the French wines? Was he reluctant to have such fare catered into the office lest The Office Wit go down the halls proclaiming an Roman orgy to be in the making? Or was he reluctant to flaunt his sybaritic luxury before the abstentious Senior Partner who might have found his behavior unseemly?

Gathering courage from one another we said, "You can't go to trial without testing your theories in focus group sessions of people comparable to your potential jury. Your circle of young associates and partners is not a valid sounding board."

"We've just been rehearsing your theories over brunch with Judith's 15-year-old son," seconded the in-house lawyer. He alternated between bafflement and hooting laughter.

"You gals have been smoking something." We were dismissed with a wave of the masterful hand.

Before we knew it, the M of the U had hired a jury consultant, a bearded 60-year-old Radical who paraded through the halls of The Firm in torn tee-shirt and bare feet. The M of the U loved to see himself as a Radical, and the Bare-Footed Wonder was confirmation thereof. After the trial, the boys in The God Squad covered their leader's rear by announcing that The Bearded Wonder had been my idea. Right!

When the jury handed out its comeuppance to the M of the U and his boys, there were many in The Firm who couldn't hide their delight.

THE DISASTER REVEALED AS A MASTER STROKE

The boys, however, explained to the other benighted ones that the disaster was in fact a master stroke planned by The Senior Partner. The decision would have to be appealed, they argued, leading to more billings. The appeal would be argued by The Senior Partner, they said, it being Firm dogma that The Senior Partner walked on water. The case would be reversed on appeal and remanded for a new trial on damages, leading to more billings. The Senior Partner would restore The Firm's good name and retain the grateful client.

The rationalizing optimists were right. The billions in damages were reduced to a piffling trifle for the client, $100,000,000. The Firm's honor was restored. The grateful client loyally stood by The Firm. The continuation of the hefty annual billings was assured.

That victory on the retrial of the damage issue, however, was won not by the M of the U or The Senior Partner, but by a stony, seemingly homespun Minnesota farm boy. Some farm boy! An aghast partner's wife reported that at Christmas time he had kissed her on the lips, sticking his tongue into her mouth. She hadn't the slightest doubt that it was his way of showing his contempt not his desire. Some country lawyer!

And guess what. Numerous focus group sessions were conducted before the retrial. Another surprise: it wasn't The Bare Footed, Tee-Shirted, Bearded, Old Radical Wonder who was the jury consultant.

While The Senior Partner was away for a short time, The Minnesota Farm Boy ran The Firm. He didn't have a chance to retain that position in a *mano a mano* with The Senior Partner when that one returned to take his rightful place within The Firm's hierarchy from his stint as General Counsel of The Major Client. No one was ever as straight a shooter as The Senior Partner. He never shot you in the back. He shot you right between the eyes. And he never missed.

As for the M of the U, he continued at The Firm for at least five years after his encounter with destiny. One day I was called to consult about a conflict of interest he had created for The Firm. Since The Firm never saw a conflict that couldn't be waived or disposed of by opting for the more powerful partner's client, I knew his demise was being plotted. He left shortly thereafter without fanfare to set up a litigation boutique, fed business by The Firm in continuing gratitude for all those years of multi-million dollar billings.

WHERE THE PARTNERS GO

Had he survived, he might have made his way to the "Dead Partners' Floor." That was where The Firm, during the gentlemanly pre 1990's years, put those who were out of power but nonetheless permitted to stay on. Excess office space, on a separate floor, housed "The Dead Partners," the term used at the Firm to describe them. They shared one receptionist/secretary, who answered their phones and typed an occasional letter so that the outside world would not know they were dead.

As for me, I should have known early on that this floor would not be my destiny. For years, I was told that I could not flourish, much less survive, unless I found myself a "niche."

"I don't want to be a niche player," I would say. "I am by nature and training and temperament a generalist."

"You'll never survive," was the verdict.

But I believed that in the greater evolutionary scheme of things all niche players die out when the climate changes or when the ecology shifts. Only the generalist, the omnivore, is the true survivor. So it proved to be.

Now don't get me wrong. I didn't have any illusions that someone with my sex and my ever unadoring stance would ever be permitted by The Firm to do much in a courtroom. Unless of course I was assigned to the small and "unwinnable" cases in the expectation that I would take the fall. "You did what?!" I was asked in disbelief by The Weather Vane when I reported that a case had been won rather than lost. The Weather Vane was the last of my three bosses, except they were not known as bosses, but as "Group Heads." He was so called because, as The Firm Wit explained, he could always be relied upon to signal which way the wind was blowing.

THE REFRAIN OF CRITICISM BEGINS

Over time a certain refrain, partly accurate, partly distortion, was used to label, define, and contain me.

"Too flamboyant" was one Firm verdict. "Boy, if I'm flamboyant, The M of the U must be a flammer," I would quip.

"Not a team player," was another conclusion. Years later I understood that the term "team player" was used to dismiss anyone who was unwilling to abide by the unspoken rules: Never question. Never expose. Never challenge.

"Can't write." That was the manner in which my legal ability was put down. Never mind that I had published more than anyone else in The Firm except for academics brought in for their scholarship. Never mind that judges often thanked me for the clarity of my briefs. The Firm had decreed that I couldn't write. It was their way of casting people into outer darkness legally. Since they had determined that I was to be cast out, it followed as night does unto the day that I couldn't write.

Besides, humiliation can only be effective if directed at those aspects of the self that give one pride. Had they said, "Not much of a diplomat," they would have been accurate indeed, and I wouldn't have been hurt. Or had they said: "Doesn't tolerate fools gladly," I would have said. "Right you are." Where is the humiliation in that? The surest way of controlling what seems alien and dangerous is through ostracism and humiliation. At this art the Firm leaders were past masters and I was far from their only victim.

The Firm had three women partners when I joined it in the mid-70's. In that respect The Firm was exceptional. Of course, all three were in the Probate Group. One had been with a boutique firm that merged into The Firm in one of the first megamergers in an industry that would become rife with them. She was asked to leave immediately. Another who had been with The Firm since the late 60's was eased out fifteen years later.

THE LADY IS HELL ON WHEELS

The third, Annabel Spunk, was hell on wheels: the toughest and best trial lawyer of the whole Firm. She had been allowed in during World War II when the young lawyers had gone off to battle and there weren't enough young men around to do the legal work. She was still there in the 1980's, although she earned less than most of the associates, despite her control of many important clients and her legal victories. For years The Management Committee chaffed about Annabel, wanting to put her out to pasture. She too was deemed "Too flamboyant." The Senior Partner protected her, but not to the point of assuring her a draw equal to her ability or her stable of clients or to that of her far less competent male contemporaries.

THE LAW FIRM AS MEDIEVAL FIEFDOM

The Firm was divided into working "Groups," each lead by a "Head." The Groups corresponded to a medieval fiefdom. The Group Head was the liege lord of the knights (partners) and squires (associates); he handed out work to the most loyal, not the most able. The Group Heads in turn owed their allegiance to other liege lords, in elaborate patterns of loyalty that did not correspond to organizational charts. Most of their clients were inherited from their liege lords. Most clients were cultivated over the years and passed from knight to squire.

The Firm was not entrepreneurial; far from it. Entrepreneurial tendencies would have threatened the Firm's carefully controlled structure. They would have transformed the oligarchical hierarchy into something far less controllable. Only a few entrepreneurial partners, generally Jewish, were tolerated, each for his respective political savvy and political contacts. They were the fixers. They did the jobs which were beneath the farm boys.

I was initially assigned to the group of a man instrumental in recruiting me to join The Firm.

"He has the fascination of a boa constrictor for a mongoose," one of my law school buddies had said upon meeting him on campus during the recruiting season.

THE BOA CONSTRICTOR IS MESMERIZING

For years I, like so many in his Group, was mesmerized by this Boa Constrictor. His neurotic worry drove us nuts. Yet, in the larger scheme of things he was better than the others. Determined to build an Empire, he was the only one who in so doing was willing to develop the younger lawyers who worked for him or to give women a break. Fearful of being swallowed whole, I tried to keep my distance, while nonetheless working for him.

He was an alumnus from my law school. There he had almost flunked out and thus was smitten by my grade point average. Even years after he would say in disbelief: "An A average. She had an A average! What a transcript!" He let me loose to discover the most complex of business fraud cases, knowing how well I could interview witnesses, take depositions, and wallow through documents, which spoke to me like clues did to Sherlock Holmes.

Yet The Boa Constrictor was consumed with worry. He would ask, "What will you do if *x* happens in the courtroom?" His worry was the legal equivalent of the imminent return of the comet that once upon a time had purportedly put an end to the Age of the Dinosaurs and set a little scurrying primate on its evolutionary path to Homo Sapiens.

"Punt," I would glibly answer. He would suck in his breath and turn away, speechless, in horror over my cavalier attitude.

"If I continue to work for him, I'll never see the inside of a courtroom again," I moaned to another woman associate who had joined The Firm a year ahead of me. "Or if I ever do, I'll be consumed with his neurotic worry and fear."

ADVICE TO "JUMP SHIP"

"Jump ship," she counselled. Far more adept politically than I, she wanted me out of the way as a potential rival for partnership slots she knew would not be numerous for women. Changing groups meant that you lost one liege lord and had to convince another that you were worthy of being backed for partnership.

"Do you really think I should," I asked. "How should I go about doing it? Perhaps I should tell the Group Head that I'll lose all my guts and panache if I let him make me as neurotically fearful of the courtroom as he is."

"Goodness, Judith. You can't do that."

"Well in many ways I am sure he wishes me well and would help me. After all he recruited me to this place."

"Don't be silly, Judith. You'll never get anywhere in his group. The Head will look out for the two young male associates before he looks out for you. There isn't room to make all three of you partners. Now The Big Case needs bodies. Go offer them your services."

"But they eat women alive. I'd be going from the frying pan into the fire. No woman lasts long in The God Squad."

"But Judith, you aren't like those other women; they were just young girls. You'll be showing them that you are a team player. You'll be showing them that you are willing to volunteer for hard labor.

"Should I ask the Group Head for his help and blessing?" I asked Ms. Politically Adept.

"Goodness, no, Judith. He'll be offended. The Head of The God Squad is in the office this Saturday. Go and volunteer to him. Let them work out the internal group transfer between them."

"You really think I should?" I asked.

"Believe me," she counselled sagely. "That's the way to handle a politically sensitive impasse."

THE SLENDER REED OF SISTERHOOD

Ever impulsive, I promptly did as she advised. Why leave for tomorrow what can be done today? Thereafter the grin never left her face when she saw me. Soon I realized I had lost the Boa Constrictor as a protector. And that Ms. Politically Adept had eliminated me as the rival she believed stood in her way. How slender was the reed of "sisterhood" in this large institution where getting ahead lay over someone else's prone body.

Over the years my feelings of inner corrosion grew.

Once I complained that it was unethical to bill one client for the unnecessary legal work being done on behalf of another under an indemnity agreement. I received a withering look of scorn and the tightly spat-out comment: "Stop being so emotional, Judith." The next day the case was assigned to a less emotional male.

Years before I had walked to the Annual Firm Christmas Dinner with the partner who had flung me off the case to protect his indemnified client. He muttered as we walked: "Have to remember not to have more than one drink. Can't let my guard down around the barracudas." Today the then Baby Barracuda has clawed his way to the role of Top Barracuda. He is a masterly in-fighter. And he never had one drink too many or let his guard down, within The Firm. When he let his pants down outside The Firm, The Firm covered for him in his divorce with his irate wife, taken on in Law School, discarded after his climb.

Early in my time at The Firm while the Barracuda was still a mere baby, he asked to see my time sheets.

"You're billing way too little time for the work you've done," he advised.

"But that's all the time it took me to do the work," I said.

"That's hardly the point," he explained.

There were other questions.

A DIVORCE TAILORED TO SATISFY THE FIRM

"Do you think one can get ahead at The Firm if one is divorced?" The Baby Barracuda asked me. For years there were bets about when he would ditch the wife he had acquired while in law school. When he did, it was spectacular.

"I have brain cancer," he said to explain his Christmas absences with his paramour and new baby. He must have meant it figuratively. His wife thought he meant it literally. When he remarried, the entire outpost office he then headed on his grooming to the top was invited to the wedding.

Meanwhile, I would sit, amazed, at partner meetings, while the M of the U calculated the earnings to the Firm's bottom line from the legal work The God Squad would be doing on The Big Case.

"The Big Case can readily absorb 40 associates at an average hourly rate of $150 an hour and 7 full-time partners at the average rate of $200 an hour times an average annual billing of 2,000 hours for the next 6 years," he explained, working out the math on the blackboard. The Senior Partner, who simultaneously was

General Counsel of the Client, nodded his head in happy agreement. Conflict of interest? What conflict of interest?

"How can we bill so much for worthless work?" I asked The Barracuda. "Do you know what the client's net income is?" he asked by way of reply. "Our billings are totally lost in that number. It is a mere trifle."

I never fit into The Firm. Initially, I, an Outsider, must have wanted very much to be part of The Establishment which The Firm represented. Increasingly, I didn't want to fit into The Firm or The Establishment. Increasingly, I would gag with nausea. The populist in me wanted to throw stones. Yet I did not leave. Inertia, fear of the uncertain, want of any better firm—all these kept me tied to what I did not respect and increasingly could not abide.

THE CASE THAT CAUSED THE BREAK-UP

The occasion for my break with The Firm arose out of my representation of an indigent defendant. It was the only way to keep myself in fighting trim and the only means of getting into the federal courts with case responsibility.

I represented Mike Brown, the brother of the lead defendant Jack Brown. The Brown case was more than an ordinary drug distribution conspiracy, because Jack had been tape recorded boasting that he had beaten a murder rap by bribing a state court judge. Jack was absent from the table where seven other defendants sat because the trial judge had released him from The Detention Center to visit his lawyer without the requisite escort of federal marshals. One day Jack tied up his lawyer with—a necktie!—and disappeared.

The trial judge had taken several guilty pleas from those who the evidence seemed to suggest were among the more culpable, including the insider who wore the wire that made hundreds of tape recordings for the federal authorities. Left to be tried were those who had less information to barter. My client, Jack's brother, out of a misplaced sense of family loyalty, refused to squeal. It was hard for me to see that Mike was any more culpable than Mama Brown, who had been given a total pass by the prosecutors.

In fact, on some of the tapes Mike seemed to be the voice of reason, taking guns away from his brother, although he was charged with supplying his brother with guns.

NICKNAMES THAT ANGER THE JUDGE

Some of the defendants had nicknames. James Carter also known as The Weasel. William Paterson a/k/a Bullshit Bill.

Bullshit Bill became one of the government's star witnesses in return for a plea of guilty and a prosecutorial promise that they would recommend leniency when it came time to sentence him. "Now Bullshit Bill . . ." I began my cross examination.

"Mrs. Gracchus," warned the trial judge. "You are to call him by his proper name."

"I am Your Honor. That is the name by which he is identified in the indictment."

Some of the tapes the government had not introduced into evidence suggested that Bullshit Bill had knowledge about murders for which he had never been indicted. In cross examining him, I referred to these tapes to refresh his purportedly faulty recollection.

"You are not to refer to tapes not in evidence," commanded the trial judge.

"I do not understand the scope of Your Honor's ruling. What may I be permitted to cross examine on and what am I to avoid? May I refresh his recollection with words he spoke on a prior occasion?"

"I am not here to teach you how to be a trial attorney, Mrs. Gracchus," answered the trial judge.

Two of the other defense attorneys whispered to each other at counsel table. "He's laid the trap. Watch her step into it."

STEPPING INTO THE TRAP

Sure enough, as I persisted in my line of questioning about the murders in respect of which Bullshit Bill contended he had no recollection but that he had discussed in tape recorded conversations, the judge ruled that I was in contempt of court for violating his prohibition against. . . . To this day I am not sure what he had prohibited or why he prohibited it or why he was so angry. I thought I was just trying to expose what seemed to be a perjurer in the midst of his perjury.

When I said that I could not simultaneously represent the defendant and worry about marshalling a defense for my own contempt hearing, the contempt hearing was continued to after the trial.

The trial judge ordered the United State's Attorney's Office to prosecute the Rule to Show Cause Why Judith Gracchus Should Not Be Held in Contempt of Court. The United State's Attorney's Office declined the honor. Which left the judge to fend for himself. He undertook to write up the Rule himself, but it never issued. The matter died there.

The Circuit Court of Appeals slapped the wrists of all seven lawyers, without naming them. We submitted a brief urging that double jeopardy precluded a retrial. Retrial became a possibility when the trial judge declared a mistrial only hours after he refused a request that he do so, expressly stating, as he did so, that he was certain the jury would be able to reach a verdict. Then a note issued from the jury room on the eve of Christmas Eve. It hinted that acquittals were in the making. Whereupon the judge promptly declared a mistrial.

A RESPONSE THAT CANNOT BE CHALLENGED

When someone anonymously informed the Management Committee that I was one of the seven lawyers on the appeal, the response was immediate and unappealable. It would be advisable were I to leave The Firm.

"Let me get this straight," a friend asked in disbelief. "There were seven defense attorneys? You were appointed counsel for an indigent defendant? None of you were singled out for any criticism by name? What was the possible embarrassment to The Firm? Why did they pin a rose on you?" she asked, genuinely perplexed.

''Because it was convenient.

''Because they were just waiting for an excuse.

''Because I didn't fit in.

''Because large institutions can't afford mavericks who are not cowed.

''Because they saw my flamboyance as unpredictability.

''Because from their perspective I was a loose cannon aboard their ship.

''And they were absolutely right. If I had been in their shoes, I'd have done the same thing.

''Besides they did me a favor. I never would have left without being pushed. I just would have gotten sourer and sourer. A Veritable Lemon. I would have, finally, fitted the labels that they had pinned on me for years. I would have become the monster they liked to imagine I was.''

WHY THE FIRM DIDN'T FIT

She wanted to know why I was such a misfit at The Firm.

''Maybe because they knew I wasn't prepared to pay the price so many of them had paid. I wasn't prepared to discard my husband or to ignore my children.

''Maybe some of them even found me sexy and were uncomfortable because of that. Maybe others didn't find me sexy and were uncomfortable because of that.

''Maybe they faulted my failure to wear little blue suits and the obligation issue female tie when they were all the rage.

''Maybe they didn't like the wide brim straw hats I went in for one summer or maybe they resented the velvet and leather casques I put on every winter.

''Maybe I should have dyed my hair when it started to turn grey.

''Maybe I had the wrong name, the wrong religion, the wrong sex.

''Maybe it is the nature of the herd instinctively to expel the foreign in order to retain its own fragile sense of intactness.

"Maybe they figured I'd gotten too far already without their permission or their help.

"Maybe belt tightening days were coming, and they needed someone to throw overboard first, and I was the most expendable. It would warn others but without too great an alarm.

"Maybe if pigs had wings and fish could fly, I'd be there still."

TRUTH IS NO DEFENSE

After I left The Firm, I forewarned another woman partner that she should not be surprised if her days there were numbered. She had gotten sued for purportedly representing a client too assiduously.

"Is that true?" she confronted the then Still-Growing Barracuda, who conveyed the news to another partner I still saw, who berated me over lunch in one of his multiple clubs.

"How could you be so disloyal to The Firm?" he asked.

"But I'm not in The Firm anymore. Besides, isn't what I told her true?"

"Of course it's true," he replied.

"Well then, what's the problem?" I asked.

"You've made it harder for us to do the inevitable when the time comes."

Harder, but not impossible. Once the case settled, my prediction came true.

Sometimes I go back to The Firm, visiting friends behind closed doors, each afraid to tell the others how stymied and fearful they feel. One friend I tried to blast out of a rut of depression as apparent as the grey streak in her hair. She was a Two Fer. The only Hispanic Woman partner in The Firm. She could have her pick of jobs in the private sector or in government. But the brainwashing had worked. The Firm had her reporting to senior associates now.

She sat listless and worn out, with no faith in her abilities or her self worth.

BECOMING WHAT I SET OUT TO BE

And I felt overwhelmingly grateful that I had been asked to leave years ago. Within four years, I had leased half a floor in a small but elegant office building and had eight other attorneys affiliated with me in the practice of the law. When I am asked what I do, I answer that I have become what, initially, I set out to be: A Gadfly lawyer, a Righter of Wrongs.

I never expected such an endeavor to be particularly lucrative. But there are lots of power abusers out there. By the third year, I earned substantially more than I did my last year as a partner in The Firm. Debt free, all my growth has been paid for through cash flow.

I have won or settled cases that many other attorneys had declined to undertake because they thought they could not be won. In the process I have crossed swords with managing partners of major firms and forced them to negotiate settlements with me. In the past I would not have come close to such cases or such authority and responsibility.

And best of all, when I choose, I have more time to call my own than ever before. I travel widely with my husband, delighting in my role of spouse. I fly off at every opportunity to visit with my daughter, who works on the Hill.

My older son and daughter-in-law come over on weekends, ostensibly for brunch but in fact to use the washing machine to do the week's laundry.

My other son, who ever marches to his own drummer, returns home delighed to tell us and our friends about his wanderings.

I escape to the Country with my friends, whether aged 20 or 70, when the spirit moves us and no court call requires my presence in the City. My PC, my modem, the telephone, and the fax machine keep me in total touch with my office if I so choose. They permit me to practice law at substantially less expense and with greater efficiency than my competitors at places like The Firm.

I have cared for my first grandchild in my office, answerable to no one for his presence but my delighted self. Daily, I pop over to the child care center where he is cared for, to hold him, feed him, and watch him learn to crawl, while he takes me totally for granted.

TAKING UP THE FEMALE DOMESTIC ARTS

And once again I have taken up certain of the female domestic arts. I always baked. Now I also knit and crochet. I even take out my handiwork at professional meetings, for it makes me endlessly patient no matter how "windy" the discussion. One of these days I'll pull it out in settlement negotiations with a particularly quarrelsome young Rambo, who mistakenly measures his effectiveness in terms of the quantum of obnoxiousness.

And of late, I've gone back to writing poetry, just as I did when I was a girl. Everything is a fitting subject for a poem: my grandson's first words, a dead finch, my wartime memories, my loves, my hates, my hopes, my fears.

For those of us over the age of fifty, the task for the remaining portion of our lives is to knit into a more harmonious whole the disparate skeins of our individual histories and talents and, accordingly, our identities.

I would not be an American of my generation, both in my upbringing and the values I absorbed, if I did not respect hard work and the success we were promised it would bring.

I would not be a European in my roots, if I did not know that a life well-lived involves more than worshipping at the feet of the Bitch Goddess, Success, and giving into the deadliest of the Seven Deadly Sins—Greed, never satiated, never able to say Enough is Enough.

But then, if I were only a European, I would have less of my American sense of outrage over unfairness and injustice, or of my optimism and the hope which springs eternal that something must and can be done to set matters aright.

CHAPTER 16

Going Solo: The How's and The Why's for Women Litigators

by
ROBIN PAGE WEST

ROBIN PAGE WEST

Robin Page West, is a solo practitioner based in Baltimore City whose practice focuses on complex civil litigation, including products liability, class actions, and negligence. A Maryland native, she attended St. John's College in Annapolis, and received her undergraduate and law degrees from the University of Maryland in 1976 and 1979, respectively. She is admitted to practice in the State of Maryland, in the U.S. Courts of Appeals for the Fourth and Seventh Circuits, and in the United States Supreme Court.

Ms. West, who maintains a national practice, counts among her clients the Sara Lee Corporation, for whom she has recovered millions of dollars in fire loss and subrogation cases. In her fifteen years of litigating, Ms. West has handled cases in Alaska, the U.S. Virgin Islands and Puerto Rico, as well as some less exotic jurisdictions, such as her home state.

Ms. West is a former member of the Council of the Section of Litigation of the American Bar Association, where she has also served as Director of the Publications Division and Editor-in-Chief of the Section's bi-monthly *Litigation News*. She holds leadership positions on the publications and editorial boards of the ABA's General Practice Section, and serves on the Council of the Maryland State Bar Association's General Practice Section. She lectures frequently on law firm efficiency and lifestyle issues.

Ms. West uses her autonomy as a solo practitioner to maximize her time with her two children, Garrett (7) and Esme (2). "I finally had the courage to go out on my own when I learned I was pregnant with Garrett," Ms. West recalls. "I continued to have a substantive, lucrative law practice without sacrificing time with the baby," observes Ms. West, who has taken her son on out-of-state deposition and document review trips. "Going on the 'mommy track' at a firm just wouldn't have worked for me, because people wouldn't have taken me seriously as a litigator."

Ms. West often works at home after the children are asleep, returning phone calls and relying on her notebook computer and fax machine to communicate information back to the office. "I find some of my clients really appreciate being able to talk to me at night, because they often cannot, or prefer not to, speak to me from their offices," observes Ms. West, who also handles whistleblower, hostile workplace, and sexual abuse matters.

"Over the years, the philosophy of my practice has gone through some changes that I attribute to my experiences as a female litigator," Ms. West says. "In the beginning, I very much wanted to fit into the male-dominated litigation field. I believed that if women were good lawyers, we would be accepted into the club. Successful women litigators, whom I looked to as role models, denied having experienced sex discrimination. So I started out believing gender bias in the legal profession wasn't a significant problem.

"But after being a part of the profession for fifteen years, I have come to learn otherwise. Those role models have left their firms and started telling the real truth—if your gender can be used against you, it will be. Not only by the lawyers on the other side, but by your own partners," Ms. West says. "I used to be reluctant to make an issue of these things, for fear of making a bad situation even worse. But now I speak up, because I know that what makes it worse is allowing it to continue.

"I think the final change occurred with the birth of my daughter in 1992. Being accepted into a male-dominated field means nothing to me now. Instead, I want to change it. Having a daughter has made me realize there is no reason whatsoever to tolerate gender bias in any form," Ms. West concludes.

CHAPTER 16

Going Solo:
The How's and the Why's for
Women Litigators

by
ROBIN PAGE WEST

If you're in a firm now and thinking that perhaps you should strike out on your own, take this little quiz. I did, and the results convinced me to open my own firm.

- Have you ever wondered why, instead of being assigned to some first-chair jury trials of your own, you just get more research assignments, while men with less experience and seniority try most of your firm's cases?

- Have you observed that women who object to being given research are disparaged for not being team players, while men who complain are rewarded with courtroom work?

- Have you been criticized for not bringing in business, only to find that, when you do bring in business, you're threatening someone's ego?

- Have you done your best to be a tenacious, forceful litigator, only to be labeled bitchy or too aggressive?

- Have you done your best to be pleasant, cheerful and accommodating, only to be faulted as having no backbone?

- Worse yet, have you been disparaged as both too aggressive and not aggressive enough?

- In your firm, if a secretary challenges a woman attorney's authority, do partners question the woman attorney's ability to get along with staff?

- Are women at your firm—lawyer or nonlawyer—subjected to unwelcome advances or suggestive remarks?

If you can answer yes to any of these questions, your firm is harboring sexism. It has a set of double or triple standards that make it difficult for women to succeed. For example, you must be likeable to be partner material. Yet a woman at such a firm who has the qualities of a successful litigator will find she still cannot be likeable by the firm's definition of the term, despite the fact that aggressive male litigators never seem to have this problem. So try as you might, you run up against brick walls. And when you attempt to discuss what's happening, you are called a troublemaker or told you are overreacting. You may then begin to question your own judgment, which, for a litigator, can be devastating.

IDENTIFYING SEXISM

Like a verbally abusive marital relationship, a sexist relationship in a law firm is often difficult to identify and almost impossible to change, especially when you are in the middle of it. Without great self-esteem and the help of people who can validate your feelings, you may go along for years getting absolutely nowhere because of the sexist culture. Worse still, you may think that you are getting nowhere because there is something wrong with *you*. I encourage you to reevaluate the situation. Put aside your womanly impulses and pretend you are a client. Would you advise a client to put up with the nonsense you are going through? If not, then why are you?

Women lawyers who experience sexism are speaking out against it more and more. Senior women litigators, instead of justifying it or pretending it does not exist, are increasingly willing to help their juniors identify and eradicate such conduct. Highly visible women like Anita Hill, Hillary Clinton, and Janet Reno are sending the message to law firms, judges, and the general public that women attorneys do not have to apologize for being effective advocates. Perhaps when our daughters try their first cases, no one in the courtroom will think twice about their gender.

CHOOSING TO GO SOLO

But in the meantime, if you're trying to build a career and find personal satisfaction in what you do for a living, you probably don't have the time or the patience to wait for that change. If you glimpse yourself in these words, perhaps you should consider doing what I did—leave the discrimination behind and start your own firm.

THE RIGHT TIME TO START

Of course, there are reasons other than sex discrimination for deciding to go solo, such as the desire for flexible hours and complete control of your cases, your expenditures, and your profits. Then, too, some choose to go solo right out of law school. What follows is based on my eight years of solo practice after seven years of work in law firms.

I had practiced complex civil litigation in two major firms and one small firm when I made the decision to go solo. Although I was not as aware of it as I am now, I had been on the receiving end of large doses of sexism at one of these firms, where I always found myself wishing for more credit for my work and for the business I brought in. I felt that I was being used as a tool to generate revenue for these firms, when what I really wanted to be was the person making the decisions. Having listened for years to partners gripe about office politics and how certain "other" partners took out more of the pot than they brought in, I suspected these would always be issues for me if I stayed in a firm.

What finally pushed me into going solo was the news that I was pregnant with my first child. At age 30, with a history of endometriosis, nothing could have made me happier. Although I had always assumed I would have children one day, I never thought much about when this would happen while I was earning my degrees and starting my career. When I learned of the endometriosis and how it might make childbearing an impossibility, I suddenly felt like the cartoon character on the tee shirt who screams, "Oh my God, I forgot to have children!" So when I became pregnant, I saw it as a gift. I would have done anything to arrange my life so that I could mother that baby the way my heart told me I should.

BEING YOUR OWN BOSS

I had seen many effective women litigators leave big firms and go into government with the birth of their children. That was not for me—it did not mesh with my entrepreneurial spirit and my low threshold for bureaucracy. Nor did I want to punch a time clock or account for personal leave, sick days, and vacation days. I wanted to come and go as I pleased, with or without my baby, without having to worry about who might be judging me. While I had been willing to tolerate strict accountability when I was the only one who might suffer from the long hours and the lack of freedom, being pregnant allowed me to say no. Only when I had the excuse of a child could I say no to inappropriate demands on my time. Had I been kinder to myself and less eager to please when I first became a lawyer, I might have been spared the endometriosis. And then again, I might not be where I am today.

Eight years later, I'm still in solo practice, and I have two children. I cut back on work quite a bit with the birth of my second child, so that I could savor the experience of mothering the baby who will most likely be my last. Solo practice has allowed me to experience life the way it was intended. Having my own business, being my own boss, using my own brain to make important decisions, and being able to bask in the glory of success I created for myself have been wonderful. Not having to share the peaks of the cash flow has been even more satisfying. Since I can arrange my schedule to spend time with my children, I don't feel like a prisoner to my job, as many I know do. Interestingly, after I spend a weekend with the children, what seems like tedious legal drudgery on Friday becomes a stimulating and worthy cause by Monday morning. This is what makes my life fulfilling: the contrasts between being a litigator and being a mommy. It reminds me of drinking Pepsi and eating popcorn because each makes the other taste so much better. If you also want autonomy as well as room for something other than your job, whether it be children, skiing, or whatever, becoming a solo lawyer may be your answer.

A ROAD MAP TO FOLLOW

What follows is a roadmap to opening your own office. I have tried to include all the issues I faced with an explanation of how I dealt with each, and why. Your practice and mine will obviously have many differences, as do our personalities, so the way I handled a particular issue may not be right for you. Remember to trust your instincts. You are setting up this practice for you, so do it the way you feel is right.

How to Tell If You Are Solo Material

Even though you have a desire to be your own boss, set your own schedule, and control your own destiny, you still may not be solo material. Evaluate these factors to learn if you are:

- **Consider how much experience you have in the practice of law, and how comfortable you are with this level of experience.**

It took me six years before I felt I knew enough to practice on my own. Before I went solo, whenever I confronted a new issue, I discussed it with other attorneys in the firm. Over time, I began to recognize that they invariably had conflicting opinions. When I got to the point of being able to predict each consulting attorney's opinion, I realized I was ready to go solo. I didn't need to ask those lawyers anymore; I just had to think about what I knew they would say.

As this example illustrates, practicing law is not about knowing the answers—it's about coming up with ways to solve problems, to make things happen, to get from point A to point B. If you feel you can manage this without help, or if you would find help irritating and counterproductive, you probably have enough experience to go solo.

- **Consider your personality**.

Realize that by the nature of your profession, you are going to be on the offensive or on the defensive almost all the time. Your adversaries will say and do things just to try to upset you. Even when you are absolutely right, your opponents will not agree with you. In fact, this is when they will be their most tenacious and irrational. As long as this kind of thing rolls off your back, you will be okay as a solo. If these tactics will make you feel insecure, you probably should team up with others.

- **Consider your financial situation**.

Will you be able to afford paying all your normal living expenses in addition to the new business expenses? Will you be able to front case expenses? Will you need to borrow money, and if so, how will this affect you? Will functioning under the stress of loan payments while trying to start a business drive you over the edge, or will you feel smug because you are fully-leveraged?

- **Consider your dependents/support system**.

Do you have children, a spouse, or parents who can help you, or conversely, whom you must care for? Evaluate how this network will be affected by what you propose to do. Going solo does give you more personal autonomy. But if you need to pay for a nursing home, and the anxiety created by lack of financial certainty looms like a thundercloud over your head, going solo may not be your answer.

- **Consider your ability to keep track of money**.

I dated someone in law school who balanced his checkbook by taking the "ending balance" from his bank statement each month and transferring it into his checkbook register. Always bouncing checks, he was never able to grasp the concept of clearing. If this describes you, and you want to go solo, do so only with great caution and a very good accountant. Attorneys who cannot manage money have been known to dip into escrow accounts and wind up getting disbarred, or worse. It's up to you to stop yourself from becoming this kind of statistic.

• **Consider your abilities to manage work, priorities, and people.**

As a solo practitioner, you will be responsible for everything from getting the clients in the door to making sure there is toilet paper in the lavatory. You won't have an office administrator, paralegal coordinator, or supply clerk to lean on; at least not at first. Consider whether you have the temperament to address all aspects of the practice. Saying "I'll hire someone to take care of that" is one approach, but be mindful that hiring someone can take as much time as taking care of things yourself. You will have to set the priorities for your employees. When your carefully-constructed support team falls apart due to attrition, illness, or other problems, *you* are the one left holding the bag. I know many lawyers who are less than happy in their firms, but refuse, wisely, to go out on their own because they need the support a big firm offers—coffee, legal pads, paralegals, law clerks, and new business for the asking. If you need to focus on one thing at a time, the many demands of solo practice may drive you to distraction. Make sure you're prepared to be a jack-of-all-trades before you make the move to solo.

• **Consider your practice area and decide whether this type of law lends itself to solo practice.**

My area of preference is complex litigation that involves massive amounts of documents and lots of defendants—products liability, class actions, *qui tam* actions under the False Claims Act, and similar matters. Had I not gotten involved with heavy document cases at a firm, I probably would not have been attracted to them as a solo practitioner. In fact, I might have been scared away. But I had learned to develop "systems" using computers and contractual workers to accomplish many seemingly-daunting tasks. By applying these principles in my solo practice, I work on the kinds of cases I enjoy. More than once, I have pooled resources and skills with out-of-state counsel having more expertise and depth than I, to obtain great results. As an added bonus, these co-counsel relationships have blossomed into real friendships as well as sources of referrals. So when I say consider whether your type of practice lends itself to the solo mode, I don't mean to dissuade you. I just mean that if you want your dream of a solo practice to become a reality, you have to think about it, and think creatively.

How To Take the Plunge

There are a host of issues you will face. One way to deal with them is to make a list and work on them methodically. My list looked something like this:

- **Select a geographic location**.

Location is one of the most important decisions you will make in setting up your office. Where you are will affect your convenience, your self-image, others' perceptions of your practice, and your overhead expenses. My office is right downtown, directly across the street from the courthouse. The reasons for this are legion, but first and foremost is the message the location sends about my practice—that I'm in court so much I can't waste time coming and going. Whether this message is accurate is beside the point; what's important is the perception created for clients, potential clients, and other lawyers.

The second most important reason for my location is that the bar library is housed in the courthouse, which means I spend almost nothing on books. Instead I have a membership at the bar library and walk across the street to do research.

My office is half a block from the subway station, and close to major bus lines and a parking garage. Anyone can get there, with or without a car. A suburban location with a free parking lot would be less expensive for me, my clients, and my employees. But this is a trade-off I make to obtain other benefits, such as accessibility to mass transportation, and being within walking distance of courts and other agencies.

Another benefit of a downtown location is proximity to law schools, which are a source of law clerks and interns. Law schools also have very comprehensive law libraries, for those times when you need an esoteric item no one else seems to have. Moreover, law schools are often the site of continuing legal education seminars and other law-related presentations. If you are already downtown, it's easier to work these activities into your schedule.

- **Find space**.

Once you know where you want to be located, you have to find an office. Whether you will need an agent depends on your level of familiarity with the available office space, the amount of time you can afford to invest in the search, and how concerned you are about keeping your space search a secret.

During my first lease, which lasted five years, I shared space with two other women lawyers. We each had individual offices, and we shared a conference room and kitchen/photocopy area. We split the rent in proportion to the square footage we occupied exclusively, and our secretaries served as backup for each other. This arrangement worked very well until our practices grew in directions that were slightly different. At the end of the lease term, we each struck out on our own. I found space by myself, another woman found space with two other women lawyers, and the third leases a single office from a large firm.

In addition to arrangements like this, ready-made, furnished offices with staffed reception areas and typing pools are available in some cities. This kind of "incubator" office is a great idea that allows you to bypass many of the headaches of setting up a separate, staffed office. You may even meet potential clients there. Each time I have investigated one of these arrangements, however, they turned out to be much too expensive and too small to house my secretary and my files.

In searching for the space I have now, I worked with many agents who showed me lots and lots of space. Going with them on tours was almost a full-time job for the better part of several months. But in the end, I found space myself by reading signs on the sides of office buildings. When using agents you need to be very discriminating in what space you look at, or you may be dragged all over the face of the earth to view space that doesn't meet your most basic criteria. Be clear with your agent about what you want, and if possible, get copies of listing sheets and floor plans before looking.

Factors to consider in selecting the space are: the rent; pass-through expenses such as utilities, real estate taxes, and common area maintenance fees; whether you can sublet; whether you can expand; building security; janitorial services; maintenance and repair services; signage; elevators; overall appearance; acoustics; other tenants in the building; location and appearance of rest rooms; windows; window treatments; availability of running water; kitchen facilities; proximity to police, and fire safety.

A word about bathrooms is also in order. I have been in offices where the bathrooms were within the leased space, and where they were outside of it, in the common area on the floor. I prefer the latter for several reasons. First of all, when the lavatory is at the other end of the hall, you do not have to worry about odors or unaesthetic sounds. Secondly, the cost of cleaning your leased premises will be less if you have no bathrooms. Third, if the bathroom is in an unleased common area, then someone else will be responsible for stocking it with tissue, paper towels, and soap. And finally, if the bathroom is not included in your leased space, you won't have to pay for it, so your rent will be less.

Keep in mind that when you are leasing space, you can negotiate for all kinds of things. My current lease includes free electricity, upgraded carpeting, construction of custom built-in cabinets for storage and kitchen equipment, installation of a glass wall in the conference room, venetian blinds, daily janitorial services, right of first refusal on adjacent space, and six months' free rent. With regard to these and other extras, figure out what you want, read the landlord's proposed lease, and start negotiating. Treat yourself as the client and drive a hard bargain. After all, you will be living with the results for years to come. If possible, eliminate pass-through expenses that cannot be controlled or estimated in advance, such as building maintenance fees and real-estate taxes.

The landlord's form lease will not be good for you. And chances are, it's not carved in stone. It is a starting point for negotiations. If a clause seems unclear or unfair, speak up and make him or her change it. The effort you invest fine tuning the lease up front will pay off many times over in saved time and money later on in the lease term.

When you are negotiating the lease, you should be thinking about construction work and finishes you will want the landlord to install. You will need to set a tone and style for your new office. You will need to have some idea of the furniture you will be using so you can select the paint and carpeting colors. Will it be Chippendale furniture and oriental rugs, chrome, glass and black leather, or something else? You will also have to specify the locations of telephones and major electrical equipment like refrigerators and copy machines so the outlets can be located properly. When you get these things figured out, write them down and attach them to the lease, so you will have some recourse if the landlord fails to live up to your agreement.

• Procure Furniture and Equipment

Of all the joys of being a solo lawyer, setting the tone for the office is one of the most fun. The furniture in my personal office is very traditional, with a tufted leather chair and a Chippendale table-style desk. But with the birth of my children, the decor has cycled toward neo-baby, with high chairs, bouncy seats, porta-cribs, and rattles taking over at times. By contrast, a friend of mine who practices out of a house—not his home—has a very different tone: he brings his dog to the office and keeps dog food dishes in the conference room. You want to create a perception of professionalism and inspire confidence in your clients and other lawyers, but don't be afraid to let a little of your true personality show. After all, that's why you're striking out on your own.

You will need to obtain, through purchase, loan, gift, or rental, basic items of furniture and equipment. Shop around, scour the "scratch and dent" rooms of office furniture stores, and check the classifieds. Sometimes a bank branch closes down and you can get great furniture for a song. The fact that it's used gives the appearance that your office has been around a lot longer than it has. However, it may be more economical to buy new furniture if the used furniture doesn't come with free delivery.

The list of basic furniture and equipment items I use includes the following items:

(a) lawyer desk, chair, bookcases and credenza;

(b) lawyer computer—I use a notebook in the office and at home or on the road;

(c) conference table and chairs;

(d) secretarial setup—desk, return, chair, computer;

(e) printers;

(f) fax;

(g) storage for supplies and files—shelving, cabinets, file cabinets;

(h) photocopy machine;

(i) phones;

(j) fireproof safe;

(k) coffee station, toaster, microwave, refrigerator;

(l) wall art.

In my experience, there is no way to generalize about what to get in terms of each of these items. You need to shop around for the quality, price, and features that suit your individual needs. Pay special attention to the service policies on the photocopy machines and telephones. Sometimes equipment may seem very reasonably priced when you purchase it, but two years later you are paying an unconscionable amount for the annual service policy. Shopping for these things is a time-consuming process, which is compounded by the fact that you will be forced to compare apples and oranges. You can make it easier by 1) doing it in stages, 2) delegating all or part of it to your secretary, or 3) hiring a consultant or furniture broker to help.

In my experience, you will get the most satisfactory results by having your secretary do the preliminary shopping and make recommendations. You then study the recommendations, ask your questions, and make the ultimate decision on what to purchase. I have not found it productive to rely on consultants or salespeople who don't know me and who don't understand my practice. Sometimes, I wonder if such people have any redeeming value. One salesman trying to sell me a laser printer actually told me that federal courts do not accept pleadings printed on a dot-matrix printer. This was quite a sales pitch, considering that our federal court accepts *handwritten* pleadings!

I suggest buying just the bare minimum to get your office up and running. Then, as you learn more about your needs, you can add pieces one at a time. For example, buy the desks and chairs, but hold off on the conference room for a while until you get a sense of what you will be using it for and who you will be meeting with there. If you really need to furnish it, perhaps you can rent a table and chairs until you make up your mind. Similarly, you can purchase an inexpensive impact printer and use it for a while until you decide what kind of laser printer to add. By waiting to purchase some items, you increase the prospects of locating and acquiring exactly the right pieces to fit your needs.

• Publicize Your Office

You will also need to consider whether and/or how to publicize your new office. Unless you already have more paying clients than you want, you should publicize the opening of your office. Your budget and your taste in advertising will dictate the extent of your publicity efforts. I sent out announcements to potential clients and sources of referral business, put announcements in the local legal paper, and listed myself in Martindale-Hubbell. I obtained letterhead, envelopes, and business cards that matched. Since then, I have begun sending out a quarterly client newsletter that I obtain, pre-written and printed, from the General Practice Section of the ABA. All I do is add my letterhead/logo at the top of the page and send it out. This keeps my name in front of my clients so they do not forget about me when they need a lawyer. Many firms now have brochures, which can be an excellent way to promote yourself, if you have the skill or the funds to produce a tasteful brochure. TV and radio ads are also an option you may want to consider if your intention is to develop a volume practice. I have noticed that many lawyers place ads in the yellow pages and some even disseminate coupons offering "free initial consultations." I have not used these techniques, mainly because I fear being deluged with too many inquiries from people seeking representation in areas I do not handle, such as drunk driving, divorces, and criminal matters.

- **Obtain Insurance Coverage**.

One important and expensive item you must attend to before opening your office is insurance. For my business alone, I have the following types of insurance: professional liability, office overhead expense, business owner's, and workers' comp. I also carry life and disability insurance.

Professional liability covers me in the event of malpractice. It is expensive. If you have been in practice before, make sure, when you purchase your policy, that you are covered for prior acts either by the new insurance or the insurance you had in the past. Past malpractice committed by you or a prior partner is not covered under your new policy unless the policy covers "prior acts." If the policy in effect at the time of the malpractice was a "claims made" policy, it will not cover you for claims made outside the policy period. Therefore, you will need prior acts coverage in the new policy if you want to cover all your potential liability. Although it will be time-consuming, read the policy carefully. Sometimes the salesman will tell you things that are not reflected in the policy language. Be aware that, if you are sued, the cost of defense may be included in your liability limits. If this is the case, you should pick higher limits on your policy than you otherwise might.

Office overhead expense insurance pays my office expenses when I am disabled. This insurance is relatively inexpensive, but essential in a solo office. Without you there to generate cash flow, you could be evicted from your office and lose your secretary pretty quickly. Unlike disability income insurance, which pays you income during your disability, office overhead expense insurance is tax deductible as a business expense. So, instead of obtaining disability income insurance and using the income to pay your office expenses, buy office overhead expense insurance to cover the overhead. If you need additional insurance for disability income, you can purchase that as well, but you won't need as much since your office overhead will already be covered.

Workers' compensation insurance will probably be required by law where you practice. Talk to your insurance agent about what kind to get and why. I think the main issue is whether you should include yourself on the policy, or just your employees. Since my policy costs the same whether I am on it or not, I am insured under mine.

Business owner's insurance, if it works as planned, is supposed to cover all the other business risks not covered under your malpractice policy. For example, it should cover you in the event of fire, theft, your secretary having an auto accident while in the scope of employment, a slip and fall in your office, etc. Again, talk to your agent about what kind of policy to get. Some leases will require your policy to have certain limits and coverages; you may also have to name the landlord as an additional insured.

- **Decide Your Staffing Needs**.

Consider the people you will have to hire. You may need a secretary, receptionist, paralegal, and/or a law clerk. In my eight years, I have always had a full-time secretary, and hired others on an as-needed, project-by-project basis. My secretary functions basically as a paralegal, since I do almost all of my typing. Once I learned WordPerfect, dictating and revising became too slow and cumbersome. As a result, I became more productive, and freed up my secretary to do projects requiring more skill. Moreover, my secretary has a working knowledge of everything I am doing, so any caller can get an intelligent answer to any question at any time, regardless of whether I'm in court, conducting a deposition, or out of town.

If you cannot afford a full-time secretary, you may wish to explore sharing space with others in the same situation. In that way, you can pool your resources to hire a full-time secretary.

You will also need an accountant to advise you on money matters, such as payroll taxes, social security withholding, personal property taxes, federal and state unemployment insurance payments, income tax estimated payments, etc. Even though my law school grades in taxation were exemplary, I could not begin to deal with all the paperwork generated by the above-listed items.

• Hook Up With a Reliable Accountant and Banker.

I have used several different accountants, and find that personality is a key factor in the relationship. You need an accountant who understands the way you think, and if possible, thinks the same way, so you can communicate clearly. My first accountant could not understand me and the problem was mutual. We limped along for a year or so, without realizing the magnitude of the communication problem. Then he did my taxes. When I saw the return, it seemed to me that he was showing I had earned about double what I thought I had earned. The reason? Every time I had transferred money from my savings into my checking, the accountant had counted the transfer as income. When I brought the discrepancy to his attention and asked him to re-do the return, he blamed me for not alerting him to the error sooner. Needless to say, I had to get a new accountant. If I had trusted my instincts and gotten rid of this accountant sooner, I would have saved myself a lot of aggravation at tax time.

While we are on the subject of banking, let me recommend that you look for a bank that will assign you a living, breathing person to deal with. You can develop a relationship with this person that will save you time standing in line, finding out information, and dealing with other needs you will have. Many banks have this ability but do not advertise it. It is sometimes referred to as "corporate banking" or "private banking." Try to get hooked into this network, and your life as a business owner will be simplified.

•   Use Computer Technology

Finally, let me tell you about my approach to computers. First, I am a great advocate of computers, especially for the solo practitioner. Computers allow us to paper a big firm with ease, if that's what the case calls for. We no longer have to fear being out-staffed, out-researched, or unable to access information as long as we have our computers.

Even given my great affinity and respect for computers, I am not, and never will be, a computer nerd. I don't live on the cutting edge of technology. I find something that works for me, and have a hard time giving it up, even if it becomes obsolete. I cannot understand a computer software instruction book until I have already tried, by myself, to use the software. Once I have done that, then I can go back to the book and understand it. But before I have some hands-on experience, it means nothing to me. This is why nobody can explain anything to me about computers. It's not that I don't want to listen, it's just that I need to try it myself before I can understand it. If you fall into this category too, you may be tempted to hire a consultant to help you get set up. I do not recommend this.

You would do better to obtain the most current computers you can afford, and then purchase the basic software programs to accomplish accounting, time and billing, word processing, calendar and diary, computerized research, and data base functions. There are many programs on the market in the $30.00 to $500.00 range that perform these tasks well.

With software in hand, figure out how to use these programs by trying them out in your daily life. Some you will like and some you won't. Even if you have to throw away all the software you bought in favor of some other programs, you will still have paid less overall than you would have by hiring a consultant. And the added bonus is, you will know how to install and operate the programs yourself. In time, as your practice develops, you may want to delegate some of these functions to others, but in the beginning, you will be best served by understanding, on a very intimate level, exactly what your computer is and is not capable of doing.

* * * * * *

Many people ask me how I combat loneliness being in solo practice. This question always strikes me as odd, because the solo practitioners I know are all busier than one-armed paperhangers, with phone message slips teetering on their desks like the Leaning Tower of Pisa. I am usually so busy that I would give my eye teeth to be lonely just for an hour. But to those of you who fear being lonely if you go solo, there are many things you can do to alleviate this potential problem. Get involved with co-counsel in your cases. Refer clients who have matters in areas you do not handle to other lawyers, but continue to work with those other lawyers on the cases. In this way, you will learn new areas of law, and will develop relationships with other lawyers. Participate in bar association activities on a local, state, or national level. Chair a committee or edit a newsletter. Get involved in your children's school activities, which, incidentally, can be a goldmine for new clients. Spend time chatting on the phone with your clients' treating physicians; tell them about your practice and what you care about. You will find new friends and possible new clients this way as well. If you have never experienced solo practice, the fear of loneliness may seem to be a cause for concern, but once you make the plunge, it will be an issue you will probably never have to face.

CHAPTER 17

A Godmother Makes Good: Practice in a Government Agency

by
PRISCILLA ANNE SCHWAB

PRISCILLA ANNE SCHWAB

L ike much of the rest of the world, Priscilla Anne Schwab, didn't think much of lawyers—her few contacts with them in her journalism career confirmed her impression that they talked in gobbledy-gook and wrote in obfuscation. That impression solidified when she became a special assistant at the National Governors' Association in Washington, D.C., and tried to write articles explaining federal statutes and regulations affecting the states. "I ranted and raved, to everyone's amusement, about the way our nation's laws were written," she says. "I knew I could write laws in plain English, and I did not understand how supposedly intelligent people could express their ideas in such an unreadable manner."

After being accepted by the Columbus School of Law at Catholic University, which overlooked her college GPA and LSAT score in favor of life experience and maturity, she learned within the first year why laws and regulations cannot be clear and simple, and appreciated soon after the "full employment" impact of legal writing. "I now make my living dissecting the meaning of regulations and case law in an arcane area of employee compensation that completely reflects the convoluted workings of our democratic system and guarantees me a lifetime career," Ms. Schwab remarks.

Still, there is a small cadre of real lawyers who are also real writers and who still believe that "agree" has more impact than "reach agreement," that *Strunk and White* should be memorized by first-year associates, and that there is no writer on earth whose first draft cannot be improved in some way. Examples of this cadre's skills are found predominantly in *Litigation* magazine, which was founded for them and by them, and where Ms. Schwab volunteered for six "fulfilling" years as an associate editor.

Ms. Schwab is now a Deputy Associate General Counsel with the Benefits Review Board, U.S. Department of Labor, in Washington, D.C. "In government, the more words in the title, the lower down in the hierarchy you are," she says. "But that suits me just fine. I work with six staff attorneys who are delightful people in addition to being outstanding attorneys. The same is true for the appeals judges and all the Board's employees. I operate on the theory that if the job is at least eighty percent satisfying, you are in the right slot."

The job entails writing memoranda and draft appellate decisions for the Board in black lung claims that have been appealed from the Office of Administrative Law Judges. In the past two fiscal years, Ms. Schwab and her group produced more than 500 appellate decisions, which was 34 percent above their goal. "Not all government is bloated and inefficient," says Ms. Schwab. "But the vast amount of good that comes from the government seems always to be overwhelmed by the much publicized instances of fraud, waste, and abuse. T'was ever thus, I suppose. Good news is no news, and bad news is tonight's news, with film at eleven."

For Ms. Schwab, "going to law school was like sending my mind to aerobics class. Torts and Professor Harvey Zuckman proved the maxim, no pain, no gain." Despite a demanding job and two small children she survived the experience, with the support of a loving family and a dedicated husband. "Looking back," she says, "my mother was right, I should have stayed home with my babies, I should have delayed law school until they were older. But I didn't know then what I know now, and so I plunged ahead."

Plunging into a challenge is characteristic; Ms. Schwab plunged into journalism after college, and took the Greyhound bus for two nights and three days to start a job as a brand new reporter for a brand new newspaper in Phoenix, Arizona. From there she moved to Los Angeles and to San Francisco, and then plunged abroad to England for five years. She didn't just return to the United States in 1970, she signed on for ten days on the high seas aboard a Belgium freighter with ten other intrepid souls and danced away the night of the Force Ten gale midway across the Atlantic. Her family was hardly surprised when she started violin lessons five years ago, after her daughter, who is now 21 and a seaman in the U.S. Coast Guard, hung up her bow, and her recently expressed desire to compete in masters swimming has her swimmer son, 17, holding his breath.

"I've lived in the Washington, D.C. area for more than twenty years, and I now consider it my home town. And it really is just a big small town, with an overlay of power, wealth, and very important people, none of which or whom affects my daily life. I know Washington has a bad rep outside the Beltway, but I love this place."

CHAPTER 17

A Godmother Makes Good: Practice in a Government Agency

by
PRISCILLA ANNE SCHWAB

A fter nine years as a government lawyer, I have a private window office. That is the ultimate achievement in the federal service, but not the only measure of success. As a woman manager for whom law was a second choice but is now a true love, I have practical information to impart to other women attorneys seeking government careers. Forewarned by my experience, perhaps you will be better armed to deal with the sort of workplace scenarios, sexist and otherwise, in which I starred.

I worked as a journalist for 20 years and went to law school at night. After graduation, I obtained an appellate clerkship, passed the Maryland bar, and signed on with a small general practice law firm. Two years later, while I was practicing solo from my living room office, finally able to relish the luxury of part-time practice and full-time mothering, my husband was killed in the fire that destroyed our home. I was left with two children and a life to rebuild. I needed a steady income, and a friend suggested completing Standard Form (SF) 171, the application for a job with the federal government. In April 1985, I was hired as a government attorney by the United States Department of Labor (DOL). At the time, I was forty-three years old.

Sexism in the federal government begins with the SF 171, which consists of seemingly straightforward and employment-related questions. That is, until you start thinking about the hidden meanings of the questions.

For example, Question 6 requires you to list "other names ever used." How many male applicants ever write something besides "none?" How many older female applicants can truthfully give the same response? What the government really wants to know, but cannot legally ask, is how many times female applicants have been married and divorced. The apparent rationale is that such information is needed to conduct a complete background or reference check. Nevertheless, there is no way to determine from the SF 171 how often a male applicant has been married and divorced. Since the background check does not occur until hiring is imminent, this intrusive question should be eliminated.

Question 7 is equally blunt: "Sex [ ] Male [ ] Female (for statistical use)." Why is this question necessary? What are the statistics? Who uses them? A perfectly reasonable explanation might be that the civil rights reporting laws require this information. But if that is so, shouldn't my qualifications be assessed in an interview before my gender is officially noted? Couldn't this question be deleted as easily as "Mr.," "Mrs.," and "Miss" have been?

The real "hidden valley" of the SF 171 is the series of questions pertaining to availability. Depending on how you answer the questions in this section, you can foreclose any number of opportunities without awareness or recourse. Here they are:

12. When can you start?

13. What is the lowest pay you will accept?

14. Are you willing to work: in the Washington, D.C. metropolitan area, outside the 50 United States, any place in the United States, only in (list the location).

15. Are you willing to work: 40 hours per week (full-time); 16 or fewer hours, 17-24 hours, 25-32 hours per week (part-time); in an intermittent job (on-call/seasonal); weekends, shifts, or rotating shifts?

16. Are you willing to take a temporary job lasting: 5 to 12

months (sometimes longer); 1 to 4 months; less than 1 month?

17. Are you willing to travel away from home for: 1 to 5 nights each month; 6 to 10 nights each month; 11 or more nights each month?

What these questions do is to slot some applicants who answer honestly, as I did, into an unfavorable category. A younger person just out of law school might answer "yes" to these questions, might be ready to begin work immediately, and might be willing to accept a paltry salary for the chance to start. But what recently widowed mother of two small children could comfortably choose to travel overnight for 11 or more nights per month? Or even 6 to 10 nights?

And how does a married male answer Questions 14 and 17, as compared to a married female? Who moves for whom? The assumption seems to be that women will demand less salary and fewer hours and that they will take part-time and temporary jobs to juggle child-rearing with a career. Before you even get to "Military Service and Veteran Preference," which the vast majority of female applicants simply skips, you may have unwittingly classified yourself as something less than an eighty-hour-a-week, gung-ho lawyer.

ANSWERING QUESTIONS WITH HIDDEN MEANINGS

Indeed, during an interview I had at the Department of Education, I was told that my interest in part-time work, as indicated on my SF 171, revealed something less than a total commitment to government service. Now I never envisioned simply working during my children's school hours. I desperately needed a job and would have taken anything, regardless of the hours, yet my answer on the form had prejudiced my prospects. My answers to the travel questions on the SF 171 likewise foreclosed a later opportunity to apply for administrative trial work. The job required only six overnights a month, and I could easily have made the necessary arrangements for child care had I known that before completing the form.

Finally, there is the matter of age. Question 4 requires that you state your date and place of birth. Why? Of what relevance are age and birthplace? Private firms do not dare ask an applicant's age; yet the federal government wants to know. The potential for misuse of this information is vast.

Consider this situation. The agency's hiring official, who is male and under 30, is reviewing a dozen SF 171 applications for one opening. Eight of the twelve applicants are identified on the forms as women, and it turns out that more than half the attorneys currently on his staff are women. One of the four male applicants is 51, the same age as the hiring official's mother. Two of the remaining three males are also under 30, and the third was born in the official's home town. You don't need to guess which three applicants get interviews.

AN INTERVIEW DESPITE THE WRONG ANSWERS

Despite my "wrong" answers on the SF 171, I was granted an interview at DOL. After some initial pleasantries and a thorough interrogation on my legal background, one questioner asked me how I would feel being supervised by people much younger than I? I responded that the situation would not matter, that in all my years as a journalist I had supervised people older than myself, and had been supervised by people younger than myself, and age had been no problem.

Long after DOL hired me, I realized with the clarity of hindsight that the age question did matter to the female questioner who became my supervisor. She had interpreted my facile answer to mean that I was oblivious to the whole issue of age discrimination and had dismissed her question as supercilious.

At another point in the DOL interview, I was asked about my commitment to long hours and occasional weekend work. I explained that I had two children to care for and a house to rebuild, but that I was ready to work whatever hours were necessary to get the job done right. The trio questioning me heard only the first part of that answer and pegged me as a "mommy" attorney.

I knew that I was not DOL's first choice. Perhaps the chief interviewer sensed my desperation and took pity on me. In any event, a hiring letter arrived inviting me to join the black lung division of the Office of the Solicitor (SOL), and I accepted. I told myself that I would simply aim to please, believing that if everyone liked me, I could not fail. Well, I almost did.

A CLASH OF CULTURES

Coming from a legal milieu in which women lawyers discussed their children's doings as much as their clients' concerns, I was singularly unprepared for the federal service. My immediate supervisor was a woman, about ten years younger than I, whose work was her life, all of it. She had little time for me, once she discerned that my legal abilities were not impressive, and that my personality was hardly compatible.

To be honest, I had a hard time during my first year at DOL. I had to get used to my new role as head of the household, sole wage-earner, and single parent. I also had to adjust to the arcane area of law in which I was expected to operate. My supervisor told me bluntly that the Black Lung Benefits Act was one of the most convoluted pieces of legislation ever enacted by Congress, and asked me if I understood what I was getting into. I responded confidently that I would master it all in six months. That was not what she wanted to hear since, as I learned later, she had devoted the past six years of her life to learning this very complex subject.

FIGURING OUT THE JOB

As a government attorney, I sat behind a government-issue desk in a cubicle partitioned off by fabric-covered dividers which offered little privacy. I handled black lung benefits claims in which an administrative law judge's decision had been appealed to the internal DOL panel called the Benefits Review Board. My job was to review the parties' pleadings, the evidentiary record, and the administrative documents, and figure out what to do. The trouble was, I didn't have a clue.

No problem, I thought. I'll just ask for some guidance. My questions were always answered, but the answers had a disapproving overtone of "you should know that," and lacked the fuller explanations that would have made the review process clearer to me. What I really needed was a mentor. I didn't see that my cubicle was symbolic, that new employees were categorized almost immediately. If your supervisors begin by perceiving you as bright and aggressive, you will find yourself on the fast track. If not, your optimism and enthusiasm will be quickly doused. As one colleague put it: "I came from Georgetown University, energized and delighted to have a job, and within two months all the wind had been taken out of me."

I too was deflated by my personal Wicked Witch of the West, my supervisor. I am not, as my mother has often noted, quick on the uptake. By the time I recognize the harmful import of certain conversations or situations, it is usually too late for me to do anything about it.

CHATTING WITH THE WICKED WITCH

For example, whenever I ventured into the Wicked Witch's office with a question or two, I felt much like Alice asking why the oysters had shoes to polish but no feet. Twisting a strand of her hair with her finger, the WW would provide an unhelpful answer and leave me with the feeling that to ask further questions would only confirm my stupidity. For me there were no warm chats about the intricate medical testing involved in the Black Lung Benefits Act. Nor were there any tidbits of gossip and office news. Such things were reserved for those in the loop.

If I simply gave the case my best shot and turned in a brief without any discussion, the WW would go to work with her gold Cross pen, making pages of finely-printed comments about my pitiable efforts. The brief would then be returned to my mail box. Of course, there was never any follow-up.

I used to watch the WW go past my door to a male colleague's cubicle, where she would spend a half hour or more of quality time explaining her revisions of his work, and chatting about this and that. The same young man once made her laugh by remarking that he was leaving work early because he had to "play Mom tonight." I was playing Mom—and Dad—every night, and it was no laughing matter.

The WW never had that problem. In fact, women attorneys in the government generally take pains to appear unconcerned about their families, discussing them with a great deal of detachment, lest they be accused of putting personal matters ahead of the job. The cardinal sin, of course, is to admit openly that what really matters in life is far removed from the office. Such an admission is almost guaranteed to ostracize you from those in power.

TWO KINDS OF FEMALE SUPERVISORS

I believe that government service produces two basic types of female supervisors. The first is the Steel Magnolia (the WW, for example), a woman who has fierce determination to succeed, detached disdain for those less talented than she, and limited tolerance for the nonwork concerns of those she supervises. The second type is the Godmother, similarly fierce in determination, but protective and nurturing of those she adopts, kinder and gentler in legal approach and thinking, and tolerant of less than perfect performance. I strongly believe that the Godmother will show better results in the performance of her staff over the long run.

My experience at the Department of Labor has made me conscious of the ironies surrounding the government's efforts to combat discrimination officially. The federal government vociferously proclaims itself to be an equal opportunity employer dedicated to the concept that discrimination must be eradicated from the workplace. In reality, discrimination is alive and flourishing at federal agencies, although it is often difficult to document. In fact, the discrimination is sometimes so subtle that you do not recognize it until the damage has been done.

THE UNSTATED POLICY IS WHAT GOVERNS

Until the present administration, it was the unstated and unadmitted policy of the Department of Labor *not* to take the lead in establishing the 21st century workplace of flexitime, off-site work arrangements, job sharing, and permanent part-time, but rather to stand squarely in the middle of other government agencies and private industry. Thus, the agency that supposedly represents the American worker is not the trend-setter but the Sears Roebuck of labor-management relations.

Yes, women have been appointed as Secretary of Labor—Roosevelt did it with Frances Perkins, and the Republicans did it with Elizabeth Dole, Ann McGlaughlin, and Lynn Martin. Theoretically, a woman atop the 17,000-employee pyramid should make women within the structure feel confident. In fact, the male power framework remains unshaken, and the shadows of prejudice against women permeate all managerial levels. The female deputies, associates, and assistants are always heard. Their memoranda are noted, their ideas are welcomed, and their performance is sometimes rated outstanding. But they are not understood.

I think the habit of hearing but not understanding is ingrained in most men from childhood. They grow up practicing selective hearing to the point of stereotype. We've all seen the ubiquitous cartoon showing the husband reading the newspaper at the breakfast table while his wife babbles on. It's no different in government offices.

At meetings women are often talked over and interrupted. As a woman reaches the middle of her presentation, a man will interject, "Oh, you mean we should. . . ." and continue confidently with his own ideas and suggestions. It's a rare woman who will retaliate by saying: "No, that is not what I meant. You really need to listen harder to what I am saying, instead of mentally drafting your response."

AN ATMOSPHERE THAT ERODES A SENSE OF WORTH

The overall atmosphere in a male-dominated office slowly erodes a woman's sense of worth. She begins to tire of struggling against the tacit perception that women are failures. Little things happen daily which send subtle messages that women are less important, less talented, and less likely to make a difference than their male peers. For instance, the praise of a male supervisor, "you did fine," is delivered in a manner, unperceived by him, that says "for a woman." If the male reports in turn to a woman supervisor, she too may pick up on the hint and assume that the performance was less than stellar.

When confronted with their tendency to utter seemingly innocent but nonetheless belittling remarks to women, men respond by saying that they were "only kidding" or that women are "too sensitive." Maybe so, but the daily barrage of banter is like water wearing away stone—how many women have listened in patient silence as two men discuss last night's game? Even for a woman keenly interested in the fortunes of the Boston Red Sox, discussion with her male colleagues rarely results in their acceptance of her opinion.

Because of four years' private legal experience, I started government service as a GS 12/13. This meant that after one year, unless I became comatose, I would be promoted to Grade 13. Each grade contains 12 steps which the employee climbs automatically, provided that an annual performance rating of "fully satisfactory" is obtained. Not so with Grade 14. Here, promotion is discretionary, and I had to spend three years fighting for it. However, the same promotion was granted to nineteen other attorneys, all of whom were far younger than I, and all of whom had similar or less experience, less time in the SOL division, and similar or even lighter caseloads than I did.

I cannot honestly blame an anti-feminine bias alone for my failure to get a timely promotion, but neither can I assert my own lack of ability. It was especially galling to me to see a younger woman get promoted to Grade 14 who was not four years out of law school and who had limited litigation experience. She and the other recent graduates had benefitted from the fact that the entry-level grade was raised to GS 12/13 a year or so after I had started at that grade with four years of experience. I was the only staff attorney adversely affected by this change, but true to form I did not realize that until much too late.

Somehow less than a week after the young woman was promoted, the office decided that I too would be recommended for advancement. I did not ask when I suddenly became Grade 14 material. Perhaps the supervisors felt forced into a corner, since the young woman's good fortune provoked outrage among many staff attorneys who complained adamantly about the canyon-like performance gap between her and me. For me, the victory was bittersweet.

WHERE THE EXCEPTION UNDOES THE RULE

The governmental policy of equal access to job openings does not work for supervisory jobs. These positions are often not advertised, even though advertising is required. It seems that exceptions are always available to creative managers who want to advance their own people. And even if the agency goes through the motions of advertising the position and interviewing prospective candidates, the result is still the same. Preselection is so prevalent that grievances are routinely filed by candidates who are passed over. I know. As a union steward, I once represented an older woman who had applied for dozens of vacant positions; she was amply qualified for any one of them but never selected. In her papers she alleged age discrimination. DOL settled her case after she had retired.

When a woman makes partner in a private law firm, she becomes one of the boys and does what other partners do. But achieving Grade 14 and up—the equivalent of making partner—is different. Like the "colored" mammies in plantation households, a supervising female attorney must project a competent but submissive attitude, exercising her power in ways that are not threatening to men or to other women in power.

HOW TO STAY ALIVE

She must also become a chameleon of sorts, supporting her male mentor in public places in return for his protection, making up for his inadequacies in return for being the power behind the throne. For most women, it is an equitable trade-off because the secondary position still permits much good to be accomplished. Moreover, in government, collegiality is a key to survival, not just to success.

In one of my formal performance appraisals, for example, my legal analysis was deemed "hit-or-miss." My supervisor reported that my work showed flashes of brilliance but was not consistent. She was a Godmother type who had replaced the WW after her promotion to higher management. Eventually I learned what she meant by "hit or miss"—she felt I was not getting enough input from her before drafting my briefs.

I initially avoided her because of my previous experience with the WW. Talking out legal ideas without worrying about looking foolish was still difficult for me. Nevertheless, I faithfully pro-grammed some chat time into my schedule. Less than a year later, the new supervisor recommended me for Grade 14. The memo she drafted recommending my promotion required five days to craft. I still marvel at her mastery of bureaucratese. After reading it, I felt as if I had walked on water and distributed the loaves and fishes.

THE FINE ART OF MEMO-WRITING

Needless to say, for government lawyers, memo writing is an art in itself. You must know when to write about what to whom, and how to package the memo for its intended audience, which may not be the person to whom you address it. I once argued futilely with a supervisor over a "pay memo" in which I had carefully delineated why we should stop litigating and pay the claimant's benefits. My supervisor's editing made a hash of the reasoning and botched the most telling points. The "revised" memo failed to persuade the agency head, who called a meeting at which I reclarified the arguments for paying the benefits. I managed to prevail and justice was probably done.

Another time, I wrote a three-page memo on ways to cope with a new policy issued by the Benefits Review Board. The Board had declared that our attorneys' motions for an extension of time to file pleadings would not be granted as a matter of course. Most of our attorneys carried caseloads numbering in the hundreds, and the extensions were sometimes needed to come up with missing case records. My detailed analysis of the situation, addressed to a male supervisor, was written within a month of the announcement. It contained a simple plan for locating case files and expediting the transfer, some sample motions, a discussion of alternative bases for seeking extensions, and an offer to help implement the overall plan.

There is a special void for such memos, and mine was filed there. I asked the supervisor about the memo on a number of occasions, and he said he was working on it. Three months later, he issued some sample motions of his own, along with a cover letter. Not a word was said about my memo. Not an inkling was ever given that I had even mentioned the subject to him, let alone submitted a memo. I now realize that I should have addressed the memo to his boss, the Associate Solicitor, except that such a procedure would have been viewed as hierarchically incorrect. I also should have publicized my ideas, despite the fact that tooting my own horn has always been somewhat distasteful to me, as it is to most women. Beyond a doubt, a talent for self-promotion is vital for women in the federal service.

LIFE ON THE FAST TRACK

So if you happen to be contemplating a government career, consider the following. If you land on the fast track and are accepted by those in charge as "one of us," you will be trained and nurtured in a kinder, gentler mode, and you will progress accordingly. As "one of us," your inevitable mistakes will be minimized, and your good work trumpeted. Thus, instead of earning a flat "meets" on the critical elements of your performance appraisal, you will earn an "exceeds" rating. Enough "exceeds" and you will be rewarded with an overall "highly effective" rating, which carries a monetary bonus. Make all "exceeds" on your critical elements—knowledge of the law, legal writing, oral communication, analysis—and you will be rated "outstanding," with even more bonus money.

Performance appraisals are meant to be completely objective, an impossible goal for the subjective human beings who draft the actual reviews. Nevertheless, performance appraisals will determine whether you wallow in obscurity or run with the thoroughbreds. Our mothers were right, first impressions are crucial. In the federal service, establishing rapport with your immediate supervisor should be your first priority.

As part of the process you need to discern what drives your supervisor and what is important in his or her office life. Then you should adapt your behavior to that norm as best you can.

At some agencies, for example, you are expected to account for every hour of your time. You add up 40 hours a week by the minute from sign-in to sign-out; linger one nano-second longer than an hour at lunch, and the overage will be deducted from your annual leave or credit time. At other agencies, only flagrant abuses of work time will be noted. Therefore, you need to size up the situation immediately and take appropriate action.

The same is true about your writing. I think of myself as a good writer, and so I was disappointed when I got nothing better than "meets" in this category of the annual performance appraisal. One supervisor commented that my briefs were "overdone," like a steak broiled to greyness; another termed my memoranda "too journalistic," as if that were a sin.

WHERE NARRATIVE STRENGTH IS A HINDRANCE

In my six years of brief-writing for the government, I have learned that narrative strength is not considered an asset. Nor is readability. There really is a bureaucratic way of writing, speaking, and acting, and the supervisors generally are not comfortable with much deviation. Because of this, I have learned to curtail my straightforward approach, particularly when I have a strong argument. I also have learned to insert explanatory phrases liberally, since supervisors seem unwilling to admit that readers might actually be able to carry a thought from one sentence to the next.

Government writing at its worst is typified by the regulations that implement the various statutes administered by the DOL.

Only those to whom clear writing is an alien concept are chosen to draft regulations. That is why, whatever area of law you are in, you must read, read, read the regulations. Look upon this reading as a regular exercise bout on the weight machine. Your mind needs the repetitions. Even with constant reading, you will, at times, find the regs to be nonsensical, ungrammatical, and contradictory. Yet it is the mastery of these same regulations that will bring success in the federal service. The more you know about the regs, the more you may wax eloquent in your chats with the powers that be.

Survival in the federal service also requires personal objectivity toward supervisors and colleagues. I posit that at least 80 percent of the law administered by the government falls into a grey area where reasonable minds can disagree. And while there are right and wrong solutions to legal problems, there are few absolutes in arriving at a specific approach. Your ideas will always be subjected to a certain amount of criticism. How you respond to the criticism is crucial. In the federal government, extremism in your own defense is no virtue.

LEARN TO TURN CRITICISM TO YOUR OWN ADVANTAGE

The trick is to develop the knack of turning the criticism, no matter how bluntly or nastily presented, to your own advantage. I am no expert, but I have watched those who are truly talented in this respect turn lead into gold. I once heard a lawyer whose case-tracking skills were non-existent listen thoughtfully to criticism from two supervisors at a staff meeting and then suggest that what was really needed was a paralegal to keep a master calendar of the division's cases. Solemn nods of agreement greeted the suggestion. Superior performance appraisals are made in this fashion. Finally, if your job position is not optimal, be patient. In June 1991, I was "discovered," as they say in Hollywood. I argued two important cases before the Benefits Review Board, which helped get me promoted to Deputy Associate General Counsel. My new boss was a woman who started in government as a GS 3, attended college and law school while working and mothering, and eventually received a political appointment for a job with a six-figure income. She and I spent the greater part of the hiring interview discussing our feelings and experiences. We covered law, morality, and the win-win approach to life. We exchanged theories of teaching, leading, and motivating. We even compared bringing up teenagers and losing husbands.

Because of her, I now work in an agency which can only be described as a matriarchy. Two of its four administrative appeals judges are women, all four division heads are women, and eight of the fourteen first-line supervisors are women. In addition, women comprise almost two thirds of the staff. Among us can be counted Steel Magnolias and Godmothers; I think I might even be considered one of the latter by the four delightful women and two young men I supervise.

Although women dominate the Board's hierarchy, the men in the office seem to be coping without any loss of masculine grace. Meanwhile, the present Secretary of Labor works on "Reinventing the Department" with the able support of many female supervisors and the committed backing of the union. But the top managerial positions are still overwhelmingly occupied by men. The Office of Administrative Law Judges remains a male bastion, and only two of the eleven divisions in my former office are headed by women. Somehow, this scenario does not compute, but perhaps I am overlooking some nuance. In any event, I will welcome the day when Sandra Day O'Connor and Ruth Bader Ginsburg can go a whole term without reminding the advocates in oral argument before the United States Supreme Court that the high bench does not consist exclusively of "gentlemen."

CHAPTER 18

When I Grow Up, I Want To Work For the ACLU: On Becoming and Being a Public Interest Lawyer

by
ANN BRICK

ANN BRICK

Ann Brick, has been a staff attorney at the American Civil Liberties Union of Northern California since January, 1991. She received her J.D. degree in 1975 from the University of California at Berkeley (Boalt Hall) where she was an editor of the California Law Review and a member of the Order of the Coif. Upon graduation, she clerked for the Honorable Alfonso J. Zirpoli, Judge of the United States District Court for the Northern District of California—the judge's first woman law clerk. She then joined the law firm of Howard, Rice, Nemerovski, Canady, Robertson, Falk & Rabkin, where, in 1982, she became the firm's first woman partner.

Ann was raised in Cheyenne, Wyoming, along with her two sisters. "We were raised believing that we could be anything we wanted to be," she says. "Gender was never regarded as a barrier in our family!" It is therefore not surprising that her older sister, Sherry Snyder, has an MBA and her own management consulting business in New Orleans or that her younger sister, D. Jean Veta, is also a contributor to this book.

Ann's practice at the ACLU primarily focuses on censorship and reproductive rights. One of her favorite cases involved a school district's attempt to censor a student-designed mural on freedom of expression. When the Elk Grove High School invited each of the school's student organizations to paint a mural depicting the goals and values of the club, the students in the Model U.N./Junior Statesmen of America Club designed a mural about the Supreme Court's recent flag burning decision—a case they had spent a great deal of time studying. The mural showed a burning American flag with the text of the First Amendment showing through the flames. Underneath was a citation to the United States Supreme Court's decision in Texas v. Johnson, 491 U.S. 397 (1989). The students believed the mural illustrated the importance of freedom of speech. (As one student put it: "Sometimes you have to look behind the flag in order to understand the Constitution.") School administrators proceeded to ban the mural. Because California has special legislation protecting students' rights of free expression, the students obtained an injunction permitting them to paint their mural.

Besides litigating as an ACLU lawyer, Ann has been a member of the Board of Directors of Equal Rights Advocates since 1983. She is also a fellow of the American Bar Foundation, a former board member of the Legal Aid Society of San Francisco, and a former member of the Committee on Women in the Law of the State Bar of California and of the Judiciary Committee of the Bar Association of San Francisco. In the non-legal world, she served as a member of the Board of Directors of Park Day School.

Ann and her husband, Steve, live in Berkeley, California with their two daughters, 11-year-old Katie and 9-year-old Rachel.

CHAPTER 18

When I Grow Up, I Want To Work For the ACLU: On Becoming and Being a Public Interest Lawyer

by
ANN BRICK

I went to law school because I wanted to be a public interest lawyer. But getting there was a long time coming. For twelve years I was a commercial litigator in a "downtown" San Francisco law firm, first as an associate and then as its first woman partner. It was only after those twelve years, two children, and a re-evaluation of what is most important to me professionally that I finally did what I had set out to do: in January 1991, I became a staff attorney at the American Civil Liberties Union of Northern California.

As with so much in life, getting there was half the fun. But being there is even better. In the pages that follow I would like to tell you about the path that led me into public interest law and to describe what it's like now that I am, at last, a public interest lawyer.

GETTING THERE

Like so many other women in the class of 1975 at Boalt (the first in which women represented a full one third of the class), I did not begin law school immediately upon college graduation.

But three years of doing marketing research at the telephone company, all the while discussing with my husband the cases he was studying in law school, convinced me of three things: (1) even if I did rise through the ranks and become president of Pacific Telephone, that was not the place for me; (2) the study of law was far more interesting than I had ever thought it could be; and (3) if I truly wanted to address the injustices that seemed so apparent in the late 1960's and early '70's, I would probably accomplish more as a lawyer.

1975, however, was the heyday of public interest law. Everyone (or so it seemed) wanted to be a public interest lawyer. Although new public interest and legal services organizations were springing up all over the landscape, there were far more eager young law school graduates than there were public interest jobs—especially if you wanted to do "big-time impact" litigation.

The conventional wisdom had it that at least three years of litigation experience was the absolute minimum necessary in order to have anyone even look at your resume. Being a reasonably conventional person myself, I set out to get that experience by clerking for a judge and then joining a small but well-thought of liberal law firm. The plan was to stay for three years and then apply for a public interest position. And so it was that I went to work at what is now Howard, Rice, Nemerovski, Canady, Robertson, Falk & Rabkin in San Francisco.

A Step Along the Way to Getting There

A number of factors attracted me to Howard, Rice. For one thing, no one there took himself too seriously. This was one of the few law firms where, during a job interview, no one asked "Do you mind if I take off my jacket?" before doing so; and it was the only firm where an unmentionable word that begins with the letter "F" was actually uttered when "ladies" were around. Equally important, the firm had a reputation for doing high visibility pro bono work, including some of the key California death penalty cases. It was not a public interest law firm, but it was the next best thing.

Although, at the time, I was the only woman lawyer at the firm, I was not the first. Even so, my first day started out like the script from a bad movie: When I announced myself to the receptionist, she asked whether I was the new temp. A few hours later, I couldn't decide whether things were getting better or worse when a dozen red roses were delivered to my office with a card that read, "Welcome. From the boys." After giving the matter much thought, I decided they were getting better. I was right. Two partners became my mentors—and, as it turned out, lifelong friends. The work was exciting and satisfying, with enough opportunity to do both pro bono and paying public interest work to meet my needs. As a result, my carefully thought-out Three Year Plan went by the boards. I simply couldn't imagine leaving a place that had become as important to me as my family.

A Side Tour Before Getting There

If Steve and I had not decided to have children (a decision that, after 14 years of marriage, surprised me almost as much as it did our family and friends), I might very well still be at Howard, Rice. But, unexpectedly, becoming a mother completely altered my perspective. For the first time in my professional life, the law was no longer the be-all and the end-all of how I wanted to spend my time. While being a lawyer was still very important to me, spending time with my children was even more important. The solution was to take a year off after each child was born and to work out a part-time arrangement with the firm.

On one level, my part-time arrangement was quite successful. For the most part, others in the firm accepted what was, at the time, an extraordinary departure from traditional practice. Working three days a week let me spend my time doing the two things I loved most. But a part-time schedule meant that there was no longer a significant amount of time left for pro bono work. And, due primarily to my own egotistical desire to prove that I could "do it all," I eventually found myself working longer hours and more days than was consistent with what I had promised myself in terms of spending time with my children.

At the same time that I was changing, the practice of law was changing, as well. It was the ''go-go 80's'' when business development, firm growth, and firm earnings came to take on overriding significance in the legal profession. My firm, while doing better than most in holding on to its core values, was not entirely immune.

Deciding Where ''There'' Is

I took a long leave of absence, and began to think seriously about what I wanted to do with my life, at least in the near-term. I ultimately reached two important conclusions. First, I realized that I no more wanted to give up the practice of law than I wanted to work full time. Part-time was the right balance for me. Second, I concluded that, if I was serious about my commitment to doing public interest work, *this* was the time to make the change.

Throughout my years in private practice I had maintained close ties at the ACLU. I had been a cooperating attorney, had served on the Legal Committee, and was a member of the ACLU's Board. Thus it was natural that, in terms of interest and affiliation, I turned first to my friends at the ACLU. After some negotiating, we were able to work things out and, effective January 2, 1991, I officially joined the staff.

If there are any generalizations to be drawn from my decision to make a radical change in career, I think they are these: First, we are different people at different times in our lives. Our financial, intellectual, and emotional needs change. A career—or lifestyle—choice that is absolutely right at one point in time may not remain so.

Second, deciding to make an important change can be paralyzingly difficult if it is viewed as a change for ''all time.'' Thinking in terms of a change for ''now'' or for the near-term is far less threatening.

Finally, once you figure out what you really want (that's the hard part), GO FOR IT. While being able to compromise is important in life, you should think long and hard before giving up on a dream.

BEING THERE—WHAT'S GREAT ABOUT IT

If this chapter were a legal brief, this section would probably begin: "First, it is important to understand what being a public interest lawyer is *not* about." It is not about billable hours, business development, or worrying that the competition will steal your clients or your best lawyers—at least for the most part. However, the absence of these less-than-perfect aspects of practicing law in the private sector is not the reason one chooses public interest law. In fact, public interest lawyers do work hard; we worry about funding, and about losing our friends and colleagues to burn-out, the government, or to a better paying job.

What makes public interest law special, of course, is the work we do. Long before I joined the staff of the ACLU I knew I would often be litigating cases raising cutting edge issues. (I would be less than honest if I did not also admit that part of the attraction is in doing cases that tend to be high-profile. That aspect of our practice adds a little spice to the day-to-day work.) What I did not realize—and what I have found to be an unexpected bonus—is the degree to which we are able to determine which cases or issues we spend our time on. This is true for two reasons. First, because we have no dearth of clients (business development is *not* a problem here), we are forced to be selective in the cases we take. While we occasionally have little choice but to take on a case because it involves one of our core values (if we don't represent the Nazis who want to have a parade, no one will), in most instances we must, of necessity, pick and choose among the cases that present themselves. This allows us to have more control over how we spend our time than is often the case in private practice.

Second, while each of us is a generalist to some extent, each of the five litigators in the office takes responsibility for two or three priority areas. These priorities represent the key areas of our practice. This not only makes for a more efficient distribution of the work; it also permits each lawyer to concentrate on the issues that he or she finds to be of greatest personal interest or importance. For example, school censorship and art censorship have always been hot-button issues for me. It was thus natural for me to take them on as priorities. Similarly, Margaret Crosby and I share responsibility for reproductive rights issues.

Why Public Interest Work Is Great For Women

There are other aspects of being a public interest lawyer that are also especially satisfying. Some aspects, like our small size and the fact that I joined a group of absolutely first-rate civil liberties lawyers, are "gender-neutral." Others, however, are definitely related to being a woman here. For example, for the first time in my career, I am working with another woman lawyer who, in many senses, is a mentor. While it may seem odd to think of having a mentor after having practiced for so many years, it is a continually enriching experience on both a personal and professional level.

Part-Time Schedules Are Possible

Similarly, the way in which our office works with cooperating attorneys is ideal for a woman (or man!) who has chosen to work part-time. As a practical matter, we could never maintain a docket the size of ours if we kept all of our cases in-house. Luckily, San Francisco law firms have a long tradition of public service and many of them have strong ties with the ACLU. Thus most of our cases are handled by cooperating attorneys who do the lion's share of the work. Our role is similar to that of a senior partner in a law firm: the degree of our involvement turns on both the size of the case and the resources and experience of the cooperating attorneys working with us.

While this arrangement means that the inevitable crises are more manageable, it is not without its costs. The chief disadvantage is that our hands-on involvement in a case is often greatly diminished. The solution that has worked for me has been always to keep one or two cases in-house. To date these have tended to be reproductive rights cases, partly because the time already invested in these cases made it inefficient to bring in outside lawyers and partly because Maggie and I could work on these cases as a team. Thus we have had the benefit of one another's advice and expertise and the fun of working together.

Working On Reproductive Rights Cases

While it is striking that it is the two women lawyers on the staff who do the reproductive rights cases, I am not sure what conclusions flow from that. It certainly does not evidence an institutional indifference to the issue; the ACLU has been in the forefront in the struggle for reproductive freedom, and has been responsible for litigating the vast majority of major cases in the area. On the other hand, it remains true that, nationwide, most (although certainly not all) of the lawyers litigating reproductive rights cases, including the cases litigated by the ACLU, have been women. Indeed, some would argue that it is not only appropriate but important for women lawyers to be in the forefront on this quintessential woman's issue.

What does this all mean? I do *not* think it means that men cannot bring the same passion or commitment to the issue or that they are incapable of litigating reproductive rights cases every bit as effectively as women. I think the question is more one of education and engagement. The issue of reproductive rights affects women more directly and more concretely than it does men. Perhaps, then, it is only natural that women have taken the lead in identifying reproductive rights issues and in fighting the battle to protect and extend a woman's right to reproductive freedom. What is important is that male lawyers not come to view reproductive rights as solely the domain of women lawyers. One of our roles as public interest lawyers is to make it possible for male lawyers to bring a feminist perspective to their evaluation of civil liberties questions.

In sum, I have found that being a public interest lawyer suits me to the proverbial "T". But, as with any job, some things are hard.

BEING THERE—WHAT'S HARD

There are two things about being a public interest lawyer that I have found difficult. The first turns on who I am; the second turns on the nature of public interest work and the hard questions that are an inevitable consequence of dealing with issues that touch on our core values.

Operating in Different Worlds

I live in at least two, possibly three, different worlds. There is my life as a former member of the "downtown" bar and as the wife of someone who is still practicing in that domain. Closely related to that world is my life as a mom. Although the people in my "mom" world are not all lawyers, the group is still pretty homogeneous in terms of lifestyle and values.

And then there is my life as a public interest lawyer. The lifestyles and values there are very different. Thus it is that in my downtown lawyer world and in my mom world, my politics and values are far to the left of anyone else I know. I am sometimes amazed to find that views that seem perfectly obvious and rational to me, are seen by my friends as radical, unrealistic, or downright crazy. On the other hand, in the public interest world, I am probably the most conservative person I know. I find myself hesitating where others, whose opinions and judgment I respect, find the issue clear.

After almost four years of being an ACLU lawyer, I finally feel comfortable, for the most part, with the fact that I am operating in three very different environments and that I, like my friends and colleagues, must accept myself for who and what I am in each of these different worlds. There is one aspect of this trifurcation that remains a real concern, however.

Because I have had so many advantages in my own life, it is all too easy to slip into the habit of generalizing from my own experience, letting that experience color my perspective and judgment. For example, because I am a white middle class woman who drives a nice car, getting stopped by the police is not likely to be anything more than a mildly unpleasant experience resulting solely from the fact that I am getting a ticket for speeding (again). The officer will treat me respectfully, I will not be asked to get out of the car, and the chances of the officer searching me or my car are almost nonexistent.

On the other hand, I know that that is *not* what happens to young African American men who get stopped by the police. But how much unconscious skepticism do I bring with me when I evaluate calls that come in through our complaint desk alleging police misconduct? Similarly, when I am trying to weigh free speech values against a person's right not to be racially or sexually harassed in the workplace, to what degree is my judgment affected by the fact that, for whatever reason, in a society in which discrimination is almost a way of life, I have not had to overcome the obstacles that have stood in the paths of so many others. The list could go on and on.

This is not an issue of white liberal guilt. It is, on a very practical level, a kind of handicap that must—and, I believe, can—be overcome. What it seems to boil down to is remembering to heed that little warning light before dismissing or discounting an argument that at first blush seems unrealistic simply because it does not resonate with my own experience.

Being Part Of Public Policy Choices

An equally difficult aspect of moving from private commercial litigation into a public interest practice lies in the difficult public policy choices that are so often at the core of what we do. The great regularity with which various ACLU members cancel their membership in the organization is ample testament to the fact that the issues we deal with are inherently controversial. It is one thing, however, to decide as an outsider that a particular stand on a particular issue is correct or not; it is quite a different matter to be on the inside helping to make those decisions.

At times, the conflict arises because core ACLU values are at stake on both sides of the equation. Sometimes, however, the conflict is not so much between competing values but rather involves the tension between taking a position that is necessary to preserve civil liberties, but which, given the realities of how government operates, may have practical results that make us quite uncomfortable. For me, these are the most difficult decisions of all.

The Most Difficult Decisions

The question of coerced contraception is a good example. Considered in the abstract, it is nothing short of Orwellian to think that the government might claim the authority to decide who will be permitted to have children. To some observers, however, the notion became more palatable when a judge ordered a woman convicted of child abuse to submit to the implantation of the new contraceptive device Norplant as a condition of her probation.

From a civil liberties standpoint, it was easy to see that the court's response was ill-considered. The same logic that supports the court's decision would also support orders denying the right to procreate to those the state deems genetically, physically, or mentally unworthy of having children. Moreover, preventing this woman from having another child would do little to make her a better parent for the children she already has or to protect those children from future abuse.

A far better solution would be to require her to attend parenting classes and counseling sessions (both of which the judge had also ordered as conditions of her probation) and to carefully monitor the situation so that the state could intervene should there be evidence of further abusive conduct. However, the reality of an over-burdened Child Protective Services system makes it unrealistic to think that the necessary follow-through would actually occur. Thus, if one's only concern were to be sure that this woman would never again abuse a child, the solution would lie in taking away her existing children and ensuring that she did not give birth to any more.

This was a hard case for me precisely because of the disparity between what the result ought to be (i.e., careful monitoring) and what I knew the result might turn out to be (a failure of the system to protect the children). In the end, I concluded that we cannot permit outcomes affecting fundamental values (and, in my view, affecting the kind of nation we are and will become) to be dictated by our unwillingness or inability to expend the resources necessary to address the root causes of a problem. If we do, the price will be our freedom as a people.

Some of you may disagree. That's fine. My point here is not to give a lecture on civil liberties; it is to say that, much to my surprise, the conflicts in values were not only much easier to resolve but less frequently encountered in private practice than they are as a public interest lawyer.

There is, of course, a certain irony here. The prevailing stereotype is that commercial lawyers often wear black hats, while public interest lawyers can lay claim to doing only white-hat litigation. The truth, however, is that, for the most part, I was not plagued with doubts about whether I was doing the right thing while in private practice. I was usually able to avoid that sort of conflict by not practicing in certain areas. Thus, with but one exception, the cases I worked on did not give me reason to question whether my client's interests were at odds with larger societal interests or values. The issue is not so simple when questions of civil liberties are involved. It is sometimes very difficult to figure out which hat is the white one. Even so, I wouldn't trade places for the world.

I have now been at the ACLU for four years. They have been unbelievably happy and fulfilling years and I look forward to many more to come. As to how many more, however, I wouldn't even hazard a guess. The world has a way of surprising us with what it has in store. I look forward to my next surprise.

CHAPTER 19

The Litigating Mom

by
ANDRA BARMASH GREENE

ANDRA BARMASH GREENE

Andra Barmash Greene, is a litigation partner in the Newport Beach, California office of Irell & Manella. Ms. Greene specializes in complex civil litigation.

Ms. Greene received her undergraduate degree from Brown University and her law degree in 1981 from Harvard Law School. Upon graduation from law school, Ms. Greene clerked for the Honorable Catherine B. Kelly of the District of Columbia Court of Appeals. The experience was memorable because the judge and everyone who worked for her were women.

Following her clerkship, Ms. Greene practiced for nearly four years at the Washington, D.C. office of Akin, Gump, Strauss, Hauer & Feld, where she handled both civil and criminal cases. While at Akin, Gump, Ms. Greene did everything she could (that was legal) to obtain courtroom experience. When she left the firm, Ms. Greene had four federal court trials and five appeals under her belt.

In 1986, Ms. Greene headed west to the Golden State and joined Irell & Manella. Despite rumors to the contrary, there was nothing "laid back" about litigation in California (although Ms. Greene was fortunate enough to have a view of the ocean from her office) nor were all lawyers "blond." At Irell & Manella, Ms. Greene has handled environmental, securities fraud, professional negligence, intellectual property, and business torts cases.

At Irell & Manella, Ms. Greene broke new ground. She became the first woman partner in the firm's Newport Beach office and the first woman to play in the firm poker club. Indeed, in 1991, Ms. Greene (aka "Killer") took first place in the Irell & Manella Poker Club, Newport Beach Division, a coveted title.

Ms. Greene not only built a law practice in California, she also took on the "awesome" job of building a family. She has a (very patient) husband, a six-year-old daughter, two teenage stepsons, one dog and one goldfish. Ms. Greene was one of those working mothers who (initially) believed in the theory of "having it all." She soon found that anyone who said it would be easy for a working mother to "have it all" was crazy. Ms. Greene has learned that managing both a household and a litigation practice require time, energy, patience, and humor (actually, quite a bit of humor). For example, during a recent two and one-half month jury trial in which the plaintiffs sought $34 million from Ms. Greene's clients, Ms. Greene insisted on making dinner for her family nearly every night after court. Who says quality time can't be achieved via a microwave? Happily, Ms. Greene won a motion for judgment of nonsuit in that case, and dinner now proceeds at a more leisurely pace. Okay, so she still uses the microwave.

Ms. Greene is currently Chair of the Program Evaluation & Utilization Committee of the Section of Litigation of the American Bar Association. She served as Co-Chair of the 1993 Conference on the Woman Advocate. She is a frequent speaker at both ABA and continuing legal education programs.

CHAPTER 19

The Litigating Mom

by
ANDRA BARMASH GREENE

The law student seated across from me was making all the right moves. Confident and energetic, she asked intelligent questions about our summer associate program and early responsibility for junior lawyers. As our twenty minutes drew to a close, the young woman glanced over to the photos on my credenza—pictures of my five-year-old daughter, my teenage stepsons, and my husband.

"That's the other part of my life," I said, acknowledging that I knew where she was looking. She answered, "Someday, I'll have a family, too. I have it all worked out. My boyfriend and I will get married when I'm 26. I'll work at a firm, have children after I become a partner, and hire a live-in for the baby. It should be no problem." "I hope not," I smiled at her. "But you know what they say about the best laid plans." Quickly, the young woman changed the subject to her law review article.

After the student left, I asked myself if I had ever thought that life would be that simple. Of course the answer is yes. If I had not, I would never have tried to do it all. I am a litigator, and I am a wife, mother, and stepmother, roles which I believe are compatible.

But meshing the demands of a family with the demands of a litigation practice is not easy. It takes energy, efficiency, a thick skin, and a sense of humor. For me, the rewards are worth the effort. I have learned to enjoy my life as a litigating mother, and I have developed certain strategies to make the situation work.

I would like to share my experience because I feel it touches on the basic issues, doubts, and fears that women who wish to combine raising children with a private law practice will inevitably encounter. Of course, what worked for me will not work for everyone. Some readers will disagree with the choices I made or question my values. In such a personal matter, every woman must strike the appropriate balance for herself.

CAN WE HAVE IT ALL?

I had no role model for the life I now lead. My mother did not work outside the home, defining herself instead as a "wife and mother." She was critical of mothers who did hold down jobs. While growing up, I knew that I did not want her life for myself. I wanted a career as well as a family, and I just assumed everything would work out.

I went to law school in the late 1970's, at the height of the feminist movement, when women were told that they could have it all. We could be superlawyers, supermoms, superwives, superlovers, and supercooks, all at the same time. (I still remember the commercial in which the woman sang, "I can bring home the bacon, fry it up in a pan.") No one talked about how difficult it was to do any of these things well, let alone all of them. No one talked about the personal toll. And no one acknowledged that "having it all" in the sense of juggling both a demanding career and a family would be a struggle.

WHEN TO HAVE KIDS

I got married for the first time during my last year of law school, at the ripe old age of 23. I knew then that I wanted to have children, but not for many years. Like many young women lawyers starting out in professional practice, I intended to become a partner at the firm first. I had an idealized notion that it would be easier to handle children once this milestone had been reached. Partners seemed to have it easy; no sixty-hour weeks, all-nighters or weekends for them. They just assigned out all the work to me and the other associates. It therefore seemed reasonable to suppose that partners had a lot more time to invest in being parents.

As a partner at a large law firm, I now know that my former perceptions were all wrong. A child-bearing decision should not be based on a firm's partnership track. No one can count on making partner, particularly in this economy. Moreover, making partner is not the paradise it seems from afar. Partners have intense pressures, more intangible than those that face associates. In fact, my busiest year as an attorney occurred when I was a second-year partner. I found that clients expected the partner on a case to be available all of the time, and that the need to develop business was incessant.

DON'T WAIT TO MAKE PARTNER

As things turned out, I did not wait until I became a partner before having a child. After five years at a Washington, D.C. law firm, my personal circumstances changed. In 1986, I moved to California with my husband and joined the Newport Beach office of a well-known litigation firm—where I continued to handle complex civil matters. I set out once again to prove that I was as good as or better than any man, a process particularly frustrating since I had to start from scratch at my new firm.

Once there, I decided that I would try to have a child. Three factors contributed to this change of heart. First, by switching firms, I lost some credit toward partnership. The earliest age I could now make partner was 33. Nor was I certain that I would make partner at my new firm, and the prospect of having to start over a third time was hard to contemplate. As I acknowledged these uncertainties, I began to hear my biological clock ticking.

Second, a number of my friends were having trouble getting pregnant. I did not want to wait until I was in my mid-thirties to discover that fertility was an issue.

Finally, many of my friends already had young children, and I began to see how much having children had changed their lives. Indeed, to my surprise, a number of my law school classmates had given up their careers entirely or had gone back to work part-time after becoming parents. Although I thought I would want to go back to work full-time immediately after my maternity leave, I knew I could not make a final decision until I had my own child. So, in 1987, three years away from partnership, I decided to have a child.

I was lucky. As soon as I decided to have a baby, I got pregnant. Wanting to keep pace with my male colleagues, I hid the fact of my pregnancy until it was no longer possible to do so. Apparently, I succeeded. A legal assistant remarked upon hearing the news, "I can't imagine you as a mother." At that time, neither could I.

A BABY CHANGES YOUR LIFE

Being a pregnant litigator was awkward for me. Like it or not, the physical manifestations of pregnancy arouse curiosity. For whatever reason, my male colleagues and opposing counsel seemed to believe that my pregnancy gave them the right to ask personal questions. Nearly everyone asked how much time I intended to take off and whether I would return to work full-time. I was bombarded with stories about women associates at various firms who had taken maternity leave and had not returned to work. Some men commented how lucky I was that mine was the "second income" in my family, as if I was merely dabbling in the law. When I told everyone that I expected to return to work full-time, I sensed a degree of skepticism. And I couldn't shake the feeling that my colleagues were taking me less seriously than they had before I became pregnant. Was I paranoid? I do not know.

NO SPECIAL TREATMENT

Even during my pregnancy, I still needed to show that I was no different, and deserved no special treatment. Determined to prove my commitment to my job, I worked until the day I went into the hospital for induced labor. I insisted on going to court right up to the last minute. My final court appearance was memorable because a chivalrous male partner insisted that I be driven to court. He would not drive me in his new Corvette, however, lest my water break on the plush seats, so an associate drove me in a more modest vehicle.

To be honest, I was not prepared for the impact my daughter's birth would have on my life. During my pregnancy I focused more on my job than on the abstract baby that I was carrying. My concerns centered on whether motherhood would adversely affect my chances for partnership. This sounds cold, but it was how I felt. I loved being a lawyer and I had devoted the last seven years to perfecting my skills. Much of my self-esteem was derived from my job satisfaction. I spent little time thinking about how my baby would change life. I assumed I could fit my child in without missing a beat.

Reality set in when my daughter Alyssa was born. No one can describe the joy a child brings to a mother. I viewed Alyssa as a miracle. The depths of my feelings for her were something I had never known before, and could not have imagined.

Nor was I prepared for the awesome responsibility of being a parent. Everyone says that children change your life; yet, until I had my daughter, I never comprehended how profound that change was. All of my plans and preconceived notions about combining career and family were suddenly thrown out of the window.

MATERNITY LEAVE BRINGS CHALLENGES

I took a 14-week maternity leave. It was barely enough time. I had all the fears of any new parent. Indeed, I was shocked that the hospital actually let me take my daughter home given my utter sense of helplessness. I felt comfortable handling multi-million dollar cases, but I felt incompetent handling a newborn baby. Slowly, but surely, I mastered that skill as well.

While on maternity leave, I faced the nemesis of every working parent—finding qualified and reliable childcare. For me, the cardinal rule for successfully combining a career and a family is to have stable childcare arrangements. But the process of finding qualified childcare is an arduous task. It takes time and patience. My advice to any new working mother is to start the search early. Explore alternatives well before maternity leave ends. Interview extensively, and check references.

Before my daughter was born, I imagined that Mary Poppins would miraculously appear at my door when I was ready to return to work. She did not. What's more, I knew I could not return to the firm if I had any misgivings about my childcare arrangements.

FINDING A NANNY

I set many requirements for my daughter's nanny, which made the task of finding a qualified caregiver all the more difficult. These requirements carried a hefty price tag, but childcare is not an area where bargain-hunting pays off. One of the benefits I derive from working as a lawyer in private practice is being able to afford a childcare provider with the qualities I want. Unfortunately, many working women do not have this luxury.

I felt that for me to resume my career as a litigator, I would need a live-in nanny during the work week. That arrangement would give me the most flexibility. When my daughter was six weeks old, I hired a woman who met my qualifications—she lived in the United States legally, spoke fluent English, loved children, and knew how to drive. She stayed with me for three years. Thanks to her, I could go to work with peace of mind, especially after my husband and I divorced. When she left, it was like saying goodbye to a member of the family. Now that my daughter is in school and I am remarried, I no longer have live-in help. However, other working mothers I know continue to employ live-in help until their children leave for college.

OTHER CHILDCARE ALTERNATIVES

There are many alternatives to live-in help—live-out nannies who come to the house each day, babysitters who watch one or more children in their homes, relatives, licensed day care centers, and pre-schools. Each option has its pluses and minuses. Each carries an emotional and financial price tag as well.

Regardless of what childcare arrangement is chosen, it is important to have a contingency plan. A litigator who is a working mother should assume that a day will come when her childcare provider fails to show up and that it will probably be a day on which the litigating-mom has to be in court at 8:00 a.m. Having a plan in place, such as a neighbor or back-up babysitter who can cover on short notice, is critical to troubleshooting this kind of emergency. Today, my daughter is in an all-day Montessori kindergarten class. I generally drive her to school in the mornings and pick her up in the afternoons. I keep a babysitter on retainer just to have someone available when unexpected problems come up. My peace of mind is worth the added price.

RETURNING TO FULL-TIME WORK

As the end of my maternity leave approached, the idea of returning to work full-time was not a pleasant one. Typical law firm maternity leaves are 12 weeks—just about the time it takes for a new mother to become confident in her parenting abilities and to find her baby irresistible. My intention wavered. I could not imagine leaving my child. For the first time, I questioned the choice I had made. How could I possibly leave my baby with a stranger? I began to understand why women who had formerly worked full-time did an about face after becoming mothers. When I went back to work I did so full of dread.

Although everyone told me that picking up at the office again would be an adjustment, I had no idea how difficult the first few months would be. I was constantly torn by conflicting feelings. On the one hand, I missed my daughter terribly. I thought about her all the time and I was worried that she would love her nanny more than me. On the other hand, I was concerned about demonstrating my commitment to my job. I wanted desperately to show my male colleagues that motherhood had not dampened my ardor for the firm or for my cases. I wanted to demonstrate that I was every bit the lawyer I had been before Alyssa's birth. In due course I began to realize that I had not lost my interest in the practice of law; rather, I had to put law practice into a new perspective. My little daughter could not be ignored.

SETTLING IN AT WORK

I hit the ground running when I went back. I was sent out of town within two weeks. What milk I had left from nursing my daughter literally dried up and my separation from her was emotionally and physically painful. To make matters worse, my client was impossible to deal with and spent a lot of time yelling at me for no particular reason. On those early days following my return, I kept asking myself if the job was worth it.

It was. Over time, I eased back into familiar routines at work. Most days, I was happy to be there. I enjoyed the intellectual stimulation of the job and the sense of accomplishment. I was glad to be with other adults during the day. My love for the practice of law and my pride in my skills returned.

Nevertheless, I was not prepared for the physical demands of being a working mother. At first, I had little patience either at home or at the office. It was exhausting to work all day and tend to a young baby at night. My daughter frequently stayed up until midnight. And since the nanny only provided childcare services, I also had scores of household chores to do. There seemed to be no time for me. To cope with these stresses, I developed a strategy that has helped me be a successful working mother—delegate as much as possible to others and let some chores go.

MAKING COMPROMISES

The women's movement notwithstanding, wives still do the majority of household chores, even when they have outside careers. That was certainly true of me during my first marriage. I got divorced when my daughter was just over a year old. After that there was no one else around to help with cooking and cleaning. So I delegated tasks to my hired help, or else I relaxed my standards. So what if the beds were not made every day or the bottom of my pots did not gleam. Even though I love cooking, I abandoned my efforts to cook fancy meals during the week. I now cook for my family of five, but I will not win any culinary awards, only awards for speed.

BEWARE OF GUILT

Despite my positive feelings about my job, however, I eventually experienced the scourge of every working mother—guilt. I felt guilty that I was not spending enough time with Alyssa and I also felt guilty that I was not spending enough time at work. The guilt came from a variety of sources—myself, my mother, friends who did not work outside the home, male colleagues with stay-at-home wives. The feeling was, at times, pervasive.

A working mother has to learn to deal with guilt if she is to be happy in either of her dual roles. Guilt goes with the territory. But learning to harness it emotionally is another matter. A working mother will generally spend less time with her child during the week than a mother who stays at home—that is a fact of life. But this by itself does not mean that the working mother is any less of a mother.

By the same token, a litigating-mom is no less a lawyer than her male or childless female counterparts. These are lessons that every working mother must learn, and they are hard ones. The process takes time. There are still days when my conviction wavers, like when my then three-year-old asked me on my wedding day, "Now that you are married can you quit your job, Mommy?"

A working mother's guilt can never be completely eliminated, but it can be minimized. I developed several ways to handle my guilt. First, I accepted the fact that my career was important to me and would make me a happier person. I know that I would never be happy being like my own mother who stayed at home without any life beyond her children. All choices have consequences. The consequence of working is that I am not home with my children all of the time. The consequence of being a mother is that I cannot work twenty-four hours a day.

WORK AS A NECESSITY

I speak of working as a choice, but sometimes work is more than an option. When I got divorced, working became a necessity.

I was faced with having to support myself and my daughter, and this was a frightening realization. Eventually I would come to understand the immense pressures that men have felt over the years in being the family breadwinners.

I also cope with my guilt by making the most of the time that I do have with my daughter. When I come home at night, I try not to do any work until after my daughter and my stepsons have gone to bed. I don't go to the office on weekends. And I try to have dinner with my family whenever possible.

JOINING YOUR CHILD'S ACTIVITIES

I also make it a point to be involved in my daughter's school and to know her teachers. I arrange my schedule so that I can participate in her activities. For example, I take her to afternoon soccer practices and stay to watch her play. Virtually all of the stay-at-home moms drop their daughters off, happy to have a free hour away from the kids. My daughter also takes speech lessons to correct a lisp. I have not missed a single lesson at the therapist's office, although I often spend the waiting period on the telephone or reviewing documents.

There is another reason why the time I spend with my daughter and stepsons is a precious commodity. They all spend time at their other parents' homes, further decreasing the time we have available to be with each other. Given this limitation, I do everything in my power not to let work or anything else interfere with the time I set aside for my family.

HELP FROM OTHER MOTHER'S

Another effective means to overcome working mother's guilt is to find a support network of other mothers who are similarly situated. If a convenient network does not exist, you should think about creating your own. I am the only woman attorney in my office who has children, and I live in a neighborhood where working mothers are a rarity. After talking to another practitioner I met who was in a similar position, I started a play group for attorney moms and their children. The group met once a month for several months. It was an excellent way to get support from women who, like me, were balancing family and career, and for my daughter to make new friends. When the group disbanded, I stayed in touch with one of the other women, and now, three years later, we still go out with our daughters once a month.

My guilt also used to make me envious of mothers who could stay home full-time. But, I have found, to my surprise, that getting to know stay-at-home mothers has actually helped me to feel more satisfied with my own lifestyle. Some of my stay-at-home friends have even told me that they envy my ability to function in the adult world. Many of them long for the day when they too can go back to work. I can see, too, that my daughter and I are as close as any mother and daughter in my neighborhood, regardless of the fact that I am the only mother who works. While I may not be around as much as the other mothers, I am always available to my daughter. I make her a priority.

I have tamed the guilt monster because I believe that my working does not handicap my daughter. Far from it. I want her to have a good role model of a strong woman who can make it on her own. I am proud when I hear her say that she wants to be a lawyer or that only girls can be lawyers. I only hope she will not be on an analyst's couch someday lamenting the fact that I worked when she was young.

BECOMING MORE EFFICIENT

To make time for my family and my job I had to increase my efficiency in new ways. When I returned to work, I adjusted my entire approach to practicing law. I could no longer spend endless hours at the office, for I had pressing and important obligations at home. It took a while for me to learn how to juggle all of these demands, and I am still looking for ways to improve.

First, I learned how to get the most out of each workday. Before I became a mother, much of my social life centered around the firm. I had friends there, and it was enjoyable to work late and have company. Efficiency was not a high priority, since I could stay late if I chose to do so. Now, however, I spend less time on idle gossip in the hallway, saving chitchat for down times. I group meetings and phone calls to maximize my time at the office. Fortunately, my firm does not require lawyers to be "seen" late at night or on weekends.

I often do two things at once. For example, my daughter likes me to sit in the bathroom while she takes a bath, but she wants to play alone in the tub. I use the time I am sitting there to edit briefs, catch up on professional reading, or make phone calls.

NEW TECHNOLOGY A MUST

I have also learned to take advantage of new technology which facilitates working outside the confines of a traditional office. My car phone is not a status symbol; it is a necessity. I can return calls from clients after dropping my daughter at school or on my way to pick her up. The car phone gives me about an hour of additional work time each day. I can also use it to check in on my daughter when I am away.

My computer and telecopier connect me to my office even when I am not there. I no longer have to sit in the firm library at night reviewing or revising documents. Instead, I can work at home after my daughter goes to sleep. Lexis software is free, so I can access statutes, case reports, and other sources from my home computer. And I use voice mail to leave messages for colleagues at all hours. This habit has not gone unnoticed. I may have the only five-year-old who dials the toy phone on her play kitchen to "check voicemail for messages."

COMBINING FAMILY AND WORK

I have also learned to be more efficient about business development activities. If possible, I plan meetings for breakfast or lunch rather than dinner, so that I do not have to miss a meal with my family. I play golf with a female client from time to time, and we typically play just nine holes, allowing us to get back to our respective families for the rest of the day. I also use children's activities as business development opportunities. If a client or prospective client has children of a compatible age, I suggest social activities that involve the whole family. When I attend professional meetings or give speeches out of town, I try to combine them with a family vacation. Indeed, my family equates the ABA annual meeting with summer vacation.

The thing I have found most difficult to manage is my trial work. In my practice trials are rare, but when they come they are long and intense. I once had to spend half a year trying three complex business cases, one of which required me to live out of town. To make matters worse, the out-of-town case occurred when I was a single mother. I flew my parents out from Chicago to take care of my daughter when I was in court. The partner in charge of the trial team offered to replace me if it would ease my personal situation; but I said no. Trials are hard to come by in large law firms, and I did not want to miss the opportunity to have an important role in a high profile case. I was glad that he gave me the option rather than unilaterally deciding that a single mother should not handle the case.

Being in that trial was both physically and emotionally draining. I worked seventeen-hour days and collapsed on the weekends. It was hard not seeing my daughter during the day, although my parents brought her to visit me on several occasions. My daughter even surprised me by coming to court on my 35th birthday. She sat patiently as I examined an expert witness. Throughout the examination, I worried that she might call out "Mommy" in front of the jury. She did not. After the trial was over, several women jurors asked me if the little girl in the courtroom was my daughter. They asked how I could try a case and be a mom, too. Apparently, everyone wonders how lawyers cope.

GETTING HELP FROM MEN

I remarried soon after that trial. I must admit that having a husband available for support and assistance helped considerably. But along with my husband, I added two teenagers to my household. The demands on my time increased, but so did the personal benefits. I hope some day to add a fourth child to the group.

Women litigators with children typically shoulder more burdens than their male counterparts. A year ago, for example, I tried a three-month jury case. There were multiple defendants represented by eight lawyers from five law firms. I was the only woman trial lawyer on the defense side. Most of the other lawyers had young children, but none of their wives worked outside the home. They did not worry about scheduling joint defense meetings or witness interviews at odd hours, at night, or on weekends. Nor did they have to worry about picking up their children or getting dinner on the table. But I had to do those things, and I did worry, even though I managed to attend all the meetings.

CARING FOR CLIENTS

Are litigating mothers accepted in our profession as equals? In this era of political correctness, few men would openly express concern about the capability of a litigating mother. However, I have often heard male attorneys say that while they personally have no problem with litigating mothers as colleagues, they worry that clients will wonder whether women with children will be as available to meet their needs. I have never found this to be a concern of my own clients, the vast majority of whom are older and male. At first, I did not advertise the fact that I was a mother, but my attitude has changed. My family is part of who I am. I have found that as long as I demonstrate my commitment to my clients, they do not feel short-changed that someone who is a mother represents them.

If anything, I "mother" my clients. I let them know that they can reach me any time, day or night, at home or at the office. Few of them take me up on the offer, but it is comforting for them to know I am available. If clients call me when my family is there, so be it. I have handled many conference calls from my home. Indeed, I am always thankful for mute buttons on telephones to drown out the sounds of boisterous children in the background. I get the work done, and my family gets me.

I do many things on my own to combine a family and a career successfully. But I am able to make the situation work because my firm provides a supportive environment for parents. Men have paved the way. One of my male partners (who is an acknowledged star) generally works from 6:30 a.m. to 3:00 p.m. (absent a court appearance) and then goes home to spend time with his young children. He finishes working after the kids have gone to bed. He is rarely seen in the office on weekends. He unabashedly tells colleagues and clients that he is going to his son's baseball practice or his daughter's recital. While he is unique, his actions have reduced the gender aspect of being a concerned parent. Indeed, many of my male partners in their fifties have expressed regret at how little time they spent with their children when they were young. As a result, I do not feel as if I have to hide the importance of my family from my colleagues, nor would anyone here expect me to do so.

WHAT ABOUT THE "MOMMY TRACK"?

Women I know at other law firms have not been as fortunate. Many of them were consciously or unconsciously placed on the "Mommy track" in terms of opportunities for advancement once they became mothers. That has not happened here. Indeed, three other women attorneys made partner with me in 1990. Three of the four of us had children and two of us were single mothers. I am certain that my firm is not unique. As the numbers of women in law firms increase, so will the numbers of litigating mothers.

Combining a career and a family should be regarded as a parenting issue, rather than a woman's issue. In this regard, I have noticed a favorable trend in recent years—men have become more forthcoming about family obligations. Here are some refreshing examples. I have one large case in which my male opposing counsel and I negotiated the scheduling of fifty depositions based on our respective family schedules. I never offered my family as a reason for selecting particular dates—he did. He told me that he was only available at those times because he was a single father with shared custody of two girls. In another matter, my male co-counsel postponed a client's board meeting for two hours after telling the client that he had to pick his son up from school. The client, the chairman of a major company, agreed. I could not imagine doing that.

These examples are noteworthy because they are unusual. When it becomes commonplace for men to openly acknowledge the importance of family obligations and to share responsibility for them, combining the demands of career and family will be far easier for women in the work place.

I have been able to combine my family and my career because I value both my roles as mother and as litigator. I am who I am because I do both. Therefore, I am willing to do whatever it takes to make the situation work. However, if I were forced to choose between my roles, there is no question but that my family would win in a heartbeat. Luckily, I do not have to make that choice.

CHAPTER 20

Life As A Mom Who Works Part-Time

by
CATHERINE HODGMAN HELM

CATHERINE HODGMAN HELM

C atherine Hodgman Helm is a labor and employment lawyer practicing at Irell & Manella, a large law firm in Los Angeles, California.

Ms. Helm came to her firm as a second-year associate in 1984 and became a partner in 1990. She has concentrated in labor and employment law throughout her career at the firm. Her practice ranges from labor litigation on behalf of large corporations to employment advising of very small employers. In recent years she has specialized in sexual harassment, labor arbitration, and employment counseling.

Ms. Helm graduated *cum laude* from Harvard Law School in 1983. She then spent a year clerking for Judge James Belson on the District of Columbia Court of Appeals. Ms. Helm was an undergraduate at Harvard College, where she majored in American History and Literature (writing her senior thesis on 19th century literary attitudes toward the American whaling industry). She graduated *magna cum laude*, Phi Beta Kappa.

Ms. Helm developed an early interest in the position of women in the law when as a first year law student she co-wrote a chapter on "The Woman Litigator" for a book on trial techniques and tactics. "I remember thinking how fortunate I was," she says, "compared to some of the women I interviewed. One described 'Ladies' Day' at her law school, when the three or four women in the class had to sit at the front of the classroom and answer all the questions for the day." The barriers and prejudices that women lawyers confront nowadays, she continues, are far more subtle, which makes them easier to ignore, but also perhaps harder to eradicate.

Ms. Helm and her husband Mark, who is also a litigator, have twin daughters, Elizabeth and Sarah. The girls were born in August 1991. After their birth Ms. Helm took nine months of maternity leave, during part of which she taught a law school class. In May 1992 she returned to Irell & Manella half-time. She hopes to remain on that schedule at least until her daughters are in school full-time.

CHAPTER 20

Life As A Mom Who Works Part-Time

by
CATHERINE HODGMAN HELM

As I sit down to begin work on this piece, my two-and-one-half-year-old twin daughters, Elizabeth and Sarah, are napping in their bedroom, the room next to our study at home. I spent the morning with them today. Eliza is currently enchanted with pens, so for quite a while she and I drew little scribbles on a legal pad. Every now and then she sang out "Old MacDonald had a farm." Sally, who has always loved blocks, wanted my help in building "a huge tower, a house, and a microwave for cooking grapes," so we worked on those for half an hour or so. In between those activities we read several books and had a fight about whether the girls had to get dressed before they could go outside, and, if so, who was going to wear which outfit.

I spend time this way almost every day, because I am lucky enough to have worked out an excellent part-time arrangement with my law firm. I joined the firm, which has about 150 lawyers, in 1984 as a second-year associate and have been a partner since 1990. I work in the labor and employment section of the litigation group, giving employers labor advice and handling cases for them. I have been working half-time at the firm since my daughters were ten months old.

Through my own experience and those of others I know who work part-time, I have formulated some ideas on:

—how to approach a law firm about setting up a part-time arrangement;

385

—how to deal with issues that may arise with clients and colleagues who may never have worked with a part-time lawyer before; and

—how to establish a daily schedule that will work for the firm, the children, and the part-timer herself.

I should say up front that my firm is more receptive to part-time arrangements than many firms may be. I am not the first young mother to work there part-time (the firm has not yet had to accommodate a part-time father), and I knew from the time I got pregnant that most people in the firm would support my wish to work something less than a full schedule upon my return from maternity leave. I also had the rare luxury of knowing that if I could not work out a good arrangement I could resign; my husband, who is also a litigator, could earn enough for the family.

These factors made it easier for me to arrive at a schedule that works well. Still, I have encountered many of the problems that anyone seeking to work part-time will likely face, and have come up with some solutions that may work for other women.

MAKING ARRANGEMENTS BEFORE THE BABY IS BORN

Anyone considering a part-time arrangement should think carefully about whether to discuss that plan in advance. If your firm has no maternity or part-time or family leave policy, you may wish to raise questions about family issues even before you are pregnant, so that there is time to solicit people's views and come up with some overall policies, before you end up being perceived as self-interested. The process of formulating initial policies would work best if a committee of men and women at various levels of seniority studied the policies of other comparable firms and drafted something that most in the firm could support. There is certainly an advantage, however, to avoiding the creation of strict policies. The firm may be willing to make *ad hoc* arrangements for women they respect but not willing to extend those arrangements to everyone.

Of course, in any event, you will need to discuss the amount of leave you wish to or can take. It also makes sense to raise, at least in a general way, the part-time option, to prepare the ground. I think it is important, however, not to commit yourself in advance to any one detailed plan, if your firm does not require you to. Often it is very hard to predict accurately how you will feel once your baby is born. I knew one woman who was certain she would want to go back to work full-time at a high-powered Washington law firm three months after her daughter's birth. She ended up not working at all for a year and then teaching one law school course until her second child was born, when she stopped working completely.

Another woman litigator I know planned to quit work after her son was born, but she found, as she said later, "I started going crazy with boredom after about a month. All the household and baby tasks that kept me so busy didn't seem nearly as satisfying as I had expected." She returned to work full time when her baby was three months old.

The questions of whom at your firm to meet with and when will come up as well. For me, the right path was to talk to the partners in the labor section who were senior to me, then to go to the head of the litigation group, and then to have him take the matter to the Executive Committee. Now that my firm has a Managing Partner, I would probably talk with him initially. In each firm the person who is appropriate to meet with will be different.

I decided to have my conversations when I was in my seventh month of pregnancy because by that time I was, of course, sure I was not going to miscarry. In addition, the news of my pregnancy was of long enough standing that I knew the firm must be wondering what my plans were. I still had at least six weeks to iron out any problems that might come up as a result of my mentioning the part-time option (none did).

I went to the head of the litigation group at my firm to discuss my plans for the coming year. I told him that I hoped to take about nine months off from the firm. For the last two-thirds of that time I would be preparing for, and then teaching, a course at a local law school. I knew privately that there was a chance that I might decide to leave the firm and move into teaching, but I didn't discuss that with him, figuring that if I decided I did *not* want to teach permanently, I would never need to bring it up. Under our firm's maternity policy, three months of the leave would be paid, and the rest would be unpaid. I told him that I planned to come back part-time but that I was not yet sure what arrangement I would want. We agreed that he would take my proposal to the Executive Committee and that we would discuss the details of a part-time arrangement sometime before my return.

A couple of weeks after I had discussed my intentions and received the Executive Committee's approval, I wrote letters to all of the clients who looked to me primarily or frequently for their labor matters. I told them that I was expecting twins in late July 1991, that I planned to take nine months off from the firm and then return, and that I could be reached either through my secretary at the office or at my home telephone number, which I gave them, during the entire period of the leave. I really meant it when I said they could call me during my leave; one of my big worries was that the relationships with clients that I had been developing would wither during my absence. I also gave the clients the names of two lawyers in the labor group whom they could call, and cc'd those two colleagues on the letters. I then wrapped up and handed off various matters, and departed for my leave.

OPTIONS FOR STRUCTURING PART-TIME WORK

While I was on my extended leave, and once my daughters began sleeping through the night, I started to focus on what kind of part-time arrangement I would want when I returned to the firm. Teaching a law school course not only gave me a chance to experiment a bit with different schedules but also convinced me that I wanted to return to practice. I considered various possible plans, and chose the one that seemed best to me. Eventually I went into work to discuss my decision.

WORKING SEVERAL FULL DAYS PER WEEK

Many women who are working part-time choose to work three or four full days every week. Each day they are in, they can devote themselves fully to the job; each day they are home, they can devote themselves fully to the children. This arrangement avoids the constant adjustments other approaches require. Since changing gears is stressful, avoiding it can be an advantage. A lawyer may also be able to get more work done when she has a longer stretch of time—an entire day—within which to do it. The full day arrangement is also fairly common, so a woman introducing the concept of part-time work to her firm might find it to be an easier sell.

It may have other advantages as well: one friend of mine in the business community works three days a week rather than several hours every day in large part because she has a long commute and does not want to drive it more often than necessary. In any event, she has told me that "Overall, my working part-time on this schedule has become a complete non-issue to my company. No one ever even talks about it."

To me the disadvantages of this arrangement seemed to outweigh the advantages. Clients might not like the idea of waiting until my next scheduled day to receive the advice or information they needed. Indeed, in a labor and employment law practice, employers often have quick questions that they need answered immediately. I also thought the arrangement might be confusing to my children, but I now realize that I probably need not have worried about that. As far as I can tell, they would have handled it fine. But the main disadvantage I saw was this: every work day I would probably feel guilty about abandoning the girls, and every day at home I would probably feel guilty about not being in the office. Eager to avoid this kind of "inner pull," I decided that an arrangement that allowed me to assuage both aspects of my guilt every day would work better for me.

WORKING AN IRREGULAR SCHEDULE

Another option is to work a schedule that completely varies in accord with the flow of work. A woman lawyer I know who does transactional work has tried this. "I might work four seventy-hour weeks when a deal is about to close," she says, "and then take a month off to be with my kids. I repeat that sequence several times during a year."

One advantage of this arrangement is that, when you are in the office, you work exactly like everyone else. You won't be concerned about showing up late or slinking off early, as you might be if you worked partial days. Maybe the people working with you won't even have to know that you are anything other than a "regular" lawyer.

Guilty feelings about carrying your weight can be a problem, so having an arrangement that minimizes them would be helpful. This schedule might also be an easier one for clients to adjust to, because you would be just as available to them as a full-time lawyer, at least at certain times. There may be particular practice areas for which the irregular schedule would also work particularly well.

However, the unpredictable nature of this arrangement can cause certain problems. If your children are upset by changes in routine, the schedule could be difficult for them. In addition, unless you have a live-in childcare person, you might have trouble finding a babysitter to meet your needs. Some kinds of clients or matters are likely to need frequent small bursts of attention rather than one sustained volley of it, so this schedule might not suit them. And I think that for this kind of schedule to work you have to be able to force yourself to take the time off after the busy periods. I was afraid that, as the end of a busy time approached, I would begin to look at all the things I had shunted aside because I was so busy, and would convince myself that I really *had* to work a few more long weeks to take care of those, by which time another truly frantic period would again have arrived. I thought that a more structured schedule would help me define my expectations of myself, and perhaps others' expectations of me, in a more balanced way.

WORKING PARTIAL DAYS

The schedule I decided would work best for me was working part of every week day. My babysitter comes to our house from

12:00 noon to 7:00 p.m. I leave for work either right when she arrives or, when I am less busy at the office, after having lunch with her and the girls. I leave the office in time to arrive home between 6:45 and 7:00. My time at the office thus ranges from four and one-half hours to six hours a day.

One advantage of this arrangement is that my children are often in their best moods in the mornings. In addition, because they nap in the afternoons, I am spared some extra guilt, as part of the time I'm away I would not be able to see them anyway. It is easier for me to come in for just afternoons than for just mornings, because when I leave at 6:30 many other people are leaving or are gone, so leaving seems more natural than it would at, say, 2:00 p.m.

The schedule is also very predictable and regular. It minimizes inconvenience to other people: a client who calls me in the morning can always talk to me in the office at some point during that same day; a meeting that might be scheduled for 11:00 a.m. can usually just as easily be held at 1:00 p.m.; the firm recruiting coordinator knows that I will be able to interview candidates in the afternoon; my secretary can plan her day to leave more time for my work in the afternoon, or can finish something for me in the morning so that it is waiting for me when I arrive. And every day I still have a good chunk of time with Sally and Eliza.

A disadvantage of this arrangement is that I feel compelled to work at top pace during the hours I am in the office. If I do not plunge into real hard work immediately upon arriving, but rather read my mail or talk to a friend for the first hour, suddenly a fifth or a quarter of my time for the whole day is gone. I feel that I am under constant high pressure during the hours I am at the office. All part-time arrangements probably give rise to this feeling but the partial day approach intensifies it.

I would also find this schedule intolerable if I did not have the flexibility to come in for a whole day when necessary. When I was interviewing babysitters I tried to find someone who could come in the morning on short notice. Four or five times a month I will go to the office for the entire work day. Certain tasks, like depositions, need a whole day. Sometimes the work will mount up so that I need a day to get caught up. Not having the ability to vary from the schedule would be very frustrating and would limit the kinds of work I could take. It could also be very inconvenient for clients and colleagues.

The need to be able to vary your schedule actually arises with respect to any part-time arrangement. I think it would be nearly impossible to do a good job at the office, and to feel as if you were doing a good job there, unless you had the ability to depart from your normal arrangement at times.

TELLING THE FIRM ABOUT THE ARRANGEMENT YOU WANT

Once I had decided on the schedule I wanted, I spent several weeks going over in my mind how I was going to tell the firm about it, what they might say, how I would respond, and so on. I came up with several different scenarios that ended in my being drummed out of the firm, and imagined conversations in which I said noble things like, "My children must come before your petty concerns about money," and then stalked out the door.

The actual event was anticlimactic. I got up the nerve to make an appointment with the head of the litigation group on a day I was planning to come to the office for a lunch. My firm uses a benchmark of 2000 billable hours against which to measure part-time percentages, and I had decided to try to work fifty percent of that. I explained that I wanted to work fifty percent and of course expected to be paid only fifty percent. He said that arrangement sounded fine, and he would check with the Executive Committee and get back to me. I thought I should explain how I was going to arrange my hours, but he waved me off, saying that he was sure I would figure out a way that would work. The whole discussion took a minute or two. The Executive Committee subsequently approved the proposal.

It will be clear by now that I thought it was important to have a well-formulated plan in mind for myself before I talked with my firm. Others might prefer just to have a general idea of the overall percentage of time they want to work, and to go into the discussions with a completely open mind about how to achieve that goal. I decided that my firm probably would not care what my arrangement was as long as it worked for clients and made economic sense, so I might just as well figure out what was best for me, my husband and twins, and my practice, and propose that.

It is important, though, to demonstrate from the very start that you are willing to be flexible and to work through whatever problems your arrangement might cause. I think you should ask the firm to be flexible as well: my compensation, like the compensation of my partners, is set prospectively for each year, but the amount can be adjusted at year-end if I work substantially more or less than 1000 hours or, presumably, if I make some other significant contribution (or a huge mistake).

Your making clear that you are willing to be flexible may help you to address one of the major potential problems of working part-time: resentment of colleagues. Everyone knows that the second thousand hours are more arduous than the first thousand; indeed, the last hundred are the hardest of all. A part-time schedule may therefore be perceived as easy. In some ways, it *is* easy, and fun. A child might hide a little plastic spaceman inside your briefcase for you to find; a client will not. I have found it best to acknowledge up front to my colleagues, "The firm has given me a very good deal, and I feel like I'm extremely lucky to be able to spend part of each day at home with the girls." This works better than trying to convince them that I really am working as hard as they are, or harder (even if that may in fact be true).

It is also useful to make explicit to colleagues that you are being paid less for working less. I have been amazed at the number of people who do not think that I am suffering any financial penalty. Indeed, if a wildly pro-family firm were to suggest that a part-time lawyer who is the mother of young children be paid the same amount as her peers, I would think she should decline that suggestion, and insist on being paid proportionately to her work percentage. It would not be comfortable for her to be paid more than she deserved, and it would certainly create resentment.

TELLING CLIENTS ABOUT THE ARRANGEMENT

What I tell clients about my part-time arrangement depends on the client. With clients I feel close to, particularly with some women clients and with male clients who have small children and professional wives, I will discuss the details of my schedule. With most, though, I will simply say that I work "a flexible schedule" (which somehow *sounds* more flexible than saying I work part-time), and that I will be available to them either at the office or at home whenever they need me. I routinely give clients my home telephone number. I no longer feel justified in trying to protect my home life from being invaded by work telephone calls or faxes, although of course I try to keep them to a minimum. Many lawyers are somewhat hard to get in touch with, so clients are used to that. What has seemed to me to matter most to them is that I make a real effort to call them back promptly after they call me, even if I have to do it from the living room with "Happy Baby Songs" playing in the background.

TELLING OPPOSING COUNSEL ABOUT THE ARRANGEMENT

I never tell opposing counsel that I work part-time. Again, many lawyers are hard to connect with over the telephone, so I do not think it will raise much suspicion if I am out of the office when opposing counsel calls, especially since I will be able to return the call a few hours later. I figure that what I do with my time is none of their business, as long as it does not impede the case or inconvenience them unduly.

A friend of mine who is a litigator at another firm takes an opposite tack. "At the beginning of a case, I'll tell opposing counsel that I'm in only three days a week and that I'll need depositions and hearings to be scheduled on those days whenever possible. Then I tell them that, if they won't cooperate with me on scheduling, I won't ever grant them an extension again in their lives. It usually seems to work pretty well."

INITIAL ADJUSTMENT TO PART-TIME WORK

I found the initial adjustment to my new schedule very difficult. I was accustomed to thinking of my job as something that filled almost all of my waking time and thoughts. Now I had other concerns that competed for a large percentage of both. I had trouble predicting how much work was half a load. I worried about how clients were perceiving me and about whether other lawyers at the firm thought I was second-class. For much of the first three months I considered quitting just about every day.

Luckily, I had told myself that I couldn't make any decision on that for at least six months after I started back at the firm. During that six-month period, I got used to many of the things that had bothered me at the beginning. I figured out how to handle some of the practical problems. I think it would be wise for any new part-time lawyer to give herself a defined amount of time during which she will make no major life decisions. I could not be happier that I stuck it out for the four or five months it took me to grow accustomed to what was really a very different kind of work.

ADVANTAGES AND DISADVANTAGES OF WORKING PART-TIME

Now that I have worked part-time for almost two years, I can see more clearly than I could have at the start what some of the advantages of the arrangement are—to my kids, to me, to my firm—and what some of the disadvantages are. I have also begun to come up with solutions to some of the problems that my schedule has created.

Advantages and Disadvantages to My Children

Of course I like to think that it is a big advantage to my children to see me more than they would if I worked full-time. I hope I don't sound too arrogant in saying that there is some objective truth in that. For example, my daughters do somewhat different kinds of activities with me than they do with their babysitter or than they would be able to do in a daycare setting. I read to them a lot, and listen to music with them. I take them out and around on errands and to friends' houses and to the library. This is usually enriching and fun for them, although, of course, depending on the trip, it could be boring.

A parent can also handle discipline differently from a babysitter. I tend more to let the girls work out their own differences, even if that means enduring fight after fight. Caretakers worry that the parent will think they are doing a bad job if the kids end the day with bruises or bite marks, so they may not feel comfortable taking the same approach. Assuming my approach is better in some way, it is an advantage to my children that I have the opportunity to put it into action for a good part of every day.

Similarly, parents can authorize risk-taking that caretakers may not wish to allow. A friend of my mother's once told me about how hard it had always been for her to allow her children to climb trees and take other physical risks, and that she had always tried to force herself to allow them to do a little more than she felt they should. "You can mend a broken leg, but not a broken spirit," was the way she summed up her reasoning. I keep that in mind when Sally and Eliza are trying to climb the ladder on a jungle-gym for the first time. Again, a babysitter may not feel as free to treat the children that way.

I suppose there are other advantages to my children from spending time with me too, like the fact that I try to imbue them with good values. A good caretaker can do a great job on most fronts as well, however. In many instances, it may just be that everybody thinks his or her own way of doing things is best, and the more time you spend with your children, the more likely they are to turn out like you.

Working part-time—indeed, working at all—has some disadvantages for my children too. They still say hopefully most days, "Are you staying with us the whole day today, Mommy?" If it's true that they benefit from being with their parents, then my leaving for part of every day is a disadvantage to them. On the other hand, I would be pretty frustrated if I stayed home all day every day, so I might lose patience with them more often if I were not working. As it is, I find that much of the time I am with them I feel lucky to be there, which enables me to be in a good mood.

Finally, there is always the standing justification of working mothers: children benefit from seeing that women work and from having a professional mother as a role model. I do think this. I recognize, however, that I could just be seeking to justify something that I want to do for myself, and that I *can* do for myself because, as a little boy I know once said to his father, "You're so big, and I'm so little." We of course have the power to take any action we want, regardless of what our children may want or what we think they want. I try to remind myself not to abuse that power and not to become complacent in my assumption that what I choose to do with my work life is necessarily okay for my children.

Advantages and Disadvantages to Me as a Mother

The primary way my arrangement benefits me as a mother is obvious: I am able to see my children more than I could if I were working full-time. This is beneficial not only because I enjoy spending time with my daughters but also because I am able to feel like a better mother than I would if I worked full-time. This is definitely not to say that women who work full-time are not good mothers. I would feel more guilt, however, if I worked full-time, and therefore I would *feel* that I was not doing as good a job as a mother, regardless of whether that was actually true.

In addition, because I have never believed in the concept of "quality time," I like having an arrangement that allows me quite a large quantity of time. In fact, I think that quantity time is the only reliable way to produce quality time. The hours that I spend with the girls during which one or another of us is cranky are just as important to our forging a relationship as are the hours we spend happily. While I still have to try constantly not to be too impatient, at least I don't feel much additional pressure from the need to provide exclusively "quality time." I know I will have time to make it up to them if I act unfairly or if I simply happen to be in a bad mood for a whole week.

Another advantage of having more time is that I have more chance of catching, among all the trivialities of the day, the really interesting things the girls do. I was the first to know the names of their imaginary friends (Doda and Choochis). I was at home when Sally first started to put Legos together rather than just being able to take them apart. I have been able to see Eliza help herself get over her fear of dogs.

Actually, the minor events have their own importance too. I like being the person who prepares lots of the girls' meals, who shops for their clothes, and who takes them to the playground. A friend of mine who works part-time once said that she did not really feel like a mother unless she was the one who cut her children's fingernails. When you work part-time, you are able to cut the kids' nails, and do most of the other tasks associated with bringing up children.

Of course, because I am at work for part of the day, there are things that I miss. My babysitter was the first to see one of my daughters start to "cruise." (She may even have been the first to see one of them walk, but I refuse to believe it.) Fairly frequently, my afternoons at work are interrupted by calls from home. One day when I was at work the babysitter decided that Sally was sick, and called me to ask if I thought she should take her to the doctor; I had no idea, because I hadn't noticed anything wrong with her when I had rushed out the door earlier that day. I do not concentrate on the girls as intensely as a full-time mother might.

On the other hand, maybe children actually benefit from not having their mothers scrutinizing their every move all day long. Or maybe that's just another self-serving justification that I've come up with because I want to work outside the home. All of these things are hard to evaluate and hard to know for sure, and I have to live with the possibility that I may never know whether I've taken the right course. All I can really do is try to work out something that both pleases me personally and seems to be fine for my children. Right now my part-time arrangement works on both counts.

Advantages and Disadvantages to Me as a Lawyer

The worst thing about working part-time is the constant worry that I am not doing as good a job as a lawyer as I would if I worked full-time. Being part-time has not affected the type of work I have—I do the same sorts of cases and matters, just fewer of them—but I always wonder if it has affected the quality of my work. I have to admit that I am not as heart-whole as I used to be about being a lawyer.

As a result of this worry I try to be more vigilant than ever about making sure I keep track of everything important. When something goes wrong, though, I attribute it to my part-time status and berate myself for not being more attentive. I'm also not as prompt as I used to be. Just a few days ago a client called me to check on something I had promised to get to her a couple of days before. Luckily I had done most of the work, and was able to get away with just asking if I could call her back in ten minutes. During the ten minutes I furiously reviewed my notes and formulated my advice. I think it all turned out fine, but it was not the best way to have handled the situation. Things like that would not have happened to me so often back in my full-time days.

Another problem with working part-time is that I often feel I am not meeting the expectations of other people. A partner at the firm had a very sensitive, important labor advice matter that he asked another labor partner to handle. I heard later that he had considered me but had thought that I might not be able to do a good enough job because I was part-time. Similarly, a client that was preparing for a strike by one of its unions questioned whether I should be on the strike team, in light of my status. In both of those instances I thought that the people making the comments were wrong. Still, I could understand their concerns, and I wonder whether others are making similar statements that never find their way back to me, or are thinking thoughts like those without voicing them.

It's probably best to confront this problem directly. For example, I could have called my partner and said, "I heard that you had some concerns about whether I would have been able to handle the XYZ matter. I just want to let you know for the future that, if I take on a matter, I will always do the best job I can on it, and I won't let my part-time status interfere with my work for the client." I could have given him some examples of how I have adjusted my schedule in the past year when I have had especially demanding matters. It would have been hard to have this conversation without sounding defensive, and probably the partner would have been embarrassed that I had even heard about his doubts. Still, looking back on it, I can see that that would have been a good way to address the situation.

Colleagues at the firm may also question the fairness of a part-time arrangement and may wonder about the commitment of a person who is working part-time. To some extent the assumption that my commitment to the firm is at a lower level than it used to be is correct. One has only so much commitment to go around, and some of mine now goes to my children. On the other hand, I still do feel extremely dedicated to the firm. The best way I have come up with to demonstrate that fact is by working on firm committees. Although it may seem that firm work could be one thing that could go when you have so many claims on your time, I have found that doing firm activities is critical to my maintaining my visibility in the firm and to my convincing people that I still care a lot about the institution.

I have more mundane concerns as well, chief among them the problem of actually getting all my work done in half a day. I am constantly shuffling elements of my life to address this problem. I've trained myself to be able to jump into a work project and start being productive almost immediately. That way, if the girls suddenly seem to want to play in the sandbox alone for fifteen minutes, I can get a little bit of work done. I got a car telephone when I returned part-time to the firm, and I always check my voice-mails as I am driving to the office, returning whatever calls I can. We also got a home fax last year. Before it broke (which was about six months ago, and I do hope to get a chance to take it to the repair place sometime in the next year or two), it was very handy when I needed to review a document that was supposed to go out before I got to the office that day. I have not quite got myself to wake up at 4:00 in the morning to do extra work, as a friend of mine does, but that's always another possible solution.

I have also tried to develop skill in doing several things at once. I read at red lights sometimes. I can make funny faces at a baby in my lap while I talk seriously about the law to the unsuspecting person on the other end of the telephone. I pay bills while

I eat my lunch. I fill out my timesheet on my way down in the elevator.

My husband also helps me tremendously. In fact, I would advise anyone who is thinking about being a part-time lawyer to marry a lawyer, because he will understand exactly what you mean when you tell him that he has to come home early tonight because you have not even started responding to a set of interrogatories and the responses are due tomorrow. We have worked out a pretty good balance, sharing the work when we are both home and covering for each other when one of us needs a break. Still, because I work part-time, there is a built-in expectation that I will usually be the one to adjust my work schedule when adjustments are necessary. A part-time law school professor I know said to me recently, "Because my husband works full-time and I'm part-time, I always end up being the one to take the kids to the doctor or to rush home if the babysitter gets locked out. I know it's kind of understandable, but it also seems a little unfair. I'm still working on figuring out the best way to deal with that particular problem."

All of this boils down to the fact that I feel under constant pressure from many directions. In some ways, though, the pressures that arise from being part-time have made me a better lawyer. I work more efficiently. Because I have less time to get involved in details and I therefore try to ignore all unimportant ones, I am more able to see the big picture in my cases. I have better perspective on criticism. A few years ago, for example, a jury consultant told me she thought my haircut was not professional enough, and I was upset for days; now I would likely either dismiss her comment or get a new haircut, but I would not waste a lot of time worrying about it.

My arrangement also makes me more valuable to my firm in recruiting new lawyers. To both female and male recruits I interviewed last fall I immediately volunteered that I work part-time and that the firm has been very flexible in allowing me and other women here to make part-time arrangements. Most of the students said something like, "Gosh, I didn't know that firms let people do that." When I told them that not all firms do, they were usually pretty impressed with our record.

The most important work-related benefit that my part-time arrangement has brought me is that I am just much happier than I used to be. I know that, despite the pressures I'm under, I won't burn out at the firm, because I get a great deal of restorative time with my family. My time at home enhances my work life in another way as well: because bringing up children can often be both strenuous and boring, I almost always drive off to work with a real sense of relief and pleasure that I am about to re-enter my other world. I appreciate more than I used to that practicing law can be extremely interesting. I'm having more fun at my job than I've ever had before, and at the same time I find that having kids is more fun than anything else I've ever done. I sometimes just can't believe my luck.

CHAPTER 21

What If Your Job Won't Take You Where You Want To Go

by
MARTHA FAY AFRICA

MARTHA FAY AFRICA

Martha Fay Africa joined the firm of Major, Wilson & Africa in 1984 after having been Placement Director at Boalt Hall for four years, and Assistant Director of Admissions for almost five years prior to that. While a Placement Director, Ms. Africa was active in both the National Association for Law Placement (NALP) and the ABA, serving as NALP's Research Chair for the years 1982-84.

Since leaving Boalt, she has remained active in the ABA, principally in the Law Practice Management Section. She co-chaired the Section's Glass Ceiling Task Force and currently is the Section's Ombudsperson, a member of *Law Practice Management Magazine* Editorial Board, and the Section's Liaison to the ABA Commission on Women. She is a member of the Bar Association of San Francisco's Committee on Employment of Minority Lawyers and has consulted with the State Bar of California on issues relating to minority attorney employment.

Ms. Africa is a frequent speaker at ABA, NALP, and state and local bar meetings, and at law schools and law firms on various topics ranging from lateral hiring, to law firm mergers, to women and business getting in the legal profession. She writes extensively, and is a frequent contributor to ABA publications, particularly multi-author books. She is the editor of a monthly column on recruiting for the *Lawyer Hiring and Training Report* and was formerly a member of the *California Lawyer* Editorial Board.

CHAPTER 21

What If Your Job Won't Take You Where You Want To Go

by
MARTHA FAY AFRICA

Don't bolt: assess. Then reassess. Too many lawyers decide to change jobs without first taking the time to understand their internal stop orders, their current workplace, and their prospective employers.

IDENTIFYING INTERNAL STOP ORDERS

Examine your attitude toward your work. Are you proactively taking full advantage of the opportunities available to you? Are you creating new ones? It is easy not to take responsibility and to blame our work place or colleagues for lack of progress toward goals: but don't fall into that trap. Have you taken a critical look at your internal landscape as a prelude to changing your external landscape?

Let me explain. All of us have stop orders programmed internally; think of them as your customized internal glass ceiling. Some of these stop orders are based on realistic assessments of who we are in terms of basic skills and talents. Others are based on faulty and limiting assumptions we make about ourselves, or others make of us and we accept. Stop orders are like a snail's shell. They are internal notions that inhibit us from growing professionally and personally to our full capacities.

If you decide your own stop orders are probably not the cause of your inability to achieve all that you want in a given professional environment, and you are satisfied that your examination is rigorous, the next step is to explore your future by considering the following:

- INCOME: What are you making now and how much do you want to make?

- EQUAL PAY: Are you making as much as men in your firm who perform similar work?

- ADVANCEMENT POTENTIAL: Where can you go from here if you stay where you are? Where do you want to go? What are your dreams?

- TRAINING: Is this a sink or swim shop or is training a priority? Are you getting work that utilizes the training you are receiving and causes you to grow?

- SUPERVISION: When you have questions, is there someone you can go to and get answers from? Are you treated with respect when you ask for an explanation because you don't understand?

- FEEDBACK: After your work is done on a project, do you ask for, or are you given, reliable, consistent feedback? Are there regular, formal reviews of your work?

- SUPPORT AND ENCOURAGEMENT: Are your colleagues and supervisors helpful and positive? Are you all pulling the oar in the same direction?

- ROLE MODELS: Are there lawyers in your workplace from whom you can learn positive, successful behaviors that will enhance your career?

- MENTORING: Is anyone in the firm taking a proactive interest in your development? Can you depend on that person for advice and counsel?

- PACE/BILLABLE HOUR EXPECTATIONS: Are you in sync with the dominant culture in the firm regarding how much of your life is consumed by work? Are you able to craft a workable time commitment and meet your external obligations? Or are you always robbing Peter to pay Paul?

- RAINMAKING EXPECTATIONS: Are you expected to bring in clients but not given the training, support, time, or encouragement to do so? Do you feel hopeful that you will eventually meet the firm's expectations or are you resigned to being a service attorney, working on someone else's clients? Is this all right with you?

- JOY AND MEANING: Do you look forward to going to work, to doing your work, to interacting with your colleagues and clients? Are you proud of the content of your work? Do you think you make a difference in the world by virtue of your work? Will your current work assignments make a difference to anyone in five years? If the answer to some or all of these questions is no, can you eventually bring in the clients who have work that excites you? Can you envision a way to transform your personal work situation so that joy and meaning are within your reach?

Discuss this list with someone you trust so you can hear yourself. On a scale of one to ten, calculate your level of satisfaction in each of the above categories and consider what, if anything, can be done to increase each rating. Say, for instance, you work with lawyers whom you consider to be excellent role models (that equals a ten) BUT there is little mentoring (so mentoring gets a two). Perhaps you can develop a mentoring relationship and get some of what you need professionally while continuing your career exploration. As you go through this process, think about what you are feeling, how you articulate those feelings, and how you sound to others. Remember, if you both feel and sound as if you are victimized, no employer will want to interview you, much less hire you.

Examine the present culture and your place in it: are you comfortable with who you are while you're at work? Do you enjoy and learn from your colleagues? Or do you feel less attractive, more guarded, less intelligent, more isolated, and less valued than you are accustomed to feeling or than you want to feel? Remember, for each of us there truly is a job that can make us feel valued and productive. Your ideal job may be tough to identify or even recognize. Often it must be crafted over time through the gradual growth and evolution of relationships with colleagues and the development of self-tailored responsibilities. In any new situation you will have to adapt to others, and they to you. Still, some adaptations are harder than others; some never mature into productive relationships no matter how hard you try. Knowing yourself and the kinds of attorneys you enjoy will help you avoid work environments that are toxic for you. You can only become a leader where you fit.

NO 'REASONABLE WOMAN' CAN SUCCEED HERE

Remember, too, that there are some work places where, no matter how hardworking, up beat, and well connected you are, you will not succeed. Examine the track record of your present firm regarding the advancement of women. Are those who are there simply tokens? Have any really made it and persisted afterwards? What are they like?

Although some workplaces are simply inhospitable to women, there are times when women do not succeed because of their own stop orders or their fit within a particular firm. Take the case of the "shadow women." Shadow women linger on the periphery of power, decrying the lack of opportunity while simultaneously failing to seize the space to create it.

For example, one of our clients, a medium-sized law firm with one woman partner and five fairly junior women associates, wanted to hire a woman partner. The firm's management committee wanted a colleague to serve as a role model to the firm's women associates, one who could demonstrate good lawyering skills, good client-getting ability, and positive leadership characteristics. The woman partner already in place was technically a fine lawyer, but she was viewed as unhappy and negative, and she was not someone the firm wanted to hold out as representative of a woman partner. She was, truly, a shadow woman. Worse, her male partners did not truly recognize her as a colleague. The new woman partner they hired was upbeat and proactive. She was a take-charge leader who had her own small client base that was compatible with the firm's existing clients. Upon joining the firm, she immediately scheduled social activities to introduce her clients to her new partners, also inviting associates when possible. What this shows is that sometimes success or failure is determined by the individual lawyer and how she fits into the firm. Remember, no one will give you your freedom to be the "best you" possible. You must create that freedom at some internal level; then take it, and run with it.

Therefore, in evaluating new work places, look at turnover among women and minority lawyers. Interview women who formerly worked at the firm. Find out why they left. Ask if they now feel they made the right decision in leaving and if they have any advice that might help you persist at the firm in light of what they now know. Understand also that people and organizations are capable of change if they recognize it as being in their own self-interest. You may be just the right teacher, even in a workplace where others before you have failed.

PREPARING TO CHANGE THE SCENE

You should go through these exercises rigorously focusing intently on a place you already know, so you can compare the information you gather after you have been there a while with what you expected when you joined. The discrepancies, both positive and negative, provide useful training for evaluating present and future employers.

What about your work? What do you learn from it? Are you busy? In changing jobs, you market your acquired skills as well as your potential. You must demonstrate a firm grasp of your substantive and experiential skills and describe a topographical map for how you will achieve your unrealized potential. If you are applying to law firms, the word "potential" is almost interchangeable with rainmaking. If you are a senior associate or a partner, your map should be in the form of a business plan that shows how and whom you will target (name industries, not specific individuals or companies). Your plan will help possible employers assess your level of seriousness about business getting and enable you to discuss the resources you need to achieve your plan. This will not only provide you with a roadmap of where to go and how to get there, but will help your progress towards your goals.

Employers focus on your experience: the work you have done. That is what you have to sell, the externals of your working past. In contrast, your internal focus should encompass not only what you have done but what you want to do: your future. Suppose you want to shift from doing straight litigation to handling real estate transactions. If what you now want to do differs vastly from what you have done, you will have difficulty persuading an employer to hire you for the new practice area. That is because your market value, billing rate, and salary are based on the experience you have, not on the experience you hope to gain. If you want to shift practice areas, don't use a headhunter; no employer wants to pay a fee for someone who requires retooling. And understand that you'll have to ''take a haircut'' in terms of credit or salary to reflect your level of knowledge about your new practice area. But, if you flourish, the haircut will be worth it. Remember, hair grows back!

WHEN NOT TO MAKE A JOB CHANGE

Painful as it is to remain, there are some situations that require sticking it out, an act of sufferance that will help you retain your market credibility. One is obvious: being pregnant. Most employers favor non-pregnant candidates unless you have a rare skill, a book of business, or a Supreme Court clerkship-type resume that is worth the potential dislocation caused by your maternity leave. This form of discrimination is illegal but, unfortunately, it exists.

Another impediment to a lateral move is having been with your current employer for less than a year. If your law firm is not dissolving and if you otherwise have the option to do so, remain with your current employer for at least a year. During the 1980's, lawyers job-hopped with ease and without opprobrium. The economic climate created brisk demand, so many moved frequently at the prospect of better deals. In the 1990's, employers are conservative; they are concerned about the stability of their hiring investments, and cognizant of culture and client satisfaction issues. High lawyer turnover seldom makes for quality work flow or happy clients. Your reasons for wanting to move may be compelling to you, but stop and evaluate them from the perspective of people deciding whether to hire you. If you have moved frequently, they may conclude that you will continue to do so. If you decide to move from your firm after less than a year, be candid with potential employers about your reasons, without maligning your present firm. Your candor may enable the potential employer to alert you to similarities in the new job, if they exist.

Most of us recognize that every firm has a few difficult partners; if you run into one, ask the firm to shift you to someone else. If your request cannot be accommodated, get the best experience you can, consider it a learning experience, and build market credibility while counting the minutes until you can leave. But, while you are there, find out if any other associates succeeded in forming a positive relationship with the tough partner. Remember the shadow woman partner described earlier? She was made partner as a reward for tolerating a partner who was intolerable but hugely profitable. Whether this was ultimately good for her, or even good for her firm, who can judge? But there are lawyers who develop successful working relationships—albeit perhaps not amicable or comfortable ones—with difficult partners. This is hardly an endorsement for tolerating the intolerable, but rather an acknowledgement that the market will get you no matter how credible your reasons for wanting to move if your timing looks flaky.

MOVING FORWARD: THE RESUME AS RORSCHACH

You'd be amazed at what I can tell about how your mind works from looking at your resume's layout, content, and length; the color of the paper you use; what you do and do not include; and the print size and type you use. To me, this is useful information about you. Because the way you structure your resume reveals so much about you, I am glad that there is no one right form for a resume. However, there is one inviolable rule governing resumes: they must be scrupulously honest and accurate.

You would think they would know better but lawyers sometimes lie on their resumes. Embarrassed by gaps in employment, the length of time it took them to pass the bar, too many jobs, the schools they went to, or the grades and degrees they got, they resort to fiction or omission. In my experience, the lawyers most likely to lie are those who least need to. I am painfully reminded of how I learned this. While a placement director, I knew a talented student whose impeccable credentials, pedigrees, and objectives were ever so subtly shaded, upgraded, obfuscated, and misrepresented. Letters to the editor became publications, weekend visits became internships, club memberships became vice-presidencies, essays became theses. This is a small world. In a job interview, the real club vice-president was encountered. He barely knew the student "vice president," whose misrepresentation gave rise to a full-scale scrutiny that ruined his otherwise extraordinary prospects.

These fictions are caught more often than people know. Usually no one asks about the "discrepancy"; they just don't give you the interview or the job. And the person who spotted the discrepancy never gives you the opportunity to correct the record. As a headhunter, I examine a resume for veracity of content as well as for typos and glitches in dates. In a tight job market, employers look for reasons to disqualify, rather than to qualify. So do I. Recently, a candidate was recommended to me in glowing terms for a high profile position. The candidate, according to the lawyers who had worked for him, was a perfect fit. Upon hearing about his background, I enthusiastically agreed he sounded like a match. The candidate sent me his resume. Absent was part of the very experience that made him so well qualified for this position: the seven years of government experience. "Well," he huffed when I queried him, "I don't have to include every summer camp experience I've had on my resume." That extraordinary lack of judgment was enough to disqualify him from consideration for a position he was both qualified for and interested in. If your resume raises concerns, and you or I haven't addressed them, the person whose resume does not raise concerns gets the interview, and maybe the job.

So keep your resume honest and brief; use reverse chronology (most recent job and school first); provide a complete list of all legal jobs; refrain from using puff words; respect your reader's aging eyes by using twelve point print; provide substantive, concise information; and use ivory or white stock so that the resume copies well. Avoid humor unless you are skilled at using it. Conceptualize your resume as the skeleton and the cover letter as its flesh.

You may want to augment the brief descriptions of your lawyering experience with a summary of your representative transactions or litigation cases. This is generally a one-page annotation of five to seven major matters you have worked on. Embedded in your description of these matters should be the substantive area of the law, the exposure to the client, and your role in the matter.

All this said, it is your resume. It should reflect your taste, values, and experience. If someone else prepares it for you, it will not say as much about you. If you are both wordy and precise, and an employer hires you based on someone else's laconic version of your professional life, the fit will be awkward and possibly short lived. So prepare your own resume. That way we, and you, know who you are. Get feedback on it and have your friends proof it. Never, EVER, rely on spell check as a substitute for rigorous proofing.

Here is one complaint I have about many lawyers' resumes: often the first entry after the obligatory name and address is a category called OBJECTIVE. This category often is self-serving ("use my exceptional case management skills"), it consumes space that could be used for substantive information, and it limits the perceptions a reader forms about you. The kind of information lawyers are tempted to include in the OBJECTIVE category far more properly belongs in the cover letter. There you have an opportunity to demonstrate your writing skills, become an individual through your writing, and organize your professional background in a way that is relevant to the position for which you are applying.

THE COVER LETTER

Think of it this way. What information would you like a potential employer to know about you? What are you proud of? What can you contribute? The rules listed for resume preparation apply to your cover letter, except the cover letter will provide more detail about your work experience. If your cover letter is longer than one page, it is too long. Lawyers are busy and they wouldn't be hiring unless there was too much work; don't add to it. Make it easy for them by answering the questions in your letter that your resume will logically raise. Some of these questions might be: Why so many jobs? Why the switch from litigation to real estate when she's now applying for a litigation position? What about three cities in six years and why is she now considering a fourth? What's that time gap about? Why is she changing jobs now? What can she offer me? Does she have portable business? Does she have management skills?

Very few professional lives are direct shots at a clear target in the distance. One job for life, one marriage for life, is a myth we all cherish, and our desire for that stability has transformed the myth into a cultural norm. But it is a myth, and the reality is that in the eighties when the economy was superheated lawyers moved continually, with impunity. Now those moves are suspect; they are taken as evidence that you won't stay put. The fact is, people cannot move as frequently in the '90's as they did in the '80's. Dealing directly in your cover letter with the negative assumptions someone might make about frequent job moves or something else in your background enables you to advocate your case, demonstrate your writing skills, and show your savvy. Personalize each cover letter, address it, if you can, to a specific person rather than to a functional title such as Hiring Partner or Recruitment Administrator. And let your unique voice shine through.

REACHING YOU

The numbers you provide at the top of your resume give a potential employer an invitation to call you, even at work. If your voicemail at work is secure, let employers know so they can leave a complete message for you. If you cannot take calls at work, provide another easy way to contact you. If you don't have a home answering machine that can take a secure message, get one. And be sure it has a tape that permits messages of up to five minutes in length. The tapes on home answering machines often provide space for more shorter messages than those at work and result in a higher number of traded phone calls.

CONFIDENTIALITY

Job seekers should be concerned about confidentiality if they are still employed. Don't assume the potential employer shares your concern. The employer may see your letter and resume and think, "Aha, I know Joe at her firm. I'll just check her out before getting back to her." To avoid this, state clearly in your letter that no one is to be contacted on your behalf without your permission.

An illustration: An associate wanting to change law firms sends her resume to a firm that she knows is looking for lawyers in her substantive area. The partner who receives the resume calls a colleague at the associate's firm to check her out. The colleague confronts the associate and threatens to fire her. The associate panics and agrees not to look further. Although this probably does not occur often in the early stages of an employment process, it could be avoided altogether. The associate should designate a safe person the employer can call who knows her work and is enthusiastic. Call this person ahead of time and ask if you can provide his or her name. Make sure you have the correct phone number, address, and general information about the person's availability to talk on the phone. Also, provide the person with a current copy of your resume and refresh his memory about the matters you worked on together, because time and rigorous work schedules can blur the mind.

A BEAUTY CONTEST: WAS BILLY CRYSTAL WRONG?

Interviews often prove the adage, 'it's not how you *feeeel*, it's how you LOOOOK!' Much as we might wish otherwise, most employers make meaningful decisions about candidates within moments of meeting them based solely on their overall appearance. Because of this, part of your pre-transition ritual should involve an objective assessment of how you look and feel and how you relate to others. Some things about you won't change: age, weight, your professional history. But sometimes how you feel about yourself must change.

Remember that internal glass ceiling, your personal and professional stop order? You must kick it aside when looking for a job. Sometimes job seekers are battered, exhausted, and dispirited by their current places of employment. Candidates who are depressed because they are unemployed or sapped by a significant loss often project negativity; and employers, unfortunately, respond unsympathetically. One employer recently told us not to send the resumes of lawyers who had been laid off, even if due to firm economics. "They are bummed out—we've seen enough of them."

Thus, you should avoid interviewing when you are not up to it. You simply won't put your best foot forward and you might misuse a valuable chance. If you must interview when you are depressed, psyche yourself up first. And don't permit intrusive questions to reduce you to your privately low state. Get up mentally, stay up mentally, and project UP. You can let your hair down when you get home.

While you can't change your personality, you can change your mood, at least temporarily. First, an interview is a chance to meet new people. That can be a lot of fun. Put your best clothes on, be punctual, be prepared, but, above all, be curious and interested in each person you meet. Getting out of yourself and into someone else changes your mood. Remember, the person on the other side of the desk who is interviewing you also has a life and might be eager to talk about how the job fits into his life (or vice versa). The person could potentially be a valuable contact for you, and perhaps even a friend.

Practice this upbeat behavior. Fabricate practice situations such as going to a store where you don't know the clerks. Practice reaching out on a human, upbeat, level. Lawyers who seem depressed do not get the job, even when they are the best qualified candidates. The cheery, interested, pleasant lawyers do.

THE INTERVIEW

Each interview constitutes an opportunity and is therefore precious. Those first few moments when the employer sizes you up are crucial. Prepare to seize this opportunity. How should you get ready? Thoroughly research the employer. In advance of the interview, call and request the firm resume, the company's annual report, or any written description that can be made available to the general public. Don't stop there. Look them up in Martindale-Hubbell and the local or national legal newspapers. Review their court opinions. Call around and ask lawyers in the community what they know about the firm, its practice, its lawyers, and its clients. This research is geared not only to making you a more impressive interviewee, but also, unfortunately, to learning negatives that employers will never willingly reveal.

Recently a promising sixth year associate announced her departure from firm X, where partnership was virtually assured based on her practice area (growing and in demand) and the amount of business she had already succeeded in bringing in. When her firm called to ask for help in replacing her and told me where she was going, I was startled. She was moving to a firm with a big reputation but one in serious economic straits that was laying off lawyers and staff in many locations. The firm's downward spiral was not privileged information; the legal newspapers had chronicled it. How had the associate failed to learn these facts? Luckily for her, her employer decided to do a Lexus search on the rival employer and make the information available to the associate who at that time firmly believed her career trajectory would be assured by joining this firm.

So do your due diligence before interviewing. Then mentally prepare and commit to memory a list of intelligent questions that are not answered by the firm's resume or by its Martindale-Hubbell listing. When appropriate, adroitly drop these questions into the interview dialogue. Lawyers adore insightful questions and admire the skill it takes to develop them. Demonstrate your interest and be prepared to describe your professional experience, your goals, and the reasons for leaving your current position. Ask what skills and experience the employer is looking for. Don't be shocked if you get a different answer each time you ask the question. There is often widespread disagreement about what skills and experience are needed; that is a reason why the hiring process takes so long.

Some interviewers ask substantive legal questions during an interview. Don't get rattled if this happens. If you don't know the answer, say so. Tell the interviewer you'll get back with the right answer swiftly after the interview. Your ability to handle this kind of stress and to think on your feet are what is being tested here. If the answer to the employer's question is essentially a judgment call based on substantive knowledge, make sure your understanding of the question (and the substantive law) is the same as the questioner's. If you are from a different jurisdiction, be especially cautious.

A skilled interviewer learns a great deal from how you handle these substantive interchanges. Your responses reveal how rapidly you think on your feet, how quick and facile your mind is, the extent of your command of the law, and how you respond to pressure. Most lawyers recognize that you can be stumped by unexpected substantive questions, given the stressful nature of interviews. But dealing with clients is similarly stressful; they frequently ask questions that require research and whose answers cannot, or should not, be guessed at. Keep this in mind, and let the knowledge help you to buy time in the interview. Don't get rattled, even if you're being interviewed by an arrogant jerk. Better not to know an answer and to acknowledge that than to make a disastrous wrong guess.

LOOKING FOR A JOB: USE ALL RESOURCES

Since 1970, most law schools have had placement offices and career services officers to guide students through elaborate on-campus interviewing programs and job searches. While this is a useful service that offers minimal distraction, it does not teach you how to look for a job on your own. Fortunately, there are many excellent written resources available, some tailored explicitly for lawyers. These publications should be consulted even if you think you know everything about job searches. Unlike cooking, job hunting has no guaranteed recipe for success. Many lawyers say they have never looked for a job; instead, jobs always came to them. The first time they look, these lawyers can't believe how much effort, stealth, networking, creativity, persistence, and concentration a job search takes. And since there are no recipes, I can't tell them how to do it. They have to create their own formula.

Most urban legal communities have regular, even daily, legal newspapers, with Want Ads that are often a great source of leads. Some ads identify the employer; others, called blind ads, do not. Use want ads in your job search and keep a record of your queries, preferably by clipping out the ad and noting the date on which you responded to it. Many lawyers get jobs by responding to ads, particularly since they can choose to respond to ads for which they are appropriately qualified.

Well-established headhunters and contract agencies advertise in legal newspapers and are additional sources of information about the market in general and about your chances in particular. View the information they give you in context; if these businesses place someone in a position, they get paid. The employers who use headhunters pay their fees upon hiring a candidate who is presented by the headhunter. Since many employers are neither willing nor able to pay these fees, and since headhunters' general knowledge of the market is often based on the needs of their client base, their knowledge of the job market may be limited. Even so, telephone calls to headhunters can provide valuable, if cursory, assessments of your prospects in the job market and can determine whether your interests (and theirs, of course) will be best served by working together to find you a new job. Even if the headhunters do not have something for you right now, developing a good relationship will encourage them to remember you when they do.

Of all the ways to find a new job, including reading newspaper ads and picking the brain of your friendly headhunter, networking is probably the single most valuable tool you can use. Even though women are natural networkers, you've probably forgotten the names of half the lawyers you know. Go through directories, call people up, suggest getting together for lunch (or for coffee if you can't afford lunch). Put the word out that you are looking. Send all contacts your resume so they'll know your qualifications and can keep you in mind. Ask them who they know, who you might contact and if you can use their name. And, if they refer you to someone, follow up on it; more than half the referrals I make never get pursued. Why should people spend time trying to help you if you don't use the help they give?

Keep lists of people you've contacted and the dates of the contacts. Remember to thank people for helping you, and return the favor when you can. Persevere. And, when you finally find a job, send a letter to all the people you contacted on your search telling them where you've gone and thanking them for their help.

ARE YOU READY TO CREATE YOUR OWN JOB?

Many lawyers are never more happy—or successful—than when they practice on their own. The most informative guide to this option is Jay Foonberg's bestselling book, published by the American Bar Association, called **How To Start And Build Your Own Law Practice**. Even if you are not considering being a solo practitioner this book is worth reading, because Foonberg is a master of uniting the discipline of law practice management with the art of promoting yourself and your business.

The ways that lawyers start practicing on their own are varied. Some practice from a home office, certainly an economical approach. Some share space, and some lease space and invest in a "real" office because they have the clients and the cash flow to do so. Depending on your practice area, your desire to work independently, and your need for steady income, solo practice may be the answer. Warning: if you go solo, it is critical to destroy your internal glass ceiling. As your own boss, you should not limit what you can achieve with a construct that gives you negative, rather than positive, inspiration.

LOYAL TO A FAULT

Do you find it hard to remain loyal when you are unhappy? It takes great effort to be as successful as you can be when you are unhappy. Hardest yet is the task of growing into a leader where you feel that you do not fit, unless you can change the factors that contribute to your unhappiness. If you work in a place where you cannot grow, you must find one where you can. If you are loyal to a fault, the fault is yours.

LEADING THE CHARGE

Law firms and legal departments, by and large, have cultures that were formed by, and for, men and their male clients. The demographics as well as the available labor supply of corporate and law firm America are changing faster than the cultures of either environment has comfortably accommodated, although many corporations are quantum leaps ahead of law firms. This creates unique opportunity for women lawyers to lead the charge in positive directions that will enable people of talent to grow and contribute. Maybe then we will read articles about satisfied, happy, and loyal lawyers, rather than dissatisfied lawyers.

THE BERLIN WALL

Remember the jubilation that accompanied the dismantling of the Berlin Wall? Remember how everyone wanted a piece of the barrier that separated people, families, and generations from each other? Well, think of our internal glass ceilings as being fully as formidable as the Berlin Wall (and potentially as lethal in their capacity to mute our dreams) and begin to dismantle them. Think of the parts of you—personal and professional—that are separated by barriers of your own making or by external barriers. Only you have the power to dismantle the barriers of your own construction. Do it, please, for yourselves and for our daughters and sons.

I believe we are entering an historic period in which we can seize the initiative, push aside internal glass ceilings, shatter external ones, help shadow women realize their potential, and enhance the profession's potential, all because of our numbers and our humane, female leadership. If you agree that the profession is in need of change, then help change it. Make it accommodate to your needs and the needs of those who follow you; each step you take is a step closer to realizing your true potential. Go for it, and bring along as many sisters as you can.

Afterword

by
MIRIAM KASS

MIRIAM KASS

Miriam Kass is an independent attorney-mediator in Houston. She started a practice devoted exclusively to mediation at the beginning of 1994, after seventeen years as a big-case litigator with major Houston law firms and fourteen years as an award-winning journalist with *The Houston Post*. Her mediation practice includes business, personal injury, employment, medical, and family disputes, as well as others.

"Mediation lets me draw on combined experience and personal strengths developed in journalism and litigation - neutrality, sensitivity to special needs and interests, communication skills, trial strategies and perceptions, public service, drama, intellectual challenge, probing questions, short-term closure, win-win victories - it really fits me," Ms. Kass says. "Even on long, hard days, I usually come home high with the satisfaction of a job well done."

As Editor-in-Chief of *Litigation*, the quarterly journal of the American Bar Association's Litigation Section, Ms. Kass also drew on her journalism and litigation backgrounds.

Ms. Kass received her undergraduate degree from Smith College and a master's degree in English literature from Rice University. As a medical, human interest, and investigative journalist, focusing on scientific, social, political, and psychological aspects of medicine, she won more than thirty major awards and honors from such diverse groups as the American Trucking Association, the Texas Association of Mental Health, the Associated Press Managing Editors Association, the Headliners Club of Texas, United Press International, and the American Society of Abdominal Surgeons.

In 1974, when she was the mother of three-year-old and eight-month-old sons (now, respectively, an aspiring New York actor and a Vassar College student), she began her law education at The University of Houston Law Center. During law school she was also a Research Associate in Law and Medicine at the University of Texas Graduate School of Biomedical Sciences under a grant from the United States Department of Human Resources and was editor of *The Houston Law Review.*

After her graduation in 1977, Ms. Kass practiced with Baker & Botts and subsequently with Sheinfeld, Maley & Kay and Bristow Hackerman Wilson & Peterson, litigating complex commercial, personal injury, medical, fraud, securities, lender liability, intentional torts, real estate, banking, employment, insurance, bankruptcy and property rights cases in state, federal, and administrative forums.

She is currently on the Council of the ABA's Litigation Section and has been a member of the Section's Task Force on the Adversary System and Emergency Task Force on Media Relations. She is also a member of the ABA's Dispute Resolution Section, the A.A. White Dispute Resolution Institute, the Association of Attorney Mediators, and the Society of Professionals in Dispute Resolution.

Ms. Kass's State Bar of Texas activities have included the Public Affairs and Plain Language Committees. Her Houston area activities have included service as trustee of *The Houston Law Review* Alumnae Association and the Vocational Guidance Service.

Ms. Kass has also been honored with the Savvy Award and the American Jewish Committee's Women of Achievement Award. She has spoken and written on topics such as evidence and discovery, lender liability, helping the jury to understand complex cases, paternity testing, many women's issues, and her own "Ba" Theory of Persuasive Writing.

Afterword

by
MIRIAM KASS

I read that the woman prosecutor in the O.J. Simpson case was advised to soften her appearance so as not to put jurors off. Maybe wear pink. This is progress. A hundred years ago, "woman advocate" would have been an oxymoron. It might have been thought ungentlemanly even to *discuss* the likes of the O.J. Simpson case with a lady. A pink dress is progress.

The prosecutor scenario assumes that the woman is rational, has the emotional stability to contemplate the gruesome details of murder, has the physical stamina to persist under grueling deadlines, and is aggressive enough to develop the case and go for the kill. The issue is not whether she can do it, but whether she can do it without offending jurors' traditional notions of womanhood.

Women are supposed to be soft and tender. Advocacy is macho and tough. Like medieval knights in armour, litigators battle as champions of others' causes. Litigators are surrogates who have shed spears and pikes, shields and swords, to joust with wits alone. That women are in the tournament is progress.

As a news reporter in the sixties, I was invited to Austin to receive a coveted journalism award. My husband came along for the ride. When we arrived for the related festivities, he was welcomed at the featured males-only luncheon, a raunchy roast of Texas's most powerful politicians. I was delicately directed to the "ladies luncheon" for the politicos' wives. I fumed. My editor warned me to button my lip.

This was a world in which men told dirty jokes to punish—or, more charitably, test—women who dared invade the city desk. Complaining meant, *prima facie*, that you didn't have the right stuff.

In the late seventies I missed another luncheon on the day that Joe the partner and Tom the senior associate invited me, one of the first women associates in a big law firm, to my first meeting with a real live client. Freed from the library, I was so heady when Joe proposed lunch at the club that I did not sense Tom behind me as I rushed to get my purse. When he caught up, he lowered his eyes and muttered, "Joe asked me to tell you—the club is for men only. He didn't think about it when he made reservations. He apologizes."

That was progress. I was *there* at least, at the mega-firm, on partnership track. And Joe *apologized*.

Ten years later, at a mid-sized firm, the women decided to gather for dinner occasionally to discuss common concerns. We laughed, hooted, let off steam. But *really* open up, no. Women partners had images to protect. Women associates feared that their words would get back to the partnership or be exploited as competitive weapons by other women associates. There were stakes to play for, flanks to guard. We were in the game, and that was progress.

It is vanity to imagine that the whole world is looking at you. Yet for years I saw myself as an embodiment of all women striving to be recognized and treated as equal in a man's world. When there are few of a kind, people judge anecdotally, not statistically. I felt I must be beyond reproach and could ask no quarter. There was one game in town, and if I wanted to play at all, I had to go by the established rules.

"It's a shame we don't wear robes like they do in England, but at least go for conservative suits and colors," a well-intentioned male litigator advised me in my first week on the job. Yet in the drab palaces of law, I soon ached for sensory stimulation—color, texture, print. I wondered why I must narrow myself because the masculine norm was narrow. Soon I concluded that appearing as a poor imitation of a man sent the most devastating of all messages for an advocate: "I have no confidence in who I am."

Wave after wave of women has entered law since my first days. Some expect "special" considerations. But when you are half of the population, why is your way more "special" than the other half's? Even that sense of entitlement is progress.

I am ready to travel light now—to shift the weight of the world to the new ones. But I worry that, spread among so many women, the burden on each will be so light that she won't remember that it is there. Not all change is progress. When change has barely begun to roll forward for some, it may already be reversing for others. In the middle of it, you may not know whether you're coming or going.

Recently a male partner in the leading law firm of a small Southern city confided that he loved to work with women lawyers because they liked the sort of details for which he had no patience. He actually said that. He said it was a pity that, after spending good years in training, most of them dropped out to be with their children.

I sometimes avoid women's issues because my flash point shames me, even when I succeed in hiding it. I told a man that the language and culture of most law firms is male and that for a woman, learning lawyering and malespeak at one time can be like spending your first year as a lawyer in Tokyo when you don't know Japanese; that women lawyers today may face subtle, even unconscious, prejudice that is harder than blatant prejudice to identify and confront; and that most women, regardless of whether they have careers, still bear primary responsibility for home and children.

I have known no passion greater than loving a child. Yet loving her new baby may not be the only reason a woman wants to leave a firm. She may feel crushed and drained—too much even to think about, much less to share—and may sense only more of the same ahead. The firm that's concerned about losing its investment in women might consider whether its own culture contributes to the problem, I suggested. His look said it all: "Hey, lady, it's not my job to change the world. I'm just trying to run a law firm."

Power in the world of law still resides primarily in men. They have progressed, too. Thirteen years ago, when I first began to meet with the leadership of the American Bar Association's Litigation Section, I was one of the odd women who was not there to accompany a husband and shop or take in the sights. I sometimes felt as if I were not there at all. Now many women are leaders, child-care is offered, and more women and minorities are being recruited for leadership opportunities.

I am not saying that every ol' boy has become pure in his heart or that all male lawyers "get it" on all women's issues. But most do know there are issues. I remember Martin Luther King saying something like, I don't care whether they love us, I just want them to give us our rights. He knew about progress.

No relationship is more fundamental in our social structure than that between a man and a woman. Over generations, centuries, millenia, that relationship has become encrusted with assumptions, projections, expectations, rules, roles, and taboos that we breathe with the air and eat with the bread of our culture. Pink is a powerful color.

As a journalist covering medicine, I wrote of babies taken for the opposite sex because their external genitals did not develop properly before birth. Surgery could correct the physical appearance, making it consistent with the chromosomes. Yet experts generally advised against surgery after age five because by then, chromosomes or not, learned gender roles were virtually fixed, and trying to change them could wreak psychological havoc.

Appearance, presentation, perception—they, too, are reality.

When Jill Ker Conway, the former president of Smith College, sought autobiographies of achievers to serve as models for students, she discovered a significant difference in the way men and women tell their own stories: Men make themselves the heroes of their lives, the active agents of their success. But women, no matter how spectacular their performances, attribute their successes to chance rather than their own active agency.

As litigators, we learn that truth has a thousand eyes and hides in fleeting glimpses, selective memories, and unconscious expectations. We learn that people have a need to make sense of isolated facts. Therefore we present a case by telling a "story" at trial. Creating transitions and inferring motivations, selecting and emphasizing, we frame a reality. If the jury embraces it, we succeed in our advocacy.

Women advocates have the power to live and tell our own stories. No two stories are alike, but each says something about all of us. I am a white, straight, divorced, remarried, red-haired, Jewish, urban, Texan, a middle-aged mother, a former journalist, a big-case litigator turned mediator. I have been privileged and exploited, humiliated and honored. One lifetime is all I have. I want to pass the torch to a hero. I don't care what she wears.

Bibliography

Bibliography

Compiled by Mary-Christine Sungaila, Esq.

Synopsis of Topics

1. Balancing Work and Family Life
2. Communication Skills
3. Discovery
4. Gender Bias in the Courts
5. Governmental Agency Practice
6. Jurors' Perspectives on Women Litigators
7. The Judiciary and Gender Issues
8. Large Firm Practice
9. Lawyers' Perceptions About How Gender Affects Courtroom Behavior
10. Legal Education
11. Legal Training
12. The Lesbian Litigator
13. Mentoring
14. The Minority Woman Lawyer
15. Prosecutorial Practice
16. Public Interest Work
17. Rainmaking
18. Settlement
19. Sexism in Legal Practice
20. Solo or Small Firm Practice
21. Women Litigators
22. Women's Progress in the Legal Profession

1. BALANCING WORK AND FAMILY LIFE

Books

Lawyers and Balanced Lives: A Guide to Drafting and Implementing Workplace Policies for Lawyers (American Bar Ass'n, 1990)

Articles

Penny Arevalo, Uneasy Balance, California Law Business (L.A. Daily J. Suppl.), May 16, 1994 at 26, 27, 32

Caviness, New Born Options for Maternity Leave, Wash. Law., Jan.-Feb. 1987, at 48

Chambers, Accommodation and Satisfaction: Women and Men Lawyers and the Balance of Work and Family, 14 L & Soc. Inquiry 251 (1989)

Lynn Dannheiser and Steve Reininger, Grape Jelly Fingerprints on Your Career: The Challenges Facing the Lawyer Parent, 58 Fla. B. J. 609 (1984)

Marcy Carey Mallory, Parents Under Pressure, 16 Pa. Law. 17 (1994)

Judith L. Maute, Balanced Lives in A Stressful Profession: An Impossible Dream?, 21 Cap. U. L. Rev. 797 (1992)

National Association for Law Placement (NALP), Developing Parental Leave Policies (1989) (available from NALP)

Sheila Nielsen, The Balancing Act: Practical Suggestions for Part-Time Attorneys, 35 N.Y.U. Sch. L. Rev. 369 (1990)

Pollock, From Here to Maternity, Am. Lawyer, Oct. 1982, at 5

Project, Law Firms & Lawyers with Children: An Empirical Analysis of Family/Work Conflict, 34 Stan. L. Rev. 1263 (1982)

Felice Schwartz, Management Women and the New Facts of Life, 67 Harv. Bus. Rev. 65 (1989)

Laurel Sorenson, Life Beyond the Law Office, in Law Office Management (1990)

2. COMMUNICATION SKILLS

Articles

Diana Morrison and Gregory P. Ladewski, Communication Challenges, in The Woman Advocate (Conference Coursebook) 199 (1993)

Diana Morrison, *The Powers of Voice: The Case for More Effective Speaking*, reprinted in *The Woman Advocate* (Conference Coursebook) 197 (1993)

Diana Morrison, *Powers of Voice: Learning to use Your Built-In Equipment*, reprinted in *The Woman Advocate* (Conference Coursebook) 239 (1993)

3. DISCOVERY

Articles

Judah Best and Bridget Bush, *What They Forgot to Tell You in Law School: How to Handle Yahoos at Depositions*, in *The Woman Advocate* (Conference Coursebook) 745 (1993)

Eugene A. Cook, Fred Hagans, and James H. Holmes III, *A Guide to the Texas Lawyer's Creed: A Mandate for Professionalism*, 10 Rev. Litig. 673 (1991)

Other

Principe v. Assay Partners, 586 N.Y.S.2d 182 (1992) (sanctioning male attorney for degrading gender-based comments he made to female opposing counsel during a deposition)

4. GENDER BIAS IN THE COURTS

Articles & Task Force Studies

Marina Angel, *Sexual Harassment by Judges*, 45 U. Miami L. Rev. 817 (1991)

California Judicial Advisory Committee on Gender Bias in the Courts, *Achieving Equal Justice for Women and Men in the Courts (1990)*, in *the Woman Advocate* (Conference Coursebook) 675 (1993)

Christine L. Carr, *Ninth Circuit Gender Bias Task Force Report: The Survey Instruments and the Compilation and Analysis of the Margin Comment Responses* (June 1993) (unpublished working paper of the Ninth

Circuit Gender Bias Task Force, on file with the Office of the Circuit Executive, United States Court of Appeals for the Ninth Circuit)

Copleman, *Sexism in the Courtroom: Report from a 'Little Girl Lawyer'*, 9 Women's Rts. L. Rep. 107 (1986)

Christine M. Durham, *Gender Equality in the Courts: Women's Work is Never Done*, 57 Fordham L. Rev. 981 (1989)

Executive Summary, The Preliminary Report of the Ninth Circuit Gender Bias Task Force (Discussion Draft, July 1992), in The Woman Advocate (Conference Coursebook) 400 (1993)

Final Report of the Task Force on Gender Bias in the Courts (District of Columbia Courts 1992)

Five Year Report of the New York Judicial Committee on Women in the Courts (June 1991), in The Woman Advocate (Conference Coursebook) 550 (1993)

Gender Bias in Courthouse Interactions, from Report of the Gender Bias Study of the Supreme Judicial Court, Commonwealth of Massachusetts (1989), *reprinted in The Woman Advocate* (Conference Coursebook) 277 (1993)

Tom Howard, *Unequal Justice? Female Lawyers Find Bias in Courtroom*, Billings Gazette, Nov. 8, 1992, at D1

Kentucky Task Force on Gender Fairness: Equal Justice for Men and Women (1992)

Barbara L. Krause, *An Open Letter to the Maine Bar on The Issue of Gender Bias*, 9 Me. B.J. 16 (1994)

Louisiana Task Force on Women in the Courts: Final Report (1992)

Rene Lynch, *Lawyers Testify to Gender Bias in Courts*, L.A. Times, Jan. 18, 1993, at B1

Vicki Quade, *Sex Bias in the Courtroom*, 69 A.B.A. J. 1017 (1983)

Report of the Fairness and Equality Committee of the Supreme Court of Idaho (1992)

Report, The Judicial Council Advisory Committee on Gender Bias in the Courts, in The Woman Advocate (Conference Coursebook) 372 (1993)

The Report of the Judicial Council Subcommittee on Gender Bias in the Courts: Evaluation, List of Modified Recommendations and Comments (California Supreme Court Task Force 1991-92)

Report of the New York Task Force on Women in the Courts, 15 Fordham Urb. L.J. 11 (1986-87)

Judith Resnik, *Housekeeping: The Nature and Allocation of Work in Federal Trial Courts*, 24 Ga. L. Rev. 909 (1990)

Deborah Ruble Round, *Gender Bias in the Judicial System*, 61 S. Cal. L. Rev. 2193 (1988)

David M. Rothman and Bobbie L. Welling, *Gender Bias in the Courts*, 4 Cal. Litigat. 25 (Winter 1991)

Lynn Hecht Schafran, *Documenting Gender Bias in the Courts: The Task Force Approach*, 70 Judicature 280 (1987)

Lynn Hecht Schafran, *Educating the Judiciary About Gender Bias: The National Judicial Education Program to Promote Equality for Women and Men in the Courts and the New Jersey Supreme Court Task Force on Women in the Courts*, 9 Women's Rts. L. Rep. 109 (1986)

Lynn Hecht Schafran, *Gender and Justice: Florida and the Nation*, 42 Fla. L. Rev. 181 (1990)

Lynn Hecht Schafran, *Gender Bias in the Courts: Time is Not the Cure*, 22 Creighton L. Rev. 413 (1987)

Lynn Hecht Schafran, *The Obligation to Intervene: New Direction from the Proposed American Bar Association Code of Judicial Conduct*, 4 Geo. J. Legal Ethics 53 (1990)

J. Stratton Shartel, *Despite Some Improvements, Women Trial Lawyers Still Face Gender Bias in Litigation*, Of Counsel, April 6, 1992, at 5

William Vogeler, *Tirade Against Women Gets Lawyer Sanctioned*, L.A. Daily J., September 16, 1993 at 1, 14

Norma Juliet Wikler and Lynn Hecht Schafran, *Learning From the New Jersey Supreme Court Task Force on Women in the Courts: Evaluation, Recommendations, Implications for Other States* (1989), *reprinted in part in The Woman Advocate* (Conference Coursebook) 333 (1993)

Norma J. Wikler, *On the Judicial Agenda for the 80's: Equal Treatment for Men and Women in the Courts*, 64 Judicature 202 (1980)

Women Lawyers and the Practice of Law in California: A Summary of Findings, Conclusions & Recommendations, The Women in the Law Committee, State Bar of California (1989)

Junda Woo, *Widespread Sexual Bias Found in Courts*, Wall St. J., Aug. 20, 1992, at B2

Other

In re Marriage of Iverson, 11 Cal. App. 4th 1495, 15 Cal. Rptr. 2d 70 (1992) (determining that court's use of gender-based stereotypes to decide validity of premarital agreement required retrial)

In the Matter of Frank Swan, 833 F. Supp. 794 (C.D. Cal. 1993) (Stotler, J.) (sanctioning male criminal defense lawyer for sending a letter to a female prosecutor which stated, in part: "MALE LAWYERS PLAY BY THE RULES, DISCOVER TRUTH AND RESTORE ORDER. FEMALE LAWYERS ARE OUTSIDE THE LAW, CLOUD THE TRUTH AND DESTROY ORDER.")

5. GOVERNMENTAL AGENCY PRACTICE

Articles

Catherine J. Lanctot, The Duty of Zealous Advocacy and the Ethics of the Federal Government Lawyer: The Three Hardest Questions, 64 S. Cal. L. Rev. 951 (1991)

6. JURORS' PERSPECTIVES ON WOMEN LITIGATORS

Articles

M. Michael Cramer, A View From the Jury Box, reprinted in The Woman Advocate (Conference Coursebook) 765 (1993)

Jeanne J. Fleming, Ph.D. and Leonard C. Schwartz, Juror Opinion Survey Reveals Obstacles for Litigators, Inside Litigation, Dec. 1991, at 5

Glaspell, A Jury of Her Peers, reprinted in The Best Short Stories of 1917 at 256 (E. O'Brien ed., 1918)

Valerie P. Hans and Krista Sweigart, Jurors' Views of Civil Lawyers: Implications for Courtroom Communications, 68 Ind. L. J. 1297 (1993)

Nancy S. Marder, Gender Dynamics and Jury Deliberations, 96 Yale L. J. 593 (1987)

Regina A. Petty and Marsha A. Redmon, Lifting the Veil: Reflections on Facing Juror Bias, in The Woman Advocate (Conference Coursebook) 794 (1993)

Soler, "A Woman's Place . . .": Combating Sex-Based Prejudices in Jury Trials Through Voir Dire, 15 Santa Clara Law 535 (1975)

Carol Weisbrod, Images of the Woman Juror, 9 Harv. Women's L. J. 59 (1986)

Williams, The Equality Crisis: Some Reflections on Culture, Courts, and Feminism, 7 Women's Rts. L. Rep. 175 (1982)

7. THE JUDICIARY AND GENDER ISSUES

Articles

Shirley S. Abrahamson, The Woman Has Robes: Four Questions, 14 Golden Gate L. Rev. 489 (1984)

David W. Allen and Diane E. Wall, Role Orientations and Women State Supreme Court Justices, 77 Judicature 156 (1993)

Gayle Binion, The Nature of Feminist Jurisprudence, 77 Judicature 140 (1993)

Miriam Goldman Cedarbaum, Women on the Federal Bench, 73 B.U. L. Rev. 39 (1993)

Cook, The Path to the Bench, Trial 48 (Aug. 1983)

Sue Davis, Do Women Judges Speak 'In a Different Voice?': Carol Gilligan, Feminist Legal Theory, and the Ninth Circuit, 8 Wis. Women's L.J. 143 (1992-93)

Sue Davis, The Voice of Sandra Day O'Connor, 77 Judicature 134 (1993)

Sue Davis, Susan Haire and Donald R. Songer, Voting Behavior and Gender on the U.S. Court of Appeals, 77 Judicature 129 (1993)

The Honorable LaDoris H. Cordell and Florence O. Keller, Pay No Attention to the Woman Behind the Bench: Musings of a Trial Court Judge, 68 Ind. L. J. 1199 (Fall 1993)

Elaine Martin, Men and Women on the Bench: Vive La Difference?, 73 Judicature 204 (1990)

Elaine Martin, The Representative Role of Women Judges, 77 Judicature 166 (1993)

Elaine Martin, Women on the Bench: A Different Voice?, 77 Judicature 126 (1993)

Judith Resnik, *On the Bias: Feminist Considerations of the Aspirations of Our Judges*, 61 S. Cal. L. Rev. 1877 (1988)

Lynn Hecht Schafran, *Eve, Mary, Superwoman: How Stereotypes About Women Influence Judges*, 24 Judges J. 13 (1985)

Susan Moloney Smith, *Diversifying the Judiciary: The Influence of Gender and Race on Judging*, 28 U. Rich. L. Rev. 179 (1994)

Carl Tobias, *The Gender Gap on the Federal Bench*, 19 Hofstra L. Rev. 171 (1988)

8. LARGE FIRM PRACTICE

Books

Making Partner: A Guide for Law Firm Associates (American Bar Ass'n, 1992)

Articles

Robert Bookman, *Helping Associates Succeed*, Ass'n of Legal Admin. News, June-July 1993, at 6

Katrina M. Dewey, *Jessica Pers Stands Alone as a Trailblazing Partner*, California L. Bus. (L.A. Daily J. Suppl.), May 16, 1994, at 24

Katrina M. Dewey, *Women and the Law: A New Reality Sets In*, California L. Bus. (L.A. Daily J. Suppl.), May 16, 1994, at 19-24

Robert W. Gordon, *Corporate Law Practice as a Pulic Calling?*, 49 Md. L. Rev. 255 (1990)

Jeffrey D. Horst, *The Application of Title VII to Law Firm Partnership Decisions: Women Struggle To Join the Club*, 44 Ohio St. L. J. 841 (1983)

Amee McKim, *The Lawyer Track: The Case for Humanizing the Career Within a Large Firm*, 55 Ohio St. L. J. 167 (1994)

Mona D. Miller, *Breaking Through the Glass Ceiling: Some Personal Reflections on Women's Climb Toward Partnership*, P.L.I./Comm., June 9, 1994, at 135

Phil Nuernberger, *From Gunfighter to Samurai: Bringing Life Quality to the Practice of Law*, 66 N.Y. St. B.J. 6 (1994)

Barbara Kate Repa, *Is There Life After Partnership?*, 74 A.B.A. J. 70 (1988)

Lawrence P. Richard, *Secrets of the Inner Sanctum: Six Key Determinations of Law Firm Behavior*, Ass'n of Legal Admin. News, April-May 1993, at 10

Sorenson, *A Woman's Unwritten Code for Success*, 69 A.B.A. J. 1414 (1983)

Joan H. Stern, *The Associate's Role in Producing Profits*, P.L.I./Comm., Nov. 8-9, 1990, at 385

Marilyn Tucker, *New Associate's Survival Guide—How to Hit the Ground Running*, Law Prac. Mgmt., Oct. 1991, at 18

Marilyn Tucker, *To Specialize or Not to Specialize: That Is The Question*, Law. Hiring & Training Rep., Apr. 1992, at 2

Susan Wubbenhorst, *Law Partnership Decisions: Title VII Applies—Will it Make A Difference?*, 53 UMKC L. Rev. 468 (1985)

9. LAWYERS' PERCEPTIONS ABOUT HOW GENDER AFFECTS COURTROOM BEHAVIOR

Articles

Nancy Blodgett, *'I Don't Think That Ladies Should Be Lawyers,'* A.B.A.J., Dec. 1986, at 48

Claire Cooper, *Men Still Rule in Rural Courts, Women Lawyers Say*, Sacramento Bee, January 25, 1987, at A10

Ellen S. Podgor and Leonard D. Portnoy, *And God Created Woman . . . But to be a Criminal Defense Attorney?*, 42 Mercer L. Rev. 713 (1991)

10. LEGAL EDUCATION

Books

Cynthia Fuchs Epstein, *Women in Law* (3d ed., 1993)

Karen Berger Morello, *The Invisible Bar: The Woman Lawyer in America 1638 to Present* (1986)

Articles

Marina Angel, *Women in Legal Education: What It's Like to Be Part of a Perpetual First Wave of the Disappearing Women*, 61 Temple L. Rev. 799 (1988)

Taunya Lovell Banks, *Gender Bias in the Classroom*, 38 J. Legal Educ. 137 (1988)

Centennial Celebration: A Tradition of Women in the Law, 66 N.Y.U. L. Rev. 1545 (1991)

Elkins, *On the Significance of Women in Legal Education*, 7 Am. Legal Stud. A.F. 290 (1983)

John D. Feerick, *The Problem of Sexism in the Classroom*, reprinted in *The Woman Advocate* (Conference Coursebook) 15 (1993)

Feminist Jurisprudence Symposium, 24 Ga. L. Rev. 795 (1990)

Sandra Janoff, *The Influence of Legal Education on Moral Reasoning*, 76 Minn. L. Rev. 193 (1991)

La Russa, *Portia's Decision: Women's Motives for Studying Law and Their Later Career Satisfaction as Attorneys*, 1 Psychol. Women Q. 350 (1977)

Special Project, *Gender, Legal Education, and the Legal Profession: An Empirical Study of Stanford Law Students and Graduates*, 40 Stan. L. Rev. 1209 (1988)

Symposium: Gender Bias in Legal Education, 14 S. Ill. U. L. J. 469 (1990)

Symposium on Gender and Legal Ethics, 4 Geo. J. Legal Ethics 1 (1990)

Abbie Willard Thorner, *Gender and the Profession: The Search for Equal Access*, 4 Geo. J. Legal Ethics 81 (1990)

Marilyn Tucker, Laurie Albright, and Patricia L. Busk, *Whatever Happened to the Class of 1983?*, 78 Geo. L. J. 153 (1989)

Voices on Women: A Symposium, 77 Iowa L. Rev. 87 (1991)

Patricia M.Wald, *Women in the Law: Stage Two*, 52 UMKC L. Rev. 45 (1983)

Catherine Weiss and Louise Melling, *Gender and the Law: The Legal Education of Twenty Women*, 40 Stan. L. Rev. 1299 (1988)

White and Roth, *The Law School Admission Test and the Continuing Minority Status of Women in Law Schools*, 2 Harv. Women's L.J. 103 (1979)

Christine M. Wiseman, *The Legal Education of Women: From "Treason Against Nature" to Sounding a "Different Voice"*, 74 Marq. L. Rev. 325 (1991)

Women and the Law: Goals for the 1990's, 42 Fla. L. Rev. 1 (1990)

Other

Sandler, *The Campus Climate Revisited: Chilly for Women Faculty, Administrators, and Graduate Students* (1986) (available from the Association of American Colleges, Washington, D.C.)

11. LEGAL TRAINING

Articles

Michael W. Coffield, *In-House Litigation Training: One Firm's Experience*, Law. Hiring & Training Rep., Mar. 1992, at 4

George W. Coombe, Jr., *Training Our Lawyers and Yours: Making Outside Counsel More Productive and Their Services More Useful to Corporation Counsel*, P.L.I./Corp., Dec. 1992-Jan. 1993, at 183

Gary Blanc Crouse, *Conference on Women Litigators Highlights Training Challenges*, Law. Hiring & Training Rep., May 1993, at 1

Carrie Menkel-Meadow, *Portia in a Different Voice: Speculations on a Woman's Lawyering Process*, 1 Berkeley Women's L. J. 39 (1985)

Lynn Hecht Schafran, *Eve, Esq.: Women in Law, in Full Disclosure: Do You Really Want to be a Lawyer?* (1989)

12. THE LESBIAN LITIGATOR

Articles

Ruthann Robson and S.E. Valentine, *Lov(h)ers: Lesbians as Intimate Partners and Lesbian Legal Theory*, 63 Temple L. Rev. 511 (1990)

Anne Melissa Rossheim, *Revised NALP Survey Tones Down Questions on Sexual Orientation*, Law. Hiring & Training Rep., May 1991, at 13

Larry Smith, *Harvard Queries on Firms' Gay Attorneys Leads to Little Controversy*, Law. Hiring & Training Rep., Aug. 1992, at 14

Symposium, Can Two Real Men Eat Quiche Together? Storytelling, Gender-Role Stereotypes, and Legal Protection for Lesbians and Gay Men, 46 U. Miami L. Rev. 511 (1992)

13. MENTORING

Books

Women Lawyers: Perspectives on Success (E. Couric ed., 1984)

Articles

Fitt and Newton, *When the Mentor is a Man and the Protege a Woman*, Harv. Bus. Rev., Mar.-Apr. 1981, at 48

Louise A. LaMothe, *Where Have the Mentors Gone?*, *in* The Woman Advocate (Conference Coursebook) 173 (1993)

Suzanne B. O'Neill, *Business Development and the Client Relationship: Don't Underestimate the Role of Mentors*, Law. Hiring & Training Rep., Jan. 1993, at 4

Oregon State Bar Affirmative Action Committee, Professional Partnership Program, *The Mentoring Relationship: Making it Work*, *in* The Woman Advocate (Conference Coursebook) 192 (1993)

Anne Melissa Rossheim, *Women's Bar Associations Sponsor Mentor Programs to Aid Law Students*, Law. Hiring & Training Rep., May 1991, at 13

14. THE MINORITY WOMAN LAWYER

Articles

Nina Burleigh, *Black Women Lawyers Coping with Dual Discrimination*, P.L.I./Comm., June 9, 1994, at 143

Diane E. Galanis, *Climbing the Mountain: Pioneer Black Lawyers Look Back*, 77 A.B.A. J. 60 (Apr. 1991)

Dannye Holley and Thomas Kleven, *Minorities and the Legal Profession: Current Platitudes, Current Barriers*, 12 T. Marshall L. Rev. 299 (1987)

Report and Recommendations of The Special Commissioner Committee re: Minority Hiring and Retention at Law Firms, 73 Mich. B.J. 204 (1994)

Anne Melissa Rossheim, *Corporation's Efforts to Attract Minorities Intensify, Increasing Pressure on Law Firms*, Law. Hiring & Training Rep., Nov. 1992, at 1

Jennifer M. Russell, *On Being a Gorilla in Your Midst, or, the Life of One Blackwoman in the Legal Academy*, 28 Harv. C.R.-C.L. L. Rev. 259 (1993)

15. PROSECUTORIAL PRACTICE

Books

James B. Stewart, *The Prosecutors: Inside the Offices of the Government's Most Powerful Lawyers* (1987)

Articles

Reena Raggi, *Prosecutors' Offices: Where Gender Is Irrelevant*, 57 Fordham L. Rev. 975 (1989)

Fred C. Zacharias, *Structuring The Ethics of Prosecutorial Trial Practice: Can Prosecutors Do Justice?*, 44 Vand. L. Rev. 45 (1991)

16. PUBLIC INTEREST WORK

Articles

Frank J. Macchiarola and Joseph Scanlon, *Lawyers in the Public Service and the Role of Law Schools*, 19 Fordham Urb. L.J. 695 (1992)

17. RAINMAKING

Lois W. Abraham, *Confessions of An Accused Rainmaker*, in *The Woman Advocate* (Conference Coursebook) 967 (1983)

Baila H. Celedonia, *Client Development: This Means You, This Means Now*, P.L.I./Comm., June 9, 1994, at 7

John Chesser, *In-House Law Practice Grows with Companies*, in *The Woman Advocate* (Conference Coursebook) 909 (1993)

Cindy Collins, *New ABA Booklet Helps Women Make Rain*, Law. Hiring & Training Rep., Jan. 1994, at 7

June Eichbaum and Jonathon Lindsey, *Women as Rainmakers: A Users Guide*, P.L.I./Comm., June 9, 1994, at 21

Horace W. Green, *Attracting Clients*, P.L.I./Lit. & Admin. Prac., Jan. 1994, at 287

Jessica Gwyn, *Littler Mendelson Works to Teach Rainmaking Skills*, California Law Business (L.A. Daily J. Suppl.), May 16, 1994, at 22

John Jefferson, *Linda, John and Rebecca's Excellent Adventure*, in *The Woman Advocate* (Conference Coursebook) 915 (1993)

Louise A. LaMothe, Jean Maclean Snyder, and Robin Page West, *Women as Rainmakers*, in *The Woman Advocate* (Conference Coursebook) 978 (1993)

David Machlowitz, *The Art of Making Money*, in *The Woman Advocate* (Conference Coursebook) 932 (1993)

Nancy J. Perry, *If You Can't Join 'Em, Beat 'Em*, in *The Woman Advocate* (Conference Coursebook) 942 (1993)

The Rainmakers, California Law Business (L.A. Daily J. Suppl.), July 1, 1991

Barbara Kate Repa, *Is There Life After Partnership?*, 74 A.B.A. J. 70 (1988)

Anne Melissa Rossheim, *Women's Rainmaking Networks: Questions About Their Effectiveness Multiply*, Of Counsel, Apr. 20, 1992, at 1

Elizabeth Roth, *Women Rainmakers: Why Only a Sprinkle?*, in *The Woman Advocate* (Conference Coursebook) 959 (1993)

Larry Smith, *Unlikely Rainmakers: Why Former Judges are Being Welcomed by Major Firms*, Of Counsel, Mar. 2, 1992, at 7

Larry Smith, *Firms De-Emphasize Rigid Formulas for Rainmaking*, Of Counsel, Nov. 19, 1990, at 4

18. SETTLEMENT

Books

Roger Fisher and William Ury, *Getting to Yes* (1981)
Howard Raiffa, *The Art and Science of Negotiation* (1982)

Articles

John W. Cooley, *Arbitration vs. Mediation—Explaining the Differences,* 69 Judicature 263 (1986)

James C. Freund, *Bridging Troubled Waters: Negotiating Disputes, in The Woman Advocate* (Conference Coursebook) 811 (1993)

James C. Freund and Marguerite S. Millhauser, *Deterring the First Strike: Contract Clauses to Handle Disputes, in The Woman Advocate* (Conference Coursebook) 821 (1993)

Deanne C. Siemer, *Perspective of Advocates and Clients on Court-Sponsored ADR, in The Woman Advocate* (Conference Coursebook) 847 (1993)

Linda R. Singer, *Origins and Growth of the Dispute Settlement Movement, in The Woman Advocate* (Conference Coursebook) 879 (1993)

Linda R. Singer, *Techniques for Settling Disputes, in The Woman Advocate* (Conference Coursebook) 890 (1993)

Sheila Prell Sonenshine, *Real Lawyers Settle: A Successful Post-Trial Settlement Program in the California Courts of Appeal,* 26 Loyola L. Rev. 1001 (1993)

Kent D. Syverud, *Getting to No! A Study of Settlement Negotiations and the Selection of Cases for Trial,* 90 Mich. L. Rev. 319 (1991)

Claudette G. Wilson, *Settlement Negotiations, in The Woman Advocate* (Conference Coursebook) 871 (1993)

19. SEXISM IN LEGAL PRACTICE

Articles

Eyster, *Analysis of Sexism in Legal Practice: A Clinical Approach,* 38 J. Legal Educ. 183 (1988)

Carrie Menkel-Meadow, *Excluded Voices: New Voices in the Legal Profession Making New Voices in the Law*, 42 U. Miami L. Rev. 29 (1987)

Rochelle Siegel, *Presumed Equal: How Women in Law School are Learning that Sexist Behavior Dies Slowly, reprinted in* The Woman Advocate (Conference Coursebook) 244 (1993)

20. SOLO OR SMALL FIRM PRACTICE

Books

Flying Solo: A Survival Guide for Solo Lawyers (American Bar Ass'n, 1994)

How to Start and Build a Law Practice (American Bar Ass'n, 1991)

Articles

Laurie Berke-Weiss, *Developing a Successful Solo Practice*, P.L.I./ Comm., July 14, 1993, at 16

Dale Ellis, *How to Build a Solo and Small Firm Network to Support Your Practice*, Law Prac. Mgmt. Oct. 1992, at 30

William J. Manassero, *Developing a Small Firm Strategic Practice Marketing Plan*, Legal Econ., Nov.-Dec. 1987, at 38

Anastasia McLaughlin, *How to Get Clients For Your Small Firm Practice: Tips for Obtaining Corporate Business*, P.L.I./Comm., July 14, 1993, at 77

21. WOMEN LITIGATORS

Articles

Catherine Therese Clark, *Missed Manners in Courtroom Decorum*, 50 Md. L. Rev. 945 (1991)

Lynn Hecht Schafran, *Eve, Mary, Superwoman: How Stereotypes About Women Influence Judges*, 24 Judges J. 13 (1985)

Lynn Hecht Schafran, *Women as Litigators—Abilities vs. Assumptions*, 19 Trial 36 (1983)

Shipp, *In Court a Woman's Character Can Dictate Her Legal Fortune* N.Y. Times, June 10, 1987, at C1

22. WOMEN'S PROGRESS IN THE LEGAL PROFESSION

Books

Cynthia Fuchs Epstein, *Women in Law* (3d ed., 1993)

Mona Harrington, *Women Lawyers: Rewriting the Rules* (1994)

Articles

Nancy Blodgett, *Whatever Happened to the Class of '81?*, 74 A.B.A. J. 56 (1988)

First Women: The Contribution of American Women to the Law, 28 Val. U. L. Rev. 1500 (1994)

Fossum, *Women in the Legal Profession: A Progress Report*, 67 A.B.A. J. 578 (1981)

Ann J. Gellis, *Great Expectations: Women in the Legal Profession, A Commentary on State Studies*, 66 Ind. L.J. 941 (1991)

Linda R. Hirshman, *Sex and Money: Is Law School a Dead-End Street for Women?*, 87 Nw. U. L. Rev. 1265 (1993)

Rand Jack and Dana Crowley Jack, *Women Lawyers: Archetype and Alternatives*, 57 Fordham L. Rev. 933 (1989)

Kandel, Davies and Raveis, *The Stressfulness of Daily Social Roles for Women: Marital, Occupational and Household Roles*, 26 J. Health & Soc. Behav. 64 (1985)

Herma Hill Kay, *The Future of Women Law Professors*, 77 Iowa L. Rev. 5 (1991)

Liefland, *Career Patterns of Male and Female Lawyers*, 35 Buffalo L. Rev. 601 (1986)

Deborah J. Merritt, *Family, Place and Career; The Gender Paradox in Law School Hiring*, 1993 Wis. L. Rev. 395 (1993)

Elizabeth Roth, *Women Lawyers Advised to Learn Rules of Male 'Law Game'*, in *The Woman Advocate* (Conference Coursebook) 957 (1993)

Virginia Sapiro, *Opening the Door to Women Attorneys: Gender Equity in Wisconsin Legal Careers*, 67 Wis. Law. 7 (1994)

Women at Work: War Stories and Other Memories, 14 Cal. Law. 64 (1994)

Women and the Law: Goals for the 1990's, 42 Fla. L. Rev. 1 (1990)

Lee E. Teitelbaum and Antoinette Sedillo Lopez, *Gender, Legal Education, and Legal Careers*, 41 J. Legal Educ. 443 (1991)

Abbie Willard Thorner, *Legal Education in the Recruitment Marketplace: Decades of Change*, 2 Duke L. J. 276 (1987)

Kanen L. Valihura, *Breaking Through the Barriers: A Reflection on the Participation of Women in the Legal Profession*, 12 Del. Law. 5 (1994)

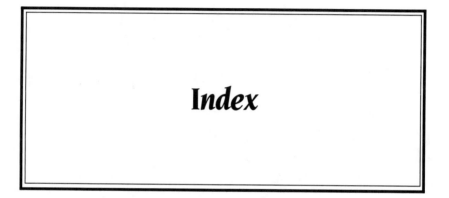

Index

Index

B

C

D

O

P

T

V

W